# THE NURTURE OF HUMAN BEHAVIOR

**Lawrence V. Harper**

University of California at Davis

ABLEX PUBLISHING CORPORATION
NORWOOD, NEW JERSEY

Printed in the United States of America.

**Library of Congress Cataloging-in-Publication Data**

Harper, Lawrence V.
    The nurture of human behavior.

    Bibliography: p.
    Includes index.
    1. Child development.    2. Developmental psychobiology.
I. Title.    [DNLM: 1. Behavior.    2. Human Development.
BF 121 H294n]
RJ131.H285    1988    155.4    88-22243
ISBN 0-89391-511-4

Ablex Publishing Corporation
355 Chestnut St.
Norwood, NJ 07648

To my Parents

# Table of Contents

# Preface

Although the nature-nurture issue has been formally laid to rest on any number of occasions (and in almost every current textbook) the conceptual framework upon which it rests lives on, unscathed, as evidenced by all-too-frequently encountered references to "innate" elements of behavior. Since Anastasi (1958) showed that the real issue was to identify "how" genes and environment act *together* to influence behavioral development, great strides have been made in developmental biology. The mechanisms underlying organismic growth, while by no means fully worked out, are certainly much better understood than they were when Anastasi's paper was written. Unfortunately, most developmental psychologists either have not kept abreast of this progress or have not attempted to incorporate these advances into their thinking. Thus the question of "how" has not been addressed in any systematic way, with the exception of a few, such as Gilbert Gottlieb (1976), who has shown how concepts drawn from embryology might be applied to understanding behavioral development. This monograph, then, represents an attempt to sketch out how advances in developmental biology might be applied to the study of behavioral development.

Many of the ideas outlined in the chapters to follow obviously involve speculative "leaps" from reasonably well-established phenomena to the development of mechanisms that might underlie complex human action. These leaps are taken in the belief that we are unlikely to solve the riddle of "how" until we become seriously committed to achieving a better appreciation for the principles underlying somatic growth and until we fully explore the implications these principles have for understanding behavioral ontogeny. Although the conceptual framework that will be elaborated in this volume is only a rough working outline, it will have served its original purpose if it encourages others to pursue and refine this line of inquiry.

I hope it also will become clear that this approach in no way should be taken to imply that we have "gone beyond" the need for careful descriptive and analytic studies of behavior. If anything became apparent as I searched for data relevant to my thesis, it was that we really are just beginning to analyze what constitutes "the environment." Similarly, our catalog of readily-observable human actions is almost embarassingly small. There remains a crying need for meticulous descriptive studies, replicated in our own and other cultures. Without a much more firm descriptive database than we now have, theoretical blind alleys will be difficult, if not impossible, to identify prior to substantial expenditures of time and effort. Efforts to test hypotheses need not be "wasted," of course, but the sad truth is that all too many of them have been so narrowly focused that the empirical yield often was disappointingly small in relation to the resources expended. Therefore, I hope that this monograph will also provide encouragement for more investigations of human behavior in the tradition of comparative ethology.

In undertaking to write this monograph, I owe a great deal to the intellectual honesty and openness of my colleagues at the University of California at Davis. Whatever coherence and clarity these ideas may have must be credited to their generous willingness to hear me out and question patiently when the flow of ideas became muddled. I would like to acknowledge special debts to Brenda Bryant for reading and commenting upon an excessively diffuse first draft and to Emmy Werner for constant encouragement and invaluable suggestions for focusing my arguments. Janet Heron Asay and Larry Carr also read and commented on early drafts. Jamie Straw typed the initial draft and Anita Gentry subsequently retyped collages of handwritten notes and pasted-together segments of earlier drafts. Jean Seay inherited the final revision and an update of the references, handling them with good humor despite my last-minute scheduling and microscopic marginal corrections.

# CHAPTER 1

# Introduction

This monograph is an attempt to broaden the choice of conceptual models of human behavioral ontogeny to include one that draws largely from developmental biology. The scheme to be developed here amounts to a rough working model which may encourage conceptual leaps from the level of behavior to analyses of the organismic substrates of action. The utility of this model may be gauged not so much by the extent to which it leads to new laboratory experiments, but, perhaps more importantly, to the extent that it inspires detailed field observations. What follows is an attempt to examine the biology of behavioral development from the perspective of three types of explanations as outlined by Tinbergen (1951). Tinbergen's first type of explanation, a consideration of evolutionary origins, will be addressed in terms of the implications of evolutionary theory for understanding the conditions necessary for behavioral development. For example, from an evolutionary perspective, one would expect that environmental conditions which are important for the development of species-typical behavioral characteristics will be simple, reliable indicators of the quality of the habitat in which ontogeny must take place. The second type of explanation, an examination of the underlying mechanisms, will be addressed in terms of the relevance of developmental genetics and embryology for understanding the ontogeny of human behavior. For example, from the standpoint of developmental biology, no behavior is "either" genetically "or" environmentally determined. The third type of explanation, the analysis of the conditions evoking responses, will be addressed in terms of an analysis of the kinds of effects that "experience" may have on the course of behavioral development. For example, it will be argued that the conditions for initiating the expression of a characteristic may be fundamentally different from the inputs that sustain and/or consolidate its growth.

## ASSUMPTIONS

The ideas that will be presented in subsequent chapters are based upon the acceptance of two, basic, working assumptions:

1

*Adaptation.* The first assumption is that the theory of evolution pro-vides us with a set of postulates that may (a) help us better understand the patterns of developmental change we observe and (b) guide our inquiries toward more fruitful investigations of the environmental conditions that affect behavioral development and performance. This means, among other things, that we begin with the supposition that most, if not all, be-havioral characteristics of animals, including *Homo sapiens*, evolved as a result of natural selection. That is, *contra* Lewontin, Rose, & Kamin, (1984)—who argue that many characteristics of a species may not be adap-tive, per se, but rather "side effects" of selection for other traits—we begin with the working assumption that phenotypic traits either have contributed to, or are currently enhancing the selective fitness of those who exhibit them. This choice is based upon the conviction that it will be more fruitful to search for demonstrable functions than to dismiss traits as "vestiges" or adaptively "neutral" epiphenomena of other attributes or processes.[1] However, acceptance of the "adaptationist" assumption does not require uncritical endorsement of functional explanations simply on the basis of their plausibility. At a minimum, such accounts also must yield at least one of the following: (a) an economical framework within which to orga-nize known phenomena, (b) testable hypotheses about the conditions under which behavioral variants develop, or are manifest, or about the consequences such behaviors will have for those displaying them.

*Reductionism.* The second assumption is that behavior ultimately can be understood in terms of underlying biological mechanisms. The utility and even the logic of "reductionism," as this strategy is often called, has been the subject of vigorous debate (e.g., Lewontin et al., 1984; Maddox, 1983). It has been argued that we simply do not understand biological phenomena well enough to predict complex physiological (let alone be-havioral) outcomes from the properties of genetic materials or even of whole cells. This undoubtedly is true (Maddox, 1983; Thomson, 1984). However, even though our biological knowledge is incomplete, it does not mean that it cannot help us ask better questions about the substrates of behavior (Medawar, 1984).

It has been argued that reductionist attempts are inherently futile be-cause the co-action of complex entities can give rise to "emergent proper-ties," processes or structures which are vastly more complex than the sum of the elements underlying them. Therefore, the argument goes, it is im-possible to predict the properties of these functional aggregates solely from

---

[1] This choice is defensible on purely logical grounds: One can never *prove* that a charac-teristic has *no* fundamental significance; *any* postulated function can be disproved by con-trary evidence.

a knowledge of the characteristics of their component elements.[2] For the moment, the argument is moot: There is no question that our understanding of molecular and cellular mechanisms is imperfect (Thomson, 1984). Therefore, the fact that molecular mechanisms do not suffice to explain cellular or organismic processes is hardly proof of the existence of emergents. Indeed, proof of the notion of emergent phenomena would require the demonstration that there remain *no* unknowns at more elemental levels, a logical impossibility.

A third objection to reductionism rests upon the assumption that changes resulting from biological or physical events are qualitatively different from those arising from (cognitive) interpretations of events. If so, it is argued, cognitive science must be fundamentally different from biological science. However, the dividing line between changes caused biologically and those caused by "inference" based upon "knowledge" has yet to be specified. Moreover, we have yet to be shown precisely how knowledge can exist (or influence other processes) independently of the substrate (Pylyshyn, 1985). Therefore, the choice of a reductionist model is not invalidated on purely logical grounds.

However, given our admittedly sketchy understanding of more complex, biological phenomena, the adoption of this strategy requires some further justification. One reason for going beyond purely psychological explanations derives from the considerable successes of students of animal behavior who have been guided by biological theory (e.g., Eisenberg & Kleiman, 1983; Marler & Hamilton, 1966; Tinbergen, 1951).

Another reason for turning to biology for models of developmental process stems from the persistence of the nature-nurture issue (Aslin, 1981; Oyama, 1985; Immelmann, Barlow, Petrinovich, & Main, 1981). Developmental biologists may not have entirely avoided the conceptual pitfalls inherent in this dichotomization of the contributors to growth, but they seem to be less hindered by it. Moreover, the notion of "maturation" simply described as a "universal pattern of development" all too often is invoked to "account" for ontogenetic change: We tend to take "operants" and species-typical development as "givens" rather than phenomena urgently requiring explanation in and of themselves (e.g., Mussen, Conger, Kagan, & Huston, 1984; Skinner, 1981). It would seem that such tendencies are favored, if not caused, by the absence of conceptual models that attempt to focus attention on the determinants of all facets of (behavioral) growth.

---

[2] The tenability of this argument has been weakened by recent advances in the mathematical theory of cellular automata (Wolfram, 1984) which allow the prediction of certain classes of emergents which are not obvious from the properties of the elements, and indicate that, as the properties of elements (including the constraints on their combinations) become known, predictability increases.

Attempts to reformulate our ideas of behavioral growth may be particularly appropriate at this time. Increasing recognition of the bidirectionality of social influence (Bell, 1968; Bell & Harper, 1977) combined with elaborations of models of "interaction" between genes and environments (Plomin, De Fries, & Loehlin, 1977; 1985; Scarr & McCartney, 1983) has important implications for understanding developmental processes. Given the heuristic value of these formulations, there is no compelling reason to adhere to the view that adequate explanations of biological processes, cognitive processes, and social behavior require separate conceptual frameworks (*contra* Lewontin et al., 1984; Pylyshyn, 1985).

This is not to say that "biologizing" will somehow solve our problems and automatically lead to a major advance in testable theory. Although provocative and capable of generating new observations and insights (as well as a new orthodoxy), biological models suffer from many of the definitional pitfalls bedevilling psychological theories.

Despite these problems, and the clumsiness encountered in bridging levels of explanation, the effort seems both necessary and timely. In the absence of a coherent theory of the ways in which heredity and environment "interact" (Aslin, 1981), traditional psychological models of behavioral development have been unable to bypass the nature-nurture problem while developmental genetics and evolutionary theory are enjoying a period of expansion. Psychologists, while ready to acknowledge that genes contribute to behavior, generally have had difficulty in conceptualizing concrete linkages. Thus, it now seems appropriate to begin the quest for a conceptual framework that might allow evolutionists, geneticists, and behavioral scientists to communicate with one another more effectively.

## TRADITIONAL CONCEPTS

One of the most common objections to the introduction of new conceptual models is that they either ignore well-established principles or simply couch them in new terms. These too, are legitimate and serious concerns. Thus, before proceeding, we need to make a very brief but critical survey of some of the major concepts typically used to account for behavioral development.

### Learning and Maturation

It is generally accepted that (associative) learning plays a major role in the ontogeny of behavior. A correlated assumption is that it is useful to distinguish learning, or experientially-induced modifications of behavior, from more or less inevitable and predictable change.

*Dichotomies.* However, to date, no concise definition has been proposed to identify what learning "is." Indeed, there is debate as to whether this rubric subsumes a variety of processes (cf. Thorpe, 1963) or a single, general mechanism (Bitterman, 1975). Evidence for situation- and stage-specific learning, such as the ease of establishing flavor-illness aversions in adult rats (Garcia, Hankins, & Rusiniak, 1974; Palmerino, Rusiniak, & Garcia, 1980) and the difficulty of establishing similar "conditioning" in nurslings (Gubernick & Alberts, 1984) suggest that the unique biology of organisms cannot be ignored.

Many students of behavior still insist on a distinction between "biological" functions such as respiration and digestion and allegedly more plastic adjustments to specific settings. The distinction can only be maintained by ignoring the facts that most animals can digest a variety of specific foodstuffs and alter their respiration rates to meet the (environmental) demands of exercise, altitude, or temperature.

Alternatively, it has been argued that it is helpful to distinguish between developmental outcomes that characterize essentially everyone and those whose precise form seems to depend upon highly specific settings. Underlying this approach is the view that maturational events are stable, or irreversible steps in a sequential progression, whereas learning involves reversible changes. However, events typically considered maturational often are not truly stable. We are constantly changing; no facet of anatomy or performance is absolutely static.

These considerations highlight the basic problem of definition: At which point should we draw the line between learning and other processes? Do learning and maturation "interact," and if so, how? Shall we accept such developmentally predictable events as imprinting under the rubric of learning? Can we draw the line between learning that occurs only during a critical period and that which depends upon the reasonably predictable acquisition of prerequisite knowledge (e.g., the transition from preoperational to concrete operational thought [Inhelder, Sinclair, & Bovet, 1974])? Should these predictabilities be considered different because they are not so closely tied to a chronological timetable as, say, a child's first words, which are clearly learned, yet as predictable as walking (Lenneberg, 1967)?

The foregoing issues would present no major problem if the underlying processes could be disentangled. They have not. The finding that it is difficult to isolate a biological change that is uniquely the result of learning (as opposed to some other process, such as hormone secretion, [Horn, Rose, & Bateson, 1973]), might be interpreted as evidence that learning is different from other biological functions. However, the failure to identify a single process unique to learning could simply mean that it is not unique. It is equally possible that we have begun with an erroneous *assumption* that learning and maturation must involve different processes. We have no empirical grounds for making that decision—it is just consistent with our habitual way of thinking.

*Continua vs. dichotomies.* The foregoing issues represent fundamental questions that must be answered before we can develop a workable taxonomy of processes underlying behavioral development. To overcome the impasse imposed by dichtomies, Mayr (1974) has suggested that we think in terms of a continuum of genetic programs from "closed," wherein the course of development is completely determined by the fertilized zygote, to "open," in which "additional input" can be "inserted" into the process of gene expression "through experience." In a similar vein, Hinde (1959) has proposed that we think of a continuum of developmental process from "environmentally stable" to "environmentally labile."

These conceptualizations, while meeting several of the objections mentioned above, leave the issue of degree (of openness) unanswered; they do not help us locate processes along the proposed continua. However, the difficulty raised by the proposed continuum of environmentally stable to environmentally labile points to an avenue of escape from our dilemma. Perhaps we have been focusing on the wrong term in the developmental equation. If we must have a model that posits continuous variation, we may do better to focus on the characteristics of the environment rather than developmental processes.

If anything typifies learning/open programs/labile development, it is that their form (a) is relatively difficult to predict in advance and (b) has an intuitively obvious relationship to some specific configuration of environmental events. Even if we knew precisely *what* a particular organism was capable of learning in its natural surroundings, we could not predict with any certainty when or whether the necessary conditions would be met. We might, therefore, focus on the *situational specificity* of events leading to phenotypic change. That is, once we can specify what environmental conditions *are* necessary or sufficient for development, we could reorder them along continua of the joint probabilities of stimuli being encountered/responded to.

Although the mechanisms underlying development of structures mediating behavioral maturation may be of only peripheral interest to many students of behavioral ontogeny, failure to investigate the dynamics of organismic development may actually cause us to overlook major environmental sources of individual variation. For example, the transition from eyes-closed smiling to auditorily- or visually-evoked smiling in infancy (Emde, Gaensbauer, & Harmon, 1976) seems to represent a universal and thus a "maturational" process (cf. Mussen et al., 1984). However, Ambrose (1961) has shown that the rate at which these changes take place varies as a function of the amount of social stimulation infants receive. Thus, to dismiss so-called maturational events as beyond the realm of developmental psychology is to arbitrarily restrict our field of inquiry, and thereby, our understanding of behavioral development (see also Hofer, 1981).

## Stimulus, Response, and Reinforcement

The foregoing analysis brings us to another issue: If one scans the literature with a critical eye to the definitions of other key concepts, it is hard to avoid the conclusion that the failures of explanatory systems derived from traditional models must largely be due to the fact that they seldom specify either stimuli or responses with real precision. For example, although the concept of generalization has some degree of descriptive utility, we have no means either for identifying the dimensions upon which similarity of input or action might be assessed or for quantifying the degrees of similarity among events.

Moreover, the key concept of reinforcement suffers from an inherent circularity of definition (Ritchie, 1973) and reward and punishment have proven to be context-dependent (See, e.g., Martin, 1975; Parke & Slaby, 1983). Although models which stress the importance of the contingency *relationship* between actions and their consequences (e.g., Watson, 1981) seem promising, that promise cannot be fully assessed until we have (a) precise definitions of the acts and their consequences, and (b) either extensive empirical data on *which* combinations of actions and putative consequences seem to capture children's attention at various ages, or predictions, in advance, of which combinations will be effective.

## Emotion and Expectation

Despite a number of thought-provoking studies (e.g., Emde et al., 1976) and working models of early emotional development (e.g., Campos, Barrett, Lamb, Goldsmith, & Steinberg, 1983; Sroufe, 1979), conceptual schemes utilizing concepts of emotion and expectation suffer from the same kind of difficulties. For example, Campos et al. (1983) argue that emotions can arise as a result of processes by which we evaluate the personal significance of goals or our success in attaining them. However, they also suggest that emotions can arise *prior* to such assessment and can energize and guide both cognitive and motor behavior. Although intuitively compelling, these conceptual distinctions are not yet articulated clearly enough to permit unambiguous predictions or tests of the model: It is not clear whether emotions are important as causes, or as effects, or both. If both, we need guidelines for deciding when or whether they will act in any particular way. Moreover, there remains another fundamental problem which will have to be addressed: Whether we should equate the apparently immediate sensory appreciation of such sensations as sweet and bitter (pleasant and unpleasant) with the putatively basic emotions of joy, fear, and sexual ardor (cf. Campos et al., 1983), and if so, whether we are to assume they involve the same mechanisms.

The undeniable existence of expectations similarly has yet to be systematically integrated into a theoretical framework. With a resurgence of interest in cognition influenced largely by Piaget's work (e.g., Piaget, 1952; Inhelder & Piaget, 1958), new attempts have been made to explain a range of behavioral developments in terms of amalgams of emotions with memories and expectations (e.g., Campos et al., 1983; Kagan, 1984). These ideas cast a number of phenomena in a new light and, in so doing, have the potential to expand our understanding of developmental events. However, concepts such as "arousal level," "schema," "assimilation," and so on need more precise definition.

It would seem that traditional formulations are not yet sufficient to account for behavioral phenomena. Whether they will be necessary for explaining human action remains an unanswered, empirical question. Indeed, many of the major concepts that have oriented the choice of research questions and have been utilized as explanatory terms (e.g., motivation) may have been miscast in those roles. What psychologists regard as well-understood processes often turn out to represent the identification or delineation of broad problem areas which themselves are in need of more precise definition and extensive investigation: For example, how can we distinguish "motivated" behavior from "emotional" or reflexive responses? How can we identify an "optimum" level of arousal? Is arousal "general" or specific to particular kinds of activities?

In the absence of answers to questions such as the foregoing, one could argue that some of the difficulties in establishing reasonable linkages between behavioral development and biological processes may arise from the fact that we have few firm anchors at any of the points in the chain of process(es) by which genes (*via* environments) affect behavior. Despite behavioral scientists' enduring "environmentalist" biases, we know relatively little about the conditions eliciting most "operants" and the permissable forms and quantitative limits of "stimulation" required for typical development (see, e.g., Wachs, 1983). On the output side, we are no better off. We seem to have fewer detailed descriptions of what children actually *do* than we have models of why they do it. If often is hard to resist the conclusion that a number of our ideas about what actually happens are based more upon hypothetical conceptions of underlying processes than on direct observation (Bronfenbrenner, 1979).

## Anastasi Revisited

Although the nature-nurture issue is routinely (and ritually) pronounced dead in essentially every developmental treatise, it continues to rear its head in the guise of distinctions between maturation and experience (See Oyama, 1985, for review). We thus begin with a consideration of the terminological and conceptual conventions that seem to have perpetuated it.

In 1958 Anastasi published a now-classic paper in the *Psychological Review* in which she decried the tendencies to (a) debate whether genes *or* environment could account for behavior, and (b) attempt to quantify *how much* genes or environment contribute to behavioral development. She presented a forceful argument in favor of the view that both genes and environment determine all behavioral development and concluded that the proper question was neither whether, or how much, but "how." This thesis is reiterated in essentially all texts that address the issue. It is equally frequently ignored—if not tacitly rejected—in subsequent discussions (Plomin, 1983). In part, this ambivalence is due to some fundamental misunderstandings about gene-behavior relationships, and in part, because of the fact that we have no general model of "how."[3]

*Heritability.* In some cases, statements about "how much" genes influence behavior may reflect a failure to make it clear that our current methods are best suited for the study of differences between *groups,* not among individuals. The concept of "heritability" is used by behavior geneticists when comparing groups who differ from one another primarily on the basis of their degree of genetic similarity. Typically, comparisons are made of the variation among genetically identical twins with the same measures of variation among comparably-reared fraternal twins (who share only half of the genes that are unique to each parent, on average). Heritability "measures" are thus ratios of variances across *groups:* they are not measures of the degree to which heredity "determines" the characteristics of individuals. If anything, they are rough indices of the range of ("genetic") responsiveness to a *given array of environments* among individuals in the sampled population.

An often overlooked but key point here is that some environment is essential for the expression of any gene. Because gene-expression is environment-dependent, heritability figures may differ from one study to another, particularly if the samples are drawn from different social strata. Such instability of measurement is not evidence against a genetic contribution: Some samples could be drawn from populations that receive insufficient stimulation to evoke the expression of the trait in question. Heritability estimates also may be essentially zero because variations in the environment are irrelevant. That is, there will be little phenotypic variation because the environments sampled are either functionally equivalent or contain the same stimuli necessary for the expression of that trait in essentially everyone observed (See Scarr-Salapatek, 1971, 1976; Scarr & Kidd, 1983).

---

[3] Even Anastasi (1958) described the relationship as a continuum of "indirectness."

If one accepts the principle that any phenotypic attribute depends upon gene-activity of some kind, then *no* trait can ever be purely environmentally determined. *Differences* between individuals, particularly among identical twins, may be attributed to their having encountered different environments.

*"Genetic" and "environmental" variance.* Geneticists' statements concerning the "sources" of differences (variation) among individuals (who were reared in similar environments) also refer to differences across *groups.* Variability *across* individuals is said to be (attributable to) "genetic" (sources) when differences among individuals (who were reared in similar environments) are correlated with known differences in genotype. Variability is said to be (attributable to) "environmental" (sources) when the differences observed across individuals exceed known degrees of genetic similarity, and they are assumed to have been exposed to different environments.[4] Unfortunately, the shorthand convention of speaking of environmental *vs.* genetic variance sometimes leads the unwary to conclude that expression of the attributes in question in a *single* individual are more or less genetic in origin. Virtually all geneticists would insist that *all* facets of the phenotype ultimately depend upon environmentally evoked and sustained gene expression.

In addition to misunderstandings arising from terminology, there also exist some common misconceptions concerning the outcomes of gene-expression.

*Uniformity.* One common misconception is that "inherited" (*vs.* "acquired") attributes must be uniformly expressed by all members of the species. This is based upon the erroneous assumption that individuals inherit a single "program" for development. In fact, individuals inherit genetic potentials to develop a variety of phenotypes, a "norm of reaction." Since environmental inputs are necessary both to initiate and to sustain gene-action, two individuals with essentially the same heredity could behave differently if they are reared in effectively different environments. Similarly, two individuals with different heredities could behave comparably—again as a result of different rearing conditions (Alland, 1972; Dobzhansky, 1970; Scarr-Salapatek, 1976).

Thus it does not follow that because an attribute is part of the species' repertoire, everyone should "possess" it. Some characteristics *are* diagnostic of vertebrates-in-general, mammals-in-general, and humans-in-general. Most people do not deviate in the sense that they develop these characteristics. Universals do exist in anatomy and behavior and reflect the common heredity of a species or genus. But essentially no two people are pheno-

---

[4] Unfortunately, in most cases, the *effective* parameters of environmental input are unknown.

typically identical; only monozygotic twins are *genetically* identical. A number of species-typical traits may involve subsets of fairly diverse but roughly equivalent sets of genes; for any particular functional slot or chromosomal "locus," there may be a substantial number of essentially equivalent genes (Dobzhansky, 1970; Mayr, 1970) for example, the blood groups. At the level of behavior, the product of complex mechanisms, we must be dealing with a spectrum of "ways of being human." Therefore, even though spoken language, including the capacity to generate new sentences, is a species-specific (defining) characteristic of *Homo*, we should not expect all humans either to inherit exactly the same potentials or to develop identical linguistic competencies.

*Inevitability.* The view that species-specific (genetic) attributes must be uniform in expression often is paralleled by the misconception that they must be expressed. That is, it is held that those attributes which are "innate" will develop *regardless* of environmental input. At the extreme, this notion implies that such development could take place in environments incapable of sustaining human life! Such a *reductio ad absurdum* points to the obvious contrary facts that drugs such as thalidomide can disrupt anatomical development in utero (Décarie, 1969) and that a certain mimimum of postnatal visual input is absolutely necessary for typical visual development (Aslin, Pisoni, & Jusczyk, 1983). Nothing is innate in the sense that it develops inevitably. A number of behaviors may appear in ontogeny despite the fact that the individual has not practiced them or has not previously encountered the environmental conditions required to elicit them (e.g., Harper, 1970). This means only that *other* conditions, some of which may involve interactions among developing tissues, suffice to prepare the organism to react properly. However, nutrients and so on are still essential for the tissue interactions themselves.

*Immediacy.* Another common misconception is that attributes present at birth represent the products of biological forces, controlled by the action of genes, whereas subsequent developments increasingly reflect psychological/cultural influences. One need only consider the development of juvenile intolerance to milk, or middle-aged baldness, and graying hair with old age to realize that gene-action is not static. Genes are "switching" on and off throughout the life-cycle (see Scarr & Kidd, 1983, for review). The process of gene-environment co-action is essentially continuous. There are changes in the environments required to activate and maintain new patterns of gene-action, and perhaps in the complexity of some of the pathways transmitting environmental signals from "outisde" to the genetic materials themselves (see below). However, there is no evidence for a shift from gene-environment co-action to some other mechanism. Nor is there any support for the view that genetically-controlled processes, once activated, are somehow unalterable or irreversible (Goldsmith, 1984).

*Inflexibility.* Classic examples of "instinctual" reactions in lower organisms typically involved stereotyped, "automatic" patterns of response (e.g., Tinbergen, 1951). Because of this, many seem to have drawn the conclusion that a biologically-based behavioral pattern must be inflexible by definition. However, if we grant that the development of nervous systems depends upon gene expression (Lund, 1978; Sutcliffe, 1984), then we must be prepared to admit to the possibility that genes can confer the potential to develop flexible responses to environmental exigencies.

For example, it was once common to speak of "the" social behavior of baboons or chimpanzees as if each (non-human) animal were endowed with the capacity for only one set of social responses and thereby limited to participation in one, "typical," kind of social organization. As a result of quasi-naturalistic experiments (e.g., Leyhausen, 1956) and more extensive field studies (See Lott, 1984 for review), we now know that many animals are capable of changing the ways in which they relate to their species-mates. These "facultative" variations in social organization reflect a repertoire of species-specific "strategies" for meeting the exigencies of particular seasonal and/or more long-term environmental fluctuations. Thus, we cannot assume, *a priori*, that such phenomena as human cultural variation represent flexibility that is based upon mechanisms which are qualitatively unique.

The foregoing arguments directly challenge the oft-encountered notions that learning replaces so-called genetically programmed behavior (e.g., Alland, 1972; Skinner, 1981).[5] If one accepts the view that phenotypes (including behavioral potentials) result from the co-action of genes and environment, then learning itself must be affected by inheritance. There is no lack of evidence that one can selectively breed strains of animals more or less capable of learning to solve various kinds of problems (Fuller & Thompson, 1960). Moreover, it is becoming increasingly clear that there exist species differences in the *kinds* of "lessons" that animals are capable of learning and/or the ease with which they will learn them (Hinde & Stevenson-Hinde, 1973).

*The capacity of the genome.* This brings us to a final point, often raised as an objection to models of genetic "determination" of behavior in general, and of learning as a gene-controlled process in particular. It is based upon assumptions concerning the "capacity" of the genome. It is argued that it is implausible to expect heredity to account for variable responses to uncertainties in the environment because the genome would be "overloaded." Yet no one denies that genes determine the actions of the immune system, a system capable of responding to a wide variety of highly discrete

---

[5] Skinner (1981, p. 501) has gone so far as to assert that since animals can quickly adjust to "any given environment" via operant conditioning, such learning will come not only to "supplement the natural selection of behavior" but even to "replace it."

"messages" (Jerne, 1985; Perlmutter, 1985). On this basis alone, the argument is open to debate, and somewhat similar mechanisms may be operative in the nervous system (Swanson, 1985).

In addition, the phenomena already referred to as "emergents" support the plausibility of a genetic "basis" for so-called environmentally labile behavior: When essentially identical circuits or mechanisms are connected in various configurations, their functional capacities often expand exponentially. Thus, a great deal of potential flexibility could derive from a simple instruction to repeat a developmental sequence. Since every cell presumably contains the same genetic potential as every other one, each "subcomponent" of a complex array need only be "coded" once. If functional capacity increases so much more rapidly, then "repeat" instructions —even including specifications of different conditions for repeating— would be economical. In view of much evidence both for very substantial (biochemical) heterogeneity of neuron cell-types in the human central nervous system, and for highly complex patterns of interconnections among these cells, it would be no less reasonable to wonder why our behavior is not *more* flexible than it is (Changeux, 1985).

In sum, then, many of the objections to reductionism and arguments in favor of a dualism of process are based on misconceptions of the biology of growth and function. Given the advances in developmental biology since Anastasi's (1958) review, another look is called for.


## TOWARD A MODEL OF HOW:
## GENE-ENVIRONMENT RELATIONS

In the next three chapters, I will review how gene-environment co-action controls embryonic development, particularly of the nervous system, consider the implications for evolutionary theory for understanding patterns of inheritance and growth, and present a descriptive model of growth. The four following chapters will indicate how these conceptions might be applied to the analysis of a range of behavioral phenomena, and in the final chapter I will discuss the implications of this model for both theory and research in behavioral development. The major themes to be developed at greater length in these chapters are as follows.


### Gene-Environment Co-Action

Gene-action involves a number of processes. Genes must replicate themselves essentially exactly as cells proliferate. Within cells, they regulate biochemical processes ranging from protein synthesis to the production of compounds that regulate their own activity or that of other genes, either within the "parent" cell, or in other cells (e.g., Barlow, 1981). In essence, they determine the structure and function possible in an organism.

Development and the differentiation of tissues, organs, and so on depends upon changes in the configurations of gene activity within different cells (tissues) in response to biochemical "messages" transmitted among and between cells making up different structures (e.g., Sargent & Dawid, 1983). The cytoplasm of the cell is the proximate environment that ultimately controls (nuclear) gene-activity.

As implied by the idea that one inherits genetic information permitting a number of developmental outcomes, the genetic potential substantially exceeds that which ultimately gains expression. Insofar as cellular function (life processes) depends upon the products of gene-action, all organismic activity must be influenced by genes. Moreover, since phenotypic change occurs continuously throughout the life-cycle, gene-expression also must constantly be changing to some degree. Finally, because the viability of the zygote and the phenotype to which it gives rise depend upon supporting environments, we must conclude that all attributes are the *joint* products of both heredity and environment; that it is meaningless to ask how much heredity or environment contributed to the phenotype of an individual (cf. Anastasi, 1958; Hebb, 1973).

Insofar as organismic change involves changing gene-action, I will argue that all development must ultimately be understood in these terms. I will attempt to show that maturation and experience must reduce to the same mechanism, and that the distinction between endogenous and exogenous sources of change is useful only in describing the origin of stimulation; the response will always be cellular. Extending Gottlieb's (1976) model and extrapolating from studies of neurogenesis, I will argue that environmental conditions affect the development of organisms in at least five different ways: Stimulation can affect the genome to *induce, facilitate, functionally validate, maintain* and *integrate* the development of structure or functional relationships underlying behavior. These effects can be seen as separate steps in the epigenetic process, each of which *may* depend upon different environmental inputs.

Finally, insofar as our responsiveness to our surroundings is constrained by our structure (receptors, etc.), I will argue that gene-environment relations throughout much of growth amount to transactions in which the developing phenotype not only serves as a "filter" and transmitter for environmental influence (cf. Aslin, 1981, 1985; Marler, 1961), but also seeks and provokes the input required to sustain it.

### Evolution and Development

Natural selection is "blind," capitalizing upon materials at hand so long as they lead to phenotypes that can successfully exploit their surroundings. It depends upon heritable variation in phenotypes. Each species can be seen as a pool of co-adapted genes that, when arranged on chromosomes at particular loci, can recombine in various ways to yield viable phenotypes. Insofar as natural selection represents a kind of "tinkering" with available materials, many attributes can be understood as compromise solutions to the problems of adapting to an environment. On the one hand, several different genetic combinations may lead to similar outcomes, and on the other, most individuals will inherit the potential to follow several developmental courses, a "norm of reaction." This variability is particularly evident in sexually reproducing species such as our own.

Variation in form and function can result either from modification of basic building blocks or the regulation of their expression. Insofar as structural and regulatory genes are inherited independently and selection does make do with what is available, much evolutionary change can be understood as modifications of rates and patterns of growth. Ontogeny thus amounts to a mosaic of developments occurring at their own rates. Because of this heterochrony of developmental rates, there are stages in development. Natural selection begins at conception and favors those developmental patterns that yield viable phenotypes at all stages and those regulatory genes that ensure that adaptive characteristics will be expressed under the proper conditions. Given that gene expression depends upon environmental inputs, the more important facets of growth will be keyed to environmental conditions that amount to reliable "signs" of conditions-to-be-encountered. Signs evoking and sustaining expression of fundamental species-characteristics will be ubiquitous. Others will be alternative equivalents and some inputs evoking alternative developmental pathways will be situationally specific. Insofar as our species has inhabited a broad spectrum of environments over much of its evolutionary history, we should expect individuals to inherit the potential for both a range of developmental (structural) variation and the capacity to adopt a range of behavioral strategies to effectively exploit their surroundings.

## Characteristics of Growth

Because growth amounts to a series of adaptive transactions between individual and environment, it must be conceptualized as an active process which is constrained, occasionally to critical periods, despite compensatory mechanisms. Given the fact that growth is heterochronous, we can conceptualize organismic activity as the resultant of the coordinated activities of a number of semi-independent components. As a result of unremitting selection of the genes governing the regulation of the timing of expression of these component structures/capacities, in species-typical surroundings, their activities will be coordinated in *functional systems* appropriate for meeting the demands of the current phase of growth and for extracting or provoking inputs required for further development.[6]

Because organismic growth *in utero,* as a neonate, and as an adult requires different adaptations, the stages of growth will be reflected in the reorganization of existing components of functional systems into new, expanded, or quite different functional systems. I will suggest that this model of growth as the ontogenetic reorganization of stage-appropriate functional systems allows us to explain both continuities and discontinuities in development as well as the ways in which early experiences can influence later appearing behaviors.

Because the expression of components occurs semi-independently and is timed to yield stage-specific, adaptive functional organization (functional systems), there will be phases in development when structures or capacities are expressed which nevertheless appear to be nonfunctional or severely limited. In addition, when reorganizations occur involving major shifts in function, it is possible that individuals will be facing developmental "choice-points" at which environmental inputs can alter or restabilize one's developmental trajectory. Since everyone inherits a unique set of genes (save identical twins), individual differences are to be expected in responsiveness to inputs, the rates of growth(s), the degrees to which expression of components is targeted, and even the variety of components that one can express.

## Infancy

An examination of prenatal and early postnatal development will be used to illustrate the utility of both an adaptionist position and the conceptions of growth developed in the preceding sections. From conception, the developing infant can be seen as in a transactional relationship with its surroundings. Fetal and infantile behavior can be understood as adaptations to the exigencies of the average, expectable environments peculiar to those stages of the life cycle. An examination of the ontogeny of visually-elicited smiling not only illustrates our model of the developmental reorganization of components, but suggests that this shift is an adaptive response to ensure that the baby provokes input required for further growth and development. The nature of the required inputs can be understood in terms of environmental signs that care will be forthcoming.

A similar examination of the ontogenies of discrimination among individuals and separation protest also reveals developmental patterns consis-

---

[6] This postulate represents a working assumption, not an "explanation" for any attribute. Although some attributes *may,* in fact, have little or no functional significance, an "adaptationist" approach encourages the search for function and thereby the generation of testable hypotheses.

tent with the model of developmental reorganizations of functional systems which are timed to promote the adaptation of infants to newly-emerging locomotor capacities. The notion of sign stimuli can also be fruitfully applied to the analysis of the conditions facilitating the development of readiness to attach and the characteristics that should cause infants to select particular figures as their "attachment-objects."

## Exploration, Play and Peer Relations

Exploration, play, and interactions with age-mates account for the majority of young children's waking hours and can be seen as examples of the ways in which developing children actively seek and provoke input. The effects of caregivers on exploration and play may be understood in terms of sign stimuli indicating that the situation is safe. The ontogeny of wariness to the unfamiliar and fear reactions also can be interpreted in terms of adaptive, stage-specific reorganization of functional systems.

Play provides an example *par excellence* of the notion of (behavioral) components and the ways in which young children may create for themselves conditions that help to facilitate, validate, maintain, and integrate expression of the substrates for developing neuromotor skills. Indeed, gross motor play may be seen as a mechanism facilitating the "tuning" of musculoskeletal growth to local conditions.

The ontogeny of peer relationships can be understood in terms of the development of functional systems and system-specific deployment of capacities. A comparison of the effects of peer-rearing and family-upbringing illustrates how sign stimuli associated with different kinds of childcare may cause youngsters to follow different trajectories of behavioral development.

## Cognition

An examination of the neurological structures underlying the way in which we make sense of our surroundings provides one of the best-documented examples of the components (modules) underlying complex, adaptive behavior. The constraints that phenotypic structures impose upon behavior are illustrated by an examination of the ways in which stimulation is filtered by receptors, neural relay mechanisms, and specialized central processing components. A review of the tuning of central "sensory analyzers" indicates how different environmental inputs affect various phases of the development of these structures.

Consideration of newborn children's responsiveness to sights and sounds indicates how stage-specific organization could provide the basis for gaining input required for further advances. The model of developmental changes in organization is shown to be applicable to a variety of cognitive phenomena from apparent regressions in sensorimotor responsiveness to the development of abstract concepts. Developmental buffering and compensatory mechanisms of growth are illustrated by a consideration of the cognitive development of children with sensory or motor handicaps.

## Language

The adaptive nature of developmental heterochrony is illustrated by the lag between language comprehension and productive speech. The tuning of the substrates for phoneme-detection provide additional examples of the ways in which environmental inputs may affect the expression of the nervous mechanisms underlying behavior. The development of non-cry vocalizations can be seen as an example of the process of ontogenetic reorganization of functional components. Children's acquisition of grammar can be used to illustrate the active nature of behavioral growth and how the lag between comprehension and production may function to "pace" caregiver input to ensure that the child is exposed to exemplars of speech that can be used to decode grammatical rules. The development of grammatical competence can fruitfully be described in terms of stages of reorganization of component competencies.

The relationship between language and thought provides a final example of the ways in which components of functional organization in apparently different domains may affect one another and how the systems sharing components in common can become (re-)integrated as development proceeds.

## Personality

An examination of the ontogeny of the major structural elements of personality, the "self" and "conscience," again illustrate how components grow and change relatively independently of one another. A study of the development of a central "map" of the human body image also indicates how inputs can operate to validate, maintain, and integrate the neural substrates of behavior. The putative integration of one's sense of self and values that may occur at adolescence or young adulthood further indicates how the reorganization of functional systems may vary according to the demands/opportunities presented by one's environment.

I suggest that the notion of functional systems may be a useful alternative to the concept of motivation in that it implies heterogeneity of process and thereby should encourage more direct and intensive analyses of the underlying determinants of sustained, goal-directed activity. Some major individual differences in personality may be understood in terms of the adoption of different facultative strategies for adaptation. These are illustrated by the effects of birth order and father absence. Finally, the model of reorganization of functional systems is proposed as a framework in which the problem of continuities and discontinuities in personality development can be fruitfully approached.

## Summary and Implications

In the final chapter, the conceptual scheme for environmental effects and the model of developmental (re)organization of functional systems are summarized briefly and I present some of their more important implications for our conceptualization of behavioral growth and the conduct of research.

# CHAPTER 2

# Gene Environment Co-Action

In the study of development we are interested not only in the final state at which the system arrives, but also in the course by which it gets there. (C.H. Waddington, 1957, p. 26)

Over the years there have been attempts to utilize concepts from developmental biology to characterize the ontogeny of human behavior. Generally speaking, these have not been very successful for reasons which often had little to do with their inherent applicability: Those whose primary interests lay in the analysis of how already-existing behaviors are modified, considered the problem of origins to be irrelevant (cf. Bijou & Baer, 1961). Others, whose interests did encompass the origins of new capabilities, expressed several misgivings concerning the use of biology for explanatory models of behavioral growth. For example, Sibylle Escalona stated:

The reduction of psychological events to physiological (and ultimately physical) processes closes the door to the investigation of psychological events in their own right.

and

a primary characteristic of the human species would appear to be the high degree to which organization and regulation of behaviors including the developmental process is mediated by psychological events that are not identical with, or reducible to, the physiological processes on which they rest. (Escalona, 1968, p. 89).

The fear that a searach for biological models will preclude investigation of psychological processes has proven unwarranted. The substantial gains in physiological psychology and neuroethology (Ewert, Capranica, & Ingle, 1983), have not inhibited vigorous research in such purely psychological domains as cognition (e.g., Bower, 1982) and personality (e.g., Damon, 1983). Indeed, one of the theses of this monograph is that we

21

need more, not less, descriptive data on psychological development and dynamics.

The view that psychological events cannot be explained in terms of underlying biological processes amounts to a matter of opinion; the issue is one that cannot admit to a purely logical solution. At present, the only apparent criteria for choosing among alternatives seems to be utility; that is, how well a formulation encompasses existing phenomena and reconciles apparently paradoxical observations. There is nothing *inherent* in the logic of scientific inquiry that accords higher status to any level of explanation. "Psychological events" do exist and, as such, they are legitimate subjects of study; so are the "physiological processes upon which they rest," and the selective pressures that gave rise to these physiological mechanisms. Analyses at *all* levels are necessary and desirable for a full appreciation of human behavior.

Although there are valid reasons for being wary of "biologizing" the study of behavior, none of them are grounds for abandoning the attempt. Moreover, an appreciation for some of the principles of contemporary developmental and evolutionary biology may help to provide useful perspectives from which to view the ontogeny of behavior.

In this chapter, we will examine some findings from developmental biology which shed light on the ways in which genes and environments co-act to yield functioning organisms. They provide a case for abandoning rigid distinctions between environmentally- and organismically-controlled development. In terms of the biological mechanisms involved, "experience" ultimately creates change via essentially the same processes that underlie "maturation."

No one seriously questions the view that the phenotype, the (developing) organism, results from environmentally-evoked and sustained gene-action. However, when it comes to explaining behavioral development, most textbooks of psychology adopt a circumspect, if not frankly ambivalent stance. We have been reminded repeatedly that psychological phenomena such as emotions or motives are not inherited "as such" (Mussen, Conger, & Kagan, 1979). This is undeniable; frequently overlooked is the fact that the same applies equally to both biological structure and function. In principle, all could be conceptualized in terms of the expression of one's genetic inheritance.

The problem, then, is to discover how inherited genetic potential (the genotype) becomes translated into a person (a phenotype). This question is complex because we inherit capacities to react to different environmental conditions with a variety of developmental responses. This "norm of reaction," or range of possible phenotypic outcomes, confers more potentials for growth that can be realized. Thus we are faced with not only the task of tracing the pathways from genotype to phenotype, but also with answering the question of how *one* of many *sets* of genetically defined possibilities gains phenotypic expression (Dobzhansky, 1970; Scarr-Salapatek, 1975).

## Gene Action—General Principles

We may conceptualize the genome as containing at least two classes of information: (a) a comparatively small number of "structural" genes that specify the production of more or less stable proteins, and (b) a larger set of redundant (i.e., repeated) genes which act to regulate or control the production of structural materials. These "regulatory" genes presumably are activated (switched on) or inactivated (switched off) in such a way as to maintain ongoing life processes and also to control the progressive changes that constitute development—which is another way of saying that development depends upon basic metabolic processes. This activation and inactivation of genes is subject to feedback control. That is, the quality and quantity of materials synthesized by structural or regulatory genes provide the signals which determine whether output will be increased, decreased, or even temporarily stopped (Davidson & Britten, 1979; Dobzhansky, 1970; McMahon, 1974; Slack, 1984).

Most, if not all genes are responsible for a variety of effects; although a given gene may be primarily responsible for the production of a particular enzyme, it also is likely to influence the action of other gene products. These "pleiotropic" effects may occur in many ways: There may be competition for the pool of available substrates: gene products may cause the activation of regulators controlling the activity of structural genes (including the ones producing the activating substance), or a gene may be affected by the concentration of its own product, to name a few possibilities (Markert & Ursprung, 1971; Rastan & Cattanach, 1983).

The phenomena of gene-gene interaction also underscore the fact that, although members of sexually reproducing species receive almost random combinations of parental genes, the number of possible (re)combinations is still bounded. The modern definition of a species revolves about the idea of a gene pool from which combinations of genetic instructions can be drawn. The potential recombinants within each species' pool are co-adapted to one another so that their mutual activities typically will coordinate to produce viable organisms (Dobzhansky, 1970; Mayr, 1970). On the other hand, even in the absence of mutation, "errors" do occur because gene complexes controlling one aspect of growth such as rate, often are inherited independently of those controlling related aspects of the same organ such as its ultimate size (Tanner, 1962).

Another phenomenon of developmental importance is that the structure of certain apparently unitary, vital gene products, such as hemoglobin or muscle myosin, change as the organism matures (Caplan, Fiszman, & Eppenberger, 1983; Kabat, 1972). Moreover, in complex creatures, many genes will not find expression until relatively late in life, for example, gray hair or some forms of balding. Thus we are brought to the problem of the timing of gene action. It seems that the control of the temporal pattern of gene activity differs from one tissue to another within the same organism (Snow & Tam, 1980).

## Gene Expression

It is generally accepted that the genetic material itself is essentially dupli-cated in every "daughter" cell. That is, each cell has all the inherited in-formation necessary for the formation of every component of the adult form (Diberardino, Hoffner, & Etkin, 1984; McLaren, 1984). Obviously, *all* these possibilities cannot be expressed at once, or even sequentially. Starting with fertilization, there is progressive expression of specific potentials in response to internal and external conditions up to the point at which cellular differentiation begins to occur. At that point, once a cell has embarked on a given course, for example, activated gene complexes leading to differentiation as a neuron, the complexes associated with other developmental pathways, such as skin, are blocked from expression (Blau, Pavlath, Hardeman, Chiu, Silberstein, Webster, Miller, & Miller, 1985; Caplan & Ordahl, 1978; Holliday & Pugh, 1975; Sutcliffe, 1984). The sequence can thus be conceptualized as progressive gene-expression up to a point at which the cell is "competent" to activate one of several as-yet-unexpressed sets of genes. During a brief "critical period" the cell has several possible genetically-defined developmental courses open to it. Once one of the genetic sets defining a particular developmental pathway is activated, the "critical period" for activating alternative sets of genes has come to a close, and the range of further gene-expression has been restricted. This whole process of "differentiation" has been described as:

> a developmental tree, where, at precise times during development, cells branch out into different sublines that later themselves become subdivided into more diverse classes. At each stage the cells become more and more tied to a specific pathway of development and more and more distinct from cells derived from other branches of the tree. (Holliday & Pugh, 1975)

## Gene-Environment Relationships

The genes present in the fertilized egg thus specify the development of "the whole individual" throughout its life cycle. The question is, how is differ-entiation accomplished if the genome is replicated with each successive cell division and every daughter cell receies essentially the same information?

*The cytoplasmic environment.* One answer seems to lie in the fact that, although the chromosomal (genetic) material in the cell nucleus is duplicated almost exactly in each succeeding cell generation, the material surrounding the nucleus (the cytoplasm) is not. The egg has a very "rich" cytoplasm containing a large store of precursor materials and organelles. With fertilization and subsequent cell division, there comes a point at which the otherwise identical genetic instructions of each of the daughter cells of the fertilized egg (the zygote) will find themselves in different surroundings (Woodland & Jones, 1986). These "environmental" differences reflect either the quality or the quantity of the cytoplasm (Anderson, 1984; Muggle-Harris, Whittingham, & Wilson, 1982), and the position of a cell *vis à vis* other cells (Taghert, Doe, & Goodman, 1984).

The changing biochemical milieu provided by the cytoplasm is thought to be responsible for two types of gene-directed activities. The first type involves maintaining basic life processes such as cellular respiration. The second type of regulation accounts for the progressive expression of the gene sets specifying particular pathways of development. Once the genes directing a given, specialized developmental course begin to function, the cell's metabolic activity and its regulation are altered. With such alteration, the cytoplasmic contents change. In multicellular organisms such as humans, these specializing cell lines are all part of an interconnected cell mass. Thus they influence each other so that the "intrinsic" regulations specified within each cell's genome ultimately are affected by the activities of neighboring cells or more distant tissues (Caplan & Ordahl, 1978; Markert & Ursprung, 1971).

*Cell-cell influences.* The first step in organismic development is thought to reflect partitioning the cytoplasm among daughter cells. The essentially identical genomes, no longer residing in identical biochemical environments, begin to show differences in gene-regulation. The next step in ontogeny reflects additional alterations in each cell's cytoplasmic contents resulting from differences in the metabolic activities of neighboring cells. In the early stages of embryonic development, these inter-cell influences seem to be mediated in part by chemical "signals" transmitted via "gap junctions," apparently open channels which connect neighboring cells (Warner, 1984).

Presumably, this intercellular exchange of chemical signals causes changes in the patterns of gene activities of adjacent cells. The particular kinds of changes so induced probably are superimposed upon prior alterations resulting from factors associated with location and unequal distribution of cytoplasmic materials (Davidson & Britten, 1979). For a brief transitional period in the early multicellular phase, each of the several cells remains capable of developing into any tissue of the body. But at some point, the critical period for commitment passes, and the genetic machinery within different sets of cells becomes restricted in terms of the range of possible responses they and their descendants can make to future signals. This restriction of developmental possibilities apparently is not a matter of losing genetic material; rather, it reflects blocking or repression of segments of the genome (Caplan & Orhahl, 1978; DiBerardino et al., 1984; Holliday & Pugh, 1975). Complementing the blocking of alternative pathways, there is activation of genes (perhaps regulator or "selector" elements) that specify the possible developmental pathways remaining open to a particular cell-lineage (Blau et al., 1985; Preiss, Rosenberg, Kienlin, Seifert, & Jackle, 1985).

*Interactions among tissues.* In subsequent developmental steps, after the formation of three basic tissue-types (mesoderm, endoderm, and ectoderm), additional restrictions of cell "fate" often result from exchanges among different tissues. For example, the juxtaposition of certain segments of ectoderm (the cell lineage that gives rise to skin, nerves, etc.) above segments of mesoderm (which differentiates into muscle, bone, etc.) normally leads to the formation of the nervous system (Gimlich & Cooke, 1983; Spemann, 1938). That is, proximity to dorsal mesoderm is thought to induce changes in the gene action cells of the overlying ectoderm, presumably *via* messages transmitted across the gap junctions. (Each cell lineage expresses different classes of gene products important in defining its distinctive qualities; see Lane & Anderton, 1982; McAllister, Scheller, Kandel, & Axel, 1983; Sutcliffe, 1984).

As specialization proceeds, signals may be produced by noncontiguous, specialized tissues. Hormonal influences are the most obvious examples; they act to regulate the expression of genes in specific tissues (e.g., Firestone, Payvar, & Yamamoto, 1982; O'Malley & Means, 1974; Parker, 1983). Whether a tissue will respond depends first upon the expression of othe genes specifying "receptor" sites (e.g., Kaufman et al., 1981) and secondly upon the expression of still other, regulator genes characterizing a particular developmental stage of that presumptive "target tissue" (Kaufman, Pinsky, & Feder-Hollander, 1981; Lim & Miller, 1984; Palmiter, Norstedt, Gelinas, Hammer, & Brinster, 1983; Spelsberg, Webster, & Pikler, 1976). That is, a tissue will not respond if it is not "ready." The most obvious outcomes of such hormonal messages are the pubertal growth spurt and development of secondary sex characteristics (e.g., Tanner, 1962; 1970).

Hormonal signals are not the only messages that work at a distance, however. The developing axons of both sensory and motor nerves appear to to be affected—guided—by products of the organs they will innervate (Levi, 1985; Lumsden & Davies, 1983; Smith & Appel, 1983). In the latter case, the signals have been identified as proteins extracted from "young" muscle tissue. In developing nerve-muscle connections, the muscle may also send a contact-dependent message to the nerve regulating expression of neurotransmitter molecules (Smith & Appel, 1983). These intertissue interactions do not cease at that point, however. Once functional neuro-motor synapses form, the pattern of nerve impulses transmitted affects the kind of contractile proteins expressed in the muscle cell (Caplan et al., 1983; Salmons & Streiter, 1976), perhaps in conjunction with priming by thyroid hormone (Ianuzzo, Williams, Chen, O'Brien, & Patel, 1977).

So far, then, the picture is one of gene-environment "interaction" even within the cell, in the sense that the activities of regulator elements affect the expression of other genes. For the genome of a cell, the cytoplasm constitutes the effective environment. The make-up of the cytoplasm is not just subject to the coactions of "its" own genes, it is also affected by the presence and activities of neighboring cells (Blau et al., 1985). Finally, all these processes depend upon the surrounding medium in which they take place, the uterus—which itself is affected by the broader environment in which the mother finds herself (Jonakait, Bohn, & Black, 1980; Zamen-hof, van Marthens, & Gravel, 1971). Thus, every step of growth represents a product of gene-environment co-action. From the individual zygote (Harris, Whittingham, & Wilson, 1982) to the "whole" organism, gene expression depends upon the "proper" environment (See also Hofer, 1981).

## Development in the Nervous System

The central nervous system (CNS) is pivotal in determining our behavior. Thus, further examination of physical growth will focus upon the ontogeny of the CNS.

As we have seen, the early development of tissues that will ultimately give rise to the nervous system (the ectoderm) depends upon exchanges with contiguous tissue layers—notably the mesoderm, which is the precursor of tissues such as muscle and bone. In this early stage of ectodermal specialization there appear to be two major phases. The first involves the expression of genetic potentials to become nerve cells in conjunction with the suppression of potentials to develop into other types of tissue such as skin. In the second phase, there is a further series of restrictions of potential as genes are activated which lead to differentiation into specific types of neurons. These developments are largely confined to proximal tissue interactions within the primordia of the brain and spinal cord (Jacobson, 1970; Lund, 1978).

*Gross morphology.* Some aspects of early embryonic structure may be explained as cellular responses to mechanical tension such as stretching or compression within tissues (Curtis & Sheehar, 1978), perhaps arising from cellular proliferation (Nakatsuji & Johnson, 1984). However, even if mechanical tension is one factor regulating cell movement among developing tissues, more specific intercellular exchanges also seem to be involved (Lewis, 1984; Ungar, Geiger, & Ben-Zeév, 1986). In the developing CNS, after they have become committed as neurons, many of the individual cells within the presumptive nervous system begin to "migrate" from their sites of origin to take up positions in newly forming nervous structures. After locating in their final positions, they begin to send out dendrites and axons, the latter often spanning considerable distances (Lund, 1978).

Some of the signals controlling migration apparently act at a distance, perhaps as a result of diffusable chemical substances (Lumsden & Davies, 1986). Although control of migration may be multiply determined, often, intercell "recognition" provides the immediate guide for migration and outgrowth of nerve cells and their processes. Cell-surface glycoproteins apparently are involved in both cell migration and neural tissue-induction in a variety of species (Boucaut, Darribère, Boulekbache, & Thiery, 1984; Lund, 1978; Rutishauser, 1984). In committed neurons, these molecules vary according to nerve cell type (McKay, Hockfield, Johansen, Thompson, & Frederiksen, 1983), and they change in structure and binding affinities as the neurons or their processes migrate and form connections (Rutishauser, 1984; Sadoul, Hirn, Deagostini-Bazin, Gorriolis, & Rougon, 1983). The particular cell-surface molecules expressed correlate quite closely with changes in nerve cell connections (Kotrla, 1984). Moreover, the same molecules may be expressed by the tissues *to be* innervated by outgrowing axons and may serve as binding sites for neural processes (Kotrla, 1984; Rutishauser, 1984).

Some initial neuronal processes may be guided by early developing muscle cells (Ho, Ball, & Goodman, 1983; Kotrla, 1984), or other tissue layers (Bentley & Keshishian, 1982; Berlot & Goodman, 1984). These pioneer neurons then are guided by other, identifiable "landmark cells" (Bentley & Keshishian, 1982; Berlot & Goodman, 1984). A nerve cell's developmental fate may be determined before it migrates or sends out processes, perhaps due to signals peculiar to its site of origin (Lumsden & Davies, 1986; McAllister et al., 1983; Walthall, 1984). As it sends out processes, however, additional signals evoked by the surroundings are transmitted back to the nerve-cell nucleus to affect gene expression in the form of changing cell surface molecules. The latter cause developing processes to follow, or to move away from, the various cells in their vicinity. (The guideposts themselves may also be induced to differentiate further after having been contacted by and exchanging molecular information with the pioneer axons [cf. Bentley & Keshishian, 1982].) If the guidepost cells are selectively destroyed, some pioneer axons may follow an abnormal course (Bentley & Caudy, 1983). In mammals, and presumably, humans, contact-guidance is furnished to growing nervous structures by glial cells (which also provide metabolic support for adult neurons and the myelin sheaths of nerve pathways [e.g., Grumet, Rutishauser, & Edelman, 1983; Lund, 1978; Silver & Ogawa, 1983]).

*Remodeling.* This is not the whole story, however. Although early inter-cellular signals provide remarkable specificity of nerve connections, among animals with relatively complex nervous systems, there is an apparent overproliferation of nerves and nerve processes (Cowan, Fawcett, O'Leary, & Stanfield, 1984). That is, for the motor nerves connecting muscles from the spinal cord and nerve processes growing to the brain from receptors, and even within the cortex itself (Rakic, Bourgeois, Eckenhoff, Zecevic, & Goldman-Rakic, 1986), there is a stage in which the number of potential nerve cells and nervous connections is considerably in excess of the number that will survive.

In the developing spinal cord of mammals (Brown & Booth, 1983) a stage of "hyperproliferation" of motor neurons is followed by cell death. The functions of these "transient" structures are uncertain. However, it seems that the pattern of connections made by outgrowing motor nerves are critical in determining whether they survive. In chick embryos, blocking neuromuscular synaptic activity during this period reduces cell death. In contrast, electrical stimulation of the musculature and nerve trunks *increase* the number of motor neurons that die (Oppenheim & Nunez, 1982). These data indicate that neuromuscular connections are critical in determining neuronal survival. Presumably, signals released at synapses stimulate production of intracellular messengers (Weill & Greene, 1984). The survival of proprioceptive neurons from muscle require signals from both the muscle and the CNS (Davies, Thoenen, & Barde, 1986).

In the sympathetic branch of the autonomic nervous system and in certain sensory neurons, similar cell death occurs. This seems to be regulated in some degree by chemical signals produced by the neurons' target tissues, called "Nerve Growth Factor" (NGF).[1] When NGF action is blocked by antibodies, there is an excess proliferation of nerve cells and nerve processes. Thus it seems that NGF is transported back to the cell body as a signal that connections have been formed and thereby sustains the life processes in the neuron (Hulsebosch, Coggeshall, & Perez-Polo, 1984). Some sensory cells may also require intact central connections for survival (Johnson & Yip, 1985).

In both the sensory and motor systems, remodeling also involves a reduction in the number of nerve processes without necessarily involving cell death. As a result of cell-surface contact, or via short-range molecular signals, the developing processes cease to express proteins typical of a "growth cone" and begin to produce proteins characteristic of synapses

---

[1] Contrary to prior belief, the "trophic" factors guiding pioneer cells to their targets may not be related to NGF (Lumsden & Davies, 1983).

(Sonderegger, Rishman, Bokoum, Bauer, & Nelson, 1983). Some of these changes depend upon outgrowing axons' responses to target organ "labels" which identify their places of origin within the embryo. If they fail to receive such information, nerve processes may be withdrawn (Brown & Booth, 1983). In neonatal rats, the fate of supernumerary neuro-muscular synapses depends upon activity. The pattern of nerve activity typical of so-called "fast" muscle neurons effectively eliminates many surplus synaptic connections. Activity characteristic of "slow" muscle innervation, however, is much less effective in pruning "extra" synapses. When motor nerves are reversibly, chemically paralyzed, extra processes are produced (Brown & Ironton, 1977; Thompson, 1983).

Reductions in connections are not limited to processes synapsing with receptors or muscle cells. Interneurons in the spinal cord also undergo remodeling as patterns of peripheral connections become stabilized (Jessell & Yamamoto, 1980). Similarly, in sensory receptors and their nervous links within the brain itself, patterns of connectivity are established as a result of "competition" among supernumerary neural processes for synapses with central structures (Stanfield, O'Leary, & Fricks, 1982)—which themselves depend upon the existence of receptors for their development (Van der Loos & Woolsey, 1973). In the developing retinal ganglion cell, dendrites apparently are overproduced; only those which make connections with axons in the optic tract survive (Perry & Linden, 1982). In fetal monkeys, there is a phase of apparent overproduction of axonal processes connecting the eyes with the brain. So long as both eyes are present during the first half of gestation, the brain strucures develop essentially normally (Rakic, 1981). In the next phase, the axonal projections from the two eyes are not segregated into separate areas in the brain as they are in adults. Then, over the course of about a month, almost one million axonal processes are eliminated, producing an adult-like segregation pattern. At the same time, rapid synapse-formation is occurring in the visual target areas in the brain. Since removal of one eye before this period of axon-reduction prevents segregation, interneuronal competition seems indicated (Rakic, 1981; Rakic & Riley, 1983b).

After birth, another half million projections are lost more gradually, presumably as the result of visually evoked activity (Rakic & Riley, 1983a). Similar dynamics characterize the development of binocular connections in developing cats and rodents (Insausti, Blakemore, & Cowan, 1984; Cunningham, 1976; Seneglaub & Finlay, 1981). These later interactions also are apparently mediated by some sort of nervous transmission (See Lund, 1978, for review). Insofar as a similar pattern of increasing connectivity in the human cortex is followed by a prolonged period of synapse-reduction from two to 16 years of age (Huttenlocher, 1979; Huttenlocher, De Courten, Garey, & Van der Loos, 1982), we may assume that the same mechanisms obtain in humans.

*Fine tuning via "experience".* The sequence of intercellular events described to this point leads to the establishment of a pattern of connections between the eye and the brain that is thought to underlie binocular vision, especially depth perception. In cats and primates, it results from interactions among tissues occurring before birth, in the uterine environment. Thus, the initial phases of synapse formation occur in the absence of light-induced nervous activity. The animal is born with the structures necessary for depth perception, but postnatal visual input is normally involved in the development of adult-like function. Although there is evidence that similar dynamics apply to the full development of other sensory functions (e.g., Webster & Webster, 1977), we will confine this discussion to an examination of the ontogeny of binocular vision.

Experimental studies of the postnatal development of binocular vision in animals are of particular interest because similar phenomena appear to occur in humans: People without binocular depth perception do not perceive an illusion of depth in moving arrays of random dots. By about three months of age, normal babies show evidence of being sensitive to such illusions of depth, as indicated by visual tracking (Fox, Aslin, Shea, & Dumais, 1980), or electrically recorded brain activity (Braddick, Atkinson, Julesz, Kropfl, Bodis-Wollner, & Raab, 1980; Petrig, Julesz, Kropfl, Baumgartner, & Anliker, 1981). These studies indicate that stereopsis in humans becomes functional between 2½ and 4½ months postnatally. Clinical studies of individuals who suffered from the onset of visual problems, such as squint (crossed eyes), at varying ages indicate that these functions are reasonably well-established by 31 months of age (Banks, Aslin, & Letson, 1975; Hohman & Creutzfeldt, 1975). Other clinical data suggest that failure to correct conditions which prevent opportunities for normal binocular visual experience before the sixth year may produce permanent stereoblindness (Blake & Cormack, 1979; Petrig, Julesz, Kropfl, Baumgartner, & Anliker, 1981). That is, there seems to be a critical period for establishing binocularity in humans which begins at about 3 months and ends at about 60 months.

Visually evoked nervous activity seems to be important in establishing normal neural circuits in the visual "analyzers" of the brain (Wiesel, 1982). The importance of receptor activity per se in mediating central, visual connections is demonstrated by experiments in which retinal activity is (reversibly) blocked by drugs. Brief inactivation of retinal cells in kittens not only reduces cell size in certain visual areas of kitten's brains (Kupperman & Kasamatsu, 1983), but if prolonged throughout the critical period, binocular retinal blockage prevents the normal formation of columns of cells serving ocular dominance (Archer, Dubin, & Stark, 1982). Other data suggest that several steps may be involved; for the final, fine-tuning of visual areas of the kitten's brain, eye movement may also be necessary. A loss of binocularity does *not* occur if the stimulated eye is paralyzed so that it can not move during an experimental period of monocular input (Freeman & Bonds, 1979).[2]

These relationships involve interactions among different populations of neurons (visual and motor) and among different organs (retina and brain). Just as the initial development of certain sensory areas in the brain depends upon the existence of the receptors from which they will receive inputs (van der Loos & Woolsey, 1973; Rakic, 1981), the fine tuning of these analyzers also depends upon signals from the receptors. Experiments have demonstrated transfer of material from the eye via the visual nerve trunks to the brain (Grafstein, 1971; LaVail & LaVail, 1972). Thus, despite species differences in details, we may assume that the mechanisms underlying development of binocularity are fundamentally the same as those involved in regulating tissue differentiation and morphogenesis—the "environmental" regulation of cellular gene action. In this case, the regulation is largely mediated via the formation and activity of synaptic connections among nerve cells (Greenberg, Ziff, & Green, 1986). (Postnatally, development of the eye itself may be affected by neuronal activity [Gottlieb, 1987; Kolata, 1985]).

*Synapse formation.* Experimental investigations of synapse formation in other species suggest that co-incident growth (Hadley, Kater, & Cohan, 1983) or simultaneous nerve firing favor the formation or maintenance of connections among nerves. Synapse formation does seem to represent a turning point in cellular gene action. In some areas of the brain, the final phase of nerve cell differentiation, and expression of specific proteins, apparently depends upon the establishment of functional synapses (Lazarides & Nelson, 1983). For example, prior to assuming its "adult" characteristics, an autonomic cell may express several types of neurotransmitters, sometimes simultaneously (Black, 1982; Bunge, Johnson, & Ross, 1978). The adult phenotype and regulation of amount of transmitter produced depend upon environmental cues from the final site taken by the neuron and the patterns of excitation to which it is exposed. The neurotransmitter(s) expressed by a neuron may change somewhat with development and with input (Black, 1982; Ip, 1984). Dendritic branching in some portions of the

---

[2] The role of postnatal visual experience may perhaps be understood as representing the evolution of a developmental "hedge" against receptor abnormality or perinatal damage (e.g., Lund, 1978). Similarly, the species-differences in adaptations related to postnatal caregiving may reflect adaptations to their environments: Infant monkeys' early visual experiences are gained passively; they are transported from place to place by their mothers. In contrast, kittens' early visuo-spatial experience is largely acquired as a result of their own locomotor activities; they are left in a "nest" by their mothers and maternal transport is largely confined to retrieving them to the nest—before their eyes open (Schneirla, Rosenblatt, & Tobach, 1963). The *details* of the environmental conditions required to initiate and sustain changes in gene expression are species-specific. However, the underlying *mechanisms* are remarkably similar (e.g., Struhl, 1984).

mammalian nervous system continues to change even in adulthood (Purves & Hadley, 1985).

Experiments with nerve cells in tissue cultures indicate that some of the signals affecting the development of central neurons are derived from the membranes of surrounding nerve cells (Prochiantz, Daquet, Herbert, & Glowinski, 1981) or schwann cells (Dinis-Donini, Glowinski, & Prochiantz, 1984; Mudge, 1984). (In central neurons, cell proliferation may be tightly regulated by CNS glia, [Benfey & Aguayo, 1982].) But synapse formation also affects differentiation. When cultured nerve cells begin to form functional synapses, there are reliable changes in the abundance of proteins in the presynaptic axon. These observations also suggest that synapse formation involves intercellular signals that affect the phenotypes of the synapsing cells (Sonderegger et al., 1983). In molluscs, where the fates of individual neurons can be followed throughout development, specific neurotransmitters and neurohormones do regulate morphogenesis prior to the establishment of functional synapses (McAllister et al., 1983). In fact, in tissue cultures, the neurotransmitter serotonin inhibits the outgrowth of "growth cones" and synapse formation in specified neurons which otherwise would have formed functional synapses. Other, serotonin-insensitive neurons continue to form connections under these conditions (Haydon, 1984). Likewise, electrical activity at physiological rates causes changes in growth cone proliferation and activity (Cohan & Kater, 1986).

Taken together, these experiments indicate that both the gross morphology and the functional fine tuning of the central nervous system can be understood in terms of (chemical) environmental regulation of (neuronal) gene action. Moreover, tissue culture studies suggest that neurotransmitters may serve as chemical messengers influencing morphogenesis and synapse *formation* as well as impulse propagation (See also Saji & Reis, 1987).

### Maturation, Experience, and Development

Although sketchy, at best, this overview of neuroembryology and the ontogeny of binocular vision suggest that we may profit from a re-examination of a number of common assumptions.

*Maturation vs. experience.* One of our more persistent conceptual problems is the distinction between maturation (sometimes used synonymously with "innate") and experience (occasionally equated with "learned"). Textbooks typically attempt to resolve problems raised by such phenomena as imprinting by asserting that maturation and experience "interact." Yet, if one examines how maturation and experience are defined, concepts of "interaction" are, at best, confusing. The logical problem derives from explicit recognition that maturation is not "purely genetic"; that all growth (gene-expression) depends upon quite specific, if often common, environmental conditions (See, e.g., Oyama, 1982; 1985). Since experience is (implicitly) defined as response to environmental stimuli, both terms refer to processes involving environmental input. The absolute distinction between maturation and experience can only be maintained by holding that "experience" alters the organism *without* affecting gene regulation. However, the development of stereoscopic vision would be a "typical" instance of so-called "interaction," and the evidence strongly suggests that it depends upon activity-dependent changes in gene regulation. Thus one class of inputs "readying" the system for receptor activation is either ignored or confused with the effects of activation.

Nor can we justify the dichotomy between maturation and experience on the grounds that the nervous system is unique in its modifiability as a result of experience. That argument could hold only if we were to accept the idea that experience is independent of neural function. Functionally induced change is widespread; it affects both the mass and enzymatic content of muscles (Caplan et al., 1983; Coulombre, 1970; Goldberger, 1974) and even the shape and consistuents of bone (Caplan et al., 1983; Goode & Rambaut, 1985; Hofer, 1981). Many other facets of growth also depend upon function in the changing tissues or organs themselves. Thus, at this level, experience reduces to nerve-action, or functionally-induced cellular change.

For humans, the most obviously unique feature of what we call experience is that we may be *aware* of the receptor-mediated events. But a strict criterion of conscious awareness would only serve to rule out much of the "early experience" literature (e.g., Wachs & Gruen, 1982). Moreover, as will be argued subsequently, many of the exteroceptive cues that may be crucial for normal development probably do *not* capture our conscious attention (See also Gazzaniga, 1985; Lumsden & Wilson, 1981).

*Endogenous vs. exogenous.* Yet there remains a strong intuitive appeal to the idea of separating "biological" from "environmental" factors. It seems natural to distinguish developmental changes which can be related to organ function within the body (such as hormonal signals) from those attributable to sensory excitation. If we could be both consistent in our usage and clear that we are only talking about immediate causes, the distinction might occasionally be useful. Unfortunately, we are trapped by our habits of thought, and these terms seem to lead our thinking back into the old nature-nurture dichotomy (cf. Immelmann, Barlow, Petrinovich, & Main, 1981; Oyama, 1985). Moreover, there exist too many instances which do not permit simple dichotomous analyses. For example, in addition to genotype, season, level of nutrition, and psychological stress all affect the age of onset of puberty, that is, changed hormonal regulation (Tanner, 1970). In such cases, little is gained by separating categories and much is lost by failing to specify the various contributors.

However, the most fundamental objection to maintaining a distinction between endogenous and exogenous influences on growth is simply that it is an inaccurate description of the mechanisms involved. Returning to our example of stereopsis, the eyes themselves are several synapses removed from the visual cortex. Thus the final mechanisms underlying this visually mediated "experience" involve interneuronal chemical effects, that is, synaptic transmission. Neurotransmitters may serve as chemical messengers for so-called endogenously regulated morphological change (Hanley, 1985; Snyder, 1980), and nerve impulses do affect gene action in various target tissues (e.g., Caplan et al., 1983; Greenberg et al., 1986; La Gamma, Adler, & Black, 1984) including other neurons (Kupperman & Kasamatsu, 1983; Wong-Riley & Carroll, 1984). Furthermore, it seems that neurotransmitters affect cellular metabolism via the same intermediary mechanisms as hormones (Cohen, 1982; Nestler & Greengard, 1982). Therefore, at best, the endogenous-exogenous distinction is irrelevant to understanding the final mechanisms by which developmental change is effected. (See also Altman, 1985; Farley, 1983).

### Environmental Effects on Development

Taxonomies have a way of creating expectations that blind us to important events that "don't fit." Nevertheless, given the persistence of the innate-learned dichotomy, it may be useful to attempt an alternative. Following Gottlieb's (1976) pioneering lead, I will use (neuro)embryology as a source of descriptive categories. From the foregoing review and Gottlieb's work, environmental effects may be classified in terms of their qualitative effects at various stages of (neuro)biological development. Although Gottlieb only identified three kinds of effects, and limited his discussion to those mediated by neural function, I will propose two more: One draws a distinction between two facets of what he called "facilitation," namely, support and guidance of precursors (here still called facilitation), and the interactions required to stabilize connections, here called "validation" (cf. Jacobson, 1970). In addition, I will add a final category called "integration" to distinguish facilitation and maintenance of components from their incorporation into a broader system. (See Aslin, 1981; 1985, for another extension of Gottlieb's scheme.)

*Induction.* As used here, environmental events can be considered "inductive" when they set in motion biological processes that are necessary conditions for the initiation of developmental change. This usage differs from Gottlieb's in that overt behavior need not be involved. An inductive event also need not suffice to ensure the full phenotypic expression of a characteristic; other events may be required subsequently. Presumably, induction involves qualitative or quantitative shifts in gene-regulation that bias the developing system toward one or another developmental course. As used here, induction refers to the initial activation of inherited potential. As Gottlieb notes, we have few examples of how various alternative developmental pathways are selected from the norm of reaction of vertebrates. Nevertheless, there are plenty of examples of "new" capacities "maturing" postnatally. Thus we should expect that there must exist developmental turning points for which postnatal environmental events are critical.

One of the simplest examples of induction in mammals, including humans, involves digestive responses to new foodstuffs. At a certain point in development, the digestive tract of the young mammal has the potential to produce and secrete enzymes involved in breaking down and/or assimilating specific proteins. This potential will not be activated until the tissues involved are "challenged" with the food-constituent in question. Upon exposure to these molecules, the tissues in the gut rapidly begin to synthesize the appropriate enzymes. Within as little as 15 minutes, measurable changes can occur in enzyme synthesis (Reisenauer, 1985; See also Hofer, 1981).

It seems likely that many events which we are accustomed to dismissing as "maturational" depend upon relatively simple environmental challenges of this sort. Some of them may be involved in determining fundamental alterations in the course of behavioral development, perhaps something like LeVine's (1973) "genotypic" personality traits. These effects must be identified if we are to be able to account for some of the major dimensions of variation between people.

*Facilitation.* Here we again part company with Gottlieb and restrict the term to reflect events contributing to developmental processes set in motion by induction. Furthermore, in contrast to Gottlieb, the notion is extended to include inputs that *may* be necessary for normal growth. That is, I would consider the tissue interactions involved in cell migration (e.g., the role of "guidepost cells" in insect embryos) to be facilitative events at that level. At the level of the organism, early inoculation or ritual "surgeries" could be examples to the extent that they affect the regulation of ultimate phenotypic stature (e.g., Landauer & Whiting, 1981). Insofar as both the rate and extent of growth of the nervous system depends upon the proper levels of certain nutrients, diet would be a condition facilitating development of the brain (Balazs, Lewis, & Patel, 1979; Bergmann & Bergmann, 1979), and potentially affecting such functions as language development and concept formation (Cravioto & Delicardie, 1979). Many of the caregiving practices identified by White, Kaban, and Attanucci (1979), such as floor freedom, could be considered environmental facilitators of the toddler's acquisition of "social competence."

*Validation.* This category is to some degree included in Gottlieb's description of "facilitation." It seems necessary to treat this as a separate effect because, in the development of neuronal connections, the induction (e.g., of motor neurons) and the facilitation of their outgrowth occur independently of whether the cells or processes survived. That is, an additional set of conditions has to be met to prevent cell death, axonal withdrawal, or inactivation. In Jacobson's (1970) terms, whether or not a cell or cell process survives the phase of neuroanatomical remodeling depends upon "functional validation" by establishing a functional connection with an appropriate target cell. (This distinction also underlies what Aslin [1981] called "attunement.")

Much of what was described as the fine tuning of binocular vision would exemplify what we mean by validation. As we will see in subsequent chapters, there are a number of reasons for believing that many perceptual phenomena depend upon similar mechanisms. Thus it may be particularly important to distinguish between the conditions that ready the organism to function and those that affect the qualitative details of that function.

*Maintenance.* Another set of conditions, one that was not elaborated at length in our discussion of neuroembryology, involves the maintenance of structures which have been formed and validated. For example, the continued viability of sympathetic nerves (Sanes, 1984) and cell connections within the CNS (Gage, Bjorklund, & Steinevi, 1984) depend upon chemical signals from their surroundings. Patterned light is required to sustain the microstructure of cells in the visual system of a number of species (Brown & Salinger, 1975; Coleman & Riesen, 1968; Rosenzweig, 1971; Valverde, 1967). On the output side, maintenance of mature muscle depends upon the existence of functional synaptic connections (Changeux & Danchin, 1976).

Moreover, at the level of the whole organism, maintenance of muscle mass and bone structure both depend upon *function* (Caplan et al., 1983; Goode & Rambaut, 1985). Similarly, maintenance of articulatory control over certain speech sounds and voice modulations seem to depend upon auditory feedback (Fry, 1966). A certain number of "reinstatements" are necessary to maintain memory in retrievable form (Campbell & Jaynes, 1966).

Thus, to the extent that facilitation and validation differ from maintenance in terms of the quality of environmental events or the cellular mechanisms whereby their effects are accomplished, a separate category is warranted.

*Integration.* Even when functional linkages have been established and sustained, more may be required to ensure that they will serve the organism. For example, a common observation in the development of cognition is that young children are capable of labeling an event, but that they do not use this capacity in the service of problem solving or memory tasks. In cats, the ability to visually discriminate the orientations of lines depends in part upon postnatal exposure to visual patterns. This phenomenon would qualify as an example of what we have called "validation." However, the ability to make a discrimination is no guarantee that it will be of use to the animal. Spinelli and Jensen (1979) showed that pairing either vertical or horizontal lines with shock during the period of visual fine tuning significantly increased the number of cortical cells "driven" by the array associated with shock. The data suggested that the additional input may have been required for an appreciation of the "significance" of the event.

Although we typically think of "integration" in terms of enhancing synaptic activation (cf. Kandel, 1983), we cannot rule out the possibility that higher levels of control can be achieved as a result of *silencing* existing connections. The receptor-activated validation of stereopsis depends upon loss or inhibition of synapses (Wiesel, 1982). In humans, the number of synapses in at least one cortical area (Greenough & Schwark, 1984; Huttenlocher et al., 1982) increases in the first postnatal year and subsequently declines over the next 15 years. Surface recordings of visually-evoked brain activity suggest that binocular summation in infants is greater than in adults (Shea, Aslin, & McCulloch, 1987) and that mutual inhibition between cells in the visual cortex affects pattern vision (Morrone & Burr, 1986).

Thus what appears to be the increasing efficiency of more "mature" behavior may reflect a reduction in the "noise" in the system in addition to, or instead of, increases in the number or excitatory activity of connections. If so, some instances of integration may be contemporaneous with validation. In others, integration may follow validation and result from increases in synaptic conductance and/or the establishment of mutually inhibitory relationships among regulatory elements.

This taxonomy has been extrapolated primarily from studies of neural development to emphasize three points: (a) That the effects of experience ultimately must be achieved by alterations at the tissue level; (b) that such alterations will involve some change in gene-activation; and (c) that development typically results from a complex array of environmental conditions, often affecting the developing organism in sequence. This latter point is seldom emphasized enough. Too often investigators have ignored the conditions underlying "maturation" and emphasize what I have called integration almost exclusively. More recently, increasing attention has been devoted to facilitation and validation as well (e.g., Held, 1985; Wachs & Gruen, 1982). However, with notable exceptions of such investigators as Aslin (1981; 1985) Gottlieb (1976), Plomin (e.g., Plomin et al., 1977; Plomin, 1981), Scarr (e.g., Scarr-Salapatek, 1976; Scarr & McCartney, 1983) and Werner and Smith (1982), rather little attention has been devoted to conceptualizing all the different ways in which various environmental conditions influence the broader course of development.

This is not to say that separate stimuli *always* govern different aspects of development. For some attributes, the same conditions may suffice to initiate and support full phenotypic expression. However, the data reviewed here on the ontogeny of vision demonstrate that one cannot *assume* that the same conditions will suffice. Each attribute must be investigated in its own right.

### Genes and Development

One of the fundamental themes of this book is that all development must be understood as the joint product of genes and environment. This is hardly a new position, but it is one that has proven inordinately difficult to maintain with any consistency. In her now-classic essay, Anastasi (1958) suggested we think in terms of two continua of "indirectness" for both hereditary and environmental contributors. Unfortunately, such a scheme permits one to envision a characteristic that is "directly" influenced by heredity but only "indirectly" affected by the environment. From there, it is only a short step back to "innate" vs. "acquired."

*The question "How"*. At the level of the individual, *no* characteristic is "more" or "less" genetically or environmentally determined. All phenotypic attributes are the products of environmentally-initiated and supported gene-action. Both genetic and environmental effects are *always* "indirect" insofar as they construct the phenotype through growth processes. The question of how this occurs, like the question of describing growth, is one that can be attacked on many levels. This brief review of embryological concepts describes an approach at one level. More detailed biochemical analyses would be appropriate for some questions, such as the metabolic regulations involved in cell migration or synapse formation. For other questions, such as the quality of input required for the fine-tuning of visual perception, more classical psychological approaches would be appropriate. All are valid and relevant issues and merit vigorous pursuit.

However, clarification of the question of "how" requires a return to the concepts of developmental biology. In an oversimplified form, the gene-to-behavior sequence can be schematically portrayed as follows:

in an environment

Genes → peptides → amino acids → cell differentiation → tissues → organs → function

where "function" can range from hemoglobin transport to thought. Without the products of gene-action, there are no life-processes, and without a supporting environment there is no gene-action. But the foregoing, linear model is only part of the picture. Progressive cell divisions ultimately result in alterations of cellular environments and, eventually, intertissue interactions. Thus a strictly linear model is not an accurate portrayal even for a single cell in a developing organism. Function, whether metabolic or locomotor, can affect the environment and thus, potentially, it can feed back to affect gene activation.

*Transactions.* At the level of analysis typically undertaken by psychologists, we are dealing with even more complex relationships. They involve not only heredity and the environment in which genes gain expression, but also the (resulting) phenotype acting as an intermediary via receptors, nerve networks, muscles, glands, and so on. Thus, the linear scheme must be transformed into one in which the coaction of genes and environment is, in a sense, mediated by the developing phenotype (Fig. 2.1).

In this scheme, the effects of the environment are "transduced" via receptors and nervous/hormonal conduction. However, as argued above, this represents no fundamental difference from so-called endogenous gene regulation. The ultimately effective signal is biochemical, and the response will involve some aspect of gene expression or regulation. Moreover, insofar as the genome defines the norm of (phenotypic) reaction, heredity influences the kinds of messages that get through. That is, the fundamental nature of receptor tuning is dependent upon one's heredity and so are the mechanisms by which receptor-initiated messages are fil-

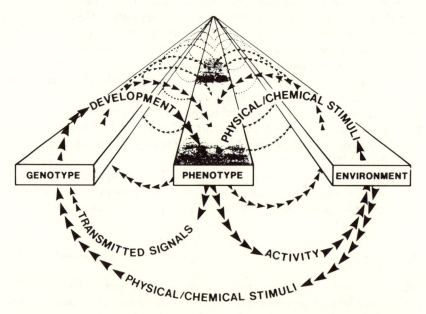

Figure 2-1:    Phenotype as Mediator of Gene-Environment Co-action.

tered. The former point is exemplified by inherited anomalies in color vision, taste sensitivities, and olfaction (e.g., Dobzhansky, 1962) and the latter by abnormalities in the "routing" of nerves from visual and auditory pathways associated with albinism (Carroll, Jay, McDonald, & Halliday, 1980; Creel, Garber, King, & Witkop, 1980).

From the foregoing, then, development must be considered as the result of an interplay between genetically determined potentials and the environment. This is just as true for child-caregiver transactions as it is for the chromosome-cytoplasm relationship. Any behavioral phenotype should ultimately be reducible to the orderly but selective expression and masking of genetic potentials. "Experience" ultimately must be reducible to receptor-activated nervous transmission. The chemical messengers involved are essentially the same as those mediating morphological growth and are not fundamentally different from those regulating what has been called "maturation." From the moment that specialized tissues form (if not simply due to the properties of cell membranes), gene-environment co-actions can be seen as embedded in a series of transactions. Heredity and environment jointly give rise to the phenotype which both filters and acts upon the environment which activates and sustains it.

# CHAPTER 3

# Evolution, Development, and Behavior

The extent to which we can hope to understand ourselves and to plan our future depends in some measure on our ability to read the riddles of the past. The present, for all its awesome importance for us who chance to dwell in it, is only a random point in the long flow of time. (Simpson, 1950, p. 9)

If we are to have a desirable biological future, we must know our biological natures, which are evolutionary, and act on that concept. (Simpson, 1972, p. 36).

In this chapter, general principles of evolutionary theory will be reviewed and their implications for understanding behavioral development discussed. The positions taken here are that: (a) *Homo sapiens* was, and continues to be, shaped by natural selection, and (b) an evolutionary approach can help not only to illuminate questions of origins, but also to provide a fruitful working framework for the analysis of ontogeny and the identification of environmental conditions that affect behavior.

Evolutionary theory is an attempt to account for the existence of the many different forms of life and the relationships among them. In its present form, the theory has two facets: They are (a) an account of the origins of different species and (b) a theory of the processes giving rise to the diversity of life forms. The account of origins involves three basic premises: (a) that existing species are the descendants of related, but different forms who lived in the past; (b) that the characteristics of some of the offspring of ancestral forms diverged in ways that eventually gave rise to new species, and (c) that the processes underlying these events have remained essentially the same to the present. The theory posits that the diversity of species represents responses of life forms to the demands—and opportunities—presented by the diversity and variability of the environments on this planet (Dobzhansky, 1951; 1970).

At present, the fossil record leaves little serious ground for challenging the premise of descendancy (Simpson, 1950). The notion of gradualism inherent in the second premise is the subject of active debate (e.g., Gould,

1982; Rose & Brown, 1984; Schankler, 1981). However, disagreement centers about rates of change of major features, changes typically measured in geologic time (e.g., Lister, 1984). The basic premise of divergence is not in question (Dawkins, 1985). Similarly, there is general acceptance of the hypothesis that the underlying, fundamental processes continue to obtain. What is debated are the details of how these processes operate (Stebbins & Ayala, 1981; Wake & Larson, 1987). Thus we turn to the second facet of the theory, the mechanisms underlying the process of speciation, which Darwin (1859/1962) dubbed "Natural Selection."

## Natural Selection

In its simplest terms, this aspect of the theory states that individuals who are the most adept sustaining themselves in a particular setting are more likely to survive and produce offspring (who are similarly happily endowed) than are individuals who are less well equipped. As a result of differential survival and reproduction, the occupants of different habitats will progressively come to possess more of the attributes which allow them to capitalize upon whatever resources may be available in their surroundings. So long as these habitats are sufficiently diverse and remain relatively consistent in their essential characteristics, over time, their inhabitants become ever more matched to them and thus increasingly different from each other.

Although ancestral forms may be gradually supplanted by better adapted, subsequent generations, and therefore eventually by "new" species, the lineage endures. Such a lineage, or branch thereof, will become extinct only if the habitat either changes too rapidly for the species inhabiting it to "keep up," or if the habitat is invaded by forms which are even better equipped to utilize it and/or are able to displace the previous occupants (Dobzhansky, 1951; 1970; Mayr, 1970; Thoday, 1975).

*Opportunism and conservatism.* On the premise that new life forms evolve from preexisting ones, natural selection is said to be "opportunistic." That is, new species arise from elaborations and/or deletions of characteristics that were exhibited by their ancestors. The process of selection can be likened to "tinkering" with the materials at hand to improve an existing match between organism and environment, to solve a new problem, or to exploit a new or underutilized habitat. In essence, the theory holds that new species are not created *de novo;* they represent restructurings of available materials (Jacob, 1977). This also implies that characteristics serving one end in a particular context may be redeployed to serve another end as conditions change. (The latter point raises an important cautionary note: One cannot assume, *a priori*, that the original adaptive significance of an attribute corresponds to its role in the present [Dobzhansky, 1970; Mayr, 1970]).

These considerations also imply that the evolutionary process is "conservative" in that workable solutions to biological problems tend to persist even though they may be utilized in different ways. For example, external morphologies of diverging species may remain quite similar despite different habits and habitats (Stebbins & Ayala, 1981), and biochemical messengers such as hormones share striking similarities in structure although they may serve somewhat different regulatory functions in different forms (Jacob, 1977; Krieger, 1983).

*Genes and selection.* Insofar as conceptions of natural selection are based upon inheritance and differential reproductive success, genetic transmission and phenotypic expression are key features of modern versions of the selective process. Although some aspects of speciation may involve the differential success of entire populations (B.J. Williams, 1981; Gould, 1982), selection ultimately acts on individuals. However, because in sexually-reproducing species, each individual inherits a unique assemblage of genes, and because chromosomes also break up and recombine ("cross-over"), the enduring "units" of selection must be the individual, replicating elements, or genes (Dawkins, 1976a; Fisher, 1930). Thus selection can be reduced to the outcome of differential reproduction of (individuals') genes via the performance of the individual phenotypes to which they give rise (See also Alexander, 1979).

The notion of what constitutes "a" gene is undergoing something of a revolution. Rather than a continuous segment of DNA which codes a specific enzyme, the basic (pan-specific) units of inheritance are now thought to represent shorter "transcription" units ("exons") which, in evolution, can recombine to form the templates for a variety of functional protein (polypeptide) chains (Gilbert, 1978; 1985). There are substantial amounts of DNA between these coding units ("introns") which seem to have no obvious function. Some of the introns apparently reflect repetitions of the same message. In addition, some coding units can be functionally equivalent although slightly different in form. Thus, it has been suggested that evolution at the molecular level often may be neutral (i.e., unaffected by natural selection, e.g., Kimura, 1983; Li, Gojobori, & Nei, 1981) and that some sequences may be essentially "parasitic" insofar as they may not contribute to individual success (Jukes, 1980). (However, if an individual has "too much" of this repeated, "junk" DNA, its metabolic costs might prove deleterious, e.g., Cavalier-Smith, 1980.) On the other hand, it is recognized that the intervening and repeated DNA sequences may provide the molecular mechanisms by which replicating segments are regulated, and/or by which transcription units can recombine, that is, the ultimate source of evolutionary variation (See Gilbert, 1985; Orgel, Crick, & Sapienza, 1980; Doolittle & Sapienza, 1980; Sudhof, Russell, Goldstein, Brown, Sanchez-Pescador, & Bell, 1985; Siegelman, Fried, Bond, Weissman, St. John, & Smith, 1986).

In essence, then, most participants in the debate about the mechanisms of evolutionary change accept the basic idea of natural selection (e.g., Li et al., 1981). The issue centers around the question of whether changing attributes of DNA structure or phenotypic expression are outcomes of "directed" natural selection or whether some of them represent incidental (evolutionary) by-products of molecular (Doolittle & Sapienza, 1980; Li et al., 1981; Vrba, 1983) or developmental (Gould, 1982) processes.[1]

At any rate, the consensus is that some genotypes will be more likely than others to lead to the development of successful phenotypes in a particular setting. Short of life-or-death differences, the degree of success is not absolute; it is relative to that of other members of the same species and can be reduced to the differential production of fertile offspring. The term "fitness" is often used to refer to the constellation of features that confer relative reproductive advantage upon individuals.

*Fitness.* If we attempted to compare individuals within a population only in terms of how well they could adapt to their environments, then we would be examining just one aspect of the issue. Although the matter is subject to debate (e.g., B.J. Williams, 1981; Vrba, 1983), a useful working definition of fitness involves a measure of the ability to *produce the most progeny* (who, in turn, can reproduce). An individual who is very adept at staying alive could still be relatively unfit as a result of any number of characteristics such as delayed reproductive maturity, a shorter reproductive period, reduced or atypical mating or caregiving activity, or, most obviously, the inability to produce gametes. In short, in Darwinian terms, fitness can be measured in terms of relative reproductive efficiency. But one must be careful here; it is not simply the number of offspring produced that is important, it is the number of offspring who survive and reproduce successfully themselves (Dobzhansky, 1962; 1970; Fisher, 1930; Thoday, 1975).

Furthermore, insofar as it is not individual genotypes, nor chromosomes that survive, but rather, the replicating units that survive, it has been argued that the ultimate test of biological success is the proportion of one's (shared) genes that are replicated in subsequent generations. Since those who are most likely to share genes in common with one another are kin, on average, the success of a kindred as a whole may be more important than the reproductive achievements of any individual member. That is, one may contribute to one's "inclusive fitness" by enhancing the perpetuation of one's own genes either via own progeny or via the progeny of close relatives, so-called "kin selection" (See Dawkins, 1976a for review). What

---

[1] I espouse the *working* hypothesis that biological phenomena are functional; it is too easy to "write off" puzzling phenomena. It seems likely that, if we begin with the assumption that attributes have utility in *some* contexts, we will learn more about human variability and the conditions that foster its expression.

counts by this logic is the relative degree to which ones (own/shared) genes appear in subsequent generations (Hamilton, 1964; 1971). This development and extension of ideas broached earlier by Fisher (1930), Haldane (1932) and Wright (1949) have led to a number of stimulating analyses (e.g., Chagnon & Irons, 1979; Wilson, 1975).

We should notice, however, that even models of kin selection are concerned with differential reproductive success of lineages *within species.* Because a single genetic complex is unlikely to be optimal over a species' range, let alone across many generations, there tend to be several variations (alleles) at a number of chromosomal loci. In large, natural populations, it is not at all unusual for somewhat different gene complexes to give rise to essentially comparable phenotypes. When we consider the contributions to fitness of "a" gene, we do so in the context of a species— members of a larger, interbreeding population. The phenotypic effects of any gene depend upon the genetic "background" against which they are expressed (e.g., Bonner & Brownstein, 1984; Lim, 1984; Nussey, Ang, Jenkins, Chowdrey, & Bisset, 1984).

*Genes and species.* Genes thus must work together harmoniously to produce viable organisms. If we can accept the idea that the "genetic code" of DNA is essentially universal (at least among "higher" forms, cf. Fox, 1985), then the total possible array of coding sequences constitutes the field within which the selective process operates. Since the number of these combinations is practically infinite, and because genes influence the effects of one another, most of the possible combinations would probably be inviable in the world as we know it. However, some combinations do give rise to life-forms capable of surviving and reproducing. These gene-"pools" define species, as they are currently understood (Dobzhansky, 1951; 1970).

Genetically, species (gene-pools) are discrete; they are unique, integrated patterns of genetic materials linked together in sets of chromosomes. Even when two species share the same number of chromosomes, the combinations and arrangements of genetic instructions on them differ. So far as we can tell, there are few intermediate forms filling the gaps across taxa. Cross-species combinations are typically incapable of surviving or reproducing. When viable interspecific hybrids are possible, they frequently are incapable of reproduction as in the case of the mule (horse × donkey). Even when hybrids can reproduce, they tend to be less vigorous themselves or to produce weaker progeny than those deriving from within-species matings. In short, the different arrays tend to be relatively incompatible with each other or favor deleterious mutations (Woodruff, Thompson, Jr., & Lyman, 1979). According to current theory, then, a species is defined as a group of organisms sharing a common gene pool through reproductive relationships within the group (Dobzhansky, 1970; Mayr, 1970).

Insofar as evolution is conceptualized in terms of the development of new species, it is a process of genetic change. Species-formation, however, involves more than just changing individual genes. It is a matter of reconstructing gene-complexes shared by a breeding group so that the average phenotypic outcomes from intra-group matings will be viable and able to produce fertile offspring—*in the surroundings typical for the species.* This latter point is particularly important; given a particular gene-pool, the critical element determining "what" will be selected is the environment. Indeed, from an ecological vantage point, evolution could be described as the filling of unoccupied habitats. A fundamental feature of evolution seems to be that if existing genetic systems will permit it, organisms will develop the capacities to exploit an available, unoccupied niche, or to more efficiently exploit the one in which they find themselves (Dobzhansky, 1970; Wright, 1960). In short, phylogeny, in many ways like ontogeny, is the resultant of the interplay between organism and environment.

Returning then, to our discussion of fitness, we find that, at the level of a species, the fitness value of a gene relative to its alleles must be gauged in terms of the average of large numbers of individuals' reproductive efficiencies over extended periods. For any individual, only a few genes may contribute to the development of a fit phenotype against an otherwise fixed genetic background. However, given a large population, and a gene-pool permitting a variety of potential genetic backgrounds, a considerably wider range of genes may contribute to fitness when one considers the species as a whole. Rare genes are unlikely to "find" compatible hereditary backgrounds simply because selection will be continuously favoring genetic environments hospitable for the most common variants. However, because physical environments do change, there will be a trade-off between (phenotypic) variability and the fine-tuning of complex systems to match existing conditions. In a population, over time, the trade-off usually results in a workable balance. For the individual, the effect of a particular allele can be all-or-nothing as in the case of a gene which is lethal to the homozygote (Mayr, 1970). Ultimately, natural selection acts on the individual's entire genetic complement and the processes that these hereditary materials govern.

A phenotype which seems well adapted at one point in time and space may be less so in another. Because the earth's environment is constantly changing, an optimal "genotype for all seasons" is exceedingly unlikely— at least among sexually reproducing species. Apparently maximally fit individuals represent only lucky combinations of inherited potentials; their offspring are unlikely to receive the same assortments (cf. G.C. Williams, 1975). This is the basis for what has been called "regression toward the mean" of measured attributes across generations. In those infrequent cases in which outstandingly fit progeny are produced across several, successive generations, these individuals probably achieve phenotypic excellence on the basis of new combinations of parental genes.

## Variation

So far, we have taken phenotypic and genotypic variability as givens. They are the raw materials upon which natural selection works. The enduring, pen-specific units of heredity may be relatively short coding sequences of DNA interspersed among other, "silent" DNA strands. Presumably, many of the genes of different species are slightly differently organized combinations of these "conserved" segments (Gilbert, 1978; Sudhof, Russell, Goldstein, Brown, Sanchez-Pescador, & Bell, 1985). For example, regulatory genes of widely varying forms, from yeast to humans, show common coding patterns, (e.g., Shepherd, 1984). Presumably, this piecemeal arrangement has provided a mechanism whereby "workable" biological (genetic) solutions could be retained without sacrificing the possibility of creating genetic "novelties." That is, selection favors genomes that can both produce fit phenotypes and store or create novelties (See Gilbert, 1978; 1985; Doolittle & Sapienza, 1980).

*Genetic variation.* Genetic material can mutate to form novel sequences via a number of mechanisms. Some genes seem to be remarkably stable. Even among these, however, the potential for novelty can arise *via* duplication so that some "copies" of the gene are supernumeraries and free to undergo structural change. Presumably, this might be one function of "silent" and/or "repeat" DNA (Jacob, 1977). Other genes apparently mutate more rapidly, perhaps due to their relative unimportance (i.e., relaxed selection pressure), or because of the peculiar characteristics of their molecular structures or of their chromosomal surroundings. With respect to the latter possibility, it is generally accepted that some genetic backgrounds favor mutations whereas others inhibit or suppress genetic novelties. It has been suggested that suppressor factors (genes) are favored by selection during periods of environmental stability (Thompson & Woodruff, 1978).

As coadapted, organized systems, the genomes of multicellular organisms seem to have intrinsic mechanisms for responding to potential threats from the environment or occasional errors in duplication. These include gene sequences that can be "transposed" within chromosomes. Indeed, when a difficulty is encountered for which it is "unprepared," a genome may even "reorganize" itself. Such restructuring may provide another mechanism whereby genetic novelties are produced (McClintock, 1984; Paulson, 1985).

Beyond changing sequences within genes and more or less permanent transpositions of gene sequences, the process of cell division can give rise to genetic novelty by inversion. This occurs when segments of two homologous chromosomes fail to segregate symmetrically, and a portion of one breaks off and becomes attached to its opposite member during meiosis (Dobzhansky, 1970).

Insofar as genomes are considered to be coadapted systems, many changes of the foregoing sorts must be deleterious, if not lethal. However, because the genetic "code" itself involves some redundancies, and because the phenotypic effects of specific sequences are not uniform across all "backgrounds," various alternative forms of "a" gene (alleles) can arise (e.g., Nathans, Thomas, & Hogness, 1986). (In species with complex life histories, several forms of such genes may be essential to cope with the demands of different environments, e.g., fetal vs. adult hemoglobins.) Such genetic "polymorphism," in conjunction with sexual reproduction, typically guarantees the continuous production of genomic novelties and thus the raw (phenotypic) materials for the selective process (Dobzhansky, 1970; G.C. Williams, 1975).

*Phenotypic variation.* Phenotypic variation, although clearly correlated with genotypic variability, does not *necessarily* index genetic polymorphism. A substantial degree of variation in a characteristic can occur if the degree of expression of these genes is variable and responsive to differences in the surroundings. Alternatively, a range of phenotypic expression may reflect variability in a limited set of genes which regulate the expression of *other* (monomorphic) genes. Therefore, the existence of a wide, even continuous range of phenotypic expression of a trait may not directly reflect the range of different alleles "for" it (Thompson, 1975). Moreover, although the transmission of nuclear DNA is closely controlled, the inheritance of cellular organelles such as mitochondria (which have "their own" DNA) in mammals is via the maternal line. Thus a substantial amount of phenotypic variation may reflect, in part, variation in non-nuclear inheritance—that is, the non-nuclear, genetic background (Birky, 1983).

*Compromise.* Presumably, the necessity to maintain genetic variability while conferring the potentials for a range of adaptations dictates that the genome must "be prepared" to meet a number of environmental demands. Insofar as selection can work with only what is available, the tinkering involved in adjusting genomes to meet even an unchanging array of environmental exigencies cannot result in either a rapid or a perfect fit. Rather, genes providing the potential to adapt to one facet of an environment (or phase of growth) must be modified or regulated so that their actions will remain compatible with genes which confer the potentials to adapt in other ways. In short, genomes—and the phenotypes that they underlie—represent evolutionary and developmental "compromises" (Dawkins, 1976a; Mayr, 1970). Even though compromises preclude a perfect match between organismic potential and situational demands, the range of phenotypic "fits" typically is more than adequate to meet the average, expectable environments. That is, the pathways for development of important phenotypic characteristics can still be programmed. The price paid for accommodations among genes may not be paid until later life (Dawkins, 1976a; Dobzhansky, 1951; Jacob, 1977).

*The norm of reaction.* The short-term payoff for mechanisms that ensure variation becomes apparent when we consider habitats. Particularly among species that exploit a heterogeneous range, the abilities to alter "strategies," or to fine-tune phenotypes to meet the demands of specific settings are critical. Therefore, most animals inherit the potentials to modify the course, and even the targets of phenotypic growth (Lowell, 1985). The norm of reaction of an individual refers to those portions of the inherited genome that specify the potential range of phenotypic variation. Theoretically, it should be substantially broader in cosmopolitan forms than in those who are specialists in exploiting a narrower range of environmental resources (Dobzhansky, 1970). Insofar as function must be adjusted to environmental variation, the potential for phenotypic flexibility should be greatest in this realm. Given the apparent conservatism and opportunism of natural selection, we should expect more heterogeneity with respect to an animal's norm of reaction for the development of function, as opposed to its gross morphology (Mayr, 1970).

Because the growing young seldom, if ever, encounter a sequence of environments identical to that encountered by their parents, a hereditary endowment that specifies a range of alternatives is often more fit in the long run as well. At the very least, an individual must have the capacity to recognize an unfavorable or a favorable setting and move or stay put as appropriate (Johnson, 1974; Thoday, 1975).

Fitness, then, is the product of a variety of adaptations. It reflects the potential to develop a phenotype that can compete with conspecifics for sustenance, shelter, and mates; resist disease; avoid predators; and efficiently exploit its habitats. In addition, an individual's genetic endowment must be one that can mix well with the hereditary combinations of available mates. But more is required; our organism must develop into an individual who is attracted to appropriate mates and who will see that its offspring will be provided for (either by self or mate). All these potentials (and many more) must be present for an individual to successfully pass on its genes. Yet for subsequent generations to survive, there must also be the ability to "store" the hereditary capacity to change in response to fluctuating environments (Simpson, 1950; G.C. Williams, 1975; Wilson, 1975).

*Sexual reproduction.* Given that species represent organized sets of genetic materials that "go together," and that novelties tend, on average, to be deleterious, how can compromises meet the need for variation and still be kept workable? One answer seems to be via sexual reproduction.

Because mutations are so unlikely to work out, most "successful" variability results from the recombinations of existing genetic materials through the union of gametes. When the egg is fertilized, the zygote obtains a new, essentially random, combination of maternal and parental chromosomes. Moreover, in the process of gamete-production genes cross over, yielding novel combinations. This phenomenon is not the same as a mutation because no genes are added or lost to the chromosome, nor are there any fundamental alterations in the arrangement of material. That is, crossing-over is a "routine" event relative to mutation because an important feature of the chromosome is the arrangement of the loci, or sites for genes which function in a given way. Genes sharing the same loci usually can be interchanged with one another without causing *serious* disruptions (as would the introduction of a mutation—a totally new gene or a drastic rearrangement of the order of alleles).

In short, a great deal of genotypic variability can result from the process of sexual reproduction (see G.C. Williams, 1975). Indeed, given random pairing of parental chromosomes and the phenomenon of crossing-over, it is highly improbable that human parents ever pass on all of their genes. Even with relatively conservative estimates of the extent of allelic variation, the variety of possible human genotypes would far exceed the total number of people who ever lived (Dobzhansky, 1962; 1970).

### Evolution and Environment

In the preceding discussion, a number of points have been qualified in terms of the degree to which a species' habitat is homogeneous or stable. To discuss evolution, adaptation, or selection without reference to some setting would be meaningless. It is the environment that determines the adaptiveness of phenotypic characteristics and thus the selective pressures exerted upon those who express them. What is frequently overlooked is the fact that a habitat cannot be understood without reference to its inhabitants. Each form depends upon sustenance, and so on, extracted from its environment and, in so doing, modifies that setting. Evolution, then, involves more than a set of inorganic constraints; much like development, natural selection is the result of transactions between organisms and their surroundings (Oyama, 1985).

### Evolution and Development

Phenotypes succeed or fail in reproducing, and a phenotype represents the expression of just one instance of an inherited norm of reaction. In complex organisms, genes achieve phenotypic expression via environmentally evoked and supported developmental processes. Thus we may say that selection does not act upon the adaptive "traits" of a species per se. Rather, it alters the probabilities that individuals will be endowed with the genetic capacities to respond to their environments with structural and functional *development* that permits survival and reproduction. Any hereditary array that is more likely than others to give rise to a developmental path ultimately leading to successful reproduction will be over-represented in subsequent generations—so long as the setting does not change in any vital ways.

A phenotype acts as a vehicle, as it were, for the transmission of genetic material. Only the developmental processes which give rise to phenotypic *variants* will be under intense selection pressure (Dobzhansky, 1960; Dawkins, 1976a; Mayr, 1970). Thus selection acts upon (genes guiding) developmental processes themselves. Major alterations in phenotype can occur as a result of changing the temporal pattern of growth of already-existing attributes (Purvis & Lichtman, 1985; Raff, Anstrom, Huffman, Leaf, Loo, Showman, & Wells, 1984; Raff & Kaufman, 1983).

*Ontogeny and evolution.* The rate of reproductive maturation, and longevity itself must be adaptations to particular habitats (Gould, 1977; Gadgil, 1982). Gould suggested that ontogeny can be conceptualized as involving three relatively separable, general processes: (a) changes in shape and complexity of organization; (b) changes in the rate at which function or activity attains adult-like form ("maturation"); and (c) increases in size. The second process, changing the timing of ontogenetic events, is thought to have repercussions on the other two processes, including those affecting structure. This is because development depends uopn the co-actions of a pool of more or less uniquely coadapted genes (e.g., Mayr, 1970; Raff & Kaufman, 1983).

These genetic coadaptations, insofar as they channel development along a limited number of pathways, also constrain the developmental changes that can take place, that is, the opportunism of selection (Gould, 1982). At present, there is debate as to whether the attributes that are modifiable represent (prior) adaptations or whether they represent "neutral" traits (cf. above, and Lewin, 1981; 1982). In either case, however, there is consensus that selection affects development and that animal evolution must have involved changes in the course of ontogeny (Raff et al., 1984; Raff & Kaufman, 1983; Wake & Larson, 1987).

Different aspects of structure are specified by relatively independent subsets of genes (e.g., Tanner, 1970; Thompson, 1975), and developmental rates vary across tissues (Snow & Tam, 1980). Although an oversimplification (Brown, 1981), one potentially useful distinction is between "structural" and "regulatory" genes. This distinction was recognized long ago by Fisher (1930) who pointed out that the "same" genes' "external effects" could be modified by other genes. This is amply verified by the fact that a single gene may be regulated differently in different tissues of the same individual—that is, against different backgrounds of activation of the *same* genome (e.g., Cooper, 1984). Thus, given the opportunism and conservatism of evolution, divergence (speciation) probably involved changes in gene-regulation more frequently than changes in the structural proteins themselves (Jacob, 1977; Markert, Shaklee, & Whitt, 1974; Raff et al., 1984).

Perhaps the most compelling illustration of this idea has come from a comparison of the major structural proteins of humans and chimpanzees. In 1975, King and Wilson reported that the structural-genetic similarities between *Homo* and *Pan* were comparable to those of "sibling" species of other forms. Speciation involving morphological divergences apparently did not depend upon major alterations in the building blocks themselves; rather, alterations in the rate and pattern of their assembly sufficed to yield substantial differences between species. These conclusions were supported by Bruce and Ayala (1978) and by Cherry, Case, and Wilson (1978) who also found that changing gene-regulation may be a major factor in morphological and behavioral evolution.

*Mosaics and heterochrony.* Generally speaking, different body parts grow at "their own" rates (Shea, 1983; Tanner, 1970), apparently as a result of genes governing the pace of cellular differentiation in specific tissues (Ambros, 1984). Growth is not unitary; it is "heterochronous." Unless the fossil evidence has been misinterpreted, many lineages seem to evolve as unevenly changing "mosaics" of characteristics (Bromage, 1985; Gould, 1977; Raff et al., 1984; White, 1980). Thus available evidence supports the view that evolutionary changes in the patterns of growth of various structures can account for many differences among species (Gould, 1977; Raff & Kaufman, 1983). Since the basic morphological elements would be structurally the same, only "minor" genetic change would be required.

Selection (and mutant genes) can either slow down or accelerate the appearance of certain attributes. Often evolution involves processes whereby juvenile characteristics are maintained (their rates of development slowed) until sexual maturity. Indeed, one frequently-encountered explanation for a number of attributes of *Homo* invokes the idea of "neoteny." It is held that our species' morphological characteristics represent the outcome of processes whereby certain juvenile characteristics of the anthropoid primate lineage were maintained as attributes of the mature organisms. For example, the ratio of the area of the forehead to the rest of the face in a juvenile chimpanzee is more similar to that of an adult human than to that of an adult chimpanzee. (See Gould, 1977 for review).

*Stages.* Whether or not the earliest phases of development are more resistant to evolutionary tinkering (Gould, 1977), a generally-established principle is that selection acts at all stages of the life-cycle (Fisher, 1930). That is, the organism must be able to maintain itself and grow (at least through reproductive maturity) in the environments typical of the species. Hofer (1981) has reviewed evidence that selection begins as soon as sperm "compete" to reach the egg through the female reproductive tract. Not all sperm are equally capable of surviving and moving in the female environment; they are subject to the action of the female's immune system. Many are thereby rendered unable to penetrate the ovum. After fertilization, the zygote must migrate, begin to differentiate, signal the uterus, implant, develop a placenta, and so on. For each phase, new patterns of gene activation and regulation are required; survival depends upon a finely-tuned genome. Thus it should be no surprise that a substantial proportion of all "fertile" human matings fail to result in full-term pregnancies (See Sameroff & Chandler, 1975).

Postnatally, the organism must be able to make the transition to extra-uterine life—to possess the physiological and behavioral attributes required for postnatal survival and growth (Bell & Harper, 1977; Harper, 1981; Galef, 1981) and finally, to compete for mates and provide the wherewithal for rearing young. This is another context in which evolutionary "compromises" are important; a "successful" mammalian genome is one which gives rise to phenotypes which remain vigorous until their progeny are capable of fending (and mating) on their own (see, Alexander, 1979; Dawkins, 1976a for reviews). As Hofer (1981) put it, selection acts upon how successfully genotypes "predict the future." (See also Lowell, 1985.)

*Genetic assimilation.* As a result of this unrelenting selection, gene-combinations will be favored which lead to the development of phenotypic attributes that represent workable solutions to the specific demands of probably-encountered settings. A mechanism by which such developmental tuning might occur was described by Waddington (1957) and dubbed "genetic assimilation." He noted that organisms from a population typically show a varying range of developmental responses to certain environmental conditions, and that one could select lines which would become increasingly reactive to a particular condition, such as temperature. That is, by deliberately interbreeding the most reactive individuals, a developmental feature that was manifested in a "base" population only under extreme temperatures could come to be expressed in the "normal" environment (see also Rendel, 1967).

According to models of developmental regulation, this selective regimen would act primarily on the regulatory genes that affected thresholds for development responses. The quality of the response itself, that is, development of a morphological or physiological attribute, would not be altered substantially, if at all. Rather, the change would involve the (regulatory) genetic mechanisms controlling expression of that (structural) genetic potential (e.g., Riddle, Swanson, & Albert, 1981).

Thus we come to one possible explanation for the origin of invariant (species-typical) outcomes of development. When characteristics are (become) adaptively important, selection should favor genotypes which lead to expression of the underlying developmental pathways in any or all settings that are compatible with growth. That is, evolution should favor regulatory genes that orchestrate developments so that the organism can be counted upon to encounter the conditions necessary for the expression of structural genes underlying the phenotypic attributes in question. This phylogenetic fine-tuning could involve the evolution of responsiveness to self-generated, proximal signals such as hormones. Alternatively, selection could lead to responsiveness to some fundamental physical parameter such as temperature—for example, the organism will respond appropriately in any temperature that will sustain its vital processes.

*Sign stimuli.* Insofar as selection is opportunistic and is more comparable to tinkering than careful preplanning, we should not expect the development of organisms to be exquisitely sensitive to all the nuances of their surroundings. Indeed, for the expression of phenotypic traits that are fundamental to the species, situational-specificity of responsiveness could be detrimental. Rather, we should expect that, just as the display of adaptive behavioral responses, the developmental expression of essential phenotypic attributes will also hinge upon more general, schematic, stimuli providing reliable "signs" that conditions are favorable (see e.g., Lumsden & Wilson, 1981; Lorenz, 1935/1957; Tinbergen, 1951).[2]

If Gould (1977) is correct, and early-appearing steps in development should be the more highly conserved, then we would predict that the sign-stimuli evoking and supporting expression of early steps will be *ubiquitous*. That is, they will involve stimuli which are encountered (at above some threshold level) throughout the species' range. Moreover, the earlier the developmental phase, the less the organism should depend upon specialized organs to detect or respond to these stimuli. (However, we must also recognize the existence of finely-tuned mechanisms within the cell—and even within the genome itself, cf. McClintock, 1984.)

For expression of attributes characteristic of later stages, more heterogenous arrays of sign stimuli might be expected. Among cosmopolitan species, the norm of reaction would be more likely to specify responsive-

---

[2] Ethologists (e.g., Tinbergen, 1951) elaborated the concept of sign stimuli in the context of the "release" of "instinctive" behavioral responses. Here we are extending the concept to include stimuli affecting developmental responses—changes *within* the organism. The extension seems warranted insofar as we are still talking about the evolution of responsiveness to stimuli that are reliable indices of environmental conditions of importance to the organism. See, e.g., Desjardins, Bronson, & Blank (1986).

ness to functionally *equivalent* sign stimuli. That is, any one (or more) of a set of different stimuli, typical of different habitats within the species' range, would suffice to evoke and support the phenotypic expression of a species-specific trait. It is an open question as to whether these stimuli will be *simple* (i.e., affecting only one receptor modality at a time) or *compound* (i.e., affecting several modalities simultaneously). Insofar as individuals can still be viable despite receptor impairment in a single modality, we would expect equivalent sign stimuli to involve compounds of inputs from different sensory avenues. The more important the phenotypic attribute, the less dependent its expression should be upon signs mediated via a single modality. (See Beach & Jaynes, 1956, for an analogy at the level of stimuli eliciting behavior).

Assuming that the inherited norm of reaction specifies several alternative pathways of development, we should also expect that some environmental sign stimuli would function as *exclusive alternatives* activating developmental "switches." The simplest mechanism of this sort would involve thresholds: Regulator genes would function so that below a certain level or concentration of input, development would follow one pathway; above that level, it would follow another (See Barlow, 1981; Dobzhansky, 1972). (Reversible) examples of such phenomena in humans might be provided by the role of nutrition (stored body fats) in the onset of female puberty and the maintenance of menstrual cycling. Presumably, a certain critical level of stored nutrient provides a sign that conditions are favorable for conceiving and/or rearing offspring (Frisch & McArthur, 1974).

In short, largely as a result of natural selection's action on the regulation of development, animals are programmed "for" the kinds of environments into which they are born. Presumably, the signs that will be most important for species-typical development should be (have been) distinctive and reliable correlates of conditions favorable for specific patterns of growth (e.g., Bergler, Negus, Sanders, & Gardner, 1981; Desjardins, Bronson, & Blank, 1986; Novotny, Jemiolo, Harvey, & Wiesler, & Marchlewska-Kay, 1986).

*Fixity and plasticity.* As indicated by the concept of the norm of reaction and heterochrony in development, species-specificity of development does not imply across-the-board fixity of ontogeny. Organisms inhabiting diverse or fluctuating habitats would be expected to inherit the potentials for different (and, on average, appropriate) developmental responses to various environmental conditions. So long as the capacity to respond differentially enhances reproductive success, selection will favor genotypes specifying a variety of developmental pathways. Even among specialized forms, one finds flexible responsiveness to fluctuating environmental demands, for example, muscle hypertrophy in response to work (Dobzhansky, 1970). This, too, is an invariant attribute insofar as expression of the muscles' potentials to respond to work are essentially universal and probably dependant upon ubiquitous stimuli. Some phenotypic attributes *will* be pan-specific. Presumably, they remained serviceable as the species evolved from ancestral stock and their phenotypic expression will be evoked and supported by ubiquitous or equivalent sign stimuli.

Alternative developmental pathways also can be closely specified. If a threshold level of stimulation is forthcoming, development will follow one course, if not, it will follow another one. An example might be the apparent switching of growth curves in response to the availability of nutrients. Children who have been subjected to severe and prolonged undernutrition or physiological stress such as disease sometimes appear to "re-set" their target for growth and follow a pathway leading to smaller final size—even after more favorable conditions are (re)instituted (Cravioto, 1968; Tanner, 1970).[3] This example might be understood in terms of an adaptation to variations in available food supplies, perhaps due to recurrent cyclic fluctuations in rainfall and temperature. To the extent that smaller size enables individuals to survive on reduced rations, selection should favor the capacity to switch channels without otherwise altering overall body form.

Finally, although development of many of the major outlines of a species' form and function may be evoked and sustained by relatively simple sign stimuli, almost all species must also be able to vary their activities according to immediate circumstances. In "complex" organisms, this means responses to *situationally-specific* stimuli mediated by specialized sensory systems. Evolutionary theory leads us to expect that each species would have evolved capacities to develop receptor/integrative mechanisms that are highly sensitive to the kinds of stimuli that are important for making such adjustments. Species-specific responsiveness to different facets of the physical environment have been well documented (e.g., von Uexkull, 1934/1957).

Some features of the environment are essential for survival, others are essentially irrelevant. Selection favors genes giving rise to development of receptors and processing mechanisms that are "tuned" to the relevant facets of the species' environments. We tend to be most keenly aware of events over which we have some (potential) control—even if it is limited to escape. The ever-increasing literature on the species-specificity of learning (e.g., Hinde & Stevenson-Hinde, 1973) strongly suggests that selection favors the development of characteristics supporting finely discriminated reactions only to those local, variable conditions animals can hope to cope with. As Plotkin and Odling-Smee (1979) have argued, each species should

---

[3] In this case, we might consider the period of early growth to be a sensitive period for adjusting the phenotype to the (probable) minimum level of resource-availability.

evolve the capacity to learn about those otherwise unpredictable events which are nevertheless both highly likely to be encountered and important to an individual's success.

The foregoing suggests that the *situation-specific* stimuli which are apparently so salient to us may be important only for the fine-tuning of behavior. The conditions that give rise to phenotypic expression of the fundamental forms of behavior may well be sign stimuli to which we are relatively oblivious. Furthermore, to the extent that behavior is the product of evolution, selection should have favored not simply adaptations for conditions existing at a single phase of growth, but also for increasing the probability of meeting the necessary conditions for development in subsequent stages.

*Facultative behavior.* For some species, individuals may have to be able to switch strategies a number of times in succession. The first, and most obvious set of pressures for versatility in mammals comes from the changing requirements of different phases of the life-cycle, for example, fetus, nursling, juvenile, and adolescent (Gadgil, 1982; Galef, 1981; Hofer, 1981). Some of these strategies are obligate, insofar as they are adaptations to predictable situations such as the presence of parents. Additional pressures will be imposed as habitats fluctuate in terms of the amount or quality of such essentials as food or shelter. Species such as *Homo*, evolving in diverse habitats, can be expected to be able to adjust behaviorally to a variety of conditions without making irreversible commitments; they should be capable of "facultative" alterations in activity patterns. An example of the latter would be seasonal changes in foraging strategies (Lott, 1984).

In order to make such adjustments, individuals must be capable of responding to features that distinguish one subhabitat from another. Selection will favor genes that provide individuals with the capacities to develop structures permitting them to discriminate distinctive attributes of the settings they are likely to encounter. The more discontinuous the habitats, or qualitatively distinct the fluctuations in living conditions, the more likely it will be that adoption of individual strategies will depend upon sign stimuli. One example of sign stimuli affecting such change is the role of day-length on the reproductive condition of seasonally-breeding animals (Bunning, 1967; Marler & Hamilton, 1966).

One can thus envision a continuum of environmental differences and correlated perceptual/integrative responses to them. At one extreme there would be essentially qualitatively discontinuous niches and more or less automatic switches in strategies in response to relatively simple sign stimuli corresponding to what we called exclusive alternatives. At the other extreme, there would be subhabitats that gradually grade into one another coupled with a corresponding range of strategic variations, including weighted amalgams of response which would be evoked by complex (polysensory), situationally-specific stimuli. Presumably, even the latter would be sign stimuli in the sense that the individual's potentials for developing sensory and information-processing capacities would exceed the minimum set(s) necessary for making the relevant distinctions.

Put another way, the range of uncertainties about which any animal, including *Homo*, has to "worry" is finite. Some events are simply irrelevant for survival, and others may be so completely beyond its control that any response is meaningless. Usually then, we can expect that the behavioral domains in which fine-grained sensory discriminations can be found will be those in which important events "outside the skin" take a variety of forms. Similarly, in each domain, the repertoire of actions from which the individual may choose and the expectations that can be formed will also be circumscribed as a function of the diversity of relevant outside events that it can influence (Alexander, 1979; Wilson, 1978). For a nursing infant, the variables to which it must be sensitive and respond in order to obtain food are different than those encountered by the two-year-old, or by the adult. Thus selection will lead not only to species-differences, but also to developmental differences in responsiveness to habitat; the effective environment for any individual changes as it grows up (Lumsden & Wilson, 1981; G.C. Williams, 1975; see also Thompson & Grusec, 1970).

# CHAPTER 4

# Characteristics of Growth

At present there is no generally accepted characterization of "development," the orderly sequence of changes in organismic growth. In part, the problem may derive from the fact that the choice of a satisfactory account ultimately depends upon the kind of question that is being asked (Immelmann et al., 1981; Robinson, 1969). For example, even though we are concerned with multicellular organisms, we could still wish to conceptualize development in the most basic terms. If so, we might describe it as RNA transcription by genes to make proteins (Waddington, 1971). At the cellular level, we could speak of "the replication of DNA and accretion of protein" (Cheek, 1968) or directional and irreversible changes in time (Sheldrake, 1974). Further along, at the tissue level, we would be concerned with increasing cellular specialization of function (Yuwiler, 1971). When we get to the level of the whole individual, all are relevant.

Additional problems arise because we typically expect to uncover a single process, or group of related processes with a specifiable beginning and a clearly defined end—"maturity." Unfortunately, between the beginning (fertilization) and the end (death), we are dealing with a substantial number of processes occurring over time, frequently simultaneously. For example, even the first steps of cellular differentiation, the development of three-dimensional form, and the beginnings of regional cellular specialization into organs overlap in time (Waddington, 1962). Thus, with so many processes going on simultaneously, it may be unrealistic to expect to achieve a simple characterization of development of the whole organism. Certainly, when we are dealing with behavior, which may be considered one product of the coordinated activity of a number of organ systems, we should be wary of sweeping generalizations. In short, we should not expect a single descriptor to accurately portray the many processes involved in growth.

What all this leads up to is the fact that development in higher organisms results from the complex orchestration of what often appear to be many contradictory trends (Ghiselin, 1974; Mayr, 1970). We often overlook the implications of the fact that humans undergo similar changes postnatally (e.g., replacing the milk teeth during childhood and the life-long changes in skeletal structure; see Arey, 1954; Meredith, 1973). In complex organisms, growth is more than a simple accretion of protoplasm or a progressive adding-on of more complex elements. At the level of the individual, we must get used to thinking in terms of many processes super-imposed upon each other to produce a viable organism (Tanner, 1970).

In this chapter we examine a number of more general attributes of the growth process: I will argue that growth tends to be self-regulated, or "active"; that the role of the environment is permissive rather than con-structive, and that growth is targeted or "canalized"; that is, that devel-opment tends to follow predictable trajectories despite environmental perturbations. Finally, I will examine the implications of the view that growth represents a complex mosaic of change in semi-independent com-ponents which are nevertheless coordinated in time to produce "functional systems." I suggest that growth does proceed by stages, and that there are changing patterns of organization of semi-independent components. Each stage represents a qualitatively different type of activity in one or more functional systems, and the developmental reorganization of components can account for longitudinal correlations between apparently dissimilar attributes and the effects of early experience on later-appearing behavior.

## AN "ACTIVE" PROCESS

The model of the developing phenotype transacting with the surroundings provides the prototype for the first of four characteristics that seems to typify growth of complex organisms at almost all levels of analysis: Growth is *active*. Development depends upon and is guided by the genome; the environment triggers and sustains growth. Forces extrinsic to the genome may induce a cell's commitment to a particular pathway of development, but the heredity of the organism determines both the pathways available and the kinds of environmental stimuli that will facilitate, validate, main-tain, and integrate newly expressed phenotypic attributes.

### Self-Regulation

While outside-the-skin conditions—including such intuitively unlikely phenomena as gravity (Cogoli, Tschopp, & Fuchs-Bislin, 1984; Cooke, 1986; Goode & Rambaut, 1985)—are essential for initiating and sustain-ing growth, many other aspects of development depend upon cell-to-cell exchanges. Interactions among tissues cause various cell lineages to be-come "committed" to specific developmental pathways. These phenomena also are relevant to our theme insofar as the various embryonic tissue layers apparently are *reciprocally* influencing each others' developmental fates. As we have seen in connection with the development of the CNS and motor nerves, when one tissue provides signals necessary for the development of another, the "inducee" may subsequently provide inputs that affect the fate of the "inducer" (See e.g., Lund, 1978). At the level of organs, the movements produced by embryonic muscle action are necessary for normal formation of joints in vertebrates (Caplan et al., 1983).

Perhaps even more striking examples of the ways in which the organism "grows itself" come from studies of the development and regulation of gonadal function. For the fetal ovary, estrogen production (by the developing gonad) is a necessary condition for further differentiation of the gland itself (George, Milewich, & Wilson, 1978; George & Wilson, 1980). At a later stage in the male, androgens produced by the testes may be necessary for the full development of Leydig cell responsiveness to pituitary luteinizing hormone (LH) (Purvis, Calandra, Naess, Attramadal, Torjesen, & Hansson, 1977). Finally, one of the events initiating puberty is a shift in regulation of brain cells controlling hormone production. The chemical release factors that lead to secretion of pituitary gonadotropins feed back upon the cells that control their own secretion in such a way that their output is increased (Grumbach, 1980).

It even has been suggested that tissues such as the developing heart may secrete their own growth-stimulating substances during specific points in development (Seifert, Schwartz, & Bowen-Pope, 1984). Insofar as mechanisms such as the foregoing "autocrine" control of growth are developmentally regulated to ensure the proper timing and amount of cell proliferation (Stiles, 1984), they may explain some aspects of the following exemplars of the active nature of growth.

## Target-seeking

Development in complex organisms involves progressive and coordinated changes over time. Each component of the organism develops along a clearly defined, species-specific pathway. Moreover, once embarked upon such a trajectory, a cell (or tissue, or organ system) tends to remain "on course" despite variation in the milieu. Presumably, this is because the genetic "instructions" of the normal, developing organism specify multiple, complex feedback relationships among its components so that the system self-regulates to yield a typical outcome. That is, the genes of complex organisms are co-adapted, not only in the sense of being good mixers, but also in that they ensure coordinated development of all components to yield a species-specific phenotype (Mayr, 1970; Waddington, 1957; 1962).

Waddington (1957) dubbed this phenomenon "canalization" and has graphically depicted canalized pathways as the ridges and valleys of a landscape. Some typical pathways are favored and they can be conceptualized as deep canyons; the steepness of the banks on either side of these channels represents the amount of pressure that must be exerted upon a developing component before it will deviate from its most favored path (see Figure 4.1). One may further conceptualize the peaks and valleys of some part of the "epigenetic landscape" as controlled by different numbers of genes. A very highly canalized pathway, with high thresholds for change (deep canyons with steep walls) represents the coordinated or redundant actions (and reactions) of many genes. (That is, some facets of development may be "buffered" via the inheritance of a set of redundant, but slightly different, "heterozygous" genetic instructions; Fleischer, Johnston, & Klitz, 1983).

Following Waddington again, this can be visually depicted by an imaginary view of the underside of the landscape (Figure 4.2). Here we might portray the landscape as a fundamentally elastic plane tightly suspended on all four sides by the limits of the species' gene pool. The topography— the peaks and valleys—is created by the "pull" of different numbers of co-acting genes, represented as guy wires affixed to the underside of the plane. The greater the number of coordinated genes involved in canalizing a pathway, the stronger the pull, and hence, the deeper the channel (Waddington, 1957).

In some cases, canalization may be achieved not simply by the independent action of specific, individually-inherited genes, but also as a result of the evolutionary linkage of whole sections of chromosomes which provide more stable, functionally coordinated, units of heredity. These larger, more stable combinations may be further buttressed by the actions of

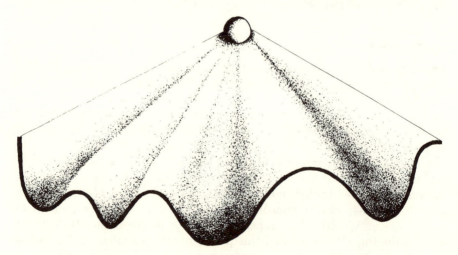

Figure 4-1:   Waddington's "Epigenetic Landscape."

other, independent genes which, however, are not as closely regulated. Together, they produce a normal phenotype (Mayr, 1970; Rendel, 1967). Any environment that suffices to permit and sustain development yields a phenotype that is obviously species-typical. That is, the *basic* pathways of development appear to be insulated from all but grossly unusual environmental conditions. Even when an environmental abnormality, such as starvation, is sufficiently extreme or prolonged to cause a child to get "off course," if enough nourishment is available to sustain *some* growth, the victim will only be deflected to a *parallel* pathway which demands less input. The result will still be a typically human phenotype but a smaller one than if the environment were able to support more virogous growth (Altman, Das, & Sudarshan, 1970; Tanner, 1970).

The resiliency of human growth is well documented. Korean infants who had lost their parents to warfare and suffered from severe malnutrition between 1 and 3 years of age caught up to their better-nourished counterparts within a few years after adoption by American families. In fact, they exceeded Korean norms for size and weight and showed normal intellectual growth (Winick, Meyer, & Harris, 1975). Youngsters often seem to be able to overcome physical trauma associated with difficult deliveries. By age 10, many children "outgrow" the effects of perinatal stress. Within limits, it takes more than two major stressors to cause most children to get off track behaviorally. A few youngsters seem to be able to

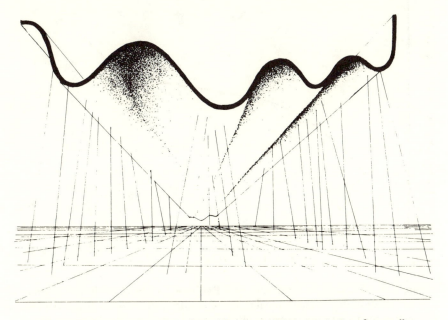

Figure 4-2:    "Underside" of Waddington's "Epigenetic Landscape."

endure even greater numbers of adverse circumstances without showing signs of deviance (Werner & Smith, 1982).

This is not to say that normal development is inevitable; unfortunately, it is not. The degree of inherited buffering varies across organ systems (Rendel, 1967; Waddington, 1957) as well as across individuals (Fuller & Clark, 1968; Ginsburg, 1969). Nevertheless, on average, most children seem to be endowed with a margin for error in development (See also Hofer, 1981).

To this point, our discussion might sound like some sort of organismic isolationism. Indeed, some interpret such data to imply that growth occurs *despite* the environment. However, it can be shown that external events often activate organismic change only after a threshold has been reached, and then, once activated, the response to environmental signals will remain essentially invariant until the "normal" level is significantly exceeded. That is, the characteristics will be remarkably stable despite apparently quite considerable variability in the intensity of input (Rendel, 1967; Fig. 4.3). Such phenomena do not mean that environmental influences are limited to what we have called induction or facilitation. What is overlooked is the fact that, assuming that we have not overestimated the

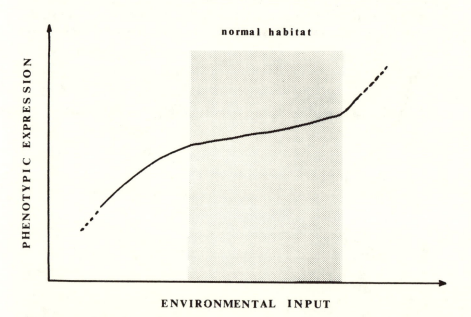

Figure 4-3:    Phenotypic Variation as a Response to Variation in Environmental "input." Within the species-typical range of habitats, some facets of growth may be insensitive to environmental variation.

actual range of input, nonresponse to variation in external conditions may simply indicate that those conditions or variations are *irrelevant*.

For example, the conditions for inducing a developmental change may not be the same as those facilitating, validating, maintaining, or integrating expression of that characteristic. Just because some step in growth may be keyed to a particular condition, one cannot assume that all other steps will also depend upon it. I suspect that much of the "inevitability" of "maturation" reflects our focus upon conditions known to affect only one facet of the trait in question, or our *a priori* expectation that it *ought* to be important. In particular, our concern with the events involved in "fine tuning" basic human characteristics may have diverted us from the search for those necessary for their initial expression.

The point is that while canalized attributes are the proximate outcomes of interactions among (cellular) components of the developing organism, these interactions still depend upon a supportive surrounding. Thus, another way of viewing canalization is to see species-typical growth as occurring because genes specify enzymes or proteins regulating growth (and metabolic processes) which normally are stable under a broad range of conditions, for example, temperature (Bensaude, Babinet, Morange, & Jacob, 1983). Relating this example to Waddington's illustration of the "underside" of the epigenetic landscape (Figure 4.2), we could reconceptualize the guy wires as elastic bands. These bands will maintain constant tension under a specified range of temperatures. If the limits are exceeded, and they get too hot, they may stretch; if they become too cold, they may become brittle and snap under stress. In either extreme, the landscape is then altered and atypical development ensues.

Viewed in this light, the apparent inevitability, or "insulation," of species-specific maturation could be understood as genetically specified dependence upon environmental conditions which: (a) are typically found within tolerance limits in all environments capable of sustaining human life ("ubiquitous" inputs), or (b) can be seen as composing functionally equivalent sets; any one ("alternative equivalents") or any combination of which ("compound equivalents") suffice to initiate and sustain species-specific growth (See also Oyama, 1982; Scarr-Salapatek, 1976).

### Constraints on Learning

In this scheme, then, what we typically call "learning" represents the fine-tuning of variations upon fundamental species-specific themes. Holliday and Pugh (1975) used the analogy of a tree to illustrate the idea of genetically-guided pathways of tissue differentiation. The analogy seems relevant here as well. As we move outward from the trunk and main branches toward the unique details of the individual phenotype, there is an increase in the number of possible alternatives. Here is where learning seems to come in; the choices become increasingly dependent upon the specific demands of the situation, what I called situationally-specific inputs.

To illustrate this notion graphically, we could amalgamate Holliday and Pugh's (1975) developmental tree with Waddington's (1957) epigenetic landscape to get a picture resembling a river delta (Figure 4.4). As the main channels progressively branch into many subsidiary ones, they become smaller and more shallow. That is, the developmental "flow" is less strongly canalized or, alternatively, is more dependent upon variations imposed by local conditions. However, even at this point, the number of channels, their locations (sensitivities to local conditions), and their banks (boundaries) are still species-specific; they remain variations on the species' theme.

Each species learns only certain things in certain ways; plasticity *is* limited by the nature of the animal (cf. Ginsburg, 1969; Hinde & Stevenson-Hinde, 1973; Sackett, Ruppenthal, Fahrenbruch, Holm, & Greenough, 1981). Indeed, a strong case can be made for the idea that the development of behavioral responsiveness to certain environmental contingencies has been canalized over the course of evolution (Plotkin & Odling-Smee, 1979; Fishbein, 1976). As Waddington (1957) pointed out, natural selection affects the capacities of genotypes to respond (phenotypically) to environments, and the responses selected are those which permit advantageous change—whether morphological or behavioral. There is no question

Figure 4-4:   The Epigenetic Landscape as a River Delta.

that behavioral modifiability plays an important role in development. Rather, the point is that plasticity will be limited to the kinds of changes that have proven "useful" to the species (Lorenz, 1965; Waddington, 1957). In short, not only is growth "targeted," modifiability is "constrained."

## Selectivity

Another way of illustrating the same ideas is to point to the fact that living systems are not indiscriminately reactive to their surroundings. Even single cells are surrounded by membranes that actively screen or filter molecules from the surround. Indeed, the basic principles of nervous function involve selective ion exchanges with the medium surrounding the neuron (e.g., Lund, 1978; Stevens, 1985). Moreover, the early development of the CNS results from actual migrations of cells from their points of origin to relatively remote regions. In this process, they do more than just move to unoccupied territory; they move *through* other tissue layers to reach their destinations on the basis of selective sensitivity to chemical signals (Lund, 1978). The "guidepost's" signals and the migrant's responses to them depend upon the genotype of the organism (e.g., Taghert et al., 1984).

Now, lest we be accused of attributing purpose or expectancies to embryonic nerve cells, it must be emphasized that they are active, not in the sense of "willing" events, but in that they react only to very specific signals, and in that their responsiveness depends upon prior differentiation occurring *within* the cell. External contingencies or signals may be necessary, but they are not sufficient to account for the form of development. The cues governing developmental responses are dependent upon the nature of the organism and upon the phenotype expressed at any point. "Information" is utilized to the extent that it is appropriate to the organism's developmental status (see Oyama, 1985).

## Critical Periods

This notion of developmentally-regulated responsiveness provides another illustration of the phenotypic contribution to the organism-environment transactions in development. At certain points in growth, a limited number of developmental pathways may be "open" insofar as the genome has become sensitive to the signal(s) inducing further differentiation. In short, there is a sequence-specificity of gene action; moreover, this phenomenon is not limited to the early stages of ontogeny. Much of the postnatal differentiation of the central nervous system seems to depend upon an organismically programmed "developmental timetable" (Jacobson, 1970; Lund, 1978; Markert & Ursprung, 1971).

As our analogy of a river delta suggests, at some points in development, the organism may be more sensitive to influence than it will be at others. The channels may be broad and lead to several alternative branches during critical periods and become narrower with steep banks subsequently. In our discussion of "remodeling" in the nervous system and the fine tuning of binocular perception, we were dealing with a series of time-tied events. Developmental processes which themselves may *not* depend upon receptor excitation by patterned light ready the organism to respond to such input. Under typical conditions, that experience will be gained shortly after the onset of the period of sensitivity. Once the receptor-sensitive pathways have been activated, visual activity induces changes that will bring the period of responsiveness (plasticity) to a close (Lichtman & Purves, 1983; Mower, Christen, & Caplan, 1983). Human children who do not get binocular input during the first three to five years appear to be stereoblind. (See Aslin, 1985; Banks & Salapatek, 1983).

### Compensatory Mechanisms

Another set of phenomena which relate to both the notions of target-seeking and critical periods are exemplified by age-dependent "restorative" capacities of the organism.

It seems to be a fairly general rule that there may be plasticity in early development that provides a margin for error to compensate for receptor anomalies (Lund, 1978) or perhaps to accommodate changing receptor-characteristics (cf. Aslin et al., 1983; Banks & Salapatek, 1983; Bower, 1982). For many, but by no means all aspects of neural ontogeny, the developing, as opposed to the adult, central nervous system seems to be more capable of compensatory (sometimes structural) adjustments to lesions or other abnormalities (See Butters, Rosen, & Stein, 1974; Goldman, 1976; Lund, 1978; McWilliams & Lynch, 1983).

At the higher levels of the brain in many species, cortical "representation" of certain receptor inputs seem to be modifiable in early development. Apparently, sensory analyzers in the cortex depend upon facilitation and functional validation by receptor-evoked impulse-transmission from lower centers. For example, the whiskers of infant mice and rats normally are connected to "barrel"-like sections of somatosensory cortex in the first few days after birth (Van der Loos & Woolsey, 1973). If neonates are lesioned in the presumptive barrel area, development proceeds so that, in adulthood, the damage falls *between* functional barrel areas. That is, in the first few days, the intact areas are capable of "taking over" the functions allotted to adjacent neurons. This plasticity presumably reflects a critical period for the formation of connections with the fibers originally destined to synapse with cells in the damaged area. If the whisker follicle itself is removed before barrels begin to form, the whole "barrel field" in the cortex is altered. Similar lesions in adulthood would lead to permanent deficits in the first case, and retrograde degeneration in the second (Ito & Seo, 1983; Van der Loos & Woolsey, 1973). As we shall see in a later section, there is evidence for a somewhat comparable critical period in the somatosensory development of humans (Simmel, 1966; Teuber & Rudel, 1962).[1]

Some cases of juvenile "sparing" of function may simply reflect a rerouting of later-developing pathways (Bregman & Goldberger, 1982; Goldman, 1976). In others, they may represent validation of "alternative" function during a phase in which some tentative synapses normally would be "silenced" by competitive mechanisms. That is, injury to an area of the brain prior to the critical period for validation of "competing" structures allows other segments to assume control of mature function (Greenough & Schwark, 1984).

There is some evidence that similar mechanisms may occur in humans. Sperry (1968) reported observations of a young woman who was born without a corpus callosum. Unlike adult neurological patients who had their callosums sectioned to alleviate *grand mal* epilepsy, this woman's cerebral hemispheres did seem to be able to "communicate" with one another. Presumably, other pathways assumed the task in the absence of competition (inhibition?) from the corpus callosum (which, in humans begins to function in an adult-like manner between 3 and 5 years of age).

In the absence of auditory input, cortical areas normally serving that modality may become recruited for the processing of input in other modalities. Neville (1985) found that congenitally deaf individuals showed more electrical activity in "auditory" areas in response to *visual* input than did hearing subjects. Subjects who lost their hearing after four years of age responded to visual inputs with somewhat more normal distributions of cortical electrical activity. Thus, in the first 4 or 5 years, there may be a sensitive period for auditory input to validate the involvement of cortical tissue for the analysis of sound stimuli. In the absence of normal auditory input, the presumptive auditory areas may become involved in processing visual information from the periphery of the visual field.

---

[1] Different areas in the brain, perhaps reflecting different receptor structures, may be less strictly "dedicated" to processing particular inputs. For example, in owl monkeys some somatosensory cortical areas subserving tactile sensitivity of the hand apparently are more flexibly organized, perhaps because local boundaries of adjacent fields may be signaled by mutually inhibitory mechanisms (Merzenich, Nelson, Stryker, Cynader, Schoppmann, & Zook, 1984). In contrast, the vibrissae of mice are individual, localized structures, each of which is served by a number of nerves. Moreover, the cortical barrels, activated by the vibrissae are located in a different cortical layer than the one studied by Merzenich et al. (see Woolsey & Van der Loos, 1970).

## GROWTH IS HETEROGENEOUS

As indicated in the preceding chapter, the evolution of many animal forms can be understood in terms of "tinkering" with rates and patterns of growth. Such modifications are possible because the genes underlying structural development of various organs, and those regulating their functions (e.g., hormone-production) can be inherited independently (Bonner & Brownstein, 1984). Moreover, genes conferring the potential to develop structures also are separable from those regulating their *rates* of development (Gould, 1977; Marx, 1984; Raff & Kaufman, 1983).

### Multiple Components

Thus, instead of regarding the growth of an organism as *a* process, we must view it as the outcome of many growth *processes*. Although they must be coordinated enough to assure viability, they can proceed at somewhat different rates. For example, within the hand, there are two groups of bones which develop at different rates at different times during growth (Masse, 1962). When we attempt to account for such complex phenomena as the overall height of the individual, over 100 different growth centers must be considered. Moreover,

> The total height of a person is influenced by many different physiological processes, including the amount of pituitary growth hormone, the efficiency of the stomach and the small intestine, and the rates of ossification of the bones of the axial skeleton. Each of these is controlled by many distinct enzymes; the production of each enzyme is, in turn, regulated by one or more pairs of genes. As gene expression may vary independently at nearly all of the relevant loci, it is clear that any reasonably complete analysis of growth in stature must be very complex. (Loehlin, Lindzey, & Spuhler, 1975, pp. 61–62)

Structures such as receptors follow this rule, as exemplified by the eyes of human infants. The peripheral retina of human neonates is well developed at birth, but, relatively speaking, the fovea is very immature with many fewer cones than in the adult eye (Abramov, Gordon, Hendrickson, Hainline, Dobson, & LaBossiere, 1982). The nervous system is no exception, either. The brain, although often considered to be *an* organ, is actually a heterogeneous structure, both anatomically and biochemically (Barnstable, 1982; Kety & Elkes, 1961). The ontogeny of different structural components of the brain, and the CNS in general, occurs unevenly with each region developing relatively independently of the other (Lund, 1978; Tanner, 1970). Even within "a" region, development can be uneven (Friedlander, 1982).

The fine-tuning of the visual cortex again provides an example of this principle within what is sometimes regarded as "a" functional area. In humans, there exists a critical period for the development of binocular vision which extends from about the second half of the first to the fourth postnatal year (Banks et al., 1975). At birth, infants also seem to discriminate horizontal and vertical lines more reliably than oblique orientations (Leehey, Moskowitz-Cook, Brill, & Held, 1975). The second half of the first year ushers in a period during which visual sensitivity to the direction of lines becomes validated (Mohindra, Held, Gwiazda, & Brill, 1978). The two effects are separable in that an ocular astigmatism can affect acuity for line orientation without necessarily affecting binocular depth perception (Aslin, 1985).

Despite the relative independence of growth in different components, the sum of these processes must give rise to an organism capable of functioning. For any kind of integrated activity to occur, all relevant components must first be operative. Then they must be properly "linked." Even at the level of the neuron, several essentially independent developmental processes must reach completion before a functioning synapse can be formed: There must be outgrowth of the neuron in the appropriate direction; there must be physiochemical compatibility between the axon and the dendrites to which it connects, and this compatibility may depend upon the timing with which these neural filaments meet (Black, 1982; Jacobson, 1970).

In short, then, we must conceptualize ontogeny as more than just the semi-autonomous development of components, but their orchestration into coherent, functional systems that are capable of maintaining life. But one may ask, how can that be, if each subcomponent of a vital organ—let alone each component organ of the whole individual—is developing at its own rate?

## Functional Systems

Evolutionary theory suggests an answer, namely, that as species evolved, selection favored phenotypes that expressed the most viable combinations of regulations. Given the opportunistic nature of evolution, these combinations were not always simple or elegant, but they were, by necessity, serviceable. We are so accustomed to viewing ontogeny from the viewpoint of the reproductively mature adult, that we often lose sight of the fact that each level of functioning is the outcome of a prior series of organized patterns, each of which has allowed the organism to adapt to average, expectable surroundings (Anokhin, 1964).

Perhaps because it is so obvious, we frequently overlook the facts that the fetus, infant, and adult all represent different levels—and kinds—of organization, and that these organizations must permit survival. This point is most vividly exemplified by considering the different demands made by the pre- and post-natal environments: The fetus' heart and blood vessels differ in form and function from those of the adult. Instead of all four chambers of the heart acting as relatively separate entities, the atria are connected by the foramen ovale so that the bulk of the oxygenated blood from the umbilical artery bypasses the lungs and flows directly to the head and upper body from the left ventricle. It thus provides the rapidly developing brain with the blood it needs. The as-yet non-"functional" lungs receive much less "fresh" blood. At birth, the lungs and other air-ways are emptied of fluid as the fetus passes through the birth canal. Then the freshly-evacuated lungs fill with air, expand, and the foramen ovale begins to grow more or less permanently shut. As a result, the blood flow now proceeds in the "adult" manner, with venous blood being oxygenated via the lungs, rather than the umbilicus. The vessels associated with the fetal system then slowly degenerate (Arey, 1954).

Since the fetus must "share" its mother's lungs, it also possesses another adaptation, a variant of hemoglobin that binds oxygen more efficiently than does the adult form. With the transition to the extrauterine environment, this fetal type is gradually replaced by an adult-type hemoglobin (Wood, 1985; Yuwiler, 1971). Clearly, even with fetal hemoglobin, the adult would be in severe difficulty if the major blood flow bypassed the lungs. Likewise, even with more efficient oxygen binding, the fetus would starve its brain cells if it had to pump a full measure of blood through non-functioning lungs. In this and a number of other ways, the fetus is adapted to its intrauterine environment.

Thus, we are dealing with a somewhat different organism at various periods in development. As Anokhin (1964) pointed out, organismic components must be organized into *functional systems* so that the individual can adapt to its environments.

For the purposes of this discussion, a functional system is a state of physiological organization in which receptor, integrator/regulator, and effector components are organized in feedback relationships that allow the individual to perform some adaptive function (e.g., breathing). The organismic components that are integrated in such systems need not all be related anatomically nor be elements of a single (adult) physiological function. That is, at different phases in early development, functional systems may be made up of components from diverse (adult) organs or organ-systems. At birth, only those elements necessary for neonatal adaptation will be fully developed.

Functional systems thus have the following characteristics: (a) They involve connections organizing central and peripheral components of the organism, for example, receptors in the infant's lips and perioral areas are linked to central processing structures sensitive to nutritional status which are in turn connected to effectors controlling head-turning and sucking; (b) they serve the adaptation of the organism, for example, neonates' sucking provides them with food; (c) their functioning is subject to some form of monitoring, for example, a receptor system sensitive to the amount and caloric value of the fluids ingested; (d) the information gained by this monitoring is fed back to a central regulating apparatus, for example, neural centers that respond to the amount of stomach loading and the level of blood sugar; (e) the central regulators control the degree of activation of the effectors, for example, the rate or continuation of sucking; and (f) all these components are ready to function at, or prior to, the moment they are required to serve the survival needs of the organism, for example, the sucking responses of human neonates and their ability to digest milk are functional as early as two months before "normal" term. In short, the systems of the neonate "anticipate" the survival demands that will be placed upon them (Peiper, 1963).

### Heterochronous Development

Functional systems in "immature" forms often consist of combinations of structural components derived from what might be considered relatively separate organ-systems. For example, infant feeding involves sucking, swallowing, and breathing, all of which must be coordinated in such a way that neonates will not choke and that their nutritional requirements will be fulfilled. This is accomplished by variations in the rates of development of the organs involved in the system and the mechanisms controlling their function: Many of the nerves controlling the musculature of the mouth and tongue are still relatively undeveloped in the neonate. However, those involved in the sucking and rooting responses are fully functional at birth. The other neural components develop later, "as needed." Finally, as implied by the fact that all aspects of an organ or organ system (as defined by adult functioning) do not always develop synchronously, functional systems frequently are reorganized insofar as the relationships and patterning of component processes may be subject to new forms of regulation (Anohkin, 1964). For example, as the infant's teeth erupt, chewing is added to sucking and swallowing in the feeding complex and the more or less "reflexive" tactual control of nipple location and sucking gives way to much more complex processes involving visual guidance and so on.

In short, then, growth involves heterochronous, rather than synchronous development of a number of components. The orchestration of these rates of growths leads to complexes of organs—or components of organs—interrelated so that they provide the means to cope with a typical environment.

An additional implication of this model is that the details, if not the form, of certain stages of growth can be influenced by environmental conditions. The genes conferring the potentials for development of each component are inherited independently of each other and the environment provides inputs that are necessary to *induce, facilitate, validate, maintain,* and *integrate* phenotypic expression of these potentials. Thus it is possible that one or another of the components of a system could become ready to function earlier or later than "usual," or they could even fail to develop at all. If so, the peculiarities of an individual's environment could affect the quality and perhaps even the timing of developmental reorganization.

## DEVELOPMENTAL STAGES

Both structurally and functionally, the developing organism changes as potentials for growth are expressed (see also Hofer, 1981). We can illustrate this point by a consideration of the development of regulation of the heart. In the early phases of embryonic growth, the contractions of individual cells are not coordinated. As more cardiac cells are generated, the activities of the individual cells' "pacemakers" become synchronized. Then intrinsic pacemaker cell control is added to and modified by extrinsic regulation by the vagus nerve, ultimately permitting heartrate to be controlled by receptors sensitive to oxygen levels, and so on (Adolph, 1968).

Distinct stages of structural and functional organization can be observed throughout the rest of growth as well. For example, the fetal and neonatal adrenal and pituitary glands are characterized by unique structures. In the adrenals, there is the "fetal cortex," an enlargement of the adrenal cortex that is apparent by the middle of gestation and which disappears in the early postnatal period (Milkovic & Milkovic, 1966). Complementing the development and regression of the fetal cortex, one area of the pituitary is detectable in fetal life and also involutes postnatally. This pituitary structure apparently accounts for the appearance of fetal variants of adrenocorticotropins which in turn regulate the development of the fetal cortex (Silman, Chard, Lowry, Smith, & Young, 1976; Silman, Holland, Chard, Lowry, & Hope, 1978).

There also is some evidence that, under stimulation from the fetal pituitary gland, which begins to show "mature" patterns of secretion near term, the immature adrenal cortex also secretes stage-specific hormones. (The adult pattern is not established until after birth.) These observations become tantalizing in view of evidence that adrenal hormones contribute to the functional development of the lungs (Fencl, Sillman, Cohen, & Tulchinsky, 1980). If so, we may have another example of self-regulation. That is, the stage-specific functional relationships in the fetal pituitary-adrenal axis may be involved in regulating the development of other structures necessary for postnatal survival.

In the early postnatal period, also, functional organization is uniquely geared to survival needs of that stage. For example, infants' protein intake is great enough so that, by adult standards, they should suffer from an excess of urea because their kidneys do not remove this substance at adult rates. This "insufficiency" of infantile kidney function once puzzled pediatricians until it was realized that, although the neonate's kidneys *can* remove urea at rates almost equalling that seen in adults, they do not do so because the "extra" nitrogen is utilized in *growth*. (Protein-tissue formation requires nitrogen). Whereas the adult's kidneys primarily respond to water deficits (by concentrating urea in urine), the infant's kidneys respond primarily to an *excess* of urea (with urine formation). In short, the regulation of renal function in the infant is organized differently than it is in the adult. In the infant, the stage-specific regulation favors nitrogen retention in the service of change, that is, growth. As the child's rate of growth slows, renal function is more geared to nitrogen excretion in order to maintain water balance (Adolph, 1968; Prader, 1962).

The ontogeny of mating behavior in guinea pigs illustrates stages of functional reorganization in behavior. The precopulatory display of the adult male guinea pig includes a slow, side-to-side swaying of the hindquarters accompanied by a guttural purring vocalization and is controlled by male sex hormones. This display pattern is also shown by estrous females, who also respond to dorsal stimulation with lordosis. Estrus is regulated by ovarian hormones; lordosis is not observed in adult males under normal conditions. Males do not usually purr and sway until the beginning of the third postnatal week, and females rarely come into first estrus before the eighth week.

However, the purring vocalization and the lordosis posture can be observed in newborn guinea pigs of both sexes. Although they are highly precocious, pups are nursed for three to four weeks postnatally and for the first two weeks (maternal) tactual stimulation of the anogenital area is necessary to induce urination. Purring and lordosis occur when the young crawl under their mothers in search of the nipple. In the first two weeks, despite the fact that both purring and lordosis are exhibited in the nursing context, neither response is affected by the administration of sex hormones even in doses adequate to cause adults to display these behaviors. Rather, the probability of lordosis is inversely related to the length of time elapsed since the pups' bladders were voided, and lordosis tends to elicit maternal licking. The purr may be more closely related to hunger, although it also precedes maternal licking and frequently accompanies lordosis (Harper, 1972; 1976).

These elements of the adult mating patterns are displayed in newborns in the context of nursing; they are organized into functional elements of the filial behavioral system. As the young reach weaning age, control of lordosis and purring is assumed by mechanisms mediating mating behavior. There is continuity in the animals' motor repertoire, but discontinuity in the mechanisms controlling the displays of these actions. Neither testosterone nor estrogen and progesterone affect the probability of occurrence of purring (and swaying) and of the lordosis until pups are over two weeks of age. In the third week, these behaviors become subject to a new level of (inhibitory) control which is sensitive to (disinhibition by) sex hormones (Harper, 1972).

### Hierarchical Organization

These observations are consistent with the idea that many facets of physiological function and behavior are subject to a "hierarchy" of controlling mechanisms (Adolph, 1968; Bruner & Bruner, 1968; Dawkins, 1976b; Tinbergen, 1951; Werner, 1948). Developmentally, there may be a progressive "layering" of control, from intrinsic, intracellular feedback to nervous or endocrine-mediated regulation of function, as in our example of the developing heart.

In some cases of severe cerebral injury or senile degeneration of higher brain centers, one can observe such "infantile" responses as reflexive palmar grasping and tactile rooting in adult humans. These observations have been taken to mean that "reflexive" responses give way to voluntary behaviors as the "higher" levels of the brain develop. Studies of fetal motor responses (Hooker, 1952; Humphrey, 1969) and the ontogeny of the control of leg movements in infancy (Thelen, 1985) support the idea that many elements of behavior become coordinated with other acts in more complex systems as children develop (See also Hofer, 1981).

Thus, one mechanism underlying reorganization of functional systems might be a kind of "layering" of specialized regulatory components in which the later-appearing apparatuses take over previously established functions. For example, the neurological control of respiration involves at least three distinct levels in the CNS: Early developing brainstem mechanisms which are later regulated by lower forebrain structures, and these centers, in turn, are finally subject to cortical control as development procedes (Aguilar & Williamson, 1968; Peiper, 1963). In short, one way of conceptualizing "stages" is in terms of periods in development in which particular levels of regulatory organization predominate. Furthermore, this progressive layering of control tends to make possible greater coordination among systems which serve common biological ends. Insofar as developmental changes do occur in the cerebral control of behavior in monkeys (Goldman-Rakic, 1985), and there exist systematic developmental changes in the cerebral function of human infants (Chugani & Phelps, 1986), this model seems applicable to human ontogeny.

## Early Experience

Our model of stages of reorganization of functional systems could also provide an explanation for the effects of early experience (as well as brain injury, cf. Amiel-Tison, 1985) on later behavior. At any developmental stage, functional systems may include elements which are components of different systems typical of another stage of development. Early experience could thus affect later behavior if a component of an early developing system were linked with some kind of environmentally sensitive circuit. To the extent that this regulatory component depends upon receptor activation for its validation, maintenance, or integration, it may be modified as a result of events occurring at that stage of development. So long as the affected component itself is not a major factor in regulating the *form* of an early system, the early effect may not be apparent. If, however, the modified component becomes (re)organized as a regulator in a later-appearing behavior, it will affect that activity.

For an example, within 12 hours of birth, guinea pig pups become capable of discriminating species-mates from other forms. Thereafter, they will respond to only their mothers or parent-surrogates; mother-reared pups will not lordose or purr to humans. In contrast, hand-reared pups will. Therefore, infantile behaviors are influenced by experience leading to what could be called species-recognition which, in turn, affects the animals' later behavior: As adults, three of five hand-reared males who directed filial lordosis and purring toward the human "surrogate parent" consistently purred and swayed in response to the human hand— even after they had successfully copulated with females (Harper, 1970; see also Beauchamp & Hess, 1971).

Thus the link between filial and mating behavior may be a perceptual component influenced by early experiences involving species-recognition as originally postulated in Lorenz' (1935/1957) concept of the "companion." That is, the early developing component governing species-recognition becomes involved in controlling hormone-responsive structures mediating sexual arousal that become functional at a later point in time. The Lorenzian model then can be seen as another example of the general process of the ontogenetic restructuring of components of functional systems to serve stage-specific adaptive needs.

## Growth is Cumulative

Whether viewed from the vantage point of the cell, or in terms of the organization and re-organization of functional systems, development involves a succession of structures and regulations. The latter often involve successive layering of one level of regulation upon another. In this process, function may be necessary for the facilitation, validation, maintenance, integration, and even the induction of structure. Indeed, the morphology of many neurons is dependent upon functional synaptic connections (Changeux & Danchin, 1976; Lund, 1978; Jacobson, 1970). Working our way backward, as it were, to embryogenesis, we also have seen how the activation of a set of genetic potentials in one group of cells leads to the formation of a tissue which, in turn, induces other cell groups to express other sets of potentials, and so on. In short, from early embryogenesis onward, we are confronted with a picture of development that is cumulative. Events succeed each other in time, each phase being based upon those that went before (cf. Fox, 1970; McMahon, 1974; Waddington, 1962).

This cumulative layering of stages by necessity is orderly. Insofar as one step is embryonic development sets the stage for a succeeding one, normal growth depends upon a more or less fixed sequence of phases. Little overall variability can be tolerated in early development if a normal phenotype is to ensue.

The succession of stages typically results in the integration of earlier appearing organismic/behavioral components into progressively broader, more closely coordinated systems. This increasing coordination results in enhanced stability of function in the organism (Adolph, 1968; Waddington, 1962; see also Piaget, 1971). That is, a consequence of the increased complexity (and redundancy) of organization in living systems is that they become increasingly resistant to disequilibratory forces (Dubos, 1968). At the same time, plasticity is also enhanced. This is because development progresses from the more basic anatomical structures and physiological functions to what might be considered the fine tuning of functional systems (cf. our analogy of the river delta). At this level (corresponding to the shallow mouths of rivulets), somewhat more variability may be possible without leading to gross pathology. One example we have already considered is the development of binocular vision. In later sections, it will be argued that the "fine tuning" of emotional life, or personality dynamics, may be understood in the same way. On the assumption that most humans are endowed with genotypes that buffer development against gross deviations from the basic human phenotype, a number of individual and cultural differences may be conceptualized as the resultants of the fine tuning of the system within the confines of the more plastic aspects of species' norm of reaction.

This model differs from more traditional notions of "integration" in that, while cumulative, growth is also seen as involving progressive reorganization. That is, although (behavioral) organization in later-appearing functional systems may include a wider number of elements, it tends to be qualitatively different in form. In addition, many of the elements are shared in common with other, coexisting systems. Finally, some of the coexisting functional systems at any stage may actually stand in antagonistic relationships with one another.

## CORRELATES OF THE GROWTH PROCESS

Several additional phenomena are frequently observed in the study of development. These phenomena follow logically from the model of semi-independent growths and have implications for understanding behavioral development.

### Delayed Regulation

In the ontogeny of regulation of the heartbeat, "autonomous" cellular contractions precede the onset of synchronized pacemaker activity (heartbeats per se) or regulation by the central nervous system. This is just one of many examples in which the onset of an activity, or the anatomical outlines of a structure are observable before the onset of centrally regulated function. Even in the development of so-called reflex arcs, motor neurons form functional linkages with muscles prior to the completion of sensory components. Many of these "incomplete" connections lead to neurally controlled muscular activity. Under these circumstances, although the organism acts, it cannot *react* (Hooker, 1952; Jacobson, 1970; Parmelee & Sigman, 1983).

This does not mean that we can dismiss such partial systems as inconsequential. Although they may have no immediately obvious role in the overall physiological adjustments of the organism, such phenomena as autonomous or strictly efferent-controlled motor activity may nevertheless contribute to the development of the muscles themselves, or the bones and joints (Caplan et al., 1983) and perhaps even influence the nature and form of dendritic connections (Bekoff, 1981; Hofer, 1981).

Such delayed regulation has a number of obvious behavioral analogues. It is common to observe that a child will engage in an activity for some time without, however, being able to "use" it to achieve an end other than the simple enactment of the activity itself (cf. Piaget, 1952). For example, the infant "practices" walking for some time before it begins to employ this skill "in order to go somewhere" or to "get something." In studies of problem-solving or memory in which verbal strategies can be employed to good advantage, a frequent observation is that younger children who are capable of conceptualizing and/or labeling the critical relationship or item often do not bring this capacity to bear on the problem. Sometimes they will even fail to employ this capability after its applicability has been explicitly pointed out to them (e.g., Flavell, 1970; Kagan & Kogan, 1970).

In the latter case we could describe the situation as one in which naming still functions in the context of vocabulary-acquisition. Presumably more complex systems involving "cognitive strategies" have yet to develop and subsume (or include) object-naming.

### Phases of Instability and Consolidation

This brings us back to a description of the development of functional systems themselves. It seems likely that few systems appear all-at-once, operating at full efficiency. Most functional systems probably require a period of time for new patterns of regulation to become fully established (validated, integrated). Initially, we may be able to see only a single component, functioning in a limited manner or perhaps even coordinated in the context of a number of other activities. Next, there may be a transient stage of apparent dysfunction which reflects the initial stages of reorganization of components. Finally, the whole system seems to "settle in" to regular, predictable function until the next phase of reorganization (e.g., Gesell, 1954; Thelen, 1985).

Events occurring at puberty provide an example of the ways in which changes in regulation (the re-organization of functional systems) can affect the organism. In pubescent girls, the "re-setting" of the mechanisms controlling hormonal secretions occurs as far as 18 months in advance of the first menstrual period. Estrogens are produced cyclically for over a year before the responses of the ovaries and uterus are coordinated in the adult manner. Moreover, a number of these cycles occur considerably in advance of the more dramatic puberal changes in bodily growth and proportions. Even when the girl begins to menstruate and has developed secondary sex characteristics, her menstrual cycles often are irregular and many of them may be anovulatory for a period of years. Thus, there can be a delay between the development of the last vital component of a system and the overt manifestations of changed function. Once overt change has occurred, there tends to be a final stage during which the new regulation becomes further consolidated to produce regular, predictable functioning (Tanner, 1970).

In some cases, the transitional stage can also represent a period of increased vulnerability of the organism to external influences. To continue with the example of pubertal development, during the early phases of settling-in, there may be apparent dysfunction in other areas besides the menstrual cycle itself. For example, acne is a frequent concomitant of the increased androgen levels associated with puberty (Donovan & van der Werff ten Bosch, 1965).

In many mammals, including humans, it appears that a period of functional activity may be a necessary condition for the validation and maintenance of the visual system (Banks & Salapatek, 1983; Lund, 1978; Wiesel, 1982). Often when structure has been validated and/or integrated during a "critical period," subsequent deprivation of input has little or no effect.

## INDIVIDUAL DIFFERENCES

The genome makes possible the expression of a rather broad array of phenotypes, but this array is still clearly limited by the nature of the species. Which phenotypes (or sequences of phenotypes) will be realized depends upon the patterning of external events. We have yet to identify those environmental events which are crucial for the expression of certain traits. Our difficulties in the search for these events are compounded by the fact that some genotypic potentials will not be expressed until a certain intensity of stimulation is present or exceeded. Still others may not co-vary in a direct manner with the amount of input even after the necessary minimum has been reached, for example, Figure 4.3 (Loehlin et al., 1975; Rendel, 1967; Scarr-Salapatek, 1971). For some canalized traits the thresholds for expression may vary genotypically. Moreover, across individuals in a population, a bare minimum of environmental stimulation may yield phenotypic variability whereas *greater* environmental input will serve to increase phenotypic similarities by guaranteeing that everyone receives enough input to surpass threshold (Coleman & Riesen, 1968).

In short, nearly identical phenotypes can result from quite different antecedent events. This phenomenon is widespread in nature. The "same" syndrome, albinism, can result from at least three separate genetic anomalies and the severity of the disorder may depend upon the presence or absence of other genes (Reed, 1975). Similarly, the external manifestations of prococious puberty may result from genetic control of the "normal" rate of development, adrenal tumors, gonadal tumors, or various neurological insults; failure to respond with the expected pubertal changes can represent pituitary malfunction, gonadal malfunction, or target-organ insensitivity (Donovan & van der Werff ten Bosch, 1965; Grumbach, Grave, & Mayer, 1974).

There are many genetic-environmental combinations that can lead to very similar outcomes. Usually, the disparate causal events leading to common outcomes turn out to "intrude" upon a common developmental pathway. They simply exert their effects at different points in the developmental chain between genotype and phenotype. Demonstrations that certain genetic or environmental manipulations suffice to produce a particular phenotype are no guarantee that all (or any) instances of that character "in nature" arose from the same conditions.

The foregoing considerations raise another interesting possibility: If development involves progressive stages of reorganization and the pathways leading to "normal" phenotypes are usually canalized, then it sometimes should be possible for an individual who has been forced slightly off course to "get back on the track" during periods of change. That is, the necessary environmental conditions favoring compensatory development may be different than those which would evoke stage-appropriate progression under normal conditions. Or, with phenotypic change, new sensitivities develop to previously-unregistered stimuli. Thus we must consider seriously the possibility that some stages of vulnerability to environmental events may also represent opportunities for restitutive growth as well as periods of sensitivity to pathogenic influences (cf. Sullivan, 1953; see also Harlow & Mears, 1979).

# CHAPTER 5

# Infancy

The environment must be relied upon to provide the right stimulus [for growth] at the right time. In this sense animals are born into "expected" environments—indeed, into "required" ones. (Tanner, 1970, p. 125.)

In this chapter, a selective review of prenatal and infantile behavior will be presented to illustrate the model of growth outlined in the preceding chapters and to demonstrate how an "adaptationist" view may yield fruitful leads for analyzing how the transactions between infants and their surroundings promote species-typical growth and development.

If evolution often works through alterations in the timing of ontogenetic events, then many of the developmental rates of species-characteristics may be adaptations in themselves. Insofar as the survival-demands of each stage of development vary, different points in the life cycle will be subjected to different selective pressures. Different patterns of (re)organization thus may be considered as adaptations to environmental conditions which have been, and are still being, shaped by natural selection. These developmental changes are likely to be initiated and sustained by ubiquitous or equivalent sign stimuli.

## THE PARENT-OFFSPRING MATCH

Theoretically, internal fertilization and development of the zygote within the mother's womb evolved as "hedges" against environmental uncertainties, whereby the remote possibility of producing large numbers of viable offspring was sacrificed in favor of increasing the chances of a few young reaching reproductive maturity. The mammalian pattern of postnatal milk feeding represents an extension of this strategy to increase the predictability of the postnatal environment (Simpson, 1950).

Most evolutionists would agree that the young are in a better position than parents or others to monitor their own internal states and the degrees to which caregiver intervention is required to sustain them. Given that the young are best suited to perform such tasks, selection should favor those who can "self-monitor" most effectively (albeit unconsciously) and elicit the appropriate responses from potential caregivers. Correspondingly, parents should co-evolve to be responsive to the signals emitted by their offspring. Thus the selective edge goes to offspring who are relatively more efficient in self-monitoring and/or in signaling, and to parents who respond to offspring signals, appropriately striking a balance between their own (including other children's) and the signaling child's needs (See Alexander, 1974; Trivers, 1974).[1]

### Prenatal Transactions

The events following fertilization illustrate the active, transactional nature of the exchanges between the conceptus and the mother: The (viable) zygote develops in ways which provoke alterations in the maternal environment that support growth, and this growth prepares the developing organism to sustain itself postnatally.

The human zygote is capable of maintaining itself while being moved from the fallopian tubes to the uterine cavity. It begins to divide during this journey and once the passage is complete, the newly-formed blastocyst produces a signal that induces nearby maternal uterine tissues to change so as to allow implantation and further growth. In order for these events to occur, the maternal fallopian tubes must secrete the appropriate fluids to suspend the zygote/blastocyst and to contract in such a way that the fluid in which the zygote is suspended is forced into the uterine cavity. Once the foregoing have been accomplished, the uterine epithelial tissues themselves respond to the blastocyst's signal and accept implantation. Then, these uterine tissues continue to vascularize while both maternal and fetal tissues contribute to the formation of the placenta, a structure which helps to sustain the pregnancy (Arey, 1954; Hofer, 1981).

In order to accommodate these changes, the mother's circulation is altered to provide more rapid oxygen exchange, her basal metabolic rate declines, and her water retention and appetite increase, presumably to provide the necessary inputs for the conceptus. Indeed, in some cases, to sustain fetal development, the mother's own tissues temporarily may be stripped of essential elements if such nutrients are not adequately provided

---

[1] From personal experience, most of us can think of examples in humans of what would appear to be both offspring "exploitation" of parents (cf. Trivers, 1974) and parental "exploitation" of young (cf. Alexander, 1974). However, the differences may be more apparent than real. A third possibility is that either sort of apparently exploitative tactics could be alternate strategies, each appropriate for maximizing the inclusive fitness of a kindred under specific circumstances. If so, our task would be to identify the circumstances favoring the expression of such behavior.

in her diet (Dugdale, 1986; Harvey, 1986). Certain of these metabolic effects are probably mediated by the extensive hormonal alterations in the mother which are occasioned by ovarian response to feedback from the zygote and the chemical messengers produced by the placenta (Eichorn, 1970; Bell & Harper, 1977). In addition, because the conceptus produces foreign proteins (fetuses obtain half their genes from their fathers), the mother's immune system must be rendered unresponsive to fetal tissues. It seems that this signal is produced by the fetus (Noonan, Halliday, Morton, & Clunic, 1979; Olding & Oldstone, 1974; Oldstone, Tishoon, & Moretta, 1977; Stahn, Fabricus, & Hartleitner, 1978).

Despite the fact that the mother's lungs oxygenate fetal blood, the fetus' lungs develop in utero. So long as the fetus is adapted to the uterine environment, the womb provides a context in which the fetal lungs become capable of oxygenating blood about one month *before* normal term. Similarly, the moderately premature infant's brain development reaches a point at which it can regulate vital processes more or less normally in the extrauterine environment (Parmelee, Schulte, Akiyama, Waldehar, Schultz, & Stern, 1968; Parmelee & Sigman, 1983). In short, the uterine development of each system "anticipates" the conditions to be met postnatally.

Consistent with the idea that the young have the responsibility of signaling their condition, not only the maintenance of pregnancy (McGregor, Kuhn, & Jaffe, 1983), but also the timing of parturition may be partly under fetal control. Mechanical factors associated with pregnancy, especially the distention of the mother's uterus, change the contractile responsiveness of these tissues to hormones associated with the birth process (Bulmer, 1970). It also seems likely that chemical signals from the fetus are involved in determining the end of the gestation period. The fetal pituitary produces age-specific forms of trophic hormones which control adrenal structure and function and a change from the "immature" to the more adult-like hormone occurs late in gestation. The adrenals of fetuses and newborns are characterized by a special "fetal cortex" which regresses rapidly after birth. Since maternal release of hormones involved in parturition is responsive to fetal adrenal output, it seems likely that the fetal pituitary-adrenal system is intimately involved in not only preparing the fetus for birth, but also in the timing of that event (Silman et al., 1976). In addition, the hormone oxytocin, which affects uterine activity, is produced by the fetus near term (Fuchs, Fuchs, Husslein, Soloff, & Fernstrom, 1982).

## Organization and Regulation of Newborn Behavior

In order for any organism to survive, all its functions—vegetative, motoric *and* cognitive—must be organized to meet the demands of the average expectable environment for the species. Every process, at every stage of development, must be regulated; what may differ developmentally are the *ways* in which processes are organized and regulated, and the ends served thereby (Adolph, 1968).

Although newborns may be "physiologically displaced persons" in the sense of having been adapted to intra-uterine environments, the average, healthy fetus is also equipped to cope with change. The basic respiratory and metabolic mechanisms are ready to function: Within three hours of birth, most normal infants' breathing is stable, functioning in an essentially adult-like manner. During this same, very brief transition period, newborns' metabolic responses to ambient temperature (corrected for weight) function essentially similarly to those of adults (Pribylova, 1968). Prenatally-developed capacities for adaptive regulation are not simply restricted to vegetative homeostasis, but can be observed in a wide variety of situations of interest to behavioral scientists. Indeed, it is possible that more extensive cross-cultural observations would reveal that many "random" or apparently vestigial responses are, in fact, adaptations to different kinds of caregiving practices.

For example, whereas the "prone head response," a tendency to raise the head when placed on the stomach, and "reflex" stepping may seem paradoxical when exhibited by a baby who spends most of its time in a crib, these movements may prevent smothering or at least serve to maintain a secure, comfortable position for an infant who is carried in a sling against its mother's body (Konner, 1972; 1982). Similarly, the Moro reflex, a circular reaching-out-and-grasping movement involving arms and hands when the baby's head suddenly falls backwards, is hardly a mere vestige as was once thought. In the sling situation, this response essentially keeps the infant from falling. This so-called reflex varies in its manifestation according to whether the baby is already clinging to something; if so, the grasp and pulling-in components are intensified and the reaching-out aspect is dropped altogether. If one hand is free, it will follow the "classic" pattern, while the occupied hand simply clings tighter (Prechtl, 1969). Other reactions, such as spontaneous startles, may also have (potential) signal value for the mother (Konner, 1972).

The motor pattern primarily involved in securing nourishment, sucking, provides another example of the complex, stage-specific, adaptive organization of the infant's motor behavior. In order for the infant to nurse, it must be able to coordinate sucking and swallowing with breathing. Even in infants who are several weeks premature the onset of sucking is associated with cessation of breathing *at the first meal*, as it must, to prevent choking. A fundamental inhibitory relationship between the nervous structures controlling sucking and those controlling breathing develops *in utero* (Johnson & Salisbury, 1975; Peiper, 1963). While the fundamental component responses involved in inspiration, suck movements, and swallowing can be elicited reflexively in early fetal life (Hooker, 1952; Humphrey, 1969), there is a delay in their integration into the organized pattern observable in the normal newborn. Whereas near-term infants suck in relatively prolonged bursts which are accompanied by several swallows, premature infants display shorter suck-bursts which are preceded and/or followed by swallows. It has been suggested that this pattern of behavioral organization in the premature infant represents a mechanism appropriate to the limited ability of the esophagus to accommodate large volumes; prolonged suck bursts and multiple swallows are observed only *after* the appearance of active esophageal transport (Gryboski, 1969).

Another example of mother-infant co-adaptation is the appropriateness of the balance between the composition of mother's milk, her nursing regimen, and the infant's bodily needs in the first few months after birth. Not only does human colostrum contain antibodies to the types of enteric bacteria to which the mother has been exposed (Goldblum, Ahlstredt, Carlsson, Hanson, Jodal, Lindin-Janson, & Sohl-Akerland, 1975), but breast milk also contains factors that facilitate the uptake of necessary nutrients (Colman, Hettiarachchy, & Herbert, 1981) and that stimulate tissue growth per se (Carpenter, 1980). Corresponding to the normal infant's ability to suck vigorously (and largely sustain itself for several days on stored fat), maternal lactation usually must be induced by the baby's sucking, and must be maintained by nursing on a regular basis. Indeed, lactation can even be induced in nulliparious, adoptive mothers (Mead & Newton, 1967).

### The Postnatal Setting—Mother

The most predictable environmental feature for a human neonate is a mother. Presumably, then, in addition to oxygen, stimuli such as those typically emanating from another human are both ubiquitous and necessary signs for postnatal survival and growth. (Lest we neglect the obvious, human milk is one of those inputs.) Warmth, especially at night, can be provided primarily by contact with the mother's body, although even low birth weight newborns are capable of some degree of endogenous homeostatic response to cool surroundings (Glass, Silverman, & Sinclair, 1968). Many metabolic/vegetative functions of premature infants can develop in the context of the largely impersonal, and randomly-patterned events characterizing the environment of the "isolette" of the premature nursery (Gottfried, Wallace-Lande, Sherman-Brown, King, & Coen, 1981). However, conditions that probably mimic the vestibular/tactile/kinesthetic inputs normally encountered when the mother moves about facilitate development/stabilization of a variety of vegitative functions in premature infants (Freedman, Boverman, & Freedman, 1966; Korner, 1979; Scofidi, Field, Schanberg, Bauer, Velga-Lahr, Garcia, Poirier, Nystrom, & Kuhn, 1986).

Human faces are among the stimulus configurations that evoke visual attention and following in newborn babies. By the second or third months, "face-ness" is largely determined by the pattern made by the eyes within an oval shape—a sign stimulus. Even a real human face turned in profile, or wearing glasses which block out the eyes (with skin-colored overlays) will not evoke as much smiling or vocalization as an *en face* presentation with both eyes visible (Bloom, 1975; Spitz & Wolf, 1946). Although there is no consensus as to whether inanimate, face-like stimuli are *uniquely* attractive to infants, there is evidence that a moving face—with two or more "eye-spots"—does elicit more attention than other stimuli by the second month (Carpenter, 1974; Cohen, DeLoache, & Strauss, 1979; Goren, 1975; Freedman, 1974; see Maurer, 1985, for review).

Babies are also selectively responsive with respect to auditory stimulation. In general, infants are more responsive to patterned sounds (vs. pure tones) with a relatively broad frequency band centered about the fundamental frequencies of the human voice (Berg & Berg, 1979; Hutt, Hutt, Lenard, Bernuth, & Muntjewerff, 1968). Although it seems to be difficult to elicit a reduction in neonates' heartrates (an aspect of "orienting") in response to variations in repeated auditory stimulation, the spoken voice is an exception. Furthermore, newborns apparently find voice-like stimulation attractive: When an instrumental or a vocal rendition of a song is made contingent upon non-nutritive sucking, only the vocal rendition will affect the neonates' sucking patterns (Siperstein, 1973). The mechanisms underlying auditory responsiveness develop and seem to be facilitated in utero. Fetuses become selectively attentive to their mothers' patterns of speech while in the womb (De Casper & Spence, 1986).

Soothing techniques typically employed to quiet crying infants also illustrate the parent-offspring match. Rocking infants horizontally while holding them in the prone position and vertically rocking them (at 60 to 70 oscillations per minute, a rate roughly equivalent to slow walking) reduces crying more than simply holding babies in a horizontal position, patting them (without holding), or talking to them. By far the most effective stimulus is holding infants upright against the shoulder; in response to such treatment, not only do babies quiet, but they also appear to become more visually alert. These effects seemed to be primarily in response to proprioceptive/vestibular stimulation involved in being placed in an upright position (Kopp, 1971; Korner, 1979; Korner & Thoman, 1972; Ter Vrugt & Pederson, 1973). All these ministrations are typically provided by caregivers and may function as "signs" that care will be forthcoming.

Perhaps the best example of stimulation associated with the presence of a caregiver is the effectiveness of the "pacifier." Several studies have demonstrated that not only do distressed newborn (and older human infants) quiet when offered a nipple, but that babies with pacifiers, as compared to babies without something to suck on, actually show markedly less heartrate responsiveness to such noxious stimulation as icewater footbaths, electric shock, or circumcision (Bridger, 1962; Kessen, Haith, & Salapatek, 1970).

Although there is continuing debate on the matter, I would side with Ainsworth (1969; Ainsworth, Bell, & Stayton, 1974, p. 99) who argues that "infants are . . . biased towards interaction with people from the beginning." Moreover, I would go further and suggest that continued development *requires* such input. We have already mentioned a number of ways in which neonates' behavior is matched to that of their caregivers. To this, we could add recent (and controversial) demonstrations that even newborns will "imitate" such actions as mouth-opening and sticking out the tongue, observations which suggest that, at some level, neonates are sensitive to correspondences between others' actions and their own (Bower, 1982; Meltzoff & Moore, 1985). Thus, not only are babies born into "required" environments, they are born with the capacities to actively deal with them.

## Vegetative Function

Most authorities seem to agree that a primary concern from the newborn period through the first month is the consolidation of metabolic and homeostatic functioning. As implied by the example of the effects of rocking premature infants, parenting is involved under normal conditions. Some cases of "failure to thrive" probably represent peculiarities in the infants that disturb the caregiver-child relationship (Sameroff & Chandler, 1975; Ullrey, 1986). Nevertheless, a number of additional findings suggest that stimuli associated with caregiving become increasingly necessary for facilitating and maintaining vegetative functioning and for eliciting and integrating motor skills in the third and subsequent months.

Throughout the first half of this century there were persistent reports of high infant mortality in orphanages and similar institutions. They tended to be ascribed to poor nutrition and sanitation. Then, a series of monographs and reports appeared which made a strong case for the contention that social stimulation in infancy played an important, if not crucial, role in all facets of development (Bowlby, 1952; Ribble, 1943; Spitz, 1945; 1946a; 1946b).

Both Ribble and Spitz described a pattern of physiological dysfunction among institutionalized infants. The syndrome became evident by the fourth month and was characterized by a failure to assimilate food, growth retardation, and increased vulnerability to infection. Although flawed, perhaps, by a lack of technology to adequately evaluate deficiencies in nutrition, sanitation, and the effects of maternal anaesthesia (according to Ribble, 1943, a large proportion of her sample of newborns could not suck "spontaneously;" see Aleksandrowitz, 1974), these studies did focus attention upon the social context as a determinant of vegetative function in early infancy.

Subsequent clinical research has confirmed the possibility that some infants and young children simply will not assimilate nutrients or develop normally in an emotionally disturbed or understimulating environment (Coddington, 1968; Powell, Brasel, & Blizzard, 1967), and controlled experiments with laboratory animals indicate that stimuli associated with mother's presence affect somatic growth (Butler, Suskind, & Schanberg, 1978; Kuhn, Butler, & Schanberg, 1978; See Hofer, 1981 for review). Moreover, studies of the effects of undernutrition in human infants suggest that a developmental shift occurs some time after the third month: Nutrient levels in the first three months do not predict later growth (for normal birth-weight infants) whereas subsequent nutritional status does predict later growth (Kim & Pollitt, 1987; Waterlow, Ashworth, & Griffiths, 1980). Sometime after the third month, babies appear to require additional social stimulation just to maintain somatic growth.

## Motor Development

Even when the levels of stimulation, nutrition, and hygiene are adequate to ensure near-normal somatic development, institutional environments often are found inadequate to support "normal" perceptual-motor performance. Insofar as his sample showed vegetative dysfunction, Spitz' observations of a developmental lag would not be at all surprising. However, Provence and Lipton (1962) conducted a study in a North American institution where the children generally conformed to the norms for growth in length and weight. They also found evidence of progressive, and apparently cumulative, behavioral deficits, which seemed to be attributable to a lack of caregiver-infant interaction.[2]

According to Provence and Lipton (1962), the behavior of the institutional sample during the first 3 to 4 weeks after birth was quite similar to that of a comparison group of home-reared infants of the same age. However, by the beginning of the second month, the institution babies began to lag behind their home-reared counterparts. For example, they did not adjust to being picked up; they failed to mold themselves to the cradle formed by the handler's arms. As their first year came to an end, the institution-reared sample lagged progressively behind the home-reared youngsters.

---

[2] Differences between home and institutional environments with respect to social and other forms of stimulation provided for infants have been clearly documented by Rheingold (1961).

They were relatively slow to sit or stand with support, and their initial walking began somewhat later. However, once they started to locomote on their own, they tended to catch up fairly rapidly. Nevertheless, there was a persistent failure of the institution babies to utilize skills that they had shown earlier. These infants had reached for and grasped objects in their cribs, and even shown rudimentary searching for dropped ones. However, as they got older, they ceased to display these skills in appropriate situations. In addition, despite the fact that they were capable of moving in their cribs, they seemed to fail to do so even when in apparently uncomfortable situations.

Although no systematic study was made, Provence and Lipton felt that babies who received "extra" stimulation by virtue of being an attendant's favorite, or simply located near to the work area, tended to be behaviorally better off.

Subsequently, White (1971) studied the conditions affecting perceptual-motor development in normal infants born in an institution serving unwed mothers. As in Provence and Lipton's setting, the babies' overall somatic growth was average, but they received a minimum of physical or social stimulation beyond that which was necessary to maintain normal vegetative functioning. White was particularly interested in the development of perceptual-motor skills and what may (loosely) be termed curiosity or exploratory behavior. Therefore he initiated a series of studies on the effects of different degrees of environmental modification. In his first study, he found that, despite having been unable to look about during their "extra" handling, infants held to the shoulder while blindfolded for 20 minutes per day appeared to be slightly more visually attentive than the controls.

Another group of infants also received an additional 20 minutes per day at the shoulder from postnatal days 6 through 36. In addition, from days 37 to 124 they were placed on their stomachs for 15-minute periods after three of the six daily feeds while the liners of their cribs were removed allowing them to observe ward activities. A colorful, multiform stabile which included rattles, was suspended above their cribs within arm's reach, and the previously white bumper pads and sheets were replaced by multicolored ones.

Under these conditions of "massive enrichment," hand regard appeared to be incidental to reaching for or touching objects and its onset was actually delayed relative to the baseline norms. Unlike home-reared babies for whom hand regard came first, visually guided reaching *preceded* it, and occurred some 45 days earlier than for the unstimulated group. A group of infants given red and white striped mitts, patterned sheets, and bumper pads and placed in the prone position from day 21 until 105 days began hand regard earlier than any other group. Although the "massively enriched" group initially seemed to be more irritable and less visually attentive than their controls, once they began touching the patterned bumpers and the stabile, the massively enriched subjects spent about 50% more time than the controls in visual exploration.

When two pacifiers were mounted against patterned backgrounds on the crib rails from days 37 to 68, and then at 68 days, the stabile replaced the pacifiers, just about all indices of manual behavior were somewhat accelerated relative to previous conditions. When an object was placed in their hands, the experimental group began viewing it one month before the controls did. Throughout the testing period, the babies who had received enviromental enrichment displayed a wider and more complex range of visual/motor behaviors than the controls. However, by day 91, their attentiveness seemed to decline in contrast to the continued increase in the massively enriched group, who were clearly more attentive by day 106.

In sum, White demonstrated that the rates of development of several visuo-motor coordinations in infancy can be facilitated by the children's surroundings. Within limits, the sequence of appearance of specific eye-hand coordinations depends upon conditions of rearing. Simple "handling," even in the absence of opportunities for visual input, affects visual responsiveness, and just providing infants with things to look at and to manipulate facilitates and maintains the expression of these potentials.

Several points stand out from these studies: Relatively meager amounts of stimulation associated with "basic caregiving" appear to maintain development in the first month or so (*contra* Ribble, 1943). However, somewhere between the second and fourth months, more is required to sustain somatic growth, and still more input is required to maintain and integrate the *use* of motor behaviors. Many motor patterns can develop in relatively sterile environments. However, the maintenance and integration of these potentials seem to require additional environmental supports: Although they *could* perform more complex "adaptive" actions, many of Provence and Lipton's sample simply failed to do so—even when apparently appropriately provoked.

A number of other studies have also shown that environmental variables are associated with motor development in infancy. Among the more important inputs seem to be the variety of inanimate stimuli available to infants and, to a lesser degree, the "responsiveness" of objects (for goal-oriented behavior and self-generated play) and overall, caregiver responsiveness to infant distress (Yarrow, Rubenstein, Pedersen, & Jankowski, 1972). All these inputs, under most conditions, would be provided in the course of typical mothering. Infants are usually moved from one setting to another—more than just from supine to prone—regularly during the day. They certainly are picked up more than six to 12 times per day and sometimes even played with (Rheingold, 1961).

## "Social" Responsiveness

If mothering is the primary source of stimuli constituting the environment to which human infants are adapted, it would follow that infants are not only dependent upon a certain modicum of mothering-like stimuli for growth and development, but they should also be capable of provoking needed stimulation, particularly when there are indications that the investment of energy in signaling their needs will yield such input.[3]

To begin with an obvious feature, babies are usually perceived as being "cute." Ethologists assert that a relatively large head, with a proportionately large forehead, large eyes at or below the middle of the skull, prominent, "chubby" cheeks, generally rounded body form with comparatively short limbs, and pudgy hands and feet all are features eliciting a judgement of cuteness (e.g., Eibl-Eibesfeldt, 1970). If one thinks of Disney's or other cartoonists' renderings of lovable animals such as Bambi, Bugs Bunny, and others, the effects of exaggerated eye-size, chubby cheeks, and so on, are readily apparent. Controlled research by experimental psychologists has generally substantiated these findings (Brooks & Hochberg, 1960; Gardner & Wallach, 1965; Fullard & Reiling, 1976; Hess, 1970; Sternglanz, Gray, & Murakami, 1977).

Presumably, some of these features originally evolved simply to accommodate the restrictions imposed by the uterine environment, given our species' considerable prenatal cortical development. However, the concept of opportunism in evolution suggests that, insofar as these attributes were distinctive of an age-class requiring special care, selection also would have favored parents who were responsive to them. Moreover, to the extent that infantile morphology and adult responsiveness co-evolved, the stage would have been set for the *exaggeration* of certain features. In humans, the prominent cheeks provide a likely example. While most mammalian young seem to be relatively large-cheeked, much of this probably represents a comparatively short snout. In humans, the fat pads in the infant and young child's cheeks are exaggerated when compared with adults and serve no other obvious function. Thus they may have evolved specifically as "releasers" for parental solicitude (Peiper, 1963). If so, infants are born attractive, as it were, especially to mothers who may have been hormonally sensitized to respond to them (Bell & Harper, 1977).

Their behavior further acts to maintain the bond. As Bowlby (1958; 1969) emphasized, neonates also cling, root, and suck. At least for a short period just after birth, they look attentively, if briefly, at interesting stimuli,

---

[3] As suggested by the foregoing studies of infants in institutions, the "minimum" input may be quite low by current American standards. See Leiderman, Tulkin, & Rosenfeld (1977).

such as human faces (Theorell, Prechtl, Blair, & Lind, 1973). They smile, too, but this occurs primarily during REM sleep (Korner, 1968; Tcheng & Laroche, 1965; Wolff, 1966), although it *may* occur a little more often among infants who get more handling (Freedman, 1974).

*Social smiling.* Sometime between one and three months after birth, babies begin to smile in response to external stimuli. This change in organization of smiling from control by sleep-state to regulation by exteroceptive stimuli cannot be explained simply as a function of social experience: Given comparable conditions, *gestational* age is the single best predictor of the onset of externally-elicited smiling (Dittrichova, 1969). Induction of the processes underlying the reorganization of this response may thus occur prenatally. However, infants born and reared in institutional settings generally begin exteroceptive smiling later than home-reared babies (Ambrose, 1961; Gewirtz, 1965; Vine, 1973). Thus it would seem that enrichment facilitates this developmental change.

Among babies reared in economically fortunate families by child-centered parents, the shift to elicited smiling begins as early as the sixth week of age, and is initially released by a fairly wide range of stimuli, especially the human voice. Later on, about two weeks after the initiation of exteroceptively-released responsiveness, smiling becomes more restricted to visual stimuli, especially the human face or caricatures thereof (Emde et al., 1976; Freedman, 1974). The facts that babies in all cultures and even blind infants begin smiling in response to auditory/tactual cues at about the same developmental age, and that the shift to exteroceptive control is contemporaneous with a number of other changes in vegetative function indicate that the behavior is more than a simple act of mimicry (Emde et al., 1976; Freedman, 1974; Sroufe & Waters, 1975; Vine, 1973).

A consideration of the kinds of stimuli eliciting smiling suggests that we are dealing with the ethologists' "sign" stimuli. In the first month or so after the onset of visually evoked smiling, babies do *not* smile at the bottle or the profile view of a familiar caregiver, and they smile almost automatically—sometimes even more regularly—at a variety of artificial stimuli whose similarities to caregivers are remote at best (Spitz & Wolf, 1946; Vine, 1973). Bloom and Erikson (1971) have shown that photographs of eyes pasted over the lenses of glasses are just as effective as clear lenses, suggesting that eye movement and reflectance may not be important features in capturing three-month-olds' attention. Institutionalized babies, in whose lives contingent social relationships are minimal (*contra* Watson, 1979) also continue to smile at people (or caricatures) for several months (Provence & Lipton, 1962; Rheingold & Bayley, 1959), and during the transition from sleep-related to exteroceptive control, babies smile at a variety of stimuli which are both familiar and unfamiliar (Emde et al.,

1976). The orientation of even a familiar caregiver's face is critical; babies smile most readily at an *en face* presentation (Watson, 1972).[4]

Other behavioral changes accompany the shift from sleep-controlled to exteroceptively-elicited smiling: Not only do babies remain awake longer, but during the day they begin to display obvious attentional responses; in particular, they seem to look at people in a more prolonged, or interested way. Whether or not they smile, they impress adults as showing "recognition." Moreover, within a week or two of the onset of visually-elicited smiling, babies also begin to "coo"—to utter non-cry, vowel-like sounds which usually strike adults as indicative of pleasure. Coos are emitted simply when adults are around—even if their parents are deaf and therefore unresponsive (Bloom & Esposito, 1975; Freedman, 1974). All these are behaviors that adults typically find endearing. Indeed, a variety of authors have remarked that the behaviors emerging at this stage function to elicit (and sustain) social involvement of adults (Ambrose, 1969; Berg & Berg, 1979; Emde et al., 1976; Robson, 1967; Vine, 1973).

The ontogeny of the smile thus provides an example of an adaptive reorganization of behavior that provokes needed input. Smiling is a motor pattern which develops in utero well before it becomes socially effective. Further, at birth, the way in which the behavior is regulated is qualitatively different than its regulation some two to three months later: Neonatal smiling occurs during REM sleep; it is essentially nonresponsive and organizationally isolated from direct, exteroceptive influence. In contrast, "social" smiling is susceptible not only to external stimulation but also to some degree of stimulus control (see Berg & Berg, 1979; Sameroff & Cavanaugh, 1979), and the shift occurs in the context of far-reaching changes in overall physiological and behavioral regulation (the sleep-wake cycle, cooing, and so on [Emde et al., 1976] and a developmental shift in cerebral function [Chugani & Phelps, 1986]).

The data suggest that the level of caregiver stimulation essential for growth and development in the first month or two is relative low—although the infant's growth rate is somewhat responsive to amount of input (cf. Ambrose, 1961)—and a shift in physiological/behavioral organization

---

[4] The facts that the earliest social smiles are elicited by a wide range of stimuli, that blind infants smile "on schedule," and that smiling does habituate all have been cited as evidence that some sort of "cognitive" interpretation is required to account for audio- or visually-evoked social smiling. The latter objections are not crucial since "released" responses can habituate, and many biologically important releasers are multidimensional amalgams of diverse stimulus qualities, which may combine more or less additively to increase the strength of a response (the so-called "Law of heterogeneous summation" e.g., Hinde, 1966). For example, smiling often is enhanced by a moving face and combined visual and auditory stimulation may further increase responsiveness (Bower, 1966; Polak, Emde, & Spitz, 1964).

occurs around the second or third months. Presumably, at this point, more, or perhaps even different kinds of input become important. If babies fail to get enough social stimulation, there may be an apparent failure of vegetative function. Even if they obtain sufficient caregiver stimulation to maintain vegetative function, more input, particularly contingent types of reactions, seems to be needed in order for babies to fully display and integrate developing potentials for motor behavior.

A behavioral reorganization favoring display of social stimulus-eliciting and stimulus-maintaining behaviors such as cooing and exteroceptively-elicited smiling at this point can be seen as a means for ensuring that needed input is forthcoming: Since the parent-offspring match works *both ways*, the requirements for infant development have evolved so that the critical postnatal period is not impossibly demanding. Mothers may be physically exhausted from labor; they must still begin to produce milk and provide it regularly around the clock. Additional, contingent exchanges with babies could simply be too much to ask. It seems that the baby is developmentally prepared to make do with less. That is, the sufficient conditions for continued development correspond to little more than warmth and regular feeding while mothers are recovering from the delivery. The fact that the shift can be facilitated by higher levels of social stimulation can be seen as a mechanism for "tracking" the environment: If caregivers do have the energy and/or resources to invest, the baby's rate of development can be accelerated.

### Parental Solicitude

If our argument is correct, newborns for whom the prognosis for survival is good, and whose mothers are in good health, should be in synchrony with their mothers from the beginning, and the (alert) newborn will augment its hormonally-primed mother's commitment to care for it (cf. Bell & Harper, 1977; Kennell, Voos, & Klaus, 1979). If either mother or baby (or both) are only temporarily rendered incapable of responding at this juncture, and the period for perinatal augmentation of solicitude passes before they recover, severing the relationship at that point would be fatal for the infant and biologically wasteful for the mother. However, if the baby still can evoke and sustain some solicitude by being cute and generally tractable, the mother may continue to provide care. Then, the healthy baby can respond to the level of maternal ministrations by sooner or later becoming "sociable" and providing a second chance for deeper maternal attachment. On the other hand, if either mother or baby is sorely debilitated, then they probably will remain out of synchrony and solicitude will not be induced permitting the mother the psychological option of abandonment. (See Freedman, 1974, for a slightly different interpretation.)

## DISCRIMINATION AMONG INDIVIDUALS

The next stage of reorganization in infancy is one in which the tendency to respond to (social) contingencies becomes modulated by the degree of familiarity with the social partner.

### Attachment

In stable family settings, babies' social responsiveness becomes progressively selective during the first year. It (usually) culminates with displays of positive emotion at the appearance of the chosen social object(s), and equally overt displays of distress and/or protest upon separation from the object. Although the specific manifestations of these social bonds vary as the infant and child get older, a common theme seems to be maintaining some form of proximity to or (social) contact with specific individuals (Bowlby, 1969).

The development of infants' differential responsiveness and ultimately their attachments to specific individuals provide another example of the heterochronous development of behavioral capacities and their adaptive, functional reorganization. Neonates display attention to stimuli which seem to be characteristic of human beings, such as the face and movement. Indeed, they even seem to be capable of some limited forms of mimicry (Collins & Olney, 1982; Meltzoff & Moore, 1985). Presumably, these attentional and motoric biases reflect peculiarities of the human newborn's nervous system. Because neonates spend most of their time asleep and do not show a clear pattern of daytime wakefulness or prolonged bouts of obvious alertness until the end of the second month (Berg & Berg, 1979; Emde et al., 1976), many of these responses have been dismissed as "reflexive." Nevertheless, when alert, very young infants are responsive to events occurring around them and may be storing information about certain features of their social environments.

*From selective responsiveness to discriminative responding.* Although there is by no means a consensus on the matter, evidence suggests that neonates under 20 *minutes* of age will visually track moving face-like stimuli (Freedman, 1974; Goren, 1975; but see Maurer, 1985). Movement is an important facet of the total configuration, as one might expect if the infant's nervous system were tuned to be responsive to stimuli reliable indicative of biologically important events—that is, caregivers. It has been claimed that infants can discriminate their mothers from adult strangers within three days from birth (Field, Cohen, Garcia, & Greenberg, 1984). Certainly, by two weeks of age, infants discriminate a moving human (mother's) face from a moving mannequin (although in the latter case, the mother's face received *less* visual regard). At this phase, *either* the mother's or the mannequin's stationary face may elicit distress, rather than attention (Freedman, 1974). (One might argue, *post hoc*, that effective caregivers don't stand immobile, staring).

In neonates, voices or other complex sounds appear to increase attention to static visual displays (Mendelson & Haith, 1976). If faces (or pictures of faces) are immobile but accompanied by sounds, infants pay more attention to them. Although, at 4 weeks of age, babies' scanning is reported to be more influenced by tones than voices, by at least 7-8 weeks, they look more at pictures of faces when voices are heard (Donnee, 1973). According to Wolff (1963), babies who are between 5 and 6 weeks old will quiet more readily to their mothers' voice than to their fathers' or an unfamiliar male's falsetto voice. (Voices are among the first effective exteroceptive stimuli in eliciting smiling [Emde et al., 1976; Wolff, 1963]).

Babies may be encoding the peculiarities of their mothers' voices much earlier. Between 3 and 4 weeks of age infants respond selectively to their mother's, as opposed to a stranger's voice (Mills & Melhuish, 1974). They suck a blind nipple at significantly higher rates and spend more time sucking (longer bursts and shorter pauses) when their mothers' voices are contingently presented. A similar contingent response for mother's voice may be demonstrated within 3 days of birth (DeCasper & Fifer, 1980). This preference may be developed in utero since *newborn* babies respond preferentially to the kinds of prose that their mothers had read aloud in the month before birth (De Casper & Spence, 1986). That is, there may be prenatal receptor-mediated facilitation or functional validation of mechanisms controlling auditory attention.

Finally, differential responsiveness to mother's, as opposed to a stranger's body odor has been reported for infants who were from 6 days (MacFarlane, 1975) to six weeks old (Russell, 1976). Thus, within at least 2 weeks of birth, infants are capable of discriminating stimulus features of a familiar caregiver from those of strangers or inanimate surrogates. Moreover, they apparently prefer stimuli typical of the mother insofar as they usually will respond more strongly (longer, more rapidly) in order to maintain mother-related as opposed to stranger-related input. Nevertheless, they will protest if anyone simply stares at them while immobile or if any moving and/or talking person suddenly disappears from view. It seems as if they can discriminate among individuals very early, but this knowledge, as it were, does not control the onset of their protest behavior. However, some infants at this age, when distressed, may more readily *quiet* in response to ministrations by a familiar than an unfamiliar caregiver (Carpenter, 1973; Emde et al., 1976).

During the third and fourth months, despite the facts that they clearly *can* discriminate familiar caregivers from strangers and will smile to their mothers more readily, babies still smile to familiar or unfamiliar faces and even schematic pictures of faces. It has been claimed that by 36 hours of birth, infants respond differentially to happy, sad, or surprised expressions (Collins & Olney, 1982), and they do seem to respond differently to visual-auditory affective displays by 10 weeks of age (Haviland & Lelwica, 1987). Nevertheless, as late as the third or fourth month, they still smile to caricatures, and show no obvious emotional—or differential—smiling response to photographs depciting various emotions or Halloween masks until around the fifth month (Schwartz, Izard, & Ansul, 1985; see Oster, 1981; Sroufe, 1979, for reviews). For whatever reason, then, the early contingent social responses of infants tend to increase in frequency and be relatively nonspecific despite evidence that they can, to some degree, distinguish their mothers from strangers on the basis of facial features, voice quality, and odor.

Something else may be going on in terms of information-processing, however. If one studies change in pupillary size, often thought to index attention, a difference emerges. In clear contrast to 1-month-old babies, who show no pupillary difference when looking at mothers or strangers, 4-month-old infants do appear to attend *more* (greater dilation) to a *stranger* (Fitzgerald, 1968). With respect to recognition of facial features, by 5 months of age, the simple presence of eyes alone is insufficient to release smiling, and infants attend to more details of features within the (schematic) outline of the head. In particular, babies at about 5 months of age attend to the nose and mouth (Caron, Caron, Caldwell, & Weiss, 1973). Around the fifth or sixth months, more smiling occurs in response to a smiling facial stimulus and by 6 months, even institution-reared infants become more selective (Spitz & Wolf, 1946; Wilcox & Clayton, 1968). In sum, although babies seem to be somewhat indiscriminately "socially" outgoing through the sixth month, they are making attentional distinctions and refining their perceptions from the first month. However, consistent with the model of heterochronous development of the components of functional systems, these discriminative capacities do not seem to play a central role in controlling filial responsiveness.

*Early bonding.* Some time around the sixth month, a new kind of organization of social responsiveness begins to appear in home-reared infants. Whereas Provence and Lipton's (1962) institutionalized infants were described as displaying behavior suggesting an "intense hunger" for personal contact even with relatively unfamiliar investigators, between 5 and 7 months of age, home-reared children tend to "sober" when confronted by strangers (Emde et al., 1976; Kagan, 1977; Schaffer, 1971). At this point, it would seem that home-reared babies' abilities to discriminate familiar caregivers from strangers are beginning to affect their social responsiveness.

For some mother-reared infants, the relationship with the familiar individual may assume tremendous significance. Spitz (1946b) studied responses to separation from their (convict) mothers in 6- to 8-month-old infants who were being reared in a penal institution. Of the babies whose prior relationships with their mothers had been rated as good, a majority displayed a suite of behaviors described as "depression" when their mothers were denied the right to care for them (for disciplinary reasons). Since this response was not observed in similarly separated babies who were not considered to have had good relations with their mothers, and because all the separated infants were assigned to other, presumably competent caregivers, their depressive reactions were interpreted to represent responses to the disruption of emotional, child-mother bonds. Many babies showed a dramatic reversal if reunions were instituted within a few weeks (Spitz, 1946b). Despite often heated criticisms, Spitz' findings have been replicated in studies of both animals and humans (see Gubernik, 1981; Hofer, 1981 for comparative reviews).

Yarrow (1963) observed the responses of infants who had been reared continuously from birth in foster homes for periods ranging from 6 weeks to 12 months prior to being adopted. Only a few infants appeared to be disturbed by a change in focal caregivers during the first 3 months, but 86% of those adopted at 6 months, and *every one* who was placed at 7 months of age or older displayed clear, negative reactions. In partial confirmation of Spitz' (1946b) data, the symptoms of disturbance included blunted social responsiveness, excessive clinging to the mother, excessive crying, unusual apathy, difficulty in adapting to routines, and the failure to display previously-acquired competencies.

Thus, within the first two to five months, infants who are reared in reasonably stimulating surroundings develop an ability to discriminate familiar caregivers from unfamiliar adults. Moreover, under such conditions, some time between the fifth and eighth months of age, most of them develop focused relationships with familiar caregivers which are so intense that their motor and social behavior and sometimes even their vegetative functioning will be noticeably disturbed by separating them from their attachment objects (see Bowlby, 1969; 1973; 1982 for reviews).

### Separation Protest

The attachment story has several additional chapters, among them the development of active protest, crying, whining, and so on, at even very brief physical separations. Although not all babies display such behavior, and few do so consistently, it seems to become more likely and/or more intense some time after the seventh or eighth months. Such behavior is not restricted to American or European infants; it can be observed in a variety of cultural settings (Ainsworth, 1977; Bretherton & Waters, 1985; Emde et al., 1976; Kagan, 1977; Konner, 1982; Lester, Kotelchuk, Spelke, Sellers, & Klein, 1974; Schaffer, 1963). Somewhat older infants in familiar settings will simply follow their mothers without apparent display of emotional upset. However, in unfamiliar surroundings, and particularly in the presence of strangers, protest behavior can be observed at least through the second year of age, and it is accompanied by such indices of emotional arousal as heart-rate acceleration and flushing (Bretherton & Waters, 1985; Marvin, 1977; Schwartz, Campos, Baisel, & Amatore, 1971).

While attachment to caregivers probably serves a variety of ends, protest at separation seems to fit nicely with Bowlby's (1969) view that much of their behavior serves to guarantee that infants are safe from predation (one seldom can ignore a crying child). It is also to the baby's advantage to be sure that it doesn't get overlooked or lost while exploring or playing. From an adaptationist viewpoint, babies should take an active role in ensuring that they get care. They do. Carr, Dabbs, and Carr (1975) observed 20- to 36-month-old infants in an unfamiliar laboratory setting, with their mothers and attractive toys available, but physically separated. So long as their mothers were looking in their general direction—and were not too far away—the babies ventured off to examine and play with the toys. If their mothers seemed to be attentive they would stray further; if their mothers seemed to be preoccupied, then they assumed more of the responsibility for maintaining contact. If the lures were out of their mothers' *line of sight,* the infants stayed much closer. Thus, whether or not one feels compelled to appeal to some cognitive process or to emotion as the immediate psychological cause of the response (e.g., Breger, 1974; Bretherton, 1985; Main, Kaplan, & Cassidy, 1985; Sroufe, 1979), separation protest clearly is more than simple "discharge" of affect or arousal and functionally represents an adaptive, organized behavior.

The development of separation protest also provides another example of reorganization—and the delayed integration—of different capacities. From birth, infants can communicate their disequilibrium states/needs by crying. They also are capable of discriminating and responding differentially to familiar and unfamiliar persons from at least the third month. Nevertheless, separation protest is not observed until after the sixth month. The change can be seen as a phase of reorganization in which vocal protest becomes controlled by social discriminatory capacities (Emde et al., 1976; Schaffer, 1971).

### Stranger Anxiety

A related phenomenon is the tendency to avoid or even to actively protest the attentions and/or the close proximity of unfamiliar persons. This "stranger anxiety" (Spitz, 1950) also has its onset some time in the second half of the first year, becoming first apparent with a "sobering" and inhibition of activity in response to a stranger's appearance as early as the fifth month and often leading to apparently fearful behavior by the ninth or tenth months. It wanes in intensity only after the second year. There is some debate as to its ubiquity (Brody & Axelrad, 1971; Rheingold & Eckerman, 1973; Sroufe, 1979), but most investigators agree that wariness or avoidance of strangers is more commonly and consistently observed than separation protest. Like the latter, stranger anxiety can be observed in a variety of cultural settings (Ainsworth, 1977; Bronson, 1972; Emde et al., 1976; Lester et al., 1974; Konner, 1971; 1982; Sagi, Lamb, Lewkowicz, Shoham, Dirr, & Estes, 1985; Schaffer, 1971).

Studies of the onset and course of negative responses to the departure of attachment-objects and to the approach of strangers indicate that, while the two behaviors may share related elements, they are not identical: Although the onset of stranger anxiety seldom precedes separation anxiety, separation protest occurs more variably, and in a few children who are otherwise apparently attached to a caregiver, one or the other response simply does not appear (Ainsworth, 1969; Emde et al., 1976; Schaffer, 1963).

The onset of protest at the approach of unfamiliar adults is correlated with the infant's apparent ability to conceive of other people as continuing to exist even when they cannot be perceived (Paradise & Curcio, 1974). But even if the relationship were a necessary one, which it may not be (Emde et al., 1976), this fact in itself is not sufficient to explain why protest *per se* should be delayed until the seventh to ninth months. After all, babies do discriminate among individuals consistently and form expectancies or "routines" of exchange much earlier (Bower, 1982). They are capable of protest from birth. Explanations based upon the relatively late development of the ability to juxtapose events in relation to one another (Schaffer, 1971) or to the late consolidation of memory and other cognitive skills required to formulate hypotheses on the basis of past experience (Kagan, 1984), might account for proximate, psychological "causation." However, they leave unexplained the important element of the timing of the integration of these previously independently-developing systems.

## Functional Significance

From the perspective taken here, a full understanding of these developments will depend upon an analysis of both the nature of developmental processes and the functional significance of the behaviors at issue. If we begin with the assumption that temporal patterning of developmental events has been subject to selection, then the problem is to account for broadening the control of vocal protest from mechanisms which are primarily concerned with monitoring internal state to include mechanisms involved in making discriminations in the social environment.

Assuming that early hominid behavioral development was similar to that of most contemporary primates and not too dissimilar from what we see in human babies today, infants have been incapable of locomoting on their own until toward the end of the first year. Furthermore, the off-spring of most terrestrial and semi-terrestrial primates and of contemporary human hunter-gatherers (a) nurse very frequently throughout the day, (b) are carried by their caregivers wherever they go, and (c) remain dependent upon their mothers for food and protection for some time *after* they can locomote on their own. Finally, mothers are less willing to nurse and risk danger for any but their own offspring. If these conditions did prevail during all—or a significant portion—of human history, then selection must have favored babies who behaved in ways which ensured that they maintained proximity to their primary caregivers, as argued by Bowlby (1969).

The timing of the control of protest then can be explained in terms of our model of development. A general principle of development is that new functional integrations will appear somewhat in advance of the moment at which they are crucial for survival. Thus emotional upset or overt protest in response to either separation from mother or to the approach of unfamiliar adults should anticipate the onset of skilled, autonomous locomotion and thereby reduce the probability of babies "walking into trouble" (See Konner, 1972).

But why stranger anxiety? For several reasons: First, human history is replete with chronicles of slaughter, including the killing of infants and young children. Attacks on infants have been observed among free-ranging primates, both within and across groups (Hausfater & Hrdy, 1984). Secondly, even though adult and juvenile female primates become very interested in infants, even solicitous, experienced adult females only rarely consummate adoptions, and juveniles are both nonlactating and frequently inept (Blaffer-Hrdy, 1976). Insofar as similar solicitous tendencies have been observed in humans (Konner, 1972; 1982), it probably was to an infant's advantage to resist even well-intentioned attentions from strangers. Consistent with the latter interpretation, among kibbutz-reared infants, separation protest is more dependent upon who *remains with* an infant than who departs in a group situation (Fox, 1975).

Thus it is irrelevant for infants to worry about where they are or who else is with them so long as their physical and social surroundings are determined almost exclusively by where their parents take them. It can be very important for them to "have a say" (and to vocally announce their whereabouts) when they can control their own movements. As Richards (1974) points out, the more or less simultaneous appearance of locomotion, protest at separation, and compliance with parental commands is probably more than simple coincidence.

Separation protest and stranger anxiety may also function to define a special relationship between infant and caregivers. In institutional settings, it often is the babies who initiate special relationships with particular caregivers by means of their selective responsiveness. As Freedman (1974) suggests, these behaviors would also function to prevent the dilution of the babies' ties while simultaneously reaffirming the special nature of existing relationships.

A functional interpretation gains further credence when one examines the conditions under which people of all ages tend to seek proximity to attachment figures. Pain, illness, fatigue, and "fear" are all conditions under which people tend to seek proximity to caregivers or family (see Bowlby, 1969; 1973; Maccoby & Masters, 1970). A familiar caregivers' presence can reduce not only the overt indices of upset in unfamiliar, stressful context, but also covert, autonomic (heart rate) responses as well (Bridger, 1962; Schwartz et al., 1971). It would make functional "sense" to conserve energy when help is at hand. Indeed, if safety from predation were a selective pressure favoring protest at separation and intrusions by strangers, it would be equally advantageous for babies and small children to be as inconspicuous as possible (not protesting) in moderately stressful settings so long as they are in close proximity to attachment figures.

### Conditions Favoring Attachment

Now we turn to another issue: Given the assumption that the phenomena subsumed under the rubric of attachment evolved as adaptations to the conditions of infancy, what can this interpretation tell us about the inputs that are necessary for the expression of these potentials?

Our evolutionary argument suggests that the stimuli necessary and sufficient to evoke and sustain species-specific developmental events are "sign stimuli" which embody components of more complex configurations diagnostic of the average expectable environments of the species, and which normally are encountered (or processed) at the *appropriate points* in the life cycle. I also have postulated that, when species-typical development depends upon a specific set of external conditions, any one of several different facets of these conditions might independently suffice to evoke or sustain developmental change. That is, the stimuli are functional equivalents which can summate.

*Input.* From these principles, we would expect that the input necessary for the development of social responsiveness in human infants are (a) typical of human environments, (b) multidimensional and semi-independent, and (c) given an above-threshold "dose," any one or a variety of combinations of them will suffice to ensure a "normal" outcome. Moreover, insofar as the most critical features for human survival in infancy are embodied in caregivers, a certain minimum of these stimuli should be characteristics of human beings, and as a result of prenatal development, infants should be *selectively* attuned to respond to them. DeCasper and Spence's (1986) data suggest that the initial functional validation of some auditory discriminations may depend upon prenatal input. If so, one might also expect the olfactory/gustatory apparatuses of neonates to be biased to be more responsive to the odor/taste of kin (cf. Pedersen, Stewart, Greer, & Shepherd, 1983). Because simple caricatures portraying "eyes" still elicit smiling and other social responses well after infants are capable of distinguishing among human faces, the discriminatory abilities probably develop somewhat independently of the mechanisms which prepare the baby to focus on an individual.

On the basis of existing data on infant attention and releasers of smiling, it seems likely that movement, "eyes" aligned to a 0° orientation (eyeball-to-eyeball, cf. Watson, 1972), the pitch/overtones of the (female) voice, and "human" odors all probably are important cues which, perhaps in conjunction with vestibular input (Korner & Thoman, 1972), serve to induce a readiness to attach. Because blind (Fraiberg, 1975), blind-deaf children (Eibl-Eibesfeldt, 1970), and even an infant who had no sense of touch at all (Caron, 1967) have been reported to form attachments, it seems unlikely that any *one* of these sensory avenues is crucial. Rather, they all contribute, (i.e., can be considered alternative equivalents). In combination, under average conditions, they provide a substantial margin for error, permitting wide variations in childrearing practices (e.g., Leiderman et al., 1977).

In addition to these basic features of human-like stimuli required for the development of readiness to respond selectively (cf. Schaffer, 1963), other qualitatively distinctive attributes, for example, hair *color*, probably help the child to discriminate among individuals. As indicated, this potential is expressed prior to stranger/separation protest and probably is also facilitated during the "priming" process.

*The chosen one.* From the literature, especially Ainsworth's studies (e.g., 1963; Ainsworth, Bell, & Stayton, 1971; 1974), it seems likely that (apart from embodying the above-mentioned characteristics diagnostic of human beings), one "quantitative" and three additional qualitative characteristics are crucial in determining to whom the infant will attach. Quantitatively, the attachment object should be someone who is generally "around" enough to become a familiar figure. Then, among the class of familiar human beings, the one to whom a baby is likely to develop a filial attachment will embody the following additional qualities: First, the individual will be a (relatively) large (mature) person. Although very young children can and do form strong personal bonds with each other, if adults are available, babies will orient toward them rather than toward their agemates.[5]

The second qualitative characteristic is that the person who gets chosen is responsive to the child. This is not synonymous with what is popularly called "warmth" or "love," (although they certainly do help). Rather, contingent reactions to the baby's signals seem to be key elements—regardless of their quality. This is the feature that Watson (1972) has emphasized as the *sine qua non* of the social partner. However, *contra* Watson, contingency *per se* probably in insufficient. It would seem likely that a contingent object must embody other features diagnostic of humans, for example, a human-like face, voice-quality, and/or odor in order to serve as an adequate mother-surrogate to support the development of an average baby.

The third qualitative characteristic that determines who gets chosen is the individual's relative salience. Here is where our commonsense notions of warmth or love may come into play. Those who have an upwelling of fondness toward an infant or who enjoy interacting with the baby probably are more animated, louder, and insistent. For example, Freud and Burlingham (1944) recounted how a London woman placed her 4-month-old twins in a residential nursery outside of the city during the bombings of World War II. Although she visited her offspring whenever she could, the twins received the bulk of their care and stimulation from the nursery staff. Nevertheless, as they grew older, they became clearly attached to their mother. Presumably, all who dealt with the babies were reasonably responsive (contingent), but their mother was a loud, rough (albeit loving) woman who hugged, squeezed, and even slapped her offspring vigorously. When she visited, the whole nursery was aware of it; her babies were too, and she was the one upon whom they focused their emotional responsiveness.

From an evolutionary perspective, all these features should be important: That the facilitating stimuli include features diagnostic of humans, for example, the face gestalt, odor, a complex voice, and so on should be obviously adaptive. It would also be adaptive if the *amount* of such input would, to some degree, regulate the infant's growth—that is, match the availability of caregiving resources. With respect to the features promoting focused attachment, other infants or toddlers simply cannot provide adequate care. A person who has a (biological) investment in an infant is more likely to be both around and attentive (if someone is frankly inattentive, the baby's chances aren't too good). Therefore, it seems reasonable to assume that selection would have favored babies who attached to fre-

---

[5] Indeed, among infants and toddlers in day care, the presence of adults (who actually hope to promote peer-directed social exchanges) often inhibits the display of agemate interaction (St. Pierre, 1981; Tizard & Tizard, 1971).

quently-encountered adults who are responsive. Similarly, those who do have strong feelings toward a baby are likely to stand out from others who interact with it either because of the quality or the intensity of their activities.[6]

This formulation has the advantage of being able to account for two apparently paradoxical facts: First, that some babies attach to abusive parents (Schneider-Rosen, Braunwald, Carlson, & Acchetti, 1985). The abusive parent would be chosen because (a) such treatment typically *is* in response to the baby's activities (i.e., contingent, although certainly inappropriate), (b) punishment, and so on, tends to mobilize one's attention, and (c) the abusive parent is an adult. In short, such an individual fills all requirements for an attachment figure. Second, some babies do not seem to focus upon their primary caregivers. If another, familiar, adult individual is more contingent and salient even though not the source of food or comfort, (or even the most frequent companion), this view can still explain the attachment.

---

[6] This position is in direct contradiction to Schneirla's (1965) view that *low*-intensity stimuli evoke approach behavior. The problem upon which resolution depends is a satisfactory measure of relative intensity—*from the baby's standpoint.*

# CHAPTER 6

# Exploration, Play, and Peer Relations

In this chapter, exploratory behavior will be used to exemplify how stage-specific phenotypic attributes may serve to focus inputs to foster growth and how youngsters actively provoke others to supply them with stimulation. The early ontogeny of wariness to the unfamiliar will be presented as an exemplar of both the ontogenetic reorganization of functional systems and the adaptive nature of such changes. Play will further illustrate the ways in which early behavior is (re)organized to serve growth. Finally, a consideration of peer relations will exemplify how different behavioral systems may relate to one another in ontogeny.

## EXPLORATION

Manifestations of "curiosity" in a variety of contexts may represent the activation of very different constallations of underlying mechanisms. Indeed, given the additional assumption that the organismic substrates for most behavioral systems undergo fundamental changes during development, exploratory behavior is probably much more complex than we would care to imagine. What follows, then, represents examples selected to further illustrate the model of development presented in preceding chapters.

Whereas older animals tend to respond with exploration only to the unfamiliar, and seem almost to avoid familiar objects (Barnett, 1958), young animals and children appear to be more curious and require greater exposure to objects before shifting to playful activities, or losing interest. This greater curiosity of younger individuals could be simply a reflection of their lack of experience and/or their limited ability to establish a stable and accessible memory store (thereby implying comparable levels of curiosity across age groups). Alternatively, it could (also) represent an inability to filter out "irrelevant" stimuli, that is, lack of focused attention (Fox, 1970; Millar, 1968).

However, if our adaptationist argument has merit, we must be careful not to confuse the (apparent) degree of functional development of underlying substrates with the ways they serve the organism. As Galef (1981) has shown for many facets of filial behavior, instances of apparently "undeveloped" physiological regulation can be seen as adaptations to the social/ecological conditions peculiar to early stages of the life cycle. Just because a particular activity is controlled differently, or because adult-like regulatory mechanisms are not operative, we should not dismiss that activity as less efficient, or less adaptive than its adult counterpart. Its functional significance and its importance to the total (developmental) economy of the individual may be quite substantial (cf. Goldman, 1976).

For example, there may be two aspects of the development of visual perception corresponding to differential rates of development of early-appearing, subcortical mechanisms and later-developing "primary" visual areas of the brain (cf. Bronson, 1974). The peripheral and subcortical mechanisms may function to direct the infant's gaze toward "salient," moving patterns which are "off center." Presumably, these mechanisms facilitate the development of cortical neuronal function subserving pattern- and color-perception (cf. Blythe, Bromley, Kennard, & Ruddock, 1986). Indeed, very young infants do try to get a "good look" at their surroundings. If one brings a shade in front of one eye of a baby, without actually touching that eye, the infant will turn away so that the view out of both eyes is unobstructed (Peiper, 1963). Four-week-old infants will even learn to vary their sucking rates on a dummy nipple in order to focus novel visual displays (Kalnins & Bruner, 1973). Thus, the retinal mechanisms underlying fixation and visual tracking might provide the necessary bases for the functional validation and maintenance of slower maturing, stimulus-dependent cortical analyzers of the so-called primary visual areas. Consistent with our model, mechanisms controlling visual localization become functional (although probably not under voluntary control) somewhat before term, and their activity controls the input available to later-maturing, stimulus-dependent elements underlying visual perception, thereby tuning the visual system to be responsive to local conditions. (See also Banks & Salapatek, 1983).

### Age-Changes

There is also the possibility that the curiosity of the human baby, the toddler, and the juvenile have different effects on their nervous systems and different importances for their immediate, successful exploitation of their environments. For example, the infant's early visual attentiveness may be essential for validating and maintaining the functional commitment of cells in the visual cortex which serve in discriminating first-order stimulus-qualities (cf. Haith, 1980), such as binocular depth. In contrast, "the same" visual attentiveness of toddlers may serve to support the development of the substrates for higher order functions such as concepts.

Discovering contingencies between their actions and events should be a primary concern of infants (Bower, 1982) and young children (Bronson, 1971; Stott, 1961). Knowing when one can affect events is one kind of information that individuals must acquire through transactions with their environments. However, from the theoretical perspective adopted here, one would expect that the kinds of contingencies that will be salient for capturing a child's attention will vary according to developmental level. For example, Piagetian theory (e.g., Piaget, 1952) would predict that, during their first half-year, babies should be maximally responsive to events contingent upon the deployment of newly-emerging motor skills such as visually-guided reaching. The existence of a contingency *per se* should be no guarantee that one's interest will be engaged (See Sameroff & Cavanagh, 1979). Indeed, Schaffer (1971) notes that infants between the ages of 4 and 8 months seem to benefit more from the opportunity to manipulate visible objects than do infants who are 9 to 12 months of age. Presumably this is because the younger infants are validating and integrating the substrates for basic sensory-motor, manipulatory coordinations.

## Seeking Change

A very substantial literature indicates that "contingent" feedback (e.g., Bower, 1982) seems to be an important determinant of infants' and young children's commerce with their surroundings. However, predictable feedback does not suffice to sustain (short-term) interest. In the first few months, infants will not only "work" to obtain auditory, visual, or audio-visual input, but they will also cease to respond unless the nature of the reward varies somewhat (Berg & Berg, 1979; Bower, 1982; Sameroff & Cavanaugh, 1979). It is also clear that, once they have voluntary hand control, babies will become more absorbed with objects or apparatus that provide varied sensory feedback (e.g., Leuba & Friedlander, 1968), as evidenced by the commercial success of the "Busy-box," and various hydraulic bathtub toys. Insofar as stimulus variety is an antecedent of infants' later cognitive development (Yarrow et al., 1972) such selectivity could be seen as another instance of the ways in which developing systems act to provide themselves with the input necessary for expressing later-appearing phenotypic attributes.

Perhaps the best example of this sort of behavior is again exemplified by the change in organization of behavior which occurs at about the third month, when continued development requires more exteroceptive input. Home-reared babies seem to come to expect a certain amount of input and will protest when they become bored (Bower, 1977; Provence & Lipton, 1962; Rheingold, 1961). In the first half-year they often can be quieted (distracted) by a mobile or some other sensory input. Although we commonly attribute their fussiness to some such distress as gas, hunger, or teething, a substantial number of these instances may, in fact, represent (unwitting) attempts to provoke parents to provide something interesting to do.

In somewhat older babies, a direct relationship between the availability of playthings and fussiness can be demonstrated. Rheingold and Samuels (1969) had mothers take their 10-month-old infants (who were able to crawl) into a sparsely-furnished room. Within a 10-minute period, most of the babies had explored the setting and, because their mothers were instructed to respond minimally, started to protest. Then, after a five-minute interlude in which the subjects were distracted by the presence of an investigator, a second 10-minute trial was conducted. For half of the subjects, the room was as before; for the remainder, the experimenter had introduced some toys. During the second period, only one of 10 babies who had toys available fussed, whereas 9 of the 10 who did not, protested. Moreover, the latency to protest was much shorter for the latter babies; infants provided with toys even emitted fewer non-cry vocalizations which, according to the point of view espoused here, could be interpreted as bids for social stimulation. Indeed, whereas all the subjects who had no toys contacted their mothers during the second 10 minutes, only 5 of the 10 babies with playthings did so. In addition, several of the toy-less subjects began to protest so vigorously during the second 10-minute period that it seemed advisable to intervene or terminate the trial early. They were then presented with toys. Every one of these five babies quieted within 5 seconds of receiving playthings, and none of them fussed again for the remainder of the period. Clearly, by at least 10 months of age, babies who have been reared in relatively stimulating settings expect—and demand—that their environments provide stimulation.

## Responses to Novelty[1]

Toward the second half of the first year, the way in which infants "use" prior experience becomes increasingly important in determining their

---

[1] While useful descriptively, "novelty" (or its presumed subjective correlate, "uncertainty") as the basis for classifying events probably should be considered only a temporary expediency. Novelty is a relative term; to adequately assess the degree of novelty of any particular stimulus, one would have to know the perceiver's history in detail. Moreover, infants and young children do not always attend preferentially to what seems intuitively to be the most unfamiliar source of stimulation. Often, they attend most to a stimulus which is quite similar, but not identical, to something with which they are well-acquainted (e.g., Kagan, 1971; El' Konin, 1969). One might postulate that infants respond most to stimuli which are only "moderately discrepant" from their stored experience. But for such a statement to be scientifically fruitful, it would be necessary to assess a child's memory store, and develop some commonly-accepted metric to measure the degree of discrepancy (or congruence) between a percept and a child's memory.

reactions to novel objects. Whereas for adults, exploration and wariness frequently are alternative—and often competing—responses to the same unfamiliar stimulus, in small infants this does not seem to be so obviously the case. Infants have developed the ability to discriminate familiar from unfamiliar objects well before they are six months old; they show increments in visual attention when, in a series of presentations of a single training object, a new "test" object is suddenly inserted in the sequence. However, their manipulatory responsiveness does not differ from that shown to the training stimulus. Six- to seven-month-old infants grasp both familiar and novel objects within seconds of presentation and their manipulatory responses to both classes of stimuli are essentially the same. Responsiveness to objects declines primarily as a function of successive presentations.

However, when similar presentations are made to infants in the last quarter of their first year, and a novel item is inserted, babies study it intently before reaching for it. Once the novel object is grasped, it receives *more* manipulatory attention than the familiar test object. Moreover, when infants in both age groups are allowed to become familiar with a complex, "salient" stimulus object and then presented with a choice between that object and a novel, but simpler one, 5- to 7-month old infants remain more attentive to the more complex object despite their greater familiarity with it. By contrast, 11- to 13-month old infants pay more attention to the less salient, but more novel, stimulus object.

Apparently, perceptual attractiveness controls both the visual and manipulative behavior of infants between 5 and 13 months of age, but familiarity is an important codeterminant of only older babies' manipulatory-investigative activity (Schaffer, 1971; Schaffer, Greenwood, & Parry, 1972). Novelty thus continues to contribute to orienting and exploratory behavior; however, the unfamiliar also evokes displays of wariness or even "fearful" behavior. Indeed, the origins of fearful responses to visual novelty have been the subject of several investigations. The evidence suggests that most infants do not become obviously apprehensive in response to changes in setting or to the presence of unfamiliar objects until around the end of their first six months (Bronson, 1969; 1971; Kagan, 1970; 1971; Schaffer, 1971).

Infants' abilities to discriminate the unfamiliar (obvious in their visual attention and operant behavior from the first or second month) thus contribute a new dimension to their investigative responsiveness when they are between 6 and 12 months of age. Mechanisms governing the recognition of the familiar apparently develop independently of those controlling the selection of manipulatory behavior. From the second or third months, discrimination of the unfamiliar and differential (motoric) responding in order to obtain stimulus variety represent the integration of stored information with processes governing motor selection. In the latter half of the first year, recognition of the unfamiliar also becomes involved in arousing behavior which is antithetical to approach or investigation (Schaffer, 1971). This is not simply an increased probability of wariness or protest responses; such behaviors are readily available to very young infants. However, these early responses *usually* are not evoked by "discrepant events."[2] Therefore, it would seem that we may be witnessing a shift in which certain facets of the avoidance/protest systems come under the influence of recognition/response selection systems which have *already* been controlling investigatory behavior.

Inelegant though this formulation may be, it is consistent with the data and the principle that organismic changes adapt developing young to stage-specific environmental challenges: In the second six months, a baby's environment involves new opportunities and dangers, resulting from the development of locomotor skills. When babies have no control over their movements, there is little reason for (and perhaps some potential danger in) protesting when confronted by the unfamiliar, especially in the absence of someone upon whom they depend for care and protection. Once they can move about on their own, such restraints can make a life-or-death difference. An adaptationist interpretation seems necessary to account for the appearance of *this* shift *at this time*. Indeed, Bertenthal, Campos, and Barrett (1984) found that permitting prelocomotor infants to move on their own with the aid of a walker does facilitate the appearance of a suite of adaptive behaviors such as wariness of heights, and increased attention to unfamiliar objects. Insofar as these changes were manifested rapidly, and occasionally antedated the onset of self-produced locomotion in some control subjects, it seems likely that their substrates were induced by different inputs. However, the fact that locomotor experience could facilitate the expression of such wariness is consistent with our model of stage-specific adaptation.

## Security

Thus, when they are in a position to get themselves into trouble and when the situation itself is unfamiliar, babies' needs for stimulation are tempered

---

[2] To account for the shift in response, "cognitive" explanations posit a "maturational" expression of infants' working memory between the ages of 6 and 8 months which permits recognition of whether the event evokes expectancies. If the baby recognizes an event as unfamiliar and can generate no prediction, then it is thought to become distressed (Kagan, 1984). Yet much younger babies both respond to familiarity and form expectancies on the basis of prior experience and they can control their behavior accordingly (Berg & Berg, 1979; Bower, 1982; Olson & Sherman, 1983). Thus, the simplest explanation would be that the affective "sign" of the unfamiliar shifts toward the negative in the second six months. However, that is *too* simple, because, *in the presence of attachment figures*, infants of this age will approach novel objects and explore in unfamiliar settings (Bronson, 1972).

with needs for security. As infants become capable of locomotion, they also become more reactive to the social context (Bertenthal et al., 1984). When accompanied by familiar caregivers, even in unfamiliar physical settings, babies will explore their immediate surroundings. The setting must provide some sort of incentive to attract their attention. But, beyond some object(s) to investigate, little more is required than the presence and apparent vigilance of a trusted attachment-object (Ainsworth & Wittig, 1969; Bretherton & Waters, 1985; Rheingold, 1963; 1969).

Differences in one-year-old infants' exploratory activity are related not only to the milieu, but also to the quality of their relationships with their mothers (Ainsworth, Bell, & Stayton, 1971). At least among middle-class Americans, mothers' sensitivities to their babies' signals, the degree to which they "reject" their infants, and the degrees to which they are accessible to and interfering with their offspring interact to determine how their youngsters react to various unfamiliar events. Generally, when mothers are unpredictable, their babies find it difficult to adapt to the apparently stressful situations of being left alone in a novel setting with toys and strangers (or entirely alone with toys), and they can not readily recover when their mothers rejoin them. Babies whose mothers are generally consistent and responsive seem to be best able to use their mothers as "bases" from which to venture forth. They can be comforted by their mothers' return—often enough to resume their object-oriented activity. However, babies whose mothers are most rejecting often seem to be most consistently attracted to the inanimate environment. Ainsworth et al. (1971) suggest that absorption with the environment could function as a defense against the anxiety that might otherwise follow from maternal rejection. (Of course, in some cases, the mothers' apparent rejection may have been in response to their babies' seeming indifference to them.)

Overall, the data are what one would expect if the behavior of infants has evolved so as to provide them with response-potentials appropriate to typical variations in their circumstances: Where mothers are likely to be responsive and succorant, babies should be comforted by their presence and feel safe in exploring their surroundings. Less fortunate infants who cannot always count on their mothers would have to expend more energy in monitoring their parents' activities to be sure that they will be protected if the need arises. The least fortunate, whose mothers seem to be unlikely to provide much protection or succor, might just as well do what they can to fend for themselves; with luck, they may garner enough information about other resources to compensate for their mothers' lack of involvement.

## Fear

What most of us call fear or incipient flight reactions do not appear until the individual's ability to recognize the familiar is integrated with other cognitive advances, motoric inhibition, and protest/locomotor behavior (Schaffer, 1971; Schaffer et al., 1972; Sroufe, 1979). We suggest that each avoidance response may have its own developmental timetable, one which has evolved so that it is expressed phenotypically in time to anticipate the exigencies of specific developmental stages. For example, although infants under six months of age are able to *discriminate* depth on the visual cliff, they do not display apparent fright until they become capable of independent locomotion (Bertenthal et al., 1984; Campos, Langer, & Krowitz, 1970). Similarly, babies do not seem to be particularly frightened by apparently impending collisions as a result of being moved until about the age at which such collisions could be self-generated (Bower, 1977; see also Yonas, Bechtold, Frankel, Gordon, McRoberts, Norcia, & Sternfels, 1977).

As young children grow older, their stated concerns also seem to be consistent with the notion of stage-specific development: Loss of parental solicitude, physical weakness or handicaps, and new socio-cultural/developmental demands are among the themes reported by grade school and adolescent children (Jersild, 1954). Insofar as the world does provide a host of dangerous stimuli, it would not be unreasonable to expect that the capacities to symbolize, to anticipate, and to imagine would be integrated with the evaluative functions at least to the extent that children could worry about possible injury. The foolhardiness of youth is already legendary. Any precocious, albeit flawed, tendency to be concerned with possible danger could be beneficial—whether or not based upon rational assessment. We may speculate that, to the extent that such concerns can cause youngsters to exercise appropriate caution, selection should favor them.

It does seem that, although youngsters do profit from experience, under everyday circumstances, many potential "associations" between situations and pain, startles, and so on, do not lead to the development of avoidance responses. For example, the frequent falls and clearly painful bumps that go with the early development of bipedal locomotion, stair-climbing, and so forth fail to inhibit the child's continued striving.

Children may become wary of certain situations as a result of observing others' avoidance response to them. It obviously would be advantageous if individuals were spared the necessity of risking injury. Thus, one would expect that children should be sensitive to the kinds of situations that seem to cause their caregivers to become alarmed. If children do, indeed, take their elders as sources of security, when these havens of safety react as if they themselves are threatened, then the situation should be perceived as dangerous (e.g., Campos & Stenberg, 1981; Klinnert, 1984). Yet we still must qualify these notions by noting that very genuine and unconcealed parental fright in response to many foolhardy juvenile activities fails to get the message across; some pursuits seem to be almost immune to such influence. Unfortunately, we can only speculate at this point with regard to which activities will be so influenced and at what points in the life-cycle. An obvious guess would be that discomforts or fright incidental to early locomotor mastery will be relatively insensitive to inhibition as a result of both direct and vicarious experience. As suggested by the functional importance of information-gathering, even in threatening situations, the early phases of exploratory behavior may also be particularly resistant to influence by example or observation.

## PLAY

As is the case with so many other psychological constructs, play still lacks a generally-acceptable definition—a situation which must raise the question of whether we are attempting to subsume diverse phenomena under a single heading. The flavor of play was captured by Millar (1968, p. 255), as "exploring what is familiar, practising what has already been mastered, friendly aggression, sex without coition, excitement about nothing, social behavior not defined by a specific common activity or by social structure, pretense not intended to deceive..."

What we call play in many ways epitomizes the concept of semi-independent (motoric) components of functional systems: Generally speaking, playful behaviors *per se* include activities that involve adult-like, apparently functional elements which are combined in unusual, "out-of-context" ways. Play patterns are performed in an exaggerated manner, often repetitively, and do not serve any obvious function. Playful behavior seems to be free from normal stimulus-response relationships and may involve members of other species; the mix of actions looks as if the elements were uncoupled from the ends that they normally serve, and are fragmented, free to (re)combine in various ways (Fagen, 1981; Lorenz, 1956; Piaget, 1962; Wilson, 1975).

Lest this description imply a lack of organization or constraint, we should note that play occurs in specific, protected, contexts, that many of the elements that are combined are clearly subject to inhibition as indexed by self-handicapping and the absence of injury during play fighting, and that much social play is preceded or accompanied by species-specific signals diagnostic of playful intent such as the preschooler's "open-mouthed smile" (Bekoff, 1972; 1974; Blurton-Jones, 1967; Fagen, 1981). Moreover, after a period of enforced inactivity, there tends to be a rebound in play-activity (Muller-Schwartze, 1968; Muller-Schwartze, Stagge, & Muller-Schwartze, 1982; Smith & Connolly, 1980).

The existence of a rebound in play after involuntary quiescence (Muller-Schwartze, 1968), the inhibition of consummatory behavior (Lorenz, 1956) and species-typical solicitation gestures (Bekoff, 1972), and sensitivity to nutritional status (Muller-Schwartze et al., 1982) suggest that readiness to play and some aspects of response-selection and modulation are systematically controlled in ways yet to be discovered. Regulation would be expected if play functions (a) to generate experience which is developmentally relevant to various situations, that is, trying out different tactics which may later prove useful, or (b) to ensure a balance between higher cortical (planful?) and subcortical control over behavior (Fagen, 1981), or (c) simply to ensure a level of stimulation necessary for normal function of the nervous system (Millar, 1968).

Play can be linked to exploration in that the novelty and complexity of elements in the environment promote its appearance as does the presence of a caregiver. The obvious difference in setting and "mood" is that play occurs only in benign, nonthreatening contexts (Fagen, 1981; Eibl-Eibesfeldt, 1970).

Aside from the common elements of novelty and complexity, the most obvious additional links between flight, exploration, and play are temporal: Initially wary, sizing-up gives way to active examination and then, finally, to exploitation of materials or the context (Nunnally & Lemond, 1973). As Hutt (1970) put it, one shifts from an interest in what objects do to what one can do *with* them; a shift from behavior that highlights the existing stimulus-properties *of* a situation to behavior that highlights the activities possible *in* that situation.

A focus exclusively on a developmental/functional role for play in humans cannot be sustained because adults also play. In part, this difficulty can be accommodated by the observation that the *form* of play changes markedly in development. Even where it does not, there is no reason to expect that similar actions have identical functional significance at different points in the life cycle. In the young, play would be primarily involved in facilitating, validating, and integrating behavioral/morphological developments; in adults play would seem to be more important for maintaining skills or condition.

### Object Play

Object-play provides the clearest links with exploration insofar as it is (nonsocial) environment-oriented behavior. Indeed, Hutt (1970) called it "diverse" exploration and considered it to differ from "specific" exploration when the following attributes were present: (a) a relaxed facial expression; (b) minimal convergence of receptor focus upon the object *per se;* (c) a variety of brief actions performed on the object in nonstereotyped order; (d) a focus upon what the actor could *do* with the object; (e) and a curvilinear decrement in activity over time.

In the early months, infants' play seems to be quite limited; most objects are mouthed and waved and, a bit later, they also are banged against something (or one another), and dropped or thrown. By 13 months of age, most babies' manipulatory/playful repertoires are more elaborate, but through their eighteenth month, they appear to limit their exploratory/ playful manipulations to a single item with little time spent on the elaboration of some obvious theme. In the next six months, toddlers' manipulatory play begins to show evidence of "imagination," and more complex "representational" objects replace brightly-colored (novel) objects as preferred playthings (Rosenblatt, 1977). Especially among older infants and preschoolers, objects that provide feedback or that can be used in some kind of goal-related activity sustain play. Among 3- to 5-year-olds, moderate stimulus changes (e.g., a clicking sound when an element is manipulated) helps to maintain interest in the play phase, after children familiarize themselves with an object (Hutt, 1970). Even among 15-month-olds, an opportunity to manipulate such devices as one which activates lights or a buzzer engages a substantial number of youngsters (Leuba & Friedlander, 1968). The richer or the more complicated the available objects, the more likely one is to observe individual (Kagan, 1971) and sex (Brooks & Lewis, 1974) differences in play behavior.

Whatever their cognitive substrates, the playful activities of young children involve the extension of newly-acquired manipulatory skills to as many additional materials as possible. To the extent that manipulatory play does highlight new aspects of objects or materials, playfully altered patterns of motor and sensory reafference might be important in the processes of functional validation and silencing or weeding out excess neuronal interconnections. Thus the role of manipulatory play in human development may serve to validate, facilitate, and integrate development of the neuromotor substrates for manual dexterity and flexibility, and as an avenue for the elaboration and consolidation of sensorimotor knowledge about the inanimate surroundings.

The opportunity to playfully manipulate objects may encourage the use of the same materials in more utilitarian contexts. Although experimental artifacts may account for the findings (Simon & Smith, 1985),[3] Schiller's (1957) classic demonstrations of such effects in chimpanzees have been paralleled with human 3- to 5-year-old children. Youngsters who were allowed to play with a series of sticks that could be joined end to end were subsequently more successful in employing them to reach a lure than were children who had similar prior experience with different objects (Sylva, Bruner, & Genova, 1976). Another study of the comparative effects of free play, imitation of adult exemplars, or no prior experience,

---

[3] Simon and Smith (1985) failed to replicate Sylva, Bruner, and Genova's (1976) findings under more stringently controlled conditions. One facet of their procedure, the adult "explaining" the use of the materials to the children, may have created a "set" antithetical to "playful" exploration of the materials (See Dansky, 1985).

suggested that 4- to 6-year-olds who had prior play opportunities with materials may be able to think of more possible "uses" for them than the other subjects (Dansky & Silverman, 1976).[4] These studies suggest that, at least when there is continuity in a "playful" situation, object-play may increase youngsters' abilities to utilize objects in solving problems and promote their conscious awareness of the (potential) properties of such materials.

### Gross Motor Play

One apparent developmental function of juvenile play is the practice and elaboration of basic skills. Some elements of apparently playful behavior in lower animals appear more or less fully-developed at the outset (Lorenz, 1956). Nevertheless, a great deal of evidence supports the view that play may serve as physical training which contributes to maximum development of bone, muscle, and neuromotor coordination, and the fine-tuning of these components to meet the demands of the environments in which the young will eventually have to fend for themselves (Fagen, 1981).

Among the more obvious forms of human gross motor play is the tendency to climb onto objects, up stairs, in trees, and so on. Another source of enjoyment/excitement for young children is traversing elevated walkways such as the top of walls (hopefully, with a trusted adult's steadying hand for support). Preschoolers and kindergartners also seem to take great delight in jumping or hanging and dropping from heights. The latter behavior sometimes causes older observers to experience vicarious bone- and joint pains, but such activities may represent one of the better examples of early play as physical training, facilitating and maintaining bone, tendon, and ligament growth when the loads are not too great and these tissues are maximally reactive to being stressed (cf. Fagen, 1981).

Strenuous exercise is most effective when intermittent, with bouts separated by light exercise and/or rest; play tends to be intermittent. In addition, as individuals grow, their body proportions change somewhat, for example, one's reach increases with age. Play provides a system whereby thorough recalibration of motor coordinations in space can be accomplished. Simple calisthenics would be less likely to demand (or provide) input relevant to the full implications of changed bodily proportions or to the variety of motor combinations possible (cf. Bower, 1982; Banks & Salapatek, 1983). Given the diversity of *Homo's* habitats, there could be real advantages to very precise channeling of development to accommodate to local conditions, including the average minimum level of sustenance.

---

[4] These data also have been questioned: Smith and Whitney (1987) reported that, with the inclusion of additional controls for unintentional prompting, even the well-controlled Dansky and Silverman study could not be replicated.

The latter consideration would also explain why play should be most prevalent during the immature stages of the life cycle: If play does function to prepare individuals to successfully meet the challenges imposed by the environment, that is, to adopt alternative adaptive strategies, then it should occur during the phases of development in which bones, ligaments, and so on are growing, and be inhibited by more pressing metabolic or situational demands. Since most of the energetic costs of early development of the mammalian young are subsidized by parents, there should be some source of information, such as play, that informs caregivers of the condition of their offspring (Fagen, 1981).

**Fantasy Play**

From an adaptationist point of view, the kinds of activities involved in play should vary according to the individual's developmental stage and should anticipate the demands of the next one. Furthermore, to the extent that such behavior is adaptive, one would expect that its expression would be facilitated by very general (i.e., ubiquitous) environmental signs. With exploration, play is much more likely in the presence of relaxed and attentive attachment-figures or other, playing children. Stimulus-novelty also promotes play once wariness has been overcome (see Hutt 1970; above).

Humans appear to be unique in manufacturing objects for children to play with (Fagen, 1981). Societies that possess enough wealth to indulge make-believe behavior foster a wide variety of creative, autonomous "pretend" play (Feitelson, 1977). Where a variety of materials is available, a range of novel and imaginative activities are first observable in children between their seventeenth and twenty-fourth months (Rosenblatt, 1977). The extent to which such behavior is elaborated depends upon additional socio-cultural factors. Whereas autocratic and restrictive parental styles tend to be associated with conformity and a lack of originality, relatively permissive parenting is associated with more original and varied play themes. One might speculate that, in the past, autocratic parental styles have signalled hostile environmental conditions that preclude the luxury of experimentation and put a premium on investing energy in pursuits that garner more immediate, practical payoffs (cf. Rosenblatt, 1977).

It is generally assumed that pretend play may foster an appreciation of adult roles. There is some evidence that make-believe play may also promote (disadvantaged) children's display of social/cognitive growth (e.g., Rosen, 1974; Saltz, Dixon, & Johnson, 1977). Whether make-believe play facilitates the growth of logical thought is more uncertain (e.g., Guthrie & Hudson, 1979). However, the fact that children can assign "pretend" functions or identities to objects or persons without losing sight of their "real" natures (Golomb & Cornelius, 1977) suggests that play may involve some capacities which, according to Piaget (Inhelder & Piaget, 1958), are crucial in the development of logico-mathematical thought.

To the extent that play embodies elements from a variety of behavioral systems, it would provide an optimum setting for the validation, maintenance, and integration of newly-developing skills. From its repetitiousness and vigor, and its "assimilative" quality (cf. Piaget, 1962) it seems likely that play serves, in addition to physical training, as a source of knowledge and a means for consolidating memory stores (Fagen, 1981; Millar, 1968). Exploratory and motor play may be most important for the early development of musculoskeletal structure, neuromotor coordination, and a working knowledge of the animate and inanimate environments. These benefits may be augmented in the second year by symbolic play. Toward middle childhood, additional benefits in the form of information regarding social status, and conventions regarding social exchange also may derive from social play (e.g., Frankel & Arbel, 1980; Sluckin & Smith, 1977; Strayer, 1980).

## PEER RELATIONS

The development of children's relationships with other youngsters further illustrates the (relative) ontogenetic independence of functional systems and suggests that, under some conditions, the facilitation of one complex of potentials may be antagonistic to the full expression of certain facets of other systems.

Harlow (1969) suggests that peer relations reflect the development of a semi-independent behavioral system which can be expressed in the absence of infant-mother experience. His observations of behavioral development in *rhesus* indicated that peer ties may have an ontogeny independent of, yet similar to, the development of parental attachment, and that peer relations may amplify, and even substitute for, the effects of parent-offspring relationships. Many would now accept the views that peer bonds in human children are not simple derivations of filial relations, and whether or not they have totally independent origins (Lewis & Rosenblum, 1975), age-mate social affiliations have a developmental history of their own (e.g., Hartup, 1983). Count (1973) suggests that, in evolution, the two systems did have independent origins. He points out that, in most vertebrate species, there is little or no adult caregiving; the first individuals with whom a newly hatched animal has dealings are siblings, and early social relationships are established in the context of interactions with age peers (e.g., reptiles, Burghardt, 1978). The mammalian tendency to orient toward adult caregivers can then be considered a "new" evolutionary development which has only preceded peer relations in time without supplanting them as important contributors to behavioral development. In short, then, the potential for developing sibling and/or agemate relationships may have ancient roots which do not depend upon adult tutelage or encouragement for their expression.

## Filial Primacy

Even though agemate attractions may have their own origins, the filial system typically predominates. According to Konner's (1972) observations of hunter/gatherer societies, young children are dependent upon their mothers for not only food and protection, but also for transportation until about the age of three years. Despite the fact that they are accomplished walkers, youngsters under three simply cannot keep up with their mothers' or the groups' movements without demanding to be carried. Moreover, children under three years of age are vulnerable to many dangers and normally cannot depend upon one another for help—or even to summon help. Thus, from an adaptive standpoint, when adults are available, infants and toddlers should not become too involved with each other—especially when in strange surroundings—until their locomotor and communicative skills permit them to rapidly seek or to effectively summon aid when necessary.

Even "secure" filial attachments would be expected to foster toddlers' interest in unrelated agemates only to a limited degree and in safe settings (Becker, 1977; St. Pierre, 1981). Indeed, simple access to agemates as afforded by day care is not sufficient to produce a predominance of peer interaction (Finkelstein, Dent, Gallacher, & Ramey, 1978; Kagan, Kearsley, & Zelazo, 1978). Even among children reared in communal, group settings 24 hours a day, the amount of time preschoolers spend in social interactions with agemates does not surpass interactions with adults (Hamer & Missakian, 1978).

## Use of Language

If the filial and peer systems are independent, one might expect that youngsters' behavioral capacities would be differentially deployed in the two contexts. Indeed, despite the fact that, by their second birthday, most children are using a number of verbal signals to regulate their interactions with parents and other caregivers, vocalizations seem to be minimally involved in ordering very early agemate relationships. Even among communally-reared infants and toddlers under 3 years of age, fewer than 10% of peer interactions are strictly verbal. The clear majority of agemate social exchanges involve combinations of brief vocalizations and motor actions (Hamer & Missakian, 1978). This apparent selectivity is not entirely due to young children's egocentrism: Children between 2½ and 3 years of age do attempt to consider the recipient's informational needs when formulating an utterance; however, this is most marked in exchanges with *adults* (Wellman & Lemper, 1977).

Insofar as they are still too young to effectively fend for themselves, it should not be surprising that 2- to 3-year-old children's decentering is manifest primarily in the context of social exchanges with adults: Grown-ups' attention is more likely to remain focused (and therefore be more predictable) than that of an agemate, and adults are far better equipped to provide succor or valid information. It thus behooves young children to direct their developing skills to those from whom they may obtain the maximum benefit. After their third birthdays, however, most preschoolers begin to employ these communicative skills in social exchanges with their fellows. By 3½ to 5 years of age, peer-directed utterances tend to be social in intent and generally produce an obvious social response from their partners (Mueller, 1972).

One might object that preschoolers' early apparent decentering when talking with adults is in response to adult queries. However, a similar asymmetry of communicative development can be observed even among much older children in *arbitrary* communication tasks. If one asks 9-year-olds to describe one of several "nonsense" figures from an array so that an agemate who has an identical array can pick out the same one, the communicator often simply points to the object (which the receiver can not see) or says "that one" or "the one in the corner" (without specifying which of the four corners). Moreover, the recipient's communicative attempts to confirm a choice or to get clarification typically are no better. The difficulty is not due to limited vocabulary: When an adult provides the information, receivers perform with near-perfect accuracy. The problem seems to be that the communicators do not employ their knowledge and/or anticipate the recipient's problems well enough to formulate an effective message (Cohen & Klein, 1968).

Thus, although children as old as 9 years of age seem to be reasonably capable of coordinating their activities with one another, and of instructing each other in the folklore of their groups (cf. Opie & Opie, 1969), they still influence their peers largely through action (Kaspar & Lowenstein, 1971), and by example (Rothenberg & Orost, 1969) rather than by communicating abstract principles.

Assuming that the foregoing findings can be replicated in non-Western cultures, one might question why children's peer relations should be regulated in such an "inefficient" manner in middle childhood when they possess the capacities for efficient symbolic communication. Although no clear answer is available, one could argue that even during this phase, youngsters still must depend upon their elders for protection and guidance.

If it is to the child's advantage to remain under the sway of adult influence, then the differential between being able to understand adult commands and directions and being able to communicate equally effectively with agemates might be one mechanism that keeps juveniles oriented toward adult authority (when the choice is available). That is, given bonds with adults, strategies for optimizing filial success might still pre-empt the full expression of similar potentials in other contexts. However, as implied by the concept of multiple pathways of growth, although the "preferred" developmental sequence (cf. Freud & Burlingham, 1944), primacy of filial bonds is not immutable.

### Precocious Peer Bonding

Precocious development of peer relationships can be achieved when children are reared under conditions of group care in residential nurseries due to the demands of war (Freud & Burlingham, 1944), as a result of more-or-less consciously designed, communal childrearing (Bettelheim, 1969; Hamer & Missakian, 1978; Spiro, 1979), or even under the extreme conditions of Nazi concentration camps (Freud & Dann, 1951). For example, in contrast to Kagan et al.'s (1978) description of 2-year-olds (who did form attachments to their parents despite all-day day care) as "not very social" with agemates, Freud and Burlingham (1944, p. 29) described children this age in residential nurseries as having developed "a surprising range of reactions [to their peers]: love, hate, jealousy, rivalry, competition, protectiveness, pity, generosity, sympathy, and even understanding."

Apparently, ties can develop under conditions of (because of?) minimal adult care-giving. Freud and Dann (1951) observed the behavior of six German-Jewish victims of the Holocaust. All of them had been orphaned and interned together in a concentration camp during their first year of life. Four of them lost their mothers at birth or within weeks thereafter, and all the children had been together from 6 to 12 months of age. According to the surviving inmate caregivers, the overworked camp staff had no opportunities to play with the infants under their care, and only one of the six children had ever shown any kind of an attachment to an adult. They remained together in various group care settings until they were sent to England, at 3 to 3½ years of age. When they were first introduced to new quarters, Freud and Dann considered their behavior to be remarkable when contrasted with home-reared children: They spontaneously took turns, shared delicacies, and showed little rivalry or jealousy of one another. Although they did argue among themselves, they did not compete with one another and showed genuine concern for each others' feelings and safety. There did seem to be special "friendships" within the group, but these relationships did not interfere with their overall intra-group solidarity.

### Adults vs Peers

From observations such as the foregoing, one might be tempted to con-clude that the acculturation of young children would be facilitated by promoting the precocious expression of the peer affectional system. How-ever, the embyrological model of developmental choice-points also raises the possibility that precocious expression of special relationships with peers might be gained at the expense of other attributes. There are some data consistent with this possibility. A number of analyses of preschoolers' social interactions suggest that, within a group, time spent interacting with adults tends to be negatively related to peer-relationships (e.g., Roper & Hinde, 1978; O'Connor, 1975; van Lieshout, 1972). Even for individual children, day-to-day variation in these two classes of social contact is negatively related for the overwhelming majority of individual preschool-ers. However, the magnitudes of the coefficients are typically moderate ($r$'s from $-0.3$ to $-0.6$), suggesting that, for preschoolers, under "nor-mal" conditions, interactions with peers and interactions with adults are alternatives, neither mutually exclusive nor equivalent forms of sociability (Harper & Huie, 1987).

Nevertheless, it would seem possible that, under unusual conditions, the two systems could work at cross purposes, as it were. For example, from a review of the effects of early childcare programs, Belsky and Stein-berg (1978) concluded that children who are enrolled in day-care or other group care programs may be relatively less cooperative toward adults than are children whose parents care for them at home. In some cases, the relationship may have reflected the *parents'* relatively smaller investment in their offspring (cf. Vandell, 1980) so that the youngsters had little choice but to turn to their peers. If so, emotional investment in agemate relation-ships would be made by default with minimal adult guidance or super-vision.

This line of reasoning is consistent with findings that, under "normal" conditions in which a child has regular, if brief, social exchanges with a responsive family caregiver, quite extensive group-care experience does not tip the balance toward peer-orientation—or precocious agemate social relationships (cf. Kagan et al., 1978). However, if home-based caregivers are not responsive, or are frankly rejecting and, in addition, most of the child's waking time is spent in a group-care situation, then the probability increases that the child will become relatively uncooperative toward adult authority figures while manifesting strong loyalties to agemates. These speculations are supported by findings that even "advantaged" children who are adult-oriented in half-day preschool tend to do better in grade school (Harper & Huie, 1987) and that peer-oriented school children and adolescents may be less adult-oriented, and more prone to engage in adult-disapproved behavior or to become truant (Condry & Siman, 1974; Hartup, 1983).

Moreover, long-term deliberate, group rearing may also blunt individualism or initiative, traits often prized by industrial societies (Bettelheim, 1969; Bronfenbrenner, 1970; Freud & Burlingham, 1944). Therefore, it is at least possible that, whether by default or design, the precocious expression of agemate social bonds may be attained at the expense of responsiveness to adults and personal initiative, as one might expect if the two developmental systems are independent and primacy of one or the other represent alternative developmental pathways, at least in the early years.

# CHAPTER 7

# Cognition

The nervous system emerges from its embryonic phase well patterned and nothing could be more misleading than the impression that embryonic neurogenesis merely fabricates blank sheets on which experiential input from the outer world is then to inscribe operative patterns. (Weiss, 1970, p. 60)

Cognition, the processes by which we make sense of the input gained from our sensory receptors, is one of the oldest areas of psychological research. In general, there is agreement that knowledge involves the detection of events external to the individual and the organization of that information. Presumably, when processed, knowledge fosters successful commerce with one's surroundings. Thanks largely to the work of Jean Piaget (e.g., 1929; 1952; 1954; 1962), most would agree that children not only actively seek new experiences, but also impose meaning upon them, "constructing" their psychological worlds.

In this chapter, we will examine several facets of the development of human thought. I will propose that the evidence is consistent with the view of development as the result of the co-action of inherited potentials and environmental inputs which give rise to heterochronous expression of quasi-independent components which become (re)organized into different age-specific configurations. That is, I will propose that cognitive development can be understood as occurring in stages, each of which permits individuals to survive and prosper in the surroundings typically encountered at that point in the life-cycle, and in addition, enables them to utilize these same surroundings to prepare to meet the challenge of subsequent stages. I will also argue that human cognitive development depends upon the development of the brain, that it is species-specific, and is both genetically canalized and functionally constrained.

## COMPONENT MODULES AND DEVELOPMENTAL STAGES

Experimental investigations of higher nervous function in animals, clinical case studies of humans with known neurological defecits, and both electrophysiological and psychophysical studies of intact humans suggest that higher mental function reflects the joint activities of semi-independent neuronal information-processing components, or "modules."

## Modules

Since the Nobel prize-winning work of Hubel and Wiesel (Hubel, 1982; Wiesel, 1982) a large body of data has accumulated suggesting that the input from each sensory modality is processed simultaneously, at a number of levels. For example, experimental studies of nonhuman mammals suggest that areas in the visual cortex are required for fine discriminations of the quality of seen objects (e.g., shape, depth, color), whereas the more "primitive," secondary visual system in the midbrain independently responds to the location of an image in the visual field. The same modular division of function apparently holds true for humans. Patients who have suffered lesions in the visual cortex rendering them "blind" to the nature of visual stimulation in a portion of the visual field can "guess" which way a stimulus is moved in the blind area correctly—despite claiming to have seen essentially nothing (Blythe et al., 1986). Similarly, other lesions in the relays to the visual cortex resulting in local blindness do not prevent the formation of aftereffects from looking at a colored target with the blind portion of the visual field (Poppel, 1986).

Investigations of the information-processing capacities of "split-brain" patients who had a variety of (additional) known, neurological deficits have led Gazzaniga (1985, p. x) to describe the human mind as "a confederation of mental systems." For example, the activities of component modules in one (disconnected) hemisphere may generate a mood in response to a stimulus which will be "interpreted" in quite different terms by modules in the other (naive) hemisphere. Even visual imagery seems to be the product of activities of components located *outside* of the cortical visual system. Thus Gazzaniga (1985) characterized human brain organization as the parallel operation of "relatively independent functioning units" (See also Luria, 1980).

## Stages

As a result of a series of studies using reversible cortical inactivation by cooling, Goldman-Rakic (1985) has concluded not only that "modular compartmentalization" of input processing occurs in the brains of other primates, but that the organization of "the same" mental function changes with development: With increasing age, "higher" cortical functions become more important in performing cognitive tasks. In infant humans, there are definite stages during which the functional activity of different higher brain areas waxes and wanes (Chugani & Phelps, 1986). Apparently transitory neuromotor abnormalities observed in the first year often predict scholastic difficulties when the same children (apparently uneventfully) reach eight to 10 years of age (Amiel-Tison, 1985). This finding can be explained by our model of developmental reorganization by assuming that neurological insults that have only minor repercussions on the sensorimotor system in early life have noticeable effects when the affected regions subsequently become involved in the regulation of higher mental functions.

The existence of behavioral stages or qualitatively different levels of cognitive function are extensively characterized in the literature on human development. Piaget (1952; 1962; Inhelder & Piaget, 1958) has described cognitive development in children as a series of stages. Each step is seen as a necessary (but not sufficient) condition for subsequent stages. Although his initial descriptions were based upon observations of Western European children, cross-cultural studies suggest that this sequence of stages of mental growth applied equally to (healthy) infants and young children the world over. Throughout infancy and early childhood, the generality of the Piagetian observations seems almost uncanny: African infants who have never before seen anything like the test items nevertheless perform in the same manner as do Genevan babies (Dasen & Heron, 1981).

Although the sequence of substages in middle childhood is more variable, the Piagetian outline *in general* continues to predict development of non-Western and nonliterate children reasonably well. The differences across cultures seem to reflect cultural variations on the kinds of materials or problems individuals are likely to encounter (Cole, Gay, Glick, & Sharp, 1971). As a whole, then, the data are consistent with the view that the (early) development of human thought progresses in stages is species-typical, and dependent upon what we have called ubiquitous stimuli (see also McCall, 1981).

### Constraints

Piaget (1929; 1952; 1954; 1962) emphasized the ideas that infants *construct* their realities; input from the environment is filtered through the child's current level of understanding. Following Marler (1961), at least three levels of phenotypic structure can be identified that filter—and thereby constrain—the nature and the effects of a child's transactions with the environment (See also Aslin, 1981; Parmelee & Sigman, 1983).

*Receptors.* The first constraints upon the contents of mind are imposed by receptor capacities. Insofar as its basic receptor equipment differs from that of other forms qualitatively or quantitatively (cf. Arvidson & Friberg, 1980; Hudspeth, 1985; von Uexkull 1934/1957), each species lives in "its own" world. Many phenomena are simply beyond our senses; cues to which we are oblivious serve to guide the behavior of other animals. Even where there is overlap across species in basic sensitivities, for example, similarly "tuned" receptor elements for color vision such as cones, (Nathans et al., 1986), their number will affect how much of that information can be exploited. A visual apparatus that projects incoming light rays on a finer-grained receptor "screen" has the potential for making more precise discriminations (Banks & Salapatek, 1983).

Thus cognition will be restricted at the outset, as it were, by the basic tuning of our sensory receptors and the course of their development in time (e.g., Banks & Salapatek, 1983). A second peripheral limitation is imposed by the degree of focusing permitted by receptor locations and/or accessory structures. For example, most herbivorous animals' eyes are situated on the sides of their heads so that they have a visual field of 270° or more. As a trade-off for this very broad field of vision, however, they sacrifice some of the information that we obtain from narrower, but overlapping visual fields (Bourlière, 1964). Although the human ear is about as sensitive as it could be within its turning range (without being overwhelmed by irrelevant molecular noise; Hudspeth, 1985), the distance between the two ears constrains our ability to locate the sources of different sounds in space without turning the head (Aslin et al., 1983).

*Central relays.* Given these limitations imposed by the receptors, we may be further limited by the degree to which individual receptor elements can make discriminable contributions to an overall picture of the world. Even if color sensitive visual cells, for example, cones, are plentiful, the visual picture will be more sketchy in systems where single neurons relay activity in groups of cones than in systems where there is closer approximation to a 1:1 corresondence between receptor units and nerve fibers (Barlow, Narasimhan, & Rosenfeld, 1972). The effects of relay apparatuses can be illustrated further by the mechanisms transmitting color information.

In principle, humans could be limited to the perception of only three hues, corresponding to the three (identified) classes of color-sensitive cells in the eye. However, the photosensitive chemicals that activate receptor elements corresponding to these different bands of the visual spectrum are so broadly tuned that their sensitivities overlap. Given complex interconnections among receptor elements (Poppel, 1986), we have the potential for distinguishing very fine gradations within the total range specified by these receptors via different configurations of neuronal activation (Barlow et al., 1972). How that information is processed depends upon more central filtering mechanisms. We possess mechanisms that permit us to perceive almost continuous gradations of color. Yet, at the same time, we are biased from early life to subdivide the spectra "categorically" (Bornstein, 1975; 1985; Bornstein, Dessen, & Weiskopf, 1976).

Along with color, shape and depth are salient visual inputs for *Homo*. Studies of the retina show that the neuronal connections among the photo-sensitive receptor cells interact in such a way that the edges or outlines of patterns of light and dark are emphasized (Barlow et al., 1972; Banks & Salapatek, 1983). Information transmitted from the eye also specifies the location in the retina of an active receptor cell. In the brain, these messages are processed further.

Corresponding to the discoveries of central neurons in animals that re-spond selectively to binocular disparities, color, (linear) orientation, and motion (Hubel et al., 1977; Hubel, 1982), a number of studies indicate that the sensory analyzers of the human brain function in a similar man-ner. Experiments using habituation, aftereffects, and illusions show that there exist mechanisms selectively tuned to respond to a variety of phe-nomena, including color, fast and slow motion (Green, Chilcoat, & Stroh-meyer, 1983), long- and short-range motion (Gregory & Harris, 1984), and the direction of motion (Green et al., 1983; Shadlen & Carney, 1986), including movement in depth (Regan & Beverley, 1973).

Illusions created by superimposed, moving gratings suggest that such percepts involve the activation of neural "feature-detectors" at several levels of visual processing (Adelson & Movshon, 1982). At earlier stages, detectors apparently are tuned to respond to moving stimuli and others are tuned to respond to movement in a specified orientation (horizontal or vertical; Morrone & Burr, 1986). Apparently coherent movement of com-plex percepts can be explained by the simultaneous activities of several "lower level" analyzers which converge and are combined at higher levels (Adelson & Movshon, 1982).

The neural mechanisms involved in relaying auditory input appear to operate in a similar manner. In humans, psychophysical evidence suggests that categorical perception of speech-sounds (phonemes) may be mediated by auditory "feature-detectors." (See Aslin et al., 1983; Eimas, 1985; Eimas & Miller, 1978, for reviews.) Although we know considerably less about other sensory systems, from neurophysiological studies of other species and psychophysical studies of humans, it appears that sensory relays also constrain what we smell and taste (Cain, 1979; Persaud & Dodd, 1982).

In short, then, the mechanisms by which receptor excitation is trans-lated into patterns of nervous activity also impose limits upon what can be experienced. Returning to the analysis of vision, there are data suggesting that, in humans, there exist at least three different classes of binocular dis-parity-detectors and that the potentials to develop each of them are in-herited independently (W. Richards, 1970).

*Specialized, central processing.* Neural relaying mechanisms and feature-detectors provide us with the capacities to see movement, edges, color, and to hear phonemes and blends of pitches, but we perceive more than just these features; we see objects, we hear words and voices. A major question thus is how we can "decompose" continuous arrays of input into discrete categories corresponding to objects and specific kinds of sounds (cf. Ballard, Hinton, & Sejnowski, 1983; Frost & Nakayama, 1983; Hudspeth, 1985). Some have sought to explain these more complex forms of information-processing in terms of "psychological" processes such as the testing of "hypotheses." To the extent that illusions do not correspond to any obvious physical patterns, hypothesis-testing interpretations are consistent with the evidence. However, they are inadequate for two reasons. In the first place, there is no way to tell in advance *which* hypotheses should be activated in any particular context. Secondly, cognitive explanations do not predict phenomena such as the appearance of an apparent reversal of brightness relations that accompany some illusory changes in contour. More damaging to arguments that "non-physiological" mechanisms are required to explain interpretations of sensory input, are data indicating that illusory phenomena give rise to aftereffects in the same way as do real visual phenomena (Smith & Over, 1975), and that real and apparent movement can *cancel* each other (Gregory & Harris, 1984).

The varoius feature detectors individually are probably broadly tuned, but, in the aggregate, given a variety of ranges of optimal tuning, they can specify very precise information. When several different processing channels converge, the potential for discrimination increases dramatically. For example, psychophysical studies of human brightness constancies suggest that they represent the integration of light intensities from objects perceived to lie adjacent to the target. That is, they result from the integration of depth cues (retinal disparity, size, etc.) and light intensities (Gilchrist, 1977).[1] Presumably, the perception of shape constancies likewise reflects the integration of textural cues such as density (Bergen & Julesz, 1983), and perhaps differences in relative motion of images corresponding both to their trajectories and our movement in space (Frost & Nakayama, 1983) and/or patterns of motion parallax (Lappan & Fuqua, 1983). Because there are inhibitory as well as excitatory interactions among both relay and central processing mechanisms (Morrone, Burr, & Ross, 1983; Schiller, 1982), the visual analyzers in principle have the potential for extracting very complex information from receptor excitation.

The ways in which a hierarchy of analyzers might interact to impose meaning upon patterns of receptor activation in humans can be illustrated by experiments on the illusion of apparent motion caused by inter-

---

[1] The constancies of hue, brightness, and shape also have been attributed to "psychological" as opposed to physiological mechanisms because the patterns of light falling on the retina do not correspond directly to the subjective percepts. Nevertheless "color constancy" cells have been found in the visual cortex of monkeys which apparently represent the integration of channels responsive to ambient and reflected hue (Wild, 1985).

mittently flashing lights. If one interposes a dim line between successive light flashes, the illusion of movement is strengthened. Moreover, curved lines create the illusion of a curved path; indeed, almost a 360° circle. The delay between flashes required to suggest motion in the latter cases increases as a function of the *curvilinear* distance of the interpolated line ("path") rather than the linear distance between light sources, consistent with the idea that the (discrete) shift across receptor-activated channels is processed as "blurred motion" (Shepard & Zare, 1983). Similarly, although the "image" on the receptors is changing, we tend to interpret certain patterns of change in two dimensions as "specifying" a rigid body moving in space (Ullman, 1979).

Presumably, impositions of meaning must represent the canalized development of structure underlying "plausible assumptions" about the world that have evolved to serve as "algorithms" to guide the processing operations of our sensory analyzers (Ballard et al., 1983; Brown, 1984; Hopfield & Tank, 1986; Poggio, Torre, & Koch, 1985; Rogers & Koenderink, 1985; Ullman, 1979).[2] They would be the cognitive responses to sensory "sign" stimuli.

### Fine Tuning

Gottlieb (1970) noted that, even among primates, human infants display accelerated sensory function relative to their overall motor maturity; their input channels are developmentally more advanced than their capacities for output. Moreover, many of the infant's motor capacities seem to be designed to facilitate the acquisition of input. The common interpretation of this state of affairs has been that early sensory precocity facilitates "learning" and "socialization." Alternatively, this sensory precocity could indicate that the maintenance, functional validation, and/or integration of processing apparatuses depend upon sensory activation.

*Vision.* In the visual modality, infants' cortical electrical responses to random dot patterns which, in adults, evoke illusions of (stereoscopic) depth suggest that human babies begin to respond to such cues between 2½ and 4½ months after birth (Braddick et al., 1980; Petrig, Julesz,

---

[2] The simian visual cortex contains cells that become activated under conditions that evoke the illusion of continuous lines in humans, such as the percept of a trangle behind a circle:

Consistent with the view that these interpretive operations represent the convergence of several levels and types of parallel feature-processing channels (cf. Ballard et al., 1983; Frost & Nakayama, 1983; Watt, 1985) they are found only in the "higher" visual centers (von der Heydt, Peterhans, & Baumgartner, 1984).

Kropfl, Baumgartner, & Anliker, 1981). This apparently marks the beginning of a critical period for the functional validation of stereopsis. Given that adult-like, binocular visual processing seems to start functioning around 2½ to 3 months of age and fully "comes on line" toward the fourth month, it may not be coincidental that visually guided reaching does not appear much before 2½ months of age even under conditions expressly designed to foster its development (White, 1971). The rough coincidence of the onset of the critical period for functional validation of binocular disparity-detectors (Banks et al., 1975; Braddick et al., 1980; Petrig et al., 1981) and Piaget's (1952) substage of spontaneously-emitted "secondary circular reactions" (which involve much visually-guided manipulation and seems to be more or less universal) is consistent with the view that the timing of many behavioral milestones serves some purpose. Presumably, newly-emerging activities ensure that the developing system obtains input required for validating and maintaining emerging capacities and/or inducing/facilitating and integrating the expression of additional ones.

The view that steropsis must be validated during a critical period is supported by studies of individuals who suffered from an early inability to keep both eyes fixated on the same point. Comparisons of the stereoscopic vision of individuals who had the problem corrected at various ages indicate that the "peak" of this critical period is between the ages of one and three years (Aslin, 1985; Banks et al., 1975; Banks & Salapatek, 1983; Hohman & Creutzfeldt, 1975). The deficiencies produced by such abnormalities are consistent with the hypothesis that in the absence of ocular convergence, binocularly-driven disparity-detectors fail to develop. Not only are such people unable to use stereoscopic cues to perceive depth, but, unlike people with normal vision, who usually are not aware of which eye is receiving any particular input, stereoblind persons tend to retain awareness of "eye-of-origin." However, they cannot "use" the disparity between images perceived by the two eyes to determine depth (Blake & Cormack, 1979). Consistent with the view that some "tuning" involves systematic inhibition of neuronal processes (cf. Sillito, Kemp, & Blakemore, 1981), psychophysiological data indicate that certain "binocular" cells in humans may receive excitatory input from one eye and inhibitory input from the other (Vidyasagar, 1976).

Perhaps as an adaptation to developmental changes in the configuration of the eye (cf. Banks & Salapatek, 1983), humans also require receptor-evoked input to detect the orientations of lines. Like cats (Leventhal & Hirsch, 1975) and monkeys (Mansfield, 1974), humans are better at discriminating horizontal or vertical orientations than diagonals (Mansfield, 1974). A study in humans of the age of optical corrections for astigmatisms which blurred one or the other orientation indicated that something like feature detectors for line-orientation are validated and integrated in the first three years (Freeman & Thibos, 1973). Visually evoked electrical responses show that activity in visual feature detectors for line-orientation become measurable in the first few weeks (Braddick, Wattam-Bell, & Atkinson, 1986) and develop inhibitory cross-connections that help to sharpen the perception of orientation by six months (Morrone & Burr, 1986).

Moreover, it seems that input that can normally achieve "meaning" is necessary for the maintenance of functional connections between the detection of patterned light and attention, or orienting. Individuals who were born with one eye normal and the other capable of detecting only diffuse light showed cortical evoked responses to light via the abnormal eye but no activation of attentional or other processing mechanisms—in contrast to such activation via the normal eye (Glass, 1977). These findings support the hypothesis that early visual tuning involved "competition" among neural processors (cf. Barlow, 1975; Sillito et al., 1981), and they also are consistent with the view that later-developing regions may pre-empt functions otherwise served by earlier-maturing, "lower" centers (Crowne, Richardson, & Ward, 1983; Ptito & Lepore, 1983). However, studies reviewed by von Senden (1960) suggest that if *neither* eye has been able to detect more than the presence of light (due to cataracts), humans can acquire a range of skills subsequent to corrective surgery.

*Audition.* Just as there exist disparity-detectors for vision (e.g., Barlow, 1975; Hubel, 1982), there are cells in the mammalian brain that "code" for differential activation of the two ears (Moore, 1983; Palmer & King, 1982). The spatial or temporal disparities are a function of the distance between the ears and this distance changes with growth. Thus, we should expect plasticity in these domains: As the child's anatomy changes, the values specifying direction of a source of sound will have to be "recalibrated" (cf. Bower, 1982; Aslin et al., 1983).

Newborns turn toward the source of a sound (Wertheimer, 1961), and according to Bower (1982), even reach in that direction. Areas in the mammalian midbrain (the superior colliculus) exist in which auditory and visual "maps" are created by converging inputs from different sensory modalities (Harris, Blakemore, & Donaghy, 1980; Pettigrew, 1984). In monkeys, at least, some of the cells in this region control eye and perhaps head movements; a few have properties typical of both sensory and motor neurons (Jay & Sparks, 1984). Therefore, it is quite possible that both auditory localization and "primitive" sensorimotor coordinations are also subject to receptor-evoked validation/tuning as the head grows and the binaural disparity detectors require recalibration (Aslin, 1985; Bower, 1982).[3]

---

[3] Knudsen (1983) has shown that, in owls, the audiovisual "map" is subject to experiential "tuning" in early life. Therefore, "recalibration" may reasonably be understood in terms of receptor-induced developmental processes.

In the auditory system, it would seem that the higher levels of information processing also operate via several "layers" of increasingly more precisely interpreted signals, each of which reflects certain aspects of the total configuration of stimulation presented to the receptors. In addition to this kind of flexible construction of the meaning of the sensory environment, there seem to be elements in the system(s) which are "pretuned" to respond to detection of predictably significant configurations of input.

Categorical perception of phonemes by infants is consistent with the notion that the hominid brain works essentially the same way as that of our simian cousins (e.g., Eimas, 1975; 1985; Eimas & Miller, 1978; Jusczyk, 1985; Kuhl, 1978). Moreover, evidence that people tend to lose the capacity to detect "irrelevant" phonemes (Eimas, 1985; Strange & Jenkins, 1978) is consistent with the model of adaptive fine-tuning of the mechanisms by which we relate to our surroundings.

At any rate, if receptor-evoked activity is required for the development of higher level processing, we may be well advised not just to be concerned with the kinds of stimuli that hold infants' attention at different ages, but we should also seek to discover those which evoke the greatest amounts of activity in different analyzers. From work reviewed above, it seems likely that a number of different processing activities are facilitated and functionally validated in the first year. If the hypotheses presented here are correct, infants' attention usually will be focused on the kinds of inputs that are most important for their "normal" development (cf. Bronson, 1974; Haith, 1980; Salapatek, 1975). Indeed, a consideration of the capacities of infants in conjunction with the development of the child's concept of "objects" would seem to call for such an interpretation.

## ONTOGENY OF KNOWLEDGE

### Object Permanence

Piaget (1952; 1954; 1962) felt that infants had no sense of the physical permanence of things and people in their environments. He held that this knowledge slowly developed as a result of babies' transactions with their surroundings. He did, however, feel that the "reflexes" with which neonates were endowed provided them with a kind of "foreknowledge" of their worlds. Whether or not one would grant them conscious concepts, it does seem that neonates are endowed with working algorithms (cf. Ballard et al., 1983; Poggio et al., 1985) that must lead to such awareness.

*Tracking.* Spelke (1985) suggests that infants begin life with a "conception" that objects move, a sense of spatio-temporal continuity of things. Neonates will track a moving face, albeit hesitantly (Freedman, 1974). Visual tracking can even be elicited by exposing babies to a row of lights which are illuminated, one at a time, in sequence, at a constant rate. Once infants turn their gaze in time to fixate on a light that is about to turn on, they will shift, smoothly, from that one to each of the remaining lights just as they were lighted (Nelson, 1968). The fact that the lights are simply going on and off in a discontinuous, albeit, regular sequence, means that the infants are, in essence, "calculating" a trajectory. Indeed, Bower (1982) has claimed that by the age of 2 months, infants will anticipate the reappearance of a moving object which disappears behind a screen, and even direct their gaze after only a few glimpses of an "object" apparently moving from one window to another as if they expected it to be moving on a specific (curved) course at a fixed rate of speed. They will show "surprise" if the object fails to appear as expected.

So long as *something* following the same trajectory reappears from behind a screen, infants under four months of age show no surprise—even if the moving object that disappears is a small red ball and the one that reappears is a large blue cube. From these observations, Bower (1982) and Spelke (1985) suggest that movement is the overriding cue initially used by babies in their conception of tangible, permanent, entities (such as mother?). A more conservative hypothesis would be that two-month-old infants' visuo-motor apparatus is so constructed that they will be able to track moving objects even when the targets pass out of sight (cf. Bronson, 1974). Surprise and upset at "disconfirmation" might be considered signals to caregivers (cf. Alexander, 1974) that "something is amiss," or simply reactions to the loss of an opportunity for continued exercise of the tracking response (cf. Piaget's [1952] "primary circular response"). Consistent with the latter interpretation, when 2- to 4-month-old babies are tracking a moving object which suddenly stops, their eye-movements stop only for a few tenths of a second and then *continue* on course, as it were, leaving the (now) stationary object behind (Bower, 1982). However, by 5 months of age, infants do appear to "expect" that only one apparently solid object can occupy the same space. If a wooden screen seems to fall flat in the space apparently "occupied" by a wooden cube, babies look at the event longer than if the screen's descent is apparently interrupted by the presence of the cube (Baillargeon, Spelke, & Wasserman, 1985).

*Intersensory coordination.* Neonates turn toward the source of a sound (Wertheimer, 1961); similarly, in darkness, Bower (1982) claims that very young infants will also reach toward a sound.[4] Thus, the substrates for a

---

[4] Bower (1982) also claims that neonates will reach toward objects in such a way that implies that they have an appreciation for the three-dimensionality of the target. Although these findings have been difficult to replicate (see Banks & Salapatek, 1983, for review), Amiel-Tison (1985) also reports that visually-guided reaching can be obtained in infants within 3 weeks of birth. She indicates that, in order to demonstrate upper-body coordinations, the infant's head must be stabilized by some form of neck support.

primitive algorithm, "noises mean things to see or touch," may develop *in utero* (See also Mendelson & Haith, 1976). Insofar as babies do turn and reach toward sound sources reasonably accurately, the substrates for auditory localization must be fairly well developed. Moreover, to control head-turning and reaching, the substrates for localizing sounds must be integrated with motor systems controlling the head and arm (Bower, 1982).

Despite the fact that, until late in the second month, babies act as if objects that remain out of sight "no longer exist," they can match oral-tactile sensations to visual input. If one allows infants to suck pacifiers upon which small, hard-rubber shapes are attached, and then presents the infants with two styrofoam shapes, one of which matches the one affixed to the pacifier, babies look longer at the shape matching the one that they had sucked on. Apparently, within the first month, infants can not only discriminate between shapes on the basis of (oral) tactual cues and store a representation of the tactual information gained thereby, they also can relate a visual percept to that stored tactual representation—which also indicates that they must be able to visually discriminate different shapes (Meltzoff & Borton, 1979).

These data and evidence concerning babies' reactions to alterations of moving patterns (above) again suggest that, well before they display clear indications of having a coherent, conscious awareness of the properties of objects *per se*, infants possess the capacities to receive and store information necessary for the formation of such a concept. Moreover, these "incomplete" items of knowledge apparently provide them with enough input to meet the demands of other developing systems.

For example, despite the fact that they may not appreciate the logical necessity for objects to remain invariant, by one year of age, babies avoid obstacles and notice when items of furniture, and so on are changed or rearranged. They can get from one room to another. In short, they do have working ideas about things in space (Acredolo, 1987). These developments may not be fortuitously timed: To be successfully mobile, one had better have developed at least an intuitive sense of space and the location of stable landmarks. Well before they can locomote on their own, babies can "locate" objects either relative to themselves or to salient landmarks, but they show little preference for one or another "strategy." However, if locomotion is fostered precociously by providing them with "walkers," prelocomotor infants tend to show greater reliance on external landmarks (Bertenthal et al., 1984).

## Expectancies and Social Objects

Infants not only habituate to repeated events, but they also change the rate and even the pattern of emission of actions such as sucking or head-turning apparently in response to attention-getting events that follow their behavior within a second or two. When awake and alert, neonates operate as if they anticipate certain activities to lead to predictable consequences (Clifton, 1974; Lipsitt, 1969; Papousek, 1969). Moreover, once neonates confirm a tentative "hypothesis," they soon lose interest in the contingency relationship. To maintain the baby's rate of responding, either the nature of the response *or* the nature of the contingent stimulus ("reward") must change (Bower, 1982). The fact that babies' post-solution response rates decline with repeated presentations of the same problem is consistent with the view that infants are "designed" to gain new information about their surroundings.

However, when left to their own devices, young babies do not seem to be particularly aware of contingency relationships; Piaget (1952) felt that expectancies were not manifest until around the fourth month. Presumably, this is because the contingent event must occur within just a few seconds of the baby's action in order to be registered. From these observations, Watson (1967; Watson & Ramey, 1972) has suggested that the first 3 months might be considered a period of "natural" intellectual deprivation for infants.

If one considers contingency-detection as *the* central element in cognitive growth, that might be cause for concern. However, before taking steps to "rectify" this state of affairs, we might do well to examine it a bit more closely.

The adaptationist position is that developmental phenomena represent the products of natural selection. If so, we must account for the paradoxical existence of a precocious potential to detect contingencies in the apparent absence of the capacity to benefit from such "knowledge." One way to resolve this apparent paradox may be to consider the infants' adaptive priorities. Of all the contingencies that are important for infants in the first 4–6 months, few could compare with establishing a mutual bond with a caregiver. Observations of mother-infant interactions (e.g., Schaffer, 1977) indicate that mothers often do respond within the 3-second interval identified by Watson.

Moreover, mothers *move* (i.e., catch the eye) and within 1 to 3 weeks after birth, infants seem to be able to detect correspondences between certain actions of an adult and their own activities. That is, when alert and interacting with adults, infants are more likely to stick out their tongues, open their mouths, protrude their lips, or move their fingers just after the adults have done so than at other times. Mimicry of tongue or mouth movements implies an ability to detect correspondences between another person's anatomy and the babies' own "equipment"—without benefit of being able to see their own actions (Meltzoff & Moore, 1985). This early "social knowledge" is accompanied by another apparently precocious cognitive attainment: Whereas the appreciation of identity, despite changes in viewing position of inanimate objects, is difficult to demonstrate until infants are at least 6 months old (cf. Banks & Salapatek, 1983), babies can identify *faces* despite changes in orientation and even expression when they are between 3 and 4 months of age (Cohen et al., 1979).

Perhaps we previously underestimated neonates' capacities because of their sensory "limitations": For adult humans, distant objects or events can be seen only; hearing usually becomes a factor at moderate distances; olfaction typically is effective only at close range, and touch requires even closer proximity (Peiper, 1963). Human newborns' visual acuity is limited to relatively short range, well within the limits of most sound-producing events, and their binocular focus is fixed at about the range of reaching. Thus, in some ways, infants live in a world of *proximal* exteroceptive stimulation. Insofar as close-range contingencies are most likely to involve caregivers, we may have an example of the adaptiveness of early limitations: The infant's early limitations may have evolved to ensure that the first contingencies that are discovered are those that lead to the establishment of social bonds. Then the baby can afford to become acquainted with inanimate objects, and gather input that will lend itself to more abstract thought.

### Intersensory Discrimination

Heterochronies in development also lead to apparently anomalous "regressions" as can be exemplified by examination of a number of cognitive attainments. Some of these apparently anomalous shifts in performance may index changing neurological function.

Observations that newborns turn to the source of a sound and that very young infants reach toward a sound-source in the dark have been interpreted to mean that neonates lack a sense of the separateness of the different sensory modalities (Bower, 1982) and that touch, sight, and sound specify "things." By 6 months of age, infants reach toward a sound less readily; by 7 months the rate is near zero. At this time, visually guided reaching is very accurate, and the grasping component has become dependent upon tactual cues even though the hand's location is monitored— and corrected—visually; yet babies *cease* to clutch an object when it is out of their view. Bower (1982) suggests that these changes occur because infants are becoming aware of the separateness of vision and touch, and temporarily regress in the sense that they seem to focus upon vision and ignore cues that once would have specified "something to see/hear/touch."[5]

By 12 to 15 months of age, infants' (apparent) conceptions of inanimate objects are somewhat better defined and they again show a willingness to

---

[5] Alternatively, it may be that babies become upset when their hands "disappear" and focus their attention on relocating the hidden member.

grope in the dark for the source of a sound (Bower, 1982). At this stage it looks as if they not only recognize the differences between modalities, but also possess an *awareness* that things can make sounds and sound is likely to indicate the presence of an object.

This does not mean that a complete integration has been achieved, however. Despite the fact that infants under one year of age seem to recognize visual displays that resemble objects they sucked on (Meltzoff & Borton, 1979), even 3-year-olds have difficulty in fully marshaling their capacities and/or in integrating the information they gain from different sensory channels. If asked to identify objects by touch and match them to visual displays, 3-year-olds do not seem to employ a focused strategy of palpitation; they tend to employ only one hand and their activities resemble playful manipulation rather than systematic exploration. In visual-haptic matching situations, 3- to 4-year-olds tend to focus upon elements of the stimuli rather than attempting to gain a picture of the whole. Yet even 2½- to 3-year-olds can learn to size up a situation before acting—if forced to: When simply given objects of different shapes to put through correspondingly-shaped holes they seem to use essentially a trial-and-error procedure. However, if they have to observe the hole-board through a screen before they are allowed to try to insert the objects, a number of 3-year-olds will shift to visually matching the object to the hole before trying to insert it. Interestingly, when 3-year-olds' trial and error activity yields a solution, they seem unable to benefit from the information available from that success. On a subsequent try they may again attempt to fit the same object into an inappropriate hole (Zaprozhets, 1969).

What may be happening here is another instance of disassembling a primitive (perhaps subcortical) sense of correspondence: As the uniqueness of the sensory modalities is recognized through the activation of higher order modes of analysis, reflection on the global visual-tactile percept is inhibited. Later, another resynthesis of the whole may be achieved with a greater appreciation for its elements (cf. Bower, 1982), only to "regress" again as a new, *conscious* appreciation of visual shape begins to emerge.

## Higher-Order Concepts

Our model of developmental reorganization may be further illustrated by the ontogeny of several more abstract intellectual attainments. If one follows the sensorimotor progression of individual children longitudinally, it becomes clear that we are not dealing with simple, linear change or "improvement." Rather, problems such as pulling on a tablecloth as a means to bring an object within reach may be solved readily at 9 months, and then appear to be difficult for the *same* children until the age of 20 months. Insofar as these infants show the expected progress with respect to other problems, such as finding hidden objects, behavioral instability would seem to represent shifts in organization and the expression and exercise of new capacities (Kopp, Sigman, & Parmelee, 1973). The solution to the problem is not lost; instead, the interim period may be one in which babies elaborate their understanding of the problem and *how* it could be solved. The "schema" expressed at 9 months may be neither erased nor abandoned; it becomes one of the substrates upon which a more complex conception is established (cf. Piaget, 1962).

*Using symbols.* In memory tasks, even though they may know the names for the items, preschool-aged children do not spontaneously *use* them as mnemonic aids. A label, for example, "cow," itself may be the focus of attention at this stage, an object no less of wonder than the infant's discovery that hands can be controlled. As they discover the utility of their newly-acquired symbolic capacities, older children who have better control over "internal," "ikonic" memory aids often refuse to use props such as photos to help them remember a scene. They seem quite captivated by the opportunity to exercise their new capacity for verbal mediation of recall (Ryan, Hegion, & Flavell, 1970). Insofar as such shifts are not unique to labeling in memory tasks, the apparently compulsive use of a new skill may be a mechanism that guarantees the substrate sufficient "exercise" for validation and maintenance, both of which may be necessary before higher levels of control will be able to regulate the integration of such skills. One might even speculate that newly-functional nervous connections cause them to pre-empt other, tried-but-true systems in benign contexts (i.e., when life-preserving or life-sustaining behavioral systems are not highly aroused). This would guarantee that, once their development was induced, they would "get enough work" to functionally validate and maintain the appropriate structures.

*Size and weight.* This kind of apparently uneven progression can be clearly illustrated by Bower's (1982) account of infants' knowledge of size and weight: At six months of age, most babies grasp all objects firmly regardless of their weight and despite the fact that they will adjust their grasping to the apparent size of objects—relative to their *hands.* However, the abstraction, "size" of one object relative to another *object*, will not be used as a basis for even nonverbal object-classification (i.e., sorting them into piles) until much later.

Although babies can discriminate objects of different lengths much earlier and, by 9 months of age, begin to adjust the force of their grasp to object-weights (after the objects are in their hands), they will not anticipate the weight of objects until they are 15 months old or older. Some time around 18 months of age they begin to anticipate the weight of objects according to their apparent length. Then, the same plasticine "sausage" will be treated as if they expected it to be heavier (babies' arms will rise after grasping the object) when one elongates it; conversely, if one rolls it into a more compact ball (while the babies watch) they respond as if anticipating a lighter object (their arms drop on initial transfer of the weight). It will be some months before they finally differentiate weight from length in the sensorimotor sphere (Bower, 1982).

At a practical level of understanding, babies recognize both size and weight before their second birthday. This knowledge permits them to manipulate things effectively enough to gain further information about the properties of objects and their potential uses. Although less complex than adults' understanding, this infantile knowledge probably also lays the foundation for more abstract and elaborated concepts, but only after new organizational levels of thought have been achieved (cf. Piaget, 1952; 1962).

Through the age of five years, an appreciation for weight as an abstract, continuous quantity is seldom achieved. If one asks children to lift unseen weights and judge them either relative to each other, or relative to a standard weight by pointing to a visual display, five-year-olds seem incapable of ordering the stimuli whether or not a standard reference weight is presented. In contrast, youngsters over six years of age not only order their arrays but also vary their heaviness-judgments of the comparison series as a function of the relative weight of the standard (O'Reilly & Steger, 1970).

Insofar as two-year-olds can use visual cues for estimating the weights of objects, five-year-olds' failure cannot entirely represent the problems inherent in using a visual representation for a tactual-kinesthetic judgment. It seems more probable that, until some time after the age of five years, the practical, sensorimotor appreciation for the heaviness of objects has not led to the elaboration of the substrates for reflective awareness of weight as an abstract concept. Five-year-olds cannot quite conceptualize heaviness as something that can be considered apart from objects. At least they cannot do so well enough to hold the "standard" (or any other weight) in mind long enough to make the appropriate comparison. Even grade-school children can be trapped by the question "which is heavier: a pound of lead or a pound of feathers?"

*Quantity.* Developmental changes in both the cognitive repertoire and its deployment also can be seen in the child's sense of number or quantity. Infants in their first year recognize the difference between arrays of two and three objects (Starkey & Cooper, 1980) and seem to recognize the similarity between two or three sound pulses and visual displays of two or three objects (Starkey, Spelke, & Gelman, 1983). Thus, some primitive sense of numerosity is available very early in life. If one presents children who are between 2½ and 5½ years of age with two rows of either clay pellets or M&M candies and asks which row has "more," all but the 3½ to 4½ year olds choose the row with the greater number of pellets, regardless of its length. The 3½ to 4½-year-olds typically choose the longer row even though it may contain only four (as opposed to six) pellets. However, when the M&Ms are presented and one tells the children to "take the row you want to eat," the number of "incorrect" choices among 3½- to 4½-year olds is much less marked, and more restricted in terms of the age-range showing dependence upon the length of the array (Mehler & Bever, 1967).[6]

These observations present us with the same sort of picture that can be seen in the sensorimotor period: Youngsters display an ability, for example, reaching very early, apparently lose it, only to recover the capacity later on in a somewhat more sophisticated form (cf. Bower, 1982).

It seems likely that all the children "see" (as opposed to count) more elements in the six-item row. However, as Mehler and Bever (1967) point out, common experience typically indicates that arrays containing greater numbers of elements take up more space. Therefore, insofar as preschoolers appear to "know" the principles underlying "counting" (Gelman & Gallistel, 1978), choosing as if the length of an array were fundamentally more salient for the judgment of quantity may only represent a transient phase in which the newly recognized correlation between numerosity and extensity is utilized *in preference* to the ability to distinguish the differences between small quantities.[7] Adopting the strategy of attending to length should, in fact, work when quantity judgments involve large numbers for children who cannot count very well. Presumably, the older children who chose the greater *number* had integrated this new knowledge of the relation between length and number and could move more flexibly from one strategy to another. The fact that M&Ms typically evoke more accurate responding even among 3½-year-olds suggests (a) that some sense of numerosity is available independent of other strategies for choosing, and (b) that in situations in which accuracy typically has the greatest payoff, such as getting enough to eat, conflicting strategies often will be resolved in favor of the one yielding the more certain return. Abstract problem solving is another matter, however.

Even 5- to 7-year old children who understand how to count discrete elements (e.g., matchsticks) to get an idea of the length of a line, have difficulty in realizing that the length of an unbroken line (a continuous string, etc.) *can* be broken up into count-able units in order to measure it.

---

[6] This study evoked quite a bit of controversy, and some evidence that choice behavior could vary according to mode of presentation (e.g., in one study, the *closer* row was most often chosen by younger children and the reverse by the older ones: Rothenberg & Courtney, 1969), and according to sequence of testing (whether clay pellets or M&Ms were presented first). Nevertheless, even in "failures to replicate" (Willoughby & Trachy, 1971) it seemed that "more" candy and "more" clay were different issues for children over 3 years of age. Calhoun (1971) did replicate Mehler and Bever's observations, and essentially all who tried to replicate the study found that some children, particularly those around 3½ years of age, were likely to "confuse" the number of elements in an array with its length.

[7] Gelman and Galistel (1978) argue persuasively that the traditional procedure of emphasizing 1:1 correspondences between rows may, in fact, cause preschoolers to adopt a "set" incompatible with utilizing their already-existing abilities to "count."

It is as if the notion of quantifying length had to derive from a sequence beginning with quantification of discrete elements (cf. Gelman & Gallistel, 1978), then recognition that the elements could be used to construct a continuous array (a line), and finally, realization that the array could again be separated to provide units of measurement (Inhelder et al., 1974). Children in the "preoperational" stage (cf. Inhelder & Piaget, 1958) appreciate distance in a practical sense; they just cannot relate it to what they know of counting and the number system.

One might be tempted to assume that once a conceptual rule or a notion of invariance gets established in one domain, it would require only a few prompts in order to be generalized to another. However, the evidence suggests that this is not the case. For example, despite the fact that most children will not be able to grasp the idea of measurement in any precise, quantitative way until they are 8 or 9 years of age, even 5- and 6-year-old preoperational youngsters display an intuitive grasp of the use of a reference standard under certain conditions. If one presents 5- and 6-year-old children with two otherwise identical wooden blocks, each of which has a hole in the top, and asks them to judge whether one hole is deeper than the other, many will spontaneously use a stick to gauge the depth of the holes. Moreover, they can use the stick to estimate relative depth of holes in blocks located on different tables. Yet the same youngsters will fail to solve traditional, Piagetian *tower* measuring tasks (Bryant & Kopytynska, 1976). What appears to be a component of a later-appearing, general (logical) system is manifested in a very limited functional context—but one which provides practical knowledge of immediate usefulness.

Thus, it seems that in order to utilize (integrate) quantitative knowledge, a number of component abilities must be coordinated. First, one must have the ability to classify the various aspects of one's experience into conceptually homogenous categories. Presumably, during the preoperational phases, children become conscious of dimensions within sensory modalities, for example, hues, distance, weight, loudness, and so on. At some point they get the notion that these aspects of experience can admit to analysis of a quantitative sort. However, consistent with the notion that component "modules" may be relatively self-contained, mastery of a principle in one context does not guarantee its application in another.

This is the phenomenon Piaget (e.g., Inhelder & Piaget, 1958) called the "horizontal décalage." Many youngsters solve problems requiring the conservation of simple number and discontinuous quantity well before they fathom problems that deal with continuous quantity. Even when a child can equate "lines" of plasticine that have been cut up into units, the same youngster may fail to conserve when these units are rejoined without stretching (Inhelder et al., 1974). The problem of volume, especially as an abstract principle, is even more difficult to master. It is especially difficult to explain coherently in terms of coordinating the relevant dimensions.

The notion of specific gravity or density is one that develops with even more difficulty. Consistent with our notion that many of these domains of thought are independent, training children to be able to conserve density may facilitate conservation of solid volume, but not liquid volume (Brainerd & Allen, 1971). For many people, broad application of a number of principles may be achieved only under extraordinary conditions and perhaps only during relatively restricted periods in ontogeny.

Thus, our model of biological development seems to be applicable to the understanding of "higher" mental functions. Our principles of cumulative development and heterochronous growth of components, as applied to the notion of quantity, may be summarized by the results of an analysis of "the number concept." From 3 to 8 years of age, a neatly scaled series can be discerned: In the first step, preschool-age children recite the (number) words in sequence. Next, they become able to match arrays of similar objects by visually noting correspondences (i.e., they can coordinate counting and matching principles cf. Footnote 7). Then, the number words—already "available"—become applied to arrays with an appreciation for absolute quantity. Finally, upon entry into the stage of concrete operations, the symbols (numerals) are conceptually linked to the abstract concept of quantity (D'Mello & Willemsen, 1969).

This cumulative sequence involves several independently developing components. Although toddlers can "count" verbally, and by 2½ years of age, apparently realize that "things" can be counted by assigning the distinctive labels (Gelman & Gallistel, 1978), simple notions of correspondences of quantity are not immediately linked to this essentially verbal skill—even though a primitive sense of quantity ("subitizing") is demonstrable in infancy (Starkey & Cooper, 1980). (This also appears to be independent of rank-ordering in a *social* context which appears by 3 years of age [Sluckin & Smith, 1977]). Similarly, learning to read number symbols is another skill that has to be mastered and integrated separately. Then children are taught to add and subtract in school, but are thrown for a loss when "word-problems" are introduced *after* they achieve reasonable proficiency at strictly numerical presentations of simple mathematical problems. The full application of mathematical logic as exemplified by algebra, calculus, and so on, usually is not mastered until adolescence.

## DEVELOPMENTAL RESILIENCY AND COGNITIVE GROWTH

### Resiliency

In the intact individual, input usually is multimodal; it involves several sensory avenues. Although the normal child typically utilizes all these impressions to build up a picture of the world, it seems that people can make do with quite restricted opportunities; that is, development is "buffered" against misfortune.

*Multiple input-channels.* We have few data on the kinds of inputs necessary for the development of cognitive potential; nevertheless, there is indirect evidence from studies of individuals who suffered from motor or sensory deficits (congenital malformations, blindness, deafness, or both blindness and deafness) from an early age. Generally speaking, these studies show that, first of all, children are remarkably persistent and ingenious in their attempts to gain knowledge. Secondly, essentially normal cognitive development may occur, albeit at a somewhat slower rate, in children who lack just one channel for input. Finally, if we (or the children themselves) are clever enough to devise means for providing input, rather atypical experiences may suffice to initiate or sustain development of the substrates for species-typical intellectual functioning (e.g., Bower, 1982; Fraiberg, 1975; Furth, 1966).

*Compensatory organization.* The resiliency of youth (as well as the success of rehabilitative efforts with adults) can be understood in terms of the existence of multiple contributors to function. Presumably, so long as other components of the total system can lend themselves to processing of the same or similar input, they may be able to "fill in" for the absent elements and thus alter the structure, while preserving the essential operation of a functional system (Luria, 1966; 1980).

Developmentally, the early hyperproliferation of (central) nervous processes may provide a margin for error against receptor or relay malfunction. In the absence of normal input, connections that would otherwise atrophy or be inhibited are validated and maintained as a result of activation via "non-preferred" channels. For example, von Senden's (1960) congenitally blind people derived spatial knowledge at least partly from a sequential analysis of tactual-kinesthetic information, and individuals who lost their hearing in the first 4 years apparently recruit portions of the auditory cortex to serve peripheral vision (Neville, 1985).

*Overcoming handicaps.* The resiliency of children's cognitive development can be illustrated by studies of infants born with severe anatomical malformations. Consistent with Piaget's views, the neurological substrates for "knowing how" (corresponding to essentially the lessons of the initial sensorimotor stages) are neurologically separable from those underlying "knowing that" (abstract, symbolic, or conceptual knowledge, cf. Cohen & Squire, 1980; Squire, 1986; Zola-Morgan, Squire, & Mishkin, 1982). However, *contra* Piaget, although the opportunity to manipulate objects facilitates early mental growth (e.g., White, 1971), manipulatory play, as we *typically* think of it is not necessary for the development of sensorimotor intelligence.

Décarie (1969) and her collaborators studied children born with severe deficiencies of limb development resulting from prenatal exposure to thalidomide. Five of the infants had almost total bilateral absence of both their arms and their legs; 10 more had total malformation of their arms, although essentially all of them had one or more fingers. (Some also suffered from other deformities such as dysgenesis of an ear, etc.) The Griffiths Scale of Mental Development was given to them and scored with allowance for physically impossible tasks. Despite their handicaps, only one-third of the children could reasonably be classified as "mentally defective," and the majority of them were the same ones who had been reared in institutions. The children's mental test scores were not consistently related to the severity of the malformations of their limbs. The subscale scores revealed that, regardless of rearing conditions, the children's "hearing and speech" was the area of functioning most impaired whereas their "eye-hand" and "performance" scores showed the *least* deviation. ("Hand" was scored successful if the child could perform the task using the feet or the mouth.)

In addition, the children all were tested on a series of tasks reflecting their understanding of the nature and permanence of objects. Despite their severe motor handicaps, all but three of them reached Piaget's final stage. Among them was one child who had essentially no arms or legs, only three fingers on either "hand," and severely malformed feet. Regardless of their handicap and rearing, between 24 and 31 months of age, *all* of the children had reached the highest stage of the object concept. They employed a variety of strategies in order to manipulate objects using their (remaining) digits, their mouths, toes, shoulders-and-chins, and so on. Décarie concluded that they could indeed form the "schemas" necessary for achieving the object concept according to Piagetian principles; that "the schema of prehension. . . has many different ways of reaching its goal" (1969, p. 181).

The latter conclusion, while consistent with the facts, assumes that "prehension" of *some* kind is a necessary condition for cognitive development. However, direct physical action on the sources of stimulation is not always required for mental growth. For example, Greenberg (1971) found that providing opportunities to simply view complex visual patterns led to an increase in the rate at which young infants developed "preferences" for more complex visual arrays, and, if Bower (1982) and Spelke (1985) are correct, babies may have the bases for acquiring a sense of "objectness" without an opportunity to touch or otherwise directly act on things via observation of movement, and so on.

Findings such as these, tentative though some of them may be, provide evidence consistent with the notion that we are dealing with a genome evolved to express a substrate that is "biased" to process information in certain ways. Moreover, while variations in different environmental conditions may correlate with the rate of development of specific facets of mental functioning (cf., White et al., 1979; Yarrow, 1972; Yarrow, Pedersen, & Rubenstein, 1977), for passing the major milestones of sensorimotor intellectual development, the *necessary* inputs are either so heterogeneous or so ubiquitous that they will be found in most environments compatible with infant survival (Dasen & Heron, 1981). For example, Sayegh and Dennis (1965) reported that providing 7- to 18-month-old, institution-reared infants with opportunities to manipulate and look at objects markedly accelerated their apparent mental development. What is most striking about the latter findings is that intervention was begun quite late in the sensorimotor period and that it lasted for only 15 days. (See Taylor, 1968, for similar observations.)

Consistent with models of growth that posit nonlinear relations between input and phenotypic response (cf. Rendel, 1967), at the other end of the spectrum, as it were, Tulkin (1977) has concluded that, although playthings may indeed affect infants' cognitive development, there probably exists an "upper limit" for enrichment beyond which additional input adds little or nothing. Indeed, White (1971) has suggested that too much stimulation too early may actually impede the attainment of a maximal rate of visuomotor development.

## Conflict and Development

Piaget (1952; 1962; 1970) argued that an essential ingredient for intellectual growth was the perception of a mismatch between one's current expectations and the results obtained by acting accordingly. To some degree this seems intuitively obvious: If our existing modes of thought serve our needs, we have no reason to do anything differently; we have to try something else only when they fail us. If one observes infants and young children at play, however, it is difficult to avoid the conclusion that they seem almost to seek out contradictory experiences. As suggested by Piaget's (e.g., 1952; 1962) notion of "assimilation," they try out new routines in what appears to be every conceivable context, many of which are (to adults) patently inappropriate. It would seem as if youngsters behave so as to make cognitive mismatches inevitable. Indeed, among other things, play probably does serve just such a function, as Piaget (1962) has argued. However, to accept the notion that psychic conflict *can* serve to promote intellectual advance is not to endorse the propositions that such conflict *must* do so, or that conflict *per se* is a necessary ingredient required for all advances.

Sensory activation seems to be required for the functional validation of feature detectors (e.g., Wiesel, 1982), and it is likely that a variety of very general experiences are essential for the facilitation, validation and even the induction of the substrates for both "basic" and "higher order" components of human thought. Conflict would seem to be a catalyst for change only when the substrates necessary for its resolution are already functional. Bower (1982) points out that if one presents infants with experiences which contradict their current expectations and for which they have no alternative solutions, they may simply cease to try to cope altogether. Similarly, Inhelder et al. (1974) report that contradictory experiences seem to promote the transition from preoperational to operational thought only in contexts in which children already have an appreciation for the essential ingredients required for solving the problems presented to them. Indeed, when both accurate and spurious feedback with respect to object-weight is provided to youngsters, only children who have already attained a concrete operational understanding of the quantitative nature of weight express surprise and question the outcome when their expectations are disconfirmed (Miller, 1971). That is, in some instances, cognitive conflict may be the *product* rather than the cause of intellectual progress. In short, conflict would appear to be useful only when it activates processes which are already in place. It seems unlikely to provide the necessary antecedents for the induction of underlying structures.

# CHAPTER 8

# Language

Newborns do not use language, and languages differ. Insofar as the development of competence in a particular tongue must be based on ontogenetic changes which depend upon exteroceptive input, language acquisition can provide a number of further examples of how our model of adaptive organism-environment transactions might be applied to the understanding of the ontogeny of human behavior.

## LANGUAGE DEVELOPMENT

Neonates communicate vocally, but the "semantic" repertoire of cry-types is limited largely to pain, hunger, and perhaps displeasure (Wasz-Hockert, Partanen, Vuorenkoski, Valanne, & Michelsson, 1964; Wolff, 1966), with graded features signaling intensity (Porter, Miller, & Marshall, 1986). The precise meanings of most of the newborn's messages are dependent upon the receiver's assessment of the situation. Although babies do exhibit a very wide range of facial expression and other gestures (Brannigan & Humphries, 1972; Haviland, 1975), it is uncertain whether they convey the same meanings as similar expressions of older children or adults. It is also not clear whether early, noncry vocalizations are controlled by functional systems organized so as to respond to distal events in the infant's environment.

### Perception

Consistent with our model of heterochronous development, some components of language-sensitive receptor/processing systems function in an adult-like manner within hours of birth. Neonates are more responsive to sounds that are complex (broadband) and within the frequency range of the human voice (Hutt et al., 1968), and some auditory analyzers are "tuned" to process speech-like sound-patterns (Eimas, Siqueland, Jusczyk, & Vigorito, 1971).

Human vocal communication conveys different meanings by varying combinations of sounds. The elemental, meaningful sounds (phonemes) are the basic elements of spoken languages. Although different languages may use somewhat different sets of phonemes to convey meaning, the human repertoire seems to be limited to about 60 such elements (Dale, 1976; Smith, 1977). Studies of phoneme perception suggest that these sound-patterns are perceived "categorically." That is, humans (and other mammals, cf. Kuhl & Miller, 1975; Kuhl, 1978; 1985)[1] tend to "break up" the continuum of auditory input into "categories" of meaning. For example, a primary difference between /b/ plus a vowel and /p/ plus the same vowel is the onset of "voicing"—before or after release of air through the lips respectively. Within about 40 ms, anything "on one side" of a remarkably uniform boundary will be heard as /b/ and anything else (on the other side) as /p/. The area of ambiguity—the boundary—is much narrower, more like a range of 5 to 10 ms. A second cue, which helps to separate /p/ from /t/ identifies the "place" of articulation; in this example, at the lips or tongue-to-upper jaw ridge (See Eimas, 1985 for review).

When we attempt to understand speech, we focus upon these limited cues diagnostic of voice onset time, place of articulation, and so on, and ignore information that falls outside these boundaries—we perceive consonants categorically. We fail to discriminate differences such as voice-onset time *within* phoneme boundaries. (Comparable differences across the same boundaries or in noise are discriminable when one adopts a set for differences in the *sound* per se). Vowels admit more readily to sensitive acoustic discriminations. Nevertheless, in context, (i.e., a "word") they too are perceived nearly categorically (Liberman, Cooper, Shankweiler, & Studdert-Kennedy, 1967) and the range of their qualitative features can be understood in terms of the constraints imposed by our auditory systems (Lindblom, 1986).[2] Apparently, parts of the brain are specialized to respond to these sound configurations; some neural auditory processing mechanisms are selectively attuned to sound-patterns diagnostic of voice-onset time, and similar mechanisms exist for detecting the auditory correlates of place of articulation (Luria, 1980).

---

[1] The fact that other forms seem to have auditory "feature detectors" that respond categorically to the same kinds of auditory stimuli humans use in speech (phonemes) (e.g., Kuhl, 1978; 1985) has occasionally been cited to refute the idea that humans possess structures specialized for speech perception. This seems to miss the point of the principle opportunism in evolution: One could argue that these basic mammalian capacities have been co-opted to serve language perception as a result of the evolution language in *Homo*. Indeed, if we adopt a *non*linguistic "set" we can discriminate sounds which, if perceived as part of speech, would be perceived as members of the same class (see Kuhl, 1978).

[2] Our ability to ignore the semantically-irrelevant fact of individual differences in pitch may rest upon a capacity to use such sounds as /u/, /y/, and /w/ to gauge the size of a speaker's vocal tract. Presumably, that "knowledge" sets a rough baseline against which all other features are judged (Lieberman, 1975; 1984).

By at least the second month, infants are capable of making a wide variety of "categorical" phonemic discriminations comparable to those made across most human languages, not just those used by their native tongue (Eimas et al., 1971; Jusczyk, 1985). More important to our model are findings that the "categorical boundaries" for certain phonemes are slightly different across languages (Eimas, 1985) and that adults often have difficulties in detecting (as well as pronouncing, cf. Eimas, 1978; Guillery, 1986) phonemes specific to a foreign tongue (Jusczyk, 1985). Since infants do process phonemes categorically, one facet of language acquisition would seem to be the auditory-evoked functional validation of the mechanisms underlying phoneme-processing peculiar to their native tongue (and either the atrophy or—more likely—inhibition of neural structures subserving categorical perception of phoneme boundaries distinctive to other languages (Eimas & Miller, 1978; Jusczyk, 1985; Strange & Jenkins, 1978).

These phenomena provide yet another example of the adaptive, heterochronous development of subcomponents: Given the diversity of human languages, before one can speak, one must know "what" to say and "how" to say it, information that is obtained by listening. In short, by the time that they are just beginning to utter noncry vocalizations regularly, infants possess very well-developed auditory (speech) sound-processing capabilities. Consistent with our contention that integration of capacities often is delayed, phoneme perception (in speech) in 1-year-olds is *less* precise than their early phoneme-detection (Jusczyk, 1985; Werker & Tees, 1984).

In addition, by 5 to 6 months of age, babies can *visually* distinguish the difference between articulatory movements corresponding to such repeated consonant-vowel sounds as "mama," "vava," and "bebi" (MacKain, Studdert-Kennedy, Speiker, & Stern, 1983). These data suggest that, with relatively little postnatal audiovisual input, infants can acquire a visual appreciation of the kinds of movements that "go with" particular patterns of sound. The latter is particularly impressive if one considers how subtle the differences are between /m/, /v/, and /b/. Findings such as these strongly suggest that pre- or perinatal events may induce the development of biases to process some auditory (and perhaps visual) stimuli in such ways (see also Kuhl & Meltzoff, 1982).

### Speech Production

*Cooing.* Around the end of the second month, well after they are capable of discriminating a wide range of speech-sounds, babies begin to utter vowel-like "cooing" vocalizations. These utterances seem to be simple reactions to an adult's presence, specifically, the visual gestalt embodying eyes (Bloom, 1974; Bloom & Esposito, 1975).[3] Cooing is communicative only in the sense that it functions to involve caregivers in social interactions and thereby provide infants with needed stimulation. Indeed, parental cooing sometimes provides a stimulus for a regular series of exchanges in which both participants seem to "take turns" (Freedman, 1974). Whether we should ascribe conscious, purposeful, communicative intent to such infantile vocalizations seems doubtful, but they do get caregivers involved with infants at a time when such input may be important in maintaining further growth. Noncrying "fussiness" overlaps with the onset of cooing (Emde et al., 1976). Presumably, fussing signals some need and thereby summons company; subsequently, reactive cooing sustains contact. Somewhat later on, infants' vocal utterances become more integrated, and noncry vocalizations begin to occur during bouts of fussiness just before crying starts (Wolff, 1969). Perhaps the noncry, coo repertoire might be shifting from reactive control by mechanisms underlying social excitement to control by systems which involve appetitive or anticipatory elements.

*Babbling.* The next major phase of vocal development is the period of "babbling," which could be seen as another stage of organization. Here the repertoire of vowel-like cooing sounds expands with the addition of consonant-like sounds and, subsequently, consonant-vowel combinations. Unlike cooing, babbling is not primarily reactive; much occurs in the absence of adults (Jones & Moss, 1971). Hearing infants seem to monitor and repeat their own utterances; although deaf infants begin babbling at about the same age, their repertoires tend to be more restricted and their rates of babbling decline sooner (Lenneberg, Rebelsky, & Nichols, 1965). The most common "social" event is simultaneous adult-child vocalization (cf. Stern, Jaffe, Beebe, & Bennett, 1975).

The similarities between infantile babbling and the sounds used in adult languages make it tempting to consider this phase as an important step in the ontogeny of speech. However, there is some question as to whether bab-

---

[3] Several early studies of operant vocalization indicated increases in vocalization rates simply in response to an adult's presence (e.g., Weisberg, 1963). An ingenious series of experiments showed that the ability to see the adult's eyes was a crucial element in socially reinforcing babies' vocalizations with smiles, touching, and a "tsk, tsk" sound. If the adult wore glasses with opaque, skin-colored inserts, then the babies, although showing no distress, failed to alter their rates of babbling. When the inserts were life-sized color photographs of eyes, the "reinforcing" procedures were effective. Moreover, in a subsequent study, when 3-month-old babies received the "standard" smile, touch, "tsk-tsk" procedure, their rates of babbling increased *whether or not* these responses were contingent upon the babies' prior vocalizations. It seemed that *any* pattern of adult responsiveness (so long as the adult face-gestalt was "intact") could increase 3-month-old infants' vocal output (Bloom, 1975; Bloom & Erickson, 1971; Bloom & Esposito, 1975). In short, although adults can affect the rate of infant vocalization it is by no means clear that the principles of (operant) conditioning are necessary or sufficient to account for the growth and development of such behavior.

bling, although similar to speech, is a direct precursor of spoken language. Sound spectrographic analyses of babies' babbling indicate that such utterances bear only slight resemblances to speech per se (Palermo, 1975). More importantly, babbling apparently does not directly facilitate later, voluntary control over vocalizations. According to McNeill (1970), the vowels and consonants *first* uttered are among the *last* organized into a linguistic system. Moreover, despite the facts that when they are babbling, babies do utter a wide variety of consonant-vowel combinations, and seem to be able to control them at least to the extent of repeating strings, when actually trying to pronounce *words*, infants' and toddlers' voluntary, combinatorial repertoires are quite restricted.

In addition, although the linguistic environment of infants may influence the rates of some articulatory activities, there exist cross-cultural similarities in the order of later acquisition of voluntary control of phonemes (Jakobson, 1968; See Dale, 1976 for review). Therefore, the early motor "fine-tuning" occurring in this phase would seem, at most, to involve the validation and maintenance of individual articulatory coordinations (Palermo, 1975) or vocal "templates" (Smith, 1977). Babbling does not seem to facilitate the development of voluntary, integrated articulatory coordinations.

Whatever the case, one or more functional reorganizations in the vocal articulatory realm occur during the first 3 to 6 months. There are shifts from vowel-like, socially-evoked cooing to coordination of vowel and consonant clusters in the state-mediated fuss-cry complex, to the "autonomous" or circular-reactive control of vowel-consonant babbling. It would seem that there is a simultaneous elaboration/emancipation of cry-type utterances (fussing) from simple state-dependence to more anticipatory, goal-directed activity.

*Substrates.* Studies of the neurological substrates of adult human speech provide evidence for the existence of multiple components underlying language production. Speech involves a variety of activities such as the choice of words, and the actual articulation/synchronization of the words themselves. These processes apparently are regulated by separate cortical structures typically located in the left cerebral hemisphere. (Interestingly enough, intonation and the control of pitch are apparently controlled by other centers, perhaps in the right cerebral hemisphere cf. Luria, 1980.) In very general terms, at least two "systems" governing production can be distinguished: The first involves the motor control of speech per se, the "final" motor pathway; the second system seems to be more concerned with the variable *sequencing* of movements. When areas in the latter system were temporarily blocked, people could repeat ongoing facial movements, but could not vary them during the period of stimulation (Ojemann & Mateer, 1979; Whitaker & Ojemann, 1977).

Among the several pathologies of language that have been identified, not only are there apparent inabilities to "think" of words but also to utilize auditory feedback to *correct oneself* after a mispronunciation (Whitaker & Ojemann, 1977). Difficulty in self-correction could represent deficiencies in several (hypothetical) subsystems: There must be a translation from one's intent to the actual muscular activities forming the utterance. Then, some perceptual mechanism must be used for comparing what actually was uttered with one's intended output. At this point, the perception and production systems must be interrelated. Indeed, a study of the effects on articulation of habituation as a result of listening to repetition of voiceless consonant-vowel ("pi"; "ti") and voiced consonant-vowel ("bi"; "di") combinations suggests that there exist processing mechanisms common to both the articulatory and perceptual systems (Cooper & Lainsten, 1974, see also Luria, 1980).

In sum, the development of communicative vocalizations seems to proceed in a series of steps in which the organization and control of sound-making is restructured several times. In addition, studies of the neural structures underlying control of speech are consistent with our contention that complex behaviors (functional systems) involve the coordination of semi-independent, contributory "components."

### Language Acquisition

Although languages clearly differ, they represent restricted sets of conventions which are drawn from what might be characterized as the hominid pool of linguistic potentials. Thus, the problem that young children face, although formidable, is not insurmountable. As Casagrande (1966, p. 290) put it, they have to choose from among "universal alternatives"—limited sets of solutions to the problem of communicating meanings to other people. The process is active; children choose and, in a sense, re-create their native languages.

If development reflects a series of stages of organization, each of which is designed to both permit survival in an average, expectable environment, and to prepare the growing organism to meet future demands, then we might expect infants to have the potential to discriminate "acceptable" phonemic combinations and intonation patterns from unacceptable or "meaningless" ones. We might also expect them to be particularly sensitive to these privileged sound-patterns when emitted by caregivers in contexts when the infant's attention is already captured by objects or events, what Roger Brown (1958) called the "original word game"—in which adults spend much time "naming" things for babies or asking them to name objects.

*Controlling input.* Not only do very young infants selectively attend to speech-patterns they heard *in utero* (DeCasper & Spence, 1986), but by the age of 3 months, they perform operant looking behavior in order to gain access to recorded speech, and they respond at a greater rate to obtain exposure to normal as opposed to random word-order (Jones-Molfese, 1975).

A consideration of the kinds of utterances infants and toddlers evoke from caregivers and the effects of toddlers' verbal competence on the complexity of caregiver speech exemplify the ways in which the young may provoke the input they require. In almost all cultures, caregivers use "baby talk," employing exaggerated expressions and intonation shifts (in an unusually high pitch) when speaking to preverbal babies, all of which seem to capture infants' attention (Blount, 1981; Fernald, 1985). The fact that infants' production tends to lag behind their understanding could be seen as another example of developmental asynchronies which facilitate the acquisition of the right input at the right time: Snow (1972) and Phillips (1973) found that the complexity of parents' speech was partially guided by their children's grammatical competencies. Perhaps youngsters' early productive limitations act to guarantee that they will receive at *least* enough exposure to simplified and direct utterances to consolidate their understanding of the more obvious grammatical principles. Although "telegraphic" commands from adults are most effective early, more fully elaborated directives subsequently become most effective in controlling child behavior—even though the youngsters are still unlikely to produce similarly complex utterances themselves (Brown, 1973). Again, it would seem that youngsters may actually control the input they receive.

*Decoding syntax.* In the acquisition of syntactical knowledge, children are selective. Given that languages represent more or less coordinated subsets of an already-limited pool of soundmaking devices, by selectively attending to a relatively restricted set of defining features, infants apparently discover inductively how meaning is to be conveyed. From an analysis of the "grammars" of young children growing up in a large number of different linguistic environments, Slobin (1973) has suggested a set of seven rules or "operating principles" by which youngsters might develop an understanding of their native language. Although these hypothetical algorithms cannot account for all instances of children's apparent grammatical development, they do seem to be applicable to a wide variety of observations and clearly support the thesis that a relatively restricted set of cues can suffice to guide a child to the discovery of the major syntactical conventions of languages. (See Table 1).

Subsequent, more detailed, prospective cross-language analyses have yielded results which support a number of these hypothetical principles. Although not all of these principles apply equally well to both decoding and encoding (Bowerman, 1981; Slobin, 1982), a relatively circumscribed set of operations can account for many facets of language acquisition. Given species-specific operating principles in conjunction with restrictions

**Table 8-1.   Slobin's Hypothetical Operating Principles for the Discovery of Grammatical Rules**

A. *Pay attention to the ends of words.* Derived from an apparently widespread tendency for early mastery locative marker at the *end* of words relative to those located before them (as in the English prepositions "to," "of," etc.)

B. *The phonological forms of words can be systematically modified.* Derived from the tendency for suffixes to be acquired readily.

C. *Pay attention to the order of words and morphemes.* Derived from a tendency of children to use word orders resembling those of adult speech—where word-order is "specified"—and to misinterpret special cases that deviate from the modal pattern.

D. *Avoid interruption or rearrangement of linguistic units.* Derived from the observations that "standard" forms are first used to express meanings that require a rearrangement of elements, e.g., the English inversion of subject- (auxiliary) verb order. Similarly, children tend to employ "continuous" morphemes before complex structures, e.g., English-speaking children's use of the progressive verb tense ending "ing" before the grammatically necessary auxiliary verb and the early development of negatives by prefacing a declarative with "no."

E. *Underlying semantic relations should be marked overtly and clearly.* Derived from the tendencies of children to pick up what seems to be the more "perceptually salient" verbal markers earlier than those which are more subtle; to "overgeneralize" the use of markers, e.g., "goed;" to fail to use contractions when acquiring a form that permits them, and to understand better when they hear the full form in complex sentences.

F. *Avoid exceptions.* Another principle suggested by overgeneralizations and the fact that these "errors" in the use of semantic markers seem to follow a regular progression until the adult form is mastered; on average, children acquire more generally-applicable grammatical rules before special cases.

G. *The use of grammatical markers should make semantic sense.* Derived from observations that, when selection of an "appropriate" inflection for a function is "arbitrary," children tend to use a single form, e.g., ignoring gender although the selection of the "wrong" form is always from within the appropriate class. Correspondingly, when rules are semantically consistent, they tend to be applied early and correctly.

on the form of adult phonology and grammars (i.e., "language universals," cf. Greenberg, 1966), the child's success in the apparently overwhelming task of language-acquisition becomes not only understandable, but, to some degree, predictable.

*Sentence production.* Consistent with our contention that development involves transactions between organism and environment that are constrained by the phenotype, in all languages, it appears that toddlers discover and employ certain ways of expressing grammatical relations, often quite different from parroted fragments of adult speech. Even at the level of two-word utterances, children create essentially unique "sentences" which are nevertheless consistent with *their own* "grammars." In linguists' terms, some of their languages even at this level is "productive" despite vocabularies that may include fewer than 100 words. When new meanings are intended, there may be a brief period during which a variety of productive strategies is apparently tried out, but then children generally settle on one way of expressing that meaning—at least until a new level of grammatical sophistication is attained (Brown, 1973; Dale, 1976).

The sequence in which children master new grammatical constructions is also consistent with the idea that development occurs in a series of stages, and that, with reorganization (to accommodate new elements), there may be a transient phase of apparent behavioral regression.

As children begin to produce more complex utterances in which they mark the tense of verbs, number of referents, and so on (Brown, 1973), forms which are clearly in their repertoires do not always appear where their use is mandatory according to adult grammar. At each level, it seems that newly-acquired skills tax children so that, even though they know several ways to shade meaning, they are unable to combine them all in a single utterance. Thus, the idea that children learn "rules" for making sentences must be tempered by the recognition that if they do so, they do not (can not?) always utilize all of the rules that apply in a given context.

Consistent with our model of species-specific phenotypic structure constraining growth (and the quality of organization), Slobin (1973) has proposed the following universal sequence in the linguistic marking of "semantic notions," such as tense: (a) no markers, (b) application only in limited cases, (c) "overgeneralization," for example, extension of the principle to irregular forms and exaggeration of the form, (d) adult-like usage. For example, he contrasted the sequence of past-tense inflections observed in the irregular English verb "to break" with the regular verb "to drop" as follows: (a) "break, drop" (b) "broke, drop" (c-1) "breaked, dropped" (c-2) "breakted, dropted" (d) "broke, dropped." This sequence is not limited to English; whenever languages lend themselves to such errors, they tend to be made in this same way.

In English, Brown (1973) has identified some 14 "morphemes" modulating or focusing the meanings expressed in simple sentences. In their average order of mastery they are: (1) the present progressive, "-ing" (2 *and* 3) "in" and "on' (4) plural, "-s" (5) past *ir*regular, "broke" (6) possessive (John's) (7) uncontractible copula, "was" (as in "it was small") (8) articles "a," "the" (9) past *regular*, "-ed" (10) third person regular, "es" (as in "goes") (11) third person irregular, "went" (12) uncontractible auxiliary, "was" (as in "I was hungry") (13) contractible copula, "-'s" (as in "*it's* small) (14) contractible auxiliary, "-'m" (as in "I'm hungry").

Consistent with our view that species-typical phenotypic alternatives are evoked by a specific set of inputs, the most striking feature of this list is that unrelated children acquire the same elements *in the same order* although at quite different ages. The order of acquisition is not related to the frequency with which caregivers utter these morphemes. For example, articles are the elements most frequently uttered by parents, yet they are acquired 8th; the next most frequenty-uttered elements among parents is the contractible copula; children master it next to *last*. (See Brown 1973, p. 358). Whereas Brown's (1973) ranking of "semantic complexity" of parental grammatical constructions yields some positive correlations with order of acquisition of these morphemes, this factor alone is inadequate to explain such observations as the much greater accuracy of children in identifying possessives in more "complex," elliptical forms ("that's John's") than the "full" possessive ("that's John's ball"). As Brown (1973) notes, the elliptical form has the advantage that the possessive marker *ends* the utterance and thus seems to conform with Slobin's first principle.

Brown also points out that: (a) the grammatical *omissions* of semantically modulated sentences do not correspond closely to parental omissions, (b) the order of acquisition of modulatory morphemes is essentially independent of adult frequency of usage and only moderately correlated with estimates of semantic complexity. Clearly, children do not simply mimic parental practice. Nor are they operating on simple feedback principles— "success" doesn't guarantee stability. For example, when the regular past tense inflection is mastered, it *supercedes* the irregular past which had been mastered and effectively utilized earlier.

The most obvious, common denominator accounting for the within-language commonalities is the language itself. If youngsters decode languages according to something akin to Slobin's "operating principles," they might be expected to proceed similarly so long as they are presented with similar "texts." In short, for language-acquisition, the form of an utterance may be more salient than its frequency.

*Syntactical elaborations.* Subsequent grammatical attainments provide further examples of developmental reorganizations. English depends upon word order to convey meaning, and several constructions such as elaborated negatives and questions involve re-ordering of elements in a sentence and the use of auxiliaries. Therefore, mastery of a new level of complexity is involved in forming sentences of this kind. This step is not, however, predicated upon complete mastery and coordination of all the grammatical elements incorporated in the preceding phases. Rather, a reasonable familiarity with the principles of semantic modulation permits the effective communication of a range of new meanings and moves toward expression of more complex ideas—or more clearly conveyed meanings of "old" themes (Brown, 1973).

To develop many negative statements in English, the auxiliary verbs "to have," and "do" must be mastered as well as the modifiers "some," "any," "none," and so on. McNeill (1970) points out that, whereas adults would say "I [do] want *some* x" and "I don't want *any* x," children, after mastering the auxiliary verb "do," say "I don't want some x"—a negation with the *affirmative* modifier "some." The next step, according to McNeill, is a double negative in which "some" is replaced by "no" yielding "I don't want no x." The adult use of "any" is attained only much later. Insofar as the samples from which these observations were drawn were middle-class families in which parents did *not* use double negatives, we again witness a progression in which various elements of the well-formed negative decla-ration are discovered and mastered more or less one at a time according to the child's own understanding. For the young child, "any" apparently takes on negative meaning and is first expressed as "no." Only later does "any" come to be used productively in the appropriate contexts.

To encode new, or expanded meanings, the grammatical units often must also be restructured in "violation" of Slobin's (1973) operating prin-ciple D, "avoid interruptions" (Table 1). For example, questions develop through a series of stages. Whereas simple questions in the early phases of grammatical development can be communicated via rising intonation, the full grammatical form of most questions in English involves not only mastery of the auxiliary verb, but, in addition, inversion of subject-verb word order of the declarative form. Menyuk (1969) outlines a series of steps that children seemed to follow: (a) declaratives with rising intona-tion, (b) declaratives with the auxiliary, and then (c) inverted auxiliary verb order.

The "wh-" questions (who, what, when, etc.) evolve similarly except that the "wh" element also must be mastered. At first, there tends to be the addition of the "wh" element to an abbreviated form of a declarative sen-tence (even when the declaratives themselves are more fully developed), for example, "where the kitty?" Then the auxiliary becomes utilized, but in declarative form, with the "wh" and intonation markers "where the kitty did go?" The next steps involve both mastery of a new element and a redundant overgeneralization ("where did the kitty goed?") and finally, the fully grammatical form ("where did the kitty go?").

As in the case of negation, the initial movement toward a new gram-matical form, adding the new "wh" element, seems to overload the sys-tem, causing children to regress to a more primitive sentence form. As each step becomes more fully consolidated ("wh," then auxiliary), the form of the whole declarative utterance "regains" its previously attained elaboration, the auxiliary gets added, and so forth (Menyuk, 1969). If a strong reductionist viewpoint can be sustained, we may be witnessing a process wherein a selection from among alternative nervous pathways controlling language is occurring and a subset of possible decoding/encod-ing systems is facilitated and/or validated at the expense of others.

The phase of grammatical acquisition Brown (1973) calls "embedding" represents yet another new level of complexity. In this stage, the child is using one sentence as a component of another one, for example, as subject, object, and so on. Although the first instances of such coordinations typically involve only two sentences, by kindergarten, four or more simple "sentences" may appear as embedded constituents of a single sentence. At this stage, further violations of principle "D," ("avoid interruptions") occur. According to Slobin (1973), the first "embeddings" often appear "external" to the core sentence, for example, "I know what is that" or "I saw the cat who had kittens, she stole the fish." Only later do children "move" the elements within the sentence, for example, "I know what that is"; "I saw the cat who had kittens steal the fish." In the latter constructions, children seem to have difficulty in choosing the correct "wh" form, and "what" often seems to serve across the board, for example, "The cat what had kittens...," (See Menyuk, 1969).

Again, the appearance of these new grammatical forms is not dependent upon complete mastery of previous acquisitions. Although possessives, number, and tense first become marked in the modulated utterances of children during an earlier stage, even as they begin to form grammatically more complex utterances, youngsters still make errors involving the use of such morphemes. Omission of obligate marking tends to be the most common form of error, but children still tend to substitute inappropriate markers. Especially common are overextensions of the regular inflection to the base form of irregular nouns, for example, "mens," and verbs, for example, "comed," or to their inflected forms, for example, "came med" or "peopleses" (Menyuk, 1969). Although closely approximating adult constructions, such errors clearly indicate that children are doing much more than simply parroting adult exemplars.

As coordinated sentences appear in children's speech, the youngsters can be said to "have" all the basic grammatical structures of the language. However, for some years, they lack the mastery and variety of semantic elements required to generate an adult-like range of utterances. Moreover, occasional violations of tense or pronoun restrictions imply that forming these constructions may require so much attention (memory load?) that "slippage" occurs in other aspects of the sentence. Still, some time after they reach the age of 4 years, many children seem to increase the rate at which they employ complex constructions such as negation, the use of the auxiliary "be," contractions, and conjunctions. After the age of 4 years, many children use complex sentences with subordinate clauses (Brannon, 1968).

The facts that most youngsters become *capable* of complex constructions between the age of 3 and 4 years, but that they do not employ them regularly and seem to produce them only with some difficulty, are compatible with the model of growth proposed here. We may be witnessing the outcomes of phases of validation, maintenance and integration of the neural substrates for encoding and decoding routines. It may not be too extreme to suggest that if one grows up in a particular linguistic environment, certain language-related subsets of analyzers and motor "command" patterns become functionally validated at the expense of a wider array corresponding to the range of human languages. The fact that adults can learn to speak another tongue argues against total involution or irreversible inhibition, although some people never lose their accents, and many never seem to master all the subtleties of a new set of grammatical conventions.

### Linguistic Awareness

Increased capacity to use new acquisitions appropriately does not mean that children, or adults, for that matter, are consciously aware of all the nuances of grammatical usage. Most grammatical rules or principles (as currently elaborated by linguists) do not apply without exception; there always seems to be a special case (e.g, Menyuk, 1977). Perhaps this is why youngsters who otherwise seem to have acquired a grammatical rule occasionally violate it. The typical pattern is (language) comprehension preceding sentence production and grammatical competence, in turn, preceding reflective awareness of syntactical rules. This sequence might be likened to Piaget's (1962) sequence of sensorimotor intelligence→intuitive operations→concrete operations. In each case, children behave in such a way that they can meet the demands of the relevant stage(s). In both, also, elements of reflective "understanding" and action develop more or less independently. Ultimately, these elements fuse, culminating in a reflective awareness of processes that previously had been carried out effectively without benefit or much apparent integration. According to Dale (1976), although both comprehension and production might be described as rule-bound, the rules governing both processes at any point in time are not necessarily identical.

Just as we "know" how to walk without consciously trying to orchestrate the movements of our limbs, changes in trunk posture, and so on, so children know how to extract meaning and, often somewhat less well, how to encode it. They are much less cognizant that (or why) they do it in a particular way.

*Pragmatics.* Yet they do begin to appreciate certain conventions at this age—those that have to do with finding one's place in society. By 2½ to 3 years of age, social exchanges in young children's peer groups are ordered according to a pecking hierarchy, and by 4 or 5 years of age a variety of dimensions of "social rank" can be distinguished (Sluckin & Smith, 1977). Between 3 and 5 years of age, children also are becoming capable of (correctly) answering questions about "who could" make certain kinds of demands or requests (Bowerman, 1981). This relatively precocious recognition of "proper forms" of address, command, and so on, provide another example of heterochrony. Whereas 3- and 4-year-olds cannot comply with requests to identify *errors* in grammatical constructions, they can identify inappropriate *usage* of perfectly grammatical constructions (Bowerman, 1981). This phenomenon would support the idea that our conscious, reflective awareness is typically focused upon cues needed for the fine tuning of our social relations. The ability to communicate verbally (or by gesture) is so basic and perhaps made possible by the activity of such a limited set of filters that we need not reflect upon it (unless we make our livings as students of development). However, correct forms of address—lexical and conventional variations—may be so varied and so crucial to survival or at least for achieving reproductive advantage as to put a premium on reflective awareness.

The timing of these sensitivities (as well as the very rapid rates of gain in productive linguistic competence) seems to coincide with the achievement of a reasonable level of locomotor competence—a level of competence often associated with emancipation from close and continuous adult protection/supervision. Perhaps the rate of language development is not so much a *reflection* of overall neuromotor "maturation" (cf. Lenneberg, 1967), as an evolutionary *product* of the rates at which the other capacities for independent action develop. If so, we would have another example of the evolutionary timing of independent developmental events to anticipate the demands of the average, stage-specific environment.

### Inputs

This raises the question of identifying the necessary inputs. Hearing children in all cultures acquire two-word "sentences" in much the same way, and they later commit similar errors such as the overextension of rules governing the syntax of regular verb forms (Blount, 1981). Such uniformity in the face of diversity may be explained in terms of a species-specific set of principles (cf. Slobin, 1973) or speech-analyzing algorithms in the speech-processing components of the auditory system.

*Induction.* Essentially normal language competencies develop in children who are blind from birth (Lenneberg, 1967), children who are reared in institutions and thereby deprived of the playful give-and-take sometimes considered to lay the groundwork for conversational exchanges (Bruner, 1977), and children who receive relatively little conversational banter relative to their interests (Greenbaum & Landau, 1977; Provence & Lipton, 1962; Tizard, Cooperman, Joseph, & Tizard, 1972). With very little focused input from adults, young children may attempt to devise or elaborate their own verbal signaling systems, for example, twins (Jespersen, 1925, cited by Eibl-Eibesfeldt, 1970; Luria & Yudovich, 1959). Expression of the potential to develop syntactic competence does not require auditory input. Goldin-Meadow and Feldman (1977) observed spontaneous generation of sign-*combinations* among 17- to 49-month-old deaf children whose parents had been advised against teaching them sign language. (Syntactic competence appears to be independent of the mode by which it is expressed, although the underlying mechanisms are located in the same hemisphere as those subserving articulation. cf. Damasio, Bellugi, Damasio, Poizner, & Van Gilder, 1986). Thus, whatever underlies these developments must be general (ubiquitous) features of human childrearing environments (See also Goldin-Meadow & Mylander, 1983).

Additional data support the idea that the conditions inducing the expression of the substrates for language are very general. Davis (1964) observed two young children who were severely neglected. One of them was reared essentially in isolation until the age of 6 years; she was severely retarded physically and behaviorally upon discovery. By the age of 10, although in delicate health (she died before age 11), she was speaking at the level of a normal 3-year-old. The second child was somewhat more fortunate. She was imprisoned in a dark room with her mother who was a deaf mute and they communicated by gesture. After this child had overcome the initial shock of freedom (and the attention of educational specialists), she acquired verbal language at an accelerated rate; she was "putting sentences together" within three months of her first communicative vocalizations. Davis likened her recovery to the catch-up growth in body weight that follows an illness.

From Davis' (1964) first case it seems that just enough stimulation to sustain a minimum of behavioral development suffices to maintain the substrates underlying a recognition of the possibility of communicating verbally and for decoding speech. Given someone with whom to interact, even if only by means of gesture in an otherwise stimulus-deprived environment (as in the case of Davis' second subject), some children may be able not only to retain the potential to decode and use speech, but also to acquire a "sense" of grammar which can be transferred from the visual-manual to the auditory-vocal realm quite rapidly.

*Facilitation.* For *speech*, aside from a corpus of more- or-less relevant input (cf. Tizard et al., 1972), caregiver behavior may facilitate the early use of language. Although it is unlikely that some of the fundamental skills underlying verbal exchanges *must* be acquired in the context of playful mother-infant interactions (Schaffer, 1977; Lewis & Freedle, 1973), other people must provide both models of semantics and syntax and feedback with regard to one's utterances (Dale, 1976; Malrieu, 1962). Rather general inputs may facilitate the use of words.[4] A study of the correlates of adopted infants' language development in the first year showed that adoptive mothers' tendencies to imitate their infants' vocalizations and to respond contingently to these utterances were associated with their infants' productive vocabularies (Hardy-Brown, Plomin, & De Fries, 1981). Thus maternal responsiveness may be one of the features important for early progress. (See also Dodd, 1972; Wachs, Uzgiris, & Hunt, 1971; Yarrow et al., 1972). However, even these findings may be confounded by (as yet unanalyzed) differences in the ability of infants to engage the interest of their caregivers (Hardy-Brown et al., 1981).

Over a wide range of inputs, variations in vocal or other social contingencies probably account for only a small proportion of the variance in the propensity to communicate verbally (cf. Greenbaum & Landau, 1977). For children with "average" endowments, the "lower" threshold for communicative input is probably quite low (Bloom, 1983; Tulkin, 1977).

*Integration.* Some caregiving practices may have more effects on the *use* of output. Both Wachs et al. (1971) and Yarrow et al. (1972) noted variations in 7- to 11-month-old infants' imitative and spontaneous (excitement-related?) vocalizations that were associated with both caregiver responsiveness to the babies' crying/non-cry vocalizing, and to intensity of ambient stimulation. Perhaps the second six months is a period in which the kinds of care received affect the *ways* in which one's later-developing communicative abilities will be employed. In contrast with home-reared babies, even after they had been placed in adoptive homes, orphanage-reared children studied by Provence and Lipton (1962) failed to *use* their language skills to obtain relief or assistance from caregivers. Children around the age of 8 or 9 months do seem to attempt to employ more complex, nonverbal vocalizations to engage adults in "dialogues" (Malrieu, 1962). Thus, this may be the age during which infants get the idea that "words" have obvious referents; they will look toward their mothers when asked "where's mama" (Dale, 1976).

From the work of Provence and Lipton (1962), the period between 9 and 24 months of age may be critical in determining whether youngsters

---

[4] Nelson (1981) suggested that language acquisition involves some elements of gestalt, wholistic perception as well as linear, sequential analysis of phonemic/semantic elements. Insofar as the children of deaf, signing parents quickly learn to sign (and to use "syntax") and the elements of meaning in sign-language are conveyed by total (gestalt) configurations of the simultaneously-occurring facets of the gestures, it seems that youngsters are capable of approaching the problem of communicating *via* several routes. Thus, we must be cautious in ascribing the development of an underlying ability to communicate symbolically according to "rules" to the development of any *one set* of decoding or encoding strategies. In adults, at least, the ability to decode or encode in a language-like manner may remain intact even if the individual is almost totally incapable of understanding or producing natural language (Baker, Berry, Gardner, Nurif, Davis, & Veroff, 1975).

will actively enlist the assistance/attention of others when in need, or seek to share/confirm an experience. Children who have been more or less the passive recipients of the early ministrations—or intrusions—of caregivers seem to use speech in a much more reactive manner than youngsters who have experienced socially contingent care (Lazar, Tanvaroff, Nir, Freund, O'Reilly, Kirkpatrick, & Kapoor, 1983). In Western, industrial societies, "competent" youngsters come from families in which young children's on-going activities become the focus for caregivers commentary, encourage-ment, or demonstrations (White et al., 1979; Schaffer, 1977).

## LANGUAGE AND THOUGHT

Cognition has been mentioned as a factor influencing children's produc-tion and comprehension of language. In this section I will argue that the ontogenies of spoken language and thought are relatively independent and provide an example of the way in which semi-independent *systems* can become reorganized in development.

### Topic and Vehicle of Expression

Cross-cultural studies of emerging grammars reveal both similarities and apparently language-related differences. The topics about which children speak at this stage seem to be almost identical across societies, reflecting toddlers' universal (cf. Dasen & Heron, 1981; Price-Williams, 1981) sen-sorimotor understanding of their worlds.

*Topics.* Brown (1973, pp. 189–198) lists some 11 meanings that were re-corded in most studies of early child grammars. Brown's analysis suggests that they can be understood as reflecting toddlers' newly-developed appre-ciation for the premanence of objects in space and time and of events that befall them, that is, the "topics" about which toddlers speak. Of these 11 meanings, at least five were recorded in samples of children's early utter-ances drawn from eight or more of a total of 11 different languages.

"Nomination" or simple naming, for example, "this [is] x," was the most commonly encountered form, apparently expressed in all languages. A second, frequently encountered meaning across unrelated languages was "agent and action"—an "animate" noun and a verb, for example, "mommy push," "car go." Third, "action and object," that is, someone or some-thing suffering a change of state, for example, "[he] cut pie." A fourth relation expressed by children in all language groups at this stage was "possessor and possession," for example, "mommy['s] sock," but including as well meanings related to part-whole relations such as "kitty['s] tail." A final semantically-expressed relationship for which the evidence strongly suggested universality was dubbed "entity and attribute," for example, "little dog." In addition, in most languages, questions were clearly marked. In English, occurrence, non-occurrence, possession, attributes, and locations of objects or events are expressed early, clearly, and consistently (in context) by toddlers using no more than two words.

At least two sets of phenotypic factors seem to underlie and constrain what children are likely to discover about language: First we have something akin to Slobin's (1973) operating principles and second, given that they recognize that vocalizations convey meaning, children are constrained by what they *understand*. Presumably, the most "meaningful" semantic/syntactic inputs for infants aside from simple naming will relate to the more basic facets of a sensorimotor appreciation of the world—something akin to the "concepts" of: (a) (object) *permanence;* (b) (primitive) *quantity,* for example, "more"; (c) *agency* (being a cause or actor); (d) *possession,* in the sense of ownership; (e) *attribute* in the sense of size, and so on; (f) *negation,* and (g) *"location."* One would not expect children between 1 and 3 years of age to be sensitive to a much wider range of ideas/concepts (cf. Piaget, 1952; 1954; 1962).

*Vehicle.* As their intellectual understanding increases, young children actively seek the means for expressing their new ideas. Words and grammatical forms that previously had little apparent meaning for youngsters —despite having been encountered frequently—begin to take on new significance as their referents become clear (Bowerman, 1981; Slobin, 1982).

According to Bower (1982) and Spelke (1985), one of the major problems infants have in gaining an adult-like sense of the permanence of physical objects involves an appreciation of (relative) location, that one object can be "in," "on," or "under" another one. It may thus be no accident that the locatives "under" and "beside" are mastered after "in" and "on," and that "between" is correctly used even later (Slobin, 1982). The idea to be conveyed apparently precedes mastery of the means for conveying it. For example, the concept of object permance is usually acquired before the use of prepositions.

Moreover, when English-speaking children begin to discover the use of prepositions as markers for location, they tend to mix them up so that "in" may be used for "on" or "under." However, articles or conjunctions, or other elements belonging to different parts of speech are *not* used in these contexts. Youngsters get the idea of prepositions-as-locatives and try to use them before mastering all the forms of expression (Brown, 1973; Bowerman, 1981; Slobin, 1982). Such errors are committed by children from well-educated, middle-class families whose parents do not model or encourage incorrect usages. Thus, early grammatical constructions must be self-generated on the basis of the children's current understanding of how (previously understood) relationships can be expressed.

Just as relative location is difficult for toddlers to express, other comparative relationships such as "more" or "less" are treated as if they were functionally identical by 3½- to 4½-year olds (Donaldson & Balfour, 1968). Children seem to know that quantity is involved, but *relative* magnitude is difficult to deal with. Spatio-temporal order poses similar difficulties. Dale (1976) lists four stages in the comprehension of "before" and "after": (a) Children focus on word order to determine which element mentioned should precede or follow; (b) They correctly interpret "before" with no apparent change in the cues used to determine what comes "after"; (c) Then, almost paradoxically, they seem to treat "after" as a synonym for "before"; (d) Finally, they recognize them as semantic opposites.

The communication of negatives may also provide an example of language (the vehicle) following thought (the topic). In English-speaking toddlers' two-word utterances, negative sentences are initially formed by simply inserting a negative element ("no"; "allgone"). Negatives usually simply express nonexistence, and "no" by itself is used to express rejection or, less frequently, nonexistence or denial. In subsequent stages of grammatical development, more complex forms develop in essentially the same order as they appeared at the two-word stage: First, nonexistence; next, rejection, and then denial. In subsequent stages, the constructions of English-speaking children tend to change from negations of the subject, "nonexistence," to predicate negation, and eventually to inclusion of the subject and an elaborated predicate which includes the (negated) verb. As negative forms become more elaborated, children "work up" more complex expressions of rejection and denial via the syntactic form already utilized to express nonexistence (cf. Bloom, 1970).

When one ponders this sequence, it seems that children's reflective awareness (preoccupations?) are among the limiting factors in determining what kinds of ideas will be expressed in sentence form. One needn't ponder the "meaning" of the impulse to reject something, and a simple "no!" usually expresses the situation clearly. Hence, one might not expect much need to develop more complex routines for getting the point across. The nonexistence of something requires some thought—an idea of the "thing" not present—and a procedure whereby that referent is specified. To the extent that "no" suffices for rejection, and occurrence/nonexistence are subject to conscious reflection, nonoccurrence might be first expressed. Denial, as Bloom (1970) points out, is more complex yet. Denial involves a referent expressed in *another's* utterance and thus a decoding of that statement before the syntactic expression of denial can be encoded.

In general, the sequence of acquisition is (a) Decoding and use of certain grammatical constructions in specific (concrete) situations followed by (b) an apparent recognition of the (grammatical) rules underlying such constructions and, finally, (c) the employment of this knowledge in more abstract cases (Menyuk, 1977). This sequence of initially restricted application of grammatical principles to concrete situations, rule-recognition, and finally, general usage may represent a parallel to the Piagetian notion of "horizontal décalage" and our model of functional reorganization.

If one peruses the sentence "types" listed by Brown (1973), in the earliest stages of grammatical acquisition, the marked forms are the affirmative and declarative; the interrogative, imperative, and negative are less well-formed. At first this would seem surprising; one might expect that children would employ their new communicative capacities primarily to express their needs and desires rather than to remark upon (their understanding of) situations or name objects. They do, but they still rely upon the more "basic" mode—crying—when they are in need.

Much like other skills, whether walking or manipulation, a period of exercise—more or less "for its own sake"—precedes the full, instrumental deployment of a new acquisition and probably serves to validate and integrate the structures underlying a competency. For example, although speech is an effective medium-range mode of communication in open spaces, toddlers playing in parks seem to restrict their conversations with their mothers to those moments when they are in close proximity (Anderson, 1972). One might almost say that, born of cognitive process, language initially is employed in the service of knowledge, knowledge of language itself, as well as the child's relations with objects and other persons.

*Questions.* In line with the idea that early language is as much or more a means for gaining as expressing information, it is interesting to note that young children begin to ask "wh" questions before they seem to be capable of answering them. This could be an exception to the notion that comprehension precedes production in that questions are asked more or less properly but not answered (Dale, 1976). However, it may be one thing for children to ask about something already salient in their own minds and quite another to reply to someone else's query. A reply may necessitate their adopting an entirely new focus or train of thought. In addition, before one can assume that children cannot understand what response is required by a question, one must be able to show that they do, in fact, have (a) the information called for and (b) the grammatical competence to express it.[5]

*Grammatical knowledge.* Even after the fundamental routines for conveying meaning are available to children, much of their further linguistic progress must await their understanding of *concepts* or relations to which

---

[5] We should also be cautious in assuming we know the ends questions serve for young children. It often seems that many forms, notably "why," are employed more as means of eliciting a response per se than as a source of specific information. If some of our functional interpretations of filial "attachment" behavior in early childhood are accurate, many early questions may simply be used to gauge whether caregivers are monitoring their charges and to ensure adult attention.

words refer. It seems that much of the preschool child's grammatical "knowledge" is subliminal. For example, Bloom (1975) points out that, although young children "recognize" parts of speech (when they substitute prepositions, pronouns, and so on, they always do so *within* the same semantic class), this "knowledge" has no effect on their mnemonic word-associations. Moreover, despite the fact that 4- and 5-year-olds may "correct" a grammatically flawed sentence when attempting to *recall* it verbatim, they appear to be unable to comply when they are directly requested to identify what is "wrong" or "funny" about that sentence. Although they possess some very real linguistic sophisication, children this age are still captured by meaning—or the decoding process—and apparently cannot attend to both the message and the means for conveying it. In terms of our model, they have not yet integrated these functions.

### Egocentric Speech

The onset and course of egocentric speech seems to track this emerging integration of function. Piaget (1928) explained the occurrence of apparently undirected comments made by young children as representing their "egocentrism," the inability to realize that others' attention might be directed toward different phenomena. He thought that, by 7 or 8 years of age, most children had come to realize that others did not automatically share the same focus. This realization caused them to adjust their commentary accordingly. However, Vygotsky (1962) pointed out that, although the frequency of "egocentric" utterances declines as children approached 7 years of age, the idiosyncratic nature of those utterances that did appear actually *increases.* The rates of such utterances increase when children are confronted with more dificult tasks. Thus Vygotsky argued that egocentric speech is not intended to communicate ideas to others. Rather, it represents one step in a process whereby speech becomes a means of regulating one's own action, a kind of self-instruction: Grammatical "fragments," usually predicate phrases referring to a child's preoccupation, represent the verbal "objectification" of the youngster's thought as a prelude to action, for example, "goes under this one."

In support of this view, Luria (1961) has shown that overt self-instruction among 3- to 4-year-olds serves only to activate or intensify responses —even when their instructions call for *inhibiting* action. However, by the ages of 5½ to 7 years, the content of verbalized self-instruction can enhance the execution of complex actions.

The fact that a 4-year-old's self-instructions tend to be ineffective while the comments of external authorities often can control the same child's behavior (Luria, 1961) illustrates the model of many independent components of behavioral systems and their heterochronous development. At least to the extent that they call for positive action (negative instructions are notoriously less effective), adult directives work, on average. Children can benefit from such guidance and, before they can encode the same information, messages from others can be decoded and translated into the realm of (appropriate) action. Nevertheless, even when they *are* capable of encoding a description of behavior, and of responding overtly and correctly to a corresponding demand made by an authority-figure, children often will be unable to link their actions appropriately to their self-instruction.

*Integration.* Some time before the age of 7 years, then, children not only become able to reflect upon the form of utterances of others but, in addition, they start to use the *meaning* of self-generated instructions to help guide their own activities. At present, we cannot say whether these emerging capacities are related to one another causally or in some other way. However, they clearly demonstrate a new level of behavioral organization in which form as well as meaning becomes accessible and one's own verbalizations may augment or supplement nonverbal processes in guiding action. In both instances, we have the beginning of an integration of thought and language.

This integration takes a while to become fully consolidated; thought still tends to "lead"—in some domains. On the other hand, some aspects of cognitive function are promoted by "language" relatively early in life. If young children are trained to name stimuli, they can apparently utilize these labels as aids to memory (Flavell, 1970). Similarly, 5-year-old children, who have been previously taught to label visual forms with distinctive names, subsequently learn discrimination tasks using these objects more rapidly than control subjects who have learned to label the objects with auditorily similar names or who have had no prior labeling training (see Bruce, 1965, for review). In the latter cases, training capitalizes upon a tendency already present and well practiced—the tendency to "name things" (cf. Brown, 1958).

It would seem that language and thought meet most closely at the stage of formal operations. Around adolescence, youngsters—who have inherited the potential to do so—may be able to develop a reflective awareness of the abstract relationships implicit in language. This awareness can then facilitate mastery of formal, symbolic logic and mathematics. Whereas natural languages allow us to refer to situations that have been encountered, or to *speculate* upon those that might be encountered, the abstract extensions of language, formal logic, and mathematics enable us to *predict* future events with some precision (Piaget, 1971). Presumably, the highest levels of abstract thought involve reflective awareness of the symbolic process itself and the rules underlying language (cf. Brown's, 1973, p. 30ff. speculations on the role of language in thought.) That is, by focusing and extending the (linguistic) expression of ideas according to conventionalized rules for conveying meaning, a new level of organization can be attained which extends the bounds of thought without sacrificing communicability or verifiability.

This uneven development might be explicable in terms of our model of adaptiveness. Assuming that a practical working knowledge of one's world would be more advantageous than the means for commenting upon it, sensorimotor intelligence should *lead*—to some extent. However, insofar as language is vital to *Homo*, some facets of information-processing should be focused to enhance the discovery of the means for communicating—at least in early life. For example, Dennis, Hampton, and Lea (1973) have shown that, whereas humans can *generate* disjunctive rules (e.g., "accept x if any two of 3 attributes obtain"), educated adults find them quite difficult to *discover* inductively from a set of exemplars. This difficulty in abstract inductive logic presents an apparent contrast to the performance of young language-learners. Their task is precisely one of induction from a corpus of exemplars that allows a variety of constructions, yet it is one at which they succeed. If Dennis et al.'s findings do reflect general features of educated adults' thought, perhaps we could explain some of the peculiarities of child logic as functionally suited (if not specific adaptations) for solving complex linguistic problems—those which are constrained by something akin to Slobin's (1973) operating principles.

In sum, "language" can and does enhance cognitive processing. Language may help to (a) enhance the identification of similarities and differences among instances, (b) focus attention on certain aspects of situations or (c) create attentional sets, and (d) increase the efficiency of storage or recall of items in memory. To the extent that language can provide the means to highlight relevant facets of experience by drawing children's attention to the reoccurrence of patterns or to relationships among variables, it may facilitate expression of the potentials to symbolize and form "concepts." However, although language may provide a vehicle to hasten the rate of acquisition of new cognitive constructions, it may only be effective under limited conditions, such as situations involving abstract relationships (Sokoloff, 1969), and only to the extent that the individual has already established a sufficiently firm foundation of experience to support a cognitive reorganization (Inhelder et al., 1974).

# CHAPTER 9

# Personality

The concept of personality is invoked to account for both individual differences in behavior and behavioral continuity across time. As Allport (1937) put it, personality refers to "the relatively enduring and unique organization" of a person's behavior. Taking Allport's (1937, p. 106) "equation": "*Personality* = $f$ (*Heredity*) × (*Environment*)" only a little further, it can be argued that "behavioral phenotype" and "personality" are, for all intents and purposes the same thing. However, people remain variable in both the short run (day to day), and in the long run, their behavior changes in roughly predictable ways. We have, then, on the one hand both momentary and developmental changes in responsiveness[1] and, on the other, continuity or individuality, the essence of one's unique "personality." Thus we cannot avoid the reality of mediating mechanisms. The issue that confronts us is to decide on how to conceptualize (and therefore how to investigate) them.

In this Chapter I will argue that the model of heterochronous development of functional systems as a result of organism-environment transactions may contribute to our understanding not only of personality "structure" and "dynamics" but also the effects of early experience on later behavior.

## STRUCTURE

With the *caveat* that we have yet to fully describe the behavior we seek to classify/understand, we will begin this chapter with an examination of the development of what have been described as the enduring, "structural" facets of personality that are thought to provide us both with a sense of continuity and some degree of predictability over time. The first of these is the sense of "self," the second is "conscience."

---

[1] Often, the determinants of momentary changes in form and intensity of response to the same situation have been attributed to personality "dynamics" and/or to "motivation." The latter concept is also employed to explain how directed activity can be sustained despite changes in the setting or the specific forms of the actions performed.

## The Self

The self refers to our awareness of ourselves as agents or actors and as (social) objects to which others react. Presumably, "it" provides us with a map, as it were, for locating ourselves within our broader surroundings. For many students of personality, the self is seen as a major—perhaps *the* major—determinant of one's enduring uniqueness (Damon, 1983). An ability to perceive one's own activities in context is important in governing some aspects of the behavior of many higher forms (Crook, 1983). With regard to such simple phenomena as reaching for an object, a sense of one's own dimensions in space is important (Bower, 1982) and simply knowing where to scratch implies a map of one's body surface, whether conscious or unconscious (Carmichael, 1954).

Although we tend to speak of "the" self or self-image, one's sense of self is, in fact, a dynamic amalgam of many component processes, or, as Harter (1983) put it, a "system." This amalgam develops over time and, as Crook (1983) suggested, functions as one element influencing the ways in which we "govern" our own behavior. In most cases, we are unaware of "ourselves"; typically, we become "self-conscious" only when difficulties are encountered or anticipated (see Harter, 1983).

## Components of the Self-Image

A classic distinction (James, 1890) is between the sense of self-as-agent (one who does things) and self-as-object (one-to-whom-others-respond/ corporeal entity). However, later students of personality distinguish a substantially greater number of components (Damon, 1983). Recognizing their essential arbitrariness, for the purpose of discussion, we will identify the following elements of one's sense of self: as causal agent; as a corporeal object embodying a variety of stimulus-attributes; as a male or female; as an object of social evaluation; and as an object of self-evaluation. In all probability, each of these components is, in itself, multifaceted. Like other aspects of knowledge, one's sense of self results from diverse inputs which seem to undergo more or less predictable changes during ontogeny. Indeed, in many ways, the concept of self exemplifies the notion of quasi-independent subcomponents which serve somewhat different ends at various stages of development, and which are subject to reorganization as new types of functioning are demanded.

*As a causal agent.* Feelings of efficacy or personal competence presumably have their origins in infancy. So long as caregivers respond reasonably reliably, and to the extent that contingencies can be detected between infants' actions and the (re)actions of babies' animate and inanimate surroundings (Watson, 1972), some sense of self-as-causal agent would be expected; indeed, infants apparently take great delight in "causing" things to happen (e.g., Bower, 1982; Piaget, 1952). The so-called circular reactions leading to "object-permanence" described by Piaget (1952; 1954; 1962) also must contribute, especially when adults add a "social" dimension to exchanges with offspring after the second month or so (e.g., Schaffer, 1977; Thoman, 1979). Through such activity as finger-play in infants during the third month (White, 1971), babies seem to gain a sense of motor agency and control of voluntary action. As self- and culturally-imposed expectations set standards for achievement, these accumulating experiences of success and failure should summate in some way. However, their origins—for example, relations with people, actions on objects—are separate and probably are stored independently at the outset. From reports of the resilience of youth (Jones, 1960; Werner & Smith, 1982) it would seem that most children are more responsive to success than to failure. At some point, when children gain the capacity to plan, a sense of self-control or voluntary agency develops (Harter, 1983).[2]

*As a corporeal object.* Babies and young children are capable of gaining a variety of relevant inputs very early. If infants can discriminate among different peoples' odors by 6 weeks of age and, as adults, can identify their own odors (Russell, 1976), we must consider the possibility that, some time after 6 weeks, babies begin to validate the substrates for establishing a rudimentary olfactory sense of self—a "template" for comparison—as other animals do (cf. Lewin, 1984).

The phenomenon of babbling poses another potential avenue for gaining knowledge-of-self. While babies probably recognize their own crying, such utterances usually occur in contexts in which the infant is more likely to be focused upon other kinds of input, for example, indications that food or comfort will be forthcoming. Babbling, however, insofar as it seems to be done for its own sake, and because it depends upon self-produced auditory feedback for its maintenance (Oller & Eilers, 1988), appears to provide an optimal situation for gaining an appreciation both of self as sound producer and producer of a *distinctive set* of sounds. (Indeed, babbling may tend to be a solitary activity *in order* to permit the infant to develop a clear template). Some capacity for identifying voices apparently develops in utero (De Casper & Fifer, 1980), so the potential for this facet of self-identification is available well before the onset of babbling. To the extent that self-monitoring is important for speech production, recognition of one's own voice would be important.

---

[2] There is an extensive literature on the antecedents of self- (or "ego") control. Unfortunately, almost all of the data reflect associations between child-characteristics and parental behavior or personality. Insofar as direction of effects and shared heredity cannot be disentangled (Bell, 1968; Scarr & McCartney, 1983), these findings will not be reviewed (see Maccoby & Martin, 1983, for review and critique).

The same experiences that contribute to a sense of agency provide input relevant to babies' concepts of their physical attributes. Some sense of self-recognition seems to be apparent before the end of the first year; by 18 months of age, American babies can use a mirror to investigate their own features (Amsterdam, 1972; Lewis & Brooks-Gunn, 1979; Pipp, Jennings, & Fischer, 1987). Therefore, we may assume that they have a visual sense of self as well.

One of the more "primitive" bases for a sense of physical self that is required for locomotion in space is a sense of one's physical body scheme. Central representations of one's body develop slowly over time and must be recalibrated with growth. Studies of the sequelae to surgical or traumatic loss of limbs suggest how a physical "body image" may be formed. Such losses in preadolescence or adulthood lead to reductions in sensory and motor nervous tissue. However, at least some pathways survive which once connected the missing member to the central motor areas that had controlled it and to the cortical sensory fields that served it (McComas, Sica, & Banerjee, 1978). The residual central afferent connections often give rise to sensations which have been dubbed "phantom limbs."

Simmel (1966) located over 100 people who had lost a limb between the ages of 2 and adulthood. She found that, of the 24 persons who had lost a limb between 2 and 4 years of age, less than one quarter ever recalled experiencing a phantom limb. Even though subjects were equated for time elapsed since limb loss and the interview, all of the 60 individuals whose loss occurred when they were over 8 years of age had experienced phantoms. Patients who underwent amputations of congenitally malformed limbs showed a similar developmental trend, but phantoms occurred only in those who could move the limb, or had feeling in the limb prior to surgery. From these findings, it seems that there may be a critical period for validating sensory representations of one's extremities. Moreover, Simmel suggested that the crucial avenues of input for maintaining and integrating a conscious, central representation of one's limbs were pressure and kinesthetic receptors. Simple touch and sight did not lead to the development of an enduring central "image."

Consistent with the idea that growing youngsters must constantly "recalibrate" their sense of self-in-space (Bower, 1982; Banks & Salapatek, 1983), Simmel (1966) also found that individuals did not report phantom limb experiences if their losses were gradual over time, for example, due to degenerative diseases. Apparently, a gradual change in innervation leads to central reorganization whereas an abrupt denervation leaves at least some central analyzers intact. From Simmel's data, it seems that a central representation of one's body image begins to consolidate between the ages of 4 and 6 years, primarily due to kinesthetic and/or pressure sensations.

*Gender identity.* While children are only gradually establishing an enduring image of their bodily boundaries during the second through fourth years, their self-identities as males or females become salient and, in some cases, resistant to change by the end of the second year (Money, 1976; Money & Ehrhardt, 1972). In this case, then, validation and maintenance begins even before children are aware (or willing to acknowledge an awareness) of the anatomical differences between the sexes and the links between gender and social role. Indeed, a (rudimentary) capacity to distinguish gender and to selectively attend to members of one's own sex can be seen by the time babies begin to distinguish strangers from familiar people (Bower, 1982; Lewis & Brooks, 1975). The work of Money and his collaborators suggests that gender-specific response-biases are induced by prenatal hormonal events and that these predispositions will affect a range of behavior from childhood play preferences to adolescent patterns of romantic involvement (Money & Ehrhardt, 1972).

*As an object of social evaluation.* Somatotype and gender often elicit reactions from others. However, despite the fact that infants can distinguish one individual from another within days or weeks of birth, a reflective awareness of another's probable reactions to one's behavior seems to develop much more slowly (Miller, Kessel, & Flavell, 1970). Presumably, affective signals received from caregivers provide relevant inputs for infants and toddlers. By the time they are four or five years of age, young children, especially boys, can locate themselves accurately in fairly complex hierarchies of age-mate social rank (e.g., Freedman, 1974; 1979; Strayer, 1980). Although social rank initially is determined largely by brute force or persuasion (Bühler, 1933), during the grade school years, children become able to locate themselves in hierarchies relative to their acquaintances in terms of relative intellectual achievement, attractiveness, affability and social skills, and, especially for boys, athletic prowess (Damon, 1983; Freedman, 1979; Hartup, 1983; Maccoby & Jacklin, 1974).

As they grow older, other, essentially universal, experiences that seem to contribute to children's developing senses of social self include culturally-ascribed identities as members of ethnic/cultural groups and of religious sects.

From the standpoint of sociobiological theory, the effects of seeing oneself as a member of a kinship group would be at least equally important as an influence on behavior as would perceived membership in racial/caste groups. In many societies, one's access to mates, material resources, and social support depend in no small measure in the number of kin one can count on (Chagnon & Irons, 1979).

As youngsters approach adulthood, new dimensions of social identity derive from economic and sociopolitical activity (Hockett, 1973; van den Berghe, 1973). Similarly, one'se sense of self-as-object and self-as-agent can be influenced by success in mating and childrearing. Begetting children represents an affirmation of one's sexuality and health; well-developed offspring provide proof of one's competence as a parent (Harper, 1975).

All these later events depend upon the cognitive ability to recognize that one is the object of evaluation by others. In this connection, it may be of more than passing interest to note that von Senden (1960) reported that, when previously "blind" cataract patients became able to see others (and themselves), they relinquished many socially inappropriate habits with regard to appearance and mannerisms. Apparently—quite literally— being able to see ourselves as others see us is important for certain aspects of what might be called self-presentation among adults.

*As an object of self-evaluation.* With an awareness that others react to them in predictable ways, and a sense of their effectiveness as agents, children are laying the groundwork for evaluating *themselves.* To the extent that young children perform for performance's sake, and recognize when they have solved a problem or succeeded on tasks before receiving any feedback from others (Kagan & Kogan, 1970), other peoples' reactions will be irrelevant or relatively unimportant. Moreover, among children who are cognitively "below" Piaget's (Inhelder & Piaget, 1958) stage of "concrete operations," it would seem unlikely that many facets of the sense of self are subjected to reflective evaluation. Indeed, overt evaluation and criticism of *others* predates self-criticism by some years (Harter, 1983).

At first, children's self-descriptions appear fairly simple and uncomplicated. Among American children, at least, preferred activities and possessions often are mentioned when youngsters are asked to describe themselves. Self-as-possessor seems to decline in importance (perhaps being supplanted by an occupational self) as youngsters grow older. Children's self-perceptions of personal characteristics (e.g., "friendly"), although present even at the preschool period, become more salient as they approach adolescence (Damon, 1983).

Presumably, with the development of adolescents' capacities to reflect upon their own thoughts (cf. Inhelder & Piaget, 1958), the potential is available to engage in extensive—and even integrative—reflection. This is only a potential, however; self-awareness or reflective consciousness of our goals seldom, if ever, extends to all facets of behavior (Freud, 1900; Gazzaniga, 1985). Aside from a number of situations in which such reflective knowledge is either clearly superfluous or dangerously inefficient, there may be contexts in which an accurate assessment of one's true intentions could actually work against one's attempts at manipulating others. Alexander (1981) points out that the most effective lies are often those in which the liar "believes"; that is, unconscious self-deception can be advantageous in some contexts. Nevertheless, people do develop feelings about themselves that are more or less available to reflection. This broader evaluation of one's self as-object-of-evaluation, or "self esteem," probably reflects various combinations of more or less autonomous self-evaluations and the evaluations of others.[3] (See Harter, 1983, for review).

*Integration.* One's sense of self thus actually refers to a variety of qualitatively different experiences, from an appreciation of self-as-actor and physical entity to awareness and acceptance of others' expectations and evaluations of social role-enactments. It seems that these components are themselves heterogeneous and change individually as one develops and encounters various challenges. New features are added in ontogeny and, as the substrates controlling behavior reorganize, the juxtaposition of components and their relative experiential salience may change.

The various components of one's self-image function as the bases for calculating one's moves in the animate as well as the inanimate environment (Crook, 1983; Damon, 1983). Insofar as adolescence is a time when one has to take one's place in the society of adults, when societies do not prescribe that place clearly and unambiguously (either through a rite of passage and/or getting the young deeply interested in "the system"), the quest for a unified, coherent sense of self may become salient (cf. Erikson, 1950; 1959). If one must have a basis for finding—or creating—one's place in society, a successful search would depend upon being able to assess what one has to offer and then to capitalize upon those assets. Indeed, the necessity to find one's own niche may have conferred additional advantages to those who could attain (or at least create a passable illusion) of self-consistency (Alexander, 1981; Humphrey, 1976).

At any rate, many students of personality would agree with Erickson that adolescence is the period during which at least some youngsters begin to attempt to integrate the various aspects of their self-images into a more or less (logically) coherent picture. From Money and Ehrhardt's (1972) work, an integration of these facets of one's identity will depend upon clear and consistent ascriptions, and role-complementary behavior by significant others in the first 2-3 years which are consonant with one's gender and biological predilections.

If behavior develops and is organized in the ways suggested herein, then the various facets of what we call the sense of self may, in fact, become effective elements of different functional systems whenever planning or an assessment of one's chances with respect to specific goals is required. If

---

[3] One major weakness in the assessments of the antecedents and dynamic significance of the sense of self is the failure to consider the role of individual (phenotypic) responses to input. We cannot rule out the possibility that some people simply are congenitally more easily devastated by failure, whether in social relationships or in instrumental strivings. Until we can assess both the range of heritable response to input and the role of the growing individual in *provoking* social reactions (Scarr & McCartney, 1983), the determinants and dynamics of the self-system will remain obscure.

so, a *unitary* sense of self or "identity" (cf. Erickson, 1950; 1959) would become an issue only under certain cultural conditions. Presumably, the luxury of self-evaluation would be reserved for those who are reared in economically secure surroundings but whose economic/political futures will be uncertain until mental development has reached the cognitive stage of "formal operations" (Inhelder & Piaget, 1958). And, among those who do attain that phase, still another set of components may be involved in the evaluative process—the conscience and/or value-system.

### Conscience

This construct was advanced to explain why people would forego capital-izing upon opportunities to further their own ends and even appear to sacrifice their personal well-being for the sake of others. It also served as a (theoretical) source for that feeling known to most of us as guilt; feelings that we have done wrong, and/or that we have failed to live up to expec-tations.

From a review of the literature up to 1970, Hoffman concluded that the development of moral behavior is "a complex, multifaceted phenome-non to which several different processes appear to contribute. . ." (Hoff-man, 1970; p. 345). He suggested that at least four developmental trends were involved, resulting in conformity, self-control, consideration for others, and a sense of the rationality of authority. Moreover, he suggested that each of these facets of moral behavior had its own, unique antece-dents and that the effective combinations of inputs changed with the changing capacities of the child. In the subsequent edition of the *Hand-book of Child Psychology* (Mussen, 1983) the topics of moral development or conscience did not appear per se. Rather, the issues traditionally con-sidered aspects of conscience were dealt with primarily under the rubrics of "self control" (Harter, 1983), "prosocial behavior" (Radke-Yarrow, Zahn-Waxler, & Chapman, 1983), and "morality"—(essentially "moral judgment" [Rest, 1983]).

*"Moral" behavior.* Insofar as actions themselves can be seen as conform-ing to or deviating from ethical standards, the "unity" of conscience can be evaluated by directly observing behavior. One of the first extensive in-vestigations in this area was the series of studies conducted by Hartshorne and May (1930/1955). They examined the verbalized moral judgments of elementary school children and, in addition, they devised an ingenious (if devious) series of tests of the same children's actual conduct in situations in which "deception, cooperation, inhibition, and persistence" could be evaluated. "Deception" included cheating, stealing and lying, and several situations were engineered for each in which children would be tempted without apparent danger of detection. A third series of situations was

devised in which children had opportunities to help others at minor personal cost (e.g., come to school early; donate money "to charity").

The results of the study suggested tath even tests of the "same" type of behavior yielded situationally-specific results. That is, whereas a child might cheat on classroom examinations, the same youngster would not violate the rules when trying to solve a puzzle even though the latter task was presented in the classroom. While peers' independent evaluations and teachers' ratings of children's "character" were in high agreement, these evaluations seemed to represent an overall assessment; the youngsters' actual behaviors were variable. Moral knowledge or judgment was not highly correlated with rule-conformity even with respect to the same issue.

Similar findings were reported for 6- to 8-year-olds some 40 years later. Walsh (1969) had teachers rate youngsters on several facets of "self-control," such as courtesy, ability to stay on task, and so on. The children's abilities to resist temptation were assessed in contrived situations at school, and at home while the observer was ostensibly interviewing the mother. The results again suggested that conscience was situation-dependent; indeed, children's self-control at home was *negatively* related to teacher ratings of classroom behavior.

The tendency to share in face-to-face situations with others also turns out to be heterogenous, even among young juveniles: Sharing toys, space on picnic blankets, and sharing food items from lunch pails all are statistically independent events in middle childhood (Dyson-Hudson & van Dusen, 1972).

From these findings, it seems that even the activities we are accustomed to considering just as one facet of conscience or moral behavior involve a variety of phenomena. In terms of overt activity, one could distinguish at least five "dimensions" of behavior: Compliance-disobedience; altruism-selfishness; truthfulness-deception; honesty-theft (of an individual's possessions); and rule-adherence-cheating (unfairly acquiring yet-to-be distributed resources). Within each of these domains, behavior shows substantial situational specificity (Radke-Yarrow et al., 1983).

*Process.* Presumably, the tendency to behave in a moral fashion reflects the outcome of a number of underlying, component processes. In order for children to behave "morally," there is consensus that they must possess at least the capacities to (a) establish a set of standards or expectations for conduct, (b) control their own behavior, and (c) assess or evaluate that behavior (Harter, 1983; Maccoby & Martin, 1983; Rest, 1983).

Of these, the establishment of standards will depend upon a child's cognitive "level" insofar as the kinds of values a society holds vary in terms of their sophistication (Edwards, 1981). Moreover, in order to behave appropriately a child must not only be able to recall standards, but be able to recognize that situations in which they are applicable; the latter will involve both cognitive and affective components (Rest, 1983). Similarly, to control their own behavior, youngsters not only have to be able to inhibit (inappropriate) actions but be able to monitor what they actually do and to modulate that action according to evaluative criteria. In order to engage in more complex ethical activities, youngsters must have the capacities both to *plan* a course of action and to anticipate its consequences (Harter, 1983).

In short, corresponding to the heterogeneity of moral activities, there seems to be a corresponding heterogeneity of underlying processes, each of which may develop more or less independently of the others. For example, although they are "moral realists" (cf. Piaget, 1932), young children may neither fully understand moral principles nor possess sufficient self-control (cf. Luria, 1961) to behave in accordance with moral precepts. Similarly, although they may recognize that a behavior is "right" or "wrong," they may not be capable of fully assessing it in terms of the actor's intent, and/or its effects on others, the social order, and so on (cf. Rest, 1983).

*Antecedents.* Both Wilson (1975) and Alexander (1981) argue that the "ethics" appropriate to one phase of the life-cycle may be inappropriate to another one. The ease with which youngsters accept (invent) notions of "immanent justice," and see even fortuitous misfortunes as "punishment" suggest that the infantile mind constructs a "moral" world (Piaget, 1929; 1932). However, given that "obedience" seems to appear at about the age of which infants are capable of independent locomotion, one could use the arguments of Ainsworth et al. (1974) to present a good case for the contention that obedience in toddlerhood represents a facet of the filial or attachment system. Indeed, infants' tendencies to share food with their caregivers or to give and to show objects to others (Eckerman, Whatley, & McGehee, 1979) may be more appropriately considered components of filial or affiliative systems in early childhood (see also Radke-Yarrow et al., 1983).

Early experience in infancy may set the tone for the later adoption of an ethical strategy, however. Presumably, youngsters who develop a sense of early "trust" and who can (accurately) anticipate their caregivers' behaviors should be better able to accept restraint or directives. (One could argue that trust may be a precondition for a child to abandon a focus on self-interest long enough to consider someone else's perspective [cf. Bryant & Crockenberg, 1980]). The relationship between children and their attachment-figures, although essentially "pre-moral," thus could contribute significantly to the course of moral development at least through early childhood.

If we translate attachment-figure to kin (or kin-surrogates), sociobiological theory also would predict that the status of such bonds continue to affect how individuals will react in a range of situations through adolescence (Werner & Smith, 1982)—and beyond. It is easier to withstand temptation and consider the feelings of others if one feels that one can count upon reciprocation when in need, and some "backing" should things go wrong (cf. Chagnon & Irons, 1979; Trivers, 1971; see also Crockenberg, 1981). In these terms, we might be able to account for the behavior of youngsters who remained in an institution until 4½ years of age and either behaved as if they cared for no one or showed indiscriminate responsiveness to anyone who showed an interest in them (Tizard & Tizard, 1971; 1974). They could be seen as having made an adjustment to extreme conditions—that is, where one has no "kin," one must seize upon any opportunity for gratification.

Thus, conscience appears to reflect a heterogeneous set of behaviors, many of which are situationally determined, and whose organization may change with age. The conditions that give rise to such behavior are not well understood. Indeed, Maccoby and Martin (1983) point out that we have been able to account for relatively little of the variance in this domain and suggest that traditional approaches may have been focusing in the wrong areas. (See also footnotes 2 and 3.) Insofar as the potentials to develop various aspects of compliance, self-control, altruism, and value-judgments, and so on are fundamental prerequisites for group membership (cf. Trivers, 1971), we may assume that the stimuli inducing and validating the developing substrates for these activities are ubiquitous. The particular acts performed, values adopted, and judgments rendered, and the degree to which they are maintained and integrated probably are more dependent upon situationally-specific stimuli. But even in the case of contextually-determined variations, some of the conditions shaping the expression of processing strategies and/or assessments underlying qualitative variations of moral behavior are likely to amount to sign stimuli.[4]

The earliest inputs facilitating expression of the potentials underlying the development of altruism probably correspond to signs of another, responsive, human being. The tendency to develop self-control may be facilitated and perhaps validated by sensitive and responsive early parenting (Ainsworth et al., 1974; Lytton, 1980; Martin, 1981). It would seem that if one can be reasonably sure that assistance or succorance will be

---

[4] With respect to the kinds of events that might "cue" an individual to adopt the ethic of mutual assistance, Axelrod and Hamilton (1981) showed that, where individuals can recognize one another and where encounters occur often enough to present opportunities for reciprocation (and retaliation for cheating), a simple rule such as "tit for tat" (with forgiveness for just one retaliation for failure to offer) would suffice to maintain the benefits of cooperative relationships even among unrelated individuals. That is, under the foregoing conditions, it can "pay" to extend a helping hand to others so long as one (a) keeps track of one's beneficiaries and (b) tolerates no more than one (retaliatory) failure to offer when one is in a position of need.

forthcoming when and if necessary, then one can afford to exercise restraint. A patient, responsive caregiver might signify not only that someone is present who cares, but that the situation is "under control." When the physical and social/economic environment is secure, caregivers *have* the time to engage young children in reciprocal, pleasurable pursuits in which they are willing to comply with the child's requests (Crockenberg, 1981).

In the preschool years it seems that a knowledge of conventional rules and "moral imperatives" of conduct can be acquired from consistent adult intervention coupled with explanation (Nucci & Turiel, 1978). However, as in infancy, youngsters' (and adults') tendencies to choose a moral course or to comply with authority varies with what might be considered "hedonic tone." That is, if one feels successful, in control, or satisfied, one is more likely to forego gratification, or display altruism than if one feels sad, disappointed, or threatened (Maccoby & Martin, 1983; Radke-Yarrow et al., 1983).

In early middle childhood, being assigned to care for younger siblings may have quite substantial effects on the sense of responsibility and "empathy" shown by youngsters, especially boys (Ember, 1973).

From the sociobiological perspective advocated by Alexander (1981), we might expect that reasoning and explanation should become more effective as guides for moral development in childhood and adolescence. He argues that, when one analyzes the content of "ethical" exhortations of parents, the guidance provided actually is consistent with the child's (or the kin-group's) self-(collective)interest. In essence, these exhortations delineate the kinds of behaviors that will be regarded as acceptable by the wider group of (potential) interactants. Such information can provide neophytes with a certain "edge" in the game of social obligation; given the knowledge gained thereby, they can present themselves as prospective altruists. If so, we should expect youngsters not only to inherit the genetic potential to develop sensitivities to these cues, but also to be attuned to exhortations, role-modeling, and so on that illustrate and highlight them.

The sense of one's self as an object of moral evaluation by others may be important as an element in the subliminal calculation of social cost/benefit ratios insofar as others' reactions/evaluations affect one's social prospects. It may be for this reason that caregiver labeling or "attribution" seem to foster the display of socially acceptable and altruistic behavior (Radke-Yarrow et al., 1983). If one tells children (who are old enough to understand such labels) that they did something because they are "honest," it could help to perpetuate such behavior, not just through "cognitive dissonance" (cf. Festinger, 1957), but by notifying them that they have accumulated some social "capital." Then, recognizing that they have something valuable to lose, youngsters may be more careful to maintain their images by behaving consistently. This should be particularly true if they believe themselves to be dealing with other people who are willing to lend a hand to those whom they value (cf. Trivers, 1971).[5]

In middle childhood, the experimental literature does suggest that rule-clarity and consistency of not only exhortation but also of observed adult practice are particularly important in determining whether or not youngsters will *exercise* moral/ethical self-control. In addition to the variable of affective tone or "mood," the attainability of standards may be an important determinant of whether or not juveniles will comply with rules, or standards of conduct, in the absence of direct supervision. (See Maccoby & Martin, 1983; Radke-Yarrow et al., 1983, for reviews.)

There is a suggestion that children become more sensitive to apparent hypocrisy in middle childhood. Children 8 and 9 years of age report "liking" adult models who espouse high ideals whether or not they abide by them. They seem not to realize the mismatch between exhortation and behavior (Bryan & Walbek, 1970). Youngsters one year older (Rosenhaan, Frederick, & Burrowes, 1968) notice the difference between verbal prescription and actual practice; they are most likely to give in to the temptation when they observe an adult doing the same. These findings deserve replication. If the age-differences across samples can be taken seriously, it would seem that children around the age of 10 (late juveniles) may become more capable of reflecting upon the mismatch between preaching and practice and be more prone to "cue in" on common observance while still cognizant of ethical standards.

### Reorganization

The ways in which these components affect moral behavior change with age. For example, most preschoolers simply don't think to consider other persons' intentions as a basis for making moral judgments about behavior. By middle grade school, youngsters clearly use this principle, but often fail to verbalize it; preadolescents are capable of describing their use of an assessment of intention; adolescents recall the principle as such and distinguish it from other bases for judgment (Breznitz & Kugelmass, 1967).

Adolescence also appears to be the phase at which the various, heretofore relatively independent component facets of self-as-agent, self-as-object, and values and ideals that relate to self-evaluation, and so on *may* be subject to simultaneous scrutiny and accommodation. Such reflective self-assessment is unlikely to take place much earlier insofar as most pre-adolescent youngsters seem to be unable—or at least unlikely—to spontaneously use

---

[5] From the foregoing, then, it may be unwise to expect young children and particularly juveniles and young adolescents to benefit from repeated, *direct* confrontations over matters of veracity or duty. Indeed, if all their deceptions and transgressions are relentlessly exposed and labeled as such, they may feel that their capital is exhausted and that they have little to gain by behaving virtuously in the future.

their developing cognitive capacities to examine the implications of their beliefs, the logical consistencies and contradictions among their beliefs, their feelings about themselves, and so on (Inhelder & Piaget, 1958).

From sociobiological theory, one would expect that additional, important contributors to an integrated, personal identity would be one's "capital" as a valued companion, as someone whose company others find pleasant and as a reciprocator of altruistic acts (Trivers, 1971). If one is to present one's self as a "good" member of society and as a person upon whom others can depend, it helps to present a morally consistent picture. For a variety of reasons, then, we should expect that under the appropriate conditions, adolescents not only become preoccupied with ethical issues but ultimately strive to reconcile these facets of their personalities with the various components comprising their self-images. Here again, one might expect that this task would be facilitated by an upbringing in which one's fundamental worth was (re)affirmed while consistent demands were being made for conformity to a set of clearly articulated standards, standards which are (a) logically compatible with one another and (b) which represent those norms to which most members of the culture expect adherence (Radke-Yarrow et al., 1983).

Under any circumstances, to the extent that a sense of self as object of evaluation, and a knowledge of social norms guide behavior, we would expect some coordination of these facets of personality in determining behavior by at least 8 years of age, if not sooner (cf. Harter, 1983).

## DYNAMICS

In this section the model of developmental reorganization of functional systems will be applied to the analysis of the ontogeny of personality "dynamics." The concept of functional systems is uncomfortably amenable to the same kinds of reification and classification that haunted notions of motivation. It will be useful in the study of personality only to the extent that it focuses our attention on the joint necessities of carefully describing behavioral patterns and investigating the mechanisms underlying them. Toward that end, I will suggest how such a system might work.

### Functional Systems

Functional ("behavioral," cf. Bowlby, 1969)[6] systems correspond to the receptor-neural/endocrine-effector pathways that direct and sustain the

---

[6] At this point, one may wonder whether anything can be gained by speaking of functional systems rather than motives or drives. To the extent that the notion of a functional system remains an abstract, hypothetical, "variable," somehow intervening between stimulus and response, nothing will have been gained. If, however, attempts are made to test this concep-

adaptive activities of a species. Different systems serve different (behavioral) ends, for example, attachment, nursing, exploration, and so on. Following Maslow (1954), they can be conceptualized as hierarchically organized and in dynamic relationships with one another. To the extent that they represent different configurations of activation of a fixed pool of phenotypic components, most of them will amount to alternative "states."

In general, according to this scheme, activating a functional system involves increasing the probability of attending to or processing relevant classes of input, probably by means of enchancing signals to analyzers for the relevant inputs and/or by inhibiting responsiveness to other kinds of stimuli (Koshland, Goldbeter, & Stock, 1982; Meredith & Stein, 1983). To the extent that a system underlies activities that relate to relatively stable or predictable features of the human environment, such as the mother for an infant, or a sexual partner for an adolescent, the effective features of these inputs will amount to what we have dubbed sign stimuli.

Certain configurations of receptor activation, such as the face-gestalt, will be more likely than other inputs to lead to specific patterns of excitation of modules within the higher-level analyzers. When these module-configurations are activated by incoming excitation, they will dominate awareness and, as appropriate, potentiate or release some reaction, internal or external. As a result of past experience, some module-configurations and memories, may be particularly relevant to only one or two functional systems. To the extent that this is true, they would be expected to be more readily and perhaps uniquely addressed by activation of such a system (Gazzaniga, 1985; Squire, 1986).

Insofar as functional systems represent stage-specific adaptations, the relative dominance of particular states will not only change in the short term to meet the demands of the immediate situation, but also developmentally in anticipation of the exigencies of different phases of the life-cycle.

*Short-term regulation.* The short-term dominance of any one organizational complex presumably is determined by multiple monitoring subsystems within the CNS. Such monitors respond selectively to biochemical signals conveying information concerning ongoing vegetative processes (blood sugar and other nutrient levels, the presence of pathogens, tissue damage, etc.) and assessments of the external situation as received via

tion of (a) quasi-independent but interrelated organismic components (b) whose hierarchical organization develops in time, (c) according to a set of inherited potentials for growth (d) which are induced, validated, facilitated, maintained, and integrated (e) in response to different arrays of environmental inputs, (f) which also lead to stages of reorganization of these components (g) where mutually antagonistic components stand in reciprocal relationships to one another, we may at least get a better idea of what does control what we do. The comparative literature suggests that mechanisms of this sort do exist (Flynn, Vanegas, Foote, & Edwards, 1970; Roberts, 1970; Krieger, 1983).

receptors and processed centrally. The latter processing would typically involve stimuli which are reliable indices of external conditions.

On average, signs of danger seem to pre-empt other states of functional organization in most phases of the life-cycle. In addition to sudden, loud sounds, abrupt changes in illumination, and so on—which release orienting and/or defensive responses—multimodal patterns of stimulation which, individually, are ineffective in gaining attention may, in combination fit the templates for danger (Meredith & Stein, 1983). Signs indexing danger typically evoke a reorganization of one's priorities, as it were, via a simultaneous pattern of inhibition of components involved in irrelevant systems, such as feeding or play, and the coordinated arousal of components involved in flight/defense reactions.

In more benign contexts, the changing short-term pattern of dominance of systems would lead to shifts in the individual's sustained, goal-directed activities such as sleeping, exploration, or proximity-seeking. At any developmental level, it also is possible that the activation of a functional system that has been reduced (inhibited?) via consummatory behavior may be reactivated by perception of a new evocative stimulus. For example, in opportunistic systems such as play and exploration, the introduction of novelty, or the discovery of new play-materials may reactivate investigative/play behavior. Apparently analogous phenomena occur in feeding behavior as well; it is not at all uncommon to feel "full" until a different dish is presented.

To the extent that certain facets of functional behavior are potentiated by relatively long-lasting messengers such as neuropeptides (Krieger, 1983) or endocrine hormones, one would also expect to find mutually antagonistic relations among substances regulating incompatible patterns. For example, the same—or same class—of messenger may simultaneously activate mechanisms involved in flight while inhibiting mechanisms involved in the display of incompatible, appetitive activities related to mating (Sirinathsinghji, Rees, Rivier, & Vale, 1983).

*Ontogeny.* As the child grows, the patterns of organization, including the specific arrays of activities appropriate to various situations, will change. For example, for an infant who cannot flee danger, the attachment system might be activated along with vocal responses and physiological preparations for coping with injury. Children who are mobile should be prepared to freeze or flee as well as vocalize and prepare for injury, and so forth. Older children and vigorous adults' activational patterns should also include physiological responses compatible with fighting as well as flight.

Beyond the flight/defense systems, we would also expect developmental changes in the probability that certain patterns of exteroceptor excitation will be able to lead to shifts in the dominance of functional systems. For example, the sight of moderately novel toys offering a range of manipulative opportunities might be expected to tip the balance in a reasonably well-fed and rested child from eating to play. A young adult otherwise in a similar state, as a result of post-puberal hormonal changes, might be more likely to respond to stimuli indicative of a potential mate. Patterns of responses to indices of impending danger might be expected to be somewhat different for adults who are parents than for those who are not parents.

Developmentally, in instances where components of functional systems such as those governing mating must be "tuned" or focused, early events such as hormone-release may affect a wide array of activities. For example, many aspects of behavior of genetic females are "masculinized" by early exposure to androgen; similarly, in males, the *absence* of androgens, or insensitivity to them combined with above threshold estrogen (the "testicular feminization syndrome"), may "feminize" the complementary behavioral proclivities (Beach, 1976; Money & Ehrhardt, 1972).

In short, then, where functional systems involve components whose simultaneous display is incompatible, these elements will be connected via inhibitory mechanisms so that the excitation (or developmental hypertrophy) of one will lead to the short-term inhibition (or developmental atrophy) of the others which are incompatible with it.

We should also expect that the stimuli necessary to initiate and sustain (behavioral) development will change. Insofar as humans exploit a wide range of habitats, beyond early infancy and toddlerhood, when the common environmental denominators for development are embodied in caregivers, the ontogenetically important facets of environments should become more varied. If so, greater proportions of the stimuli that determine the fine tuning of components of these systems will be more situationally-specific than those sustaining development in early infancy (cf. McCall, 1981). For example, just before children master language and later become motorically skilled enough to assume productive roles in their cultures, we should expect heightened sensitivities to the nuances of cultural practice: The cues diagnostic of cultural variation will play a more important part in the facilitation and integration of the components of functional systems.

To the extent that these mechanisms are neuronal, involving cells in a number of brain regions including the hypothalamus (Flynn et al., 1970; Roberts, 1970; Renaud, Martin, & Brazeau, 1975; De Weid, 1984), we should have no difficulty in seeing how preemptory stimulus patterns can not only cause a transient inhibition of activities appropriate to one functional system and the activation of another, but also cause relatively long-lasting shifts in the relative dominance of systems. Moreover, in view of developmental shifts in neuroanatomy (Greenough & Schwark, 1984) and the fact that neuromodulator peptides are expressed in slightly different forms at different periods in ontogeny (Silman et al., 1978), we have several mechanisms by which the relative salience of functional systems could change with development.

Given the foregoing, so long as people strive to achieve mastery of whatever kind, to explore the unknown, or just to walk, we can assume that such strivings represent the ontogeny and workings of the human nervous system and we can, depending upon our particular interests, directly set about the task of describing and analyzing how each class of activity develops and functions.

### Individual Differences and Early Experience

One's behavior is governed by one's momentary state, which also involves selective activation of aspects of a sense of self, values, and so on. That is, the form and direction of behavior can be understood in terms of the activation of the organizations we have called functional systems. Although the general outlines of these dynamic systems should be comparable across individuals, the quality of processing (the assessment of self-in-relation-to-others, etc.), and of the stored inputs contributing to that processing (specific values, memories, etc.) will vary from one individual to the next.

The latter point raises the issue of the origins of individual differences in personality. A basic theme of this book is that all development must be understood as the co-action of genes and environment. To the extent that essentially everyone inherits species-specific potentials, for example, to develop the organismic substrates for a self-image, the dimensions of variation should be very similar. That is, we all "do" pretty much the same things and the differences among us primarily reflect differences in degree, style, timing and, to a lesser extent, details of the underlying organization. Unfortunately, we have rather little unambiguous information concerning the range of alternative pathways for personality development or their determinants (cf. Maccoby & Martin, 1983). While it is clear that some distinctive patterns of aberrance can be related to inherited predispositions, it is equally clear that, over a range of settings, the expression of the potential for aberrance is quite variable (Scarr & Kidd, 1983; Werner & Smith, 1982).

Therefore, to illustrate the utility of an adaptationist perspective and the model of development proposed herein, we will examine two phenomena that seem to be related to the development of individual differences in personality and also reflect ways in which early experience seems to influence the course of subsequent development. Although there is no consensus on the underlying mechanisms, it is generally acknowledged that both birth-order and early father-absence are associated with individual differences in personality.

*Birth-order.* The magnitude of differences in personality attributes among members of the same families is essentially as great as that observed across members of different families (Plomin & Daniels, 1987; Rowe & Plomin, 1981; Scarr & Kidd, 1983). Unless we are to assume that the major behavior-genetic studies dealt with unusually homogeneous populations of families, to explain these data, we must look to the antecedents of individual differences among children *within* a family. Given that shared heredities between full siblings and between parents and offspring average at least 50%, and common genetic makeup among children across families must be substantially less, genetic heterogeneity alone cannot account for the differences.[7] Rather, there must be some, apparently common, dynamics that serve to magnify individual differences between children within families (Plomin & Daniels, 1987).

The most obvious conditions that might account for these phenomena would relate to birth-order and perhaps the interaction between individual children's provocative behaviors and birth order. Naturalistic observations reveal that attachments to and attempts to gain the attention of a single focal caregiver give rise to competitive situations within a family (Freud & Burlingham, 1944; Kendrick & Dunn, 1980; Lytton, 1980). Moreover, first-born and later-born youngsters experience quite different caregiving environments, particularly when the interbirth interval is less than five years or so. In general, first-borns experience greater rates of interactions with their mothers prior to the new arrival and then experience a subsequent *reduction* in attention (Lytton, 1980; Kendrick & Dunn, 1980). Later-born infants start out with caregivers whose attention is divided. For example, parents of first-born infants are more likely to follow procedures designed to provide "environmental enrichment" than are parents of second-born children who tend to feel that they are just too "busy" to take on anything new (White et al., 1979).

In essence, then, the common heredities of nontwin siblings meet quite different environmental conditions. Insofar as children must be able to adapt to various caregiving configurations, natural selection may have led to the evolution of species-typical potentials to develop different behavioral patterns in response to different caregiver/sibling configurations.[8] Extrapolating from hunter-gatherer societies, it would seem that spacing

---

[7] To the extent that mating is assortative for race, religion, intellectual attainment, and so on, there probably exists some degree of inbreeding (cf. Freedman, 1979).

[8] The degrees to which parents are unavailable—by necessity or design—and children are involved in caring for younger siblings may constitute an overriding condition: Responsibility for the care of younger children may act as a sign that inhibits expression of self-seeking behavior (e.g., Ember, 1973; Werner & Smith, 1982). Perhaps situations that highlight one's responsibilities to kin (e.g., parental inaccessibility) help to focus children's awareness of their mutual interdependence and/or of the dynamics of "reciprocal altruism"—the potential losses to be incurred as a result of violating the "tit-for-tat" principle. Group rearing (Bettelheim, 1969; Bronfenbrenner, 1970; Freud & Burlingham, 1944) shares the same element of mutual age-mate dependence and this dependence may be the critical sign for developing the alternative strategy of age-mate cooperation.

of birth intervals probably was a critical element in offspring survival for much of the human past. In such societies, the arrival of an infant sibling when a previous youngster was too young to keep up with adults (i.e., under 4 years of age or so) puts a life-threatening strain on the mother (Konner, 1972; 1977; Neel, 1970). Werner and Smith (1982) list the early arrival of a younger sibling as one (of several) "risk factors" that seems to predict later behavioral problems even in contemporary, Westernized children, and Leonard, Rhymes, and Solnit (1966) identified interbirth intervals of under 18 months as a correlate of the failure to thrive syndrome. It is thus possible that cues diagnostic of birth order and spacing (given controls for other relevant variables such as sex of sibling and the number of alternate caregivers available, cf. Bryant, 1985) might represent sign stimuli evoking a pattern of species-specific developmental responses. If so, then, on average, first-borns (or second-borns) *across* families would be more alike in some respects than first- or second-borns *within* families. Presumably, the specific outcomes of the hypothetical first- (or second-) born syndrome would depend, in part upon the caregivers' *reactions* to the toddler's behavior.

*Father absence.* In a somewhat similar vein, Draper and Harpending (1982) suggest that the syndrome of behaviors associated with early father absence may also reflect a facultative response to what we would consider a sign stimulus. Polygyny tends to occur cross-culturally in settings of relative plenty and monogamy is more typical of scarcity where a male's total energies are required to sustain a mother and her young. Therefore, they reason, early father-absence may cause youngsters to be particularly responsive to cues associated with a specific style of behavior. Presumably, under conditions favoring polygyny, males gain from self-assertive, aggressive behavior, verbal-manipulative skills, and so on, whereas the best reproductive strategy for females is early, promiscuous mating (and devaluation of males in general). In contrast, under more severe conditions, where paternal investment in (own) young is essential, males benefit more by mechanical-spatial skills (to eke out a living) and fidelity, while females benefit from being selective, and picking the best possible mate. Draper and Harpending (1982) thus postulate that early childhood is a critical period for biasing children to selectively adopt behavioral patterns appropriate for a particular reproductive strategy in adulthood, and that a father's presence (and mother's attitudes in his absence) are key stimulus-features in determining this early choice.

*Effects of early experience.* In both cases it could be argued that early signs indicating the nature of the environment-to-be-encountered induce or facilitate the substrates for a specific, stylistic component that will affect later behavior systems.

In the case of birth-interval, rearing in a nuclear family setting would seem to constitute one predisposing factor for facilitating competitiveness, particularly if interbirth intervals are on the order of 18 to 36 months *and* when adult caregivers (attachment-figures) are the primary sources of nurturance and social exchange. Given that the interbirth interval in the United States averages around 24 months (Levy, 1955), it may be significant that American youngsters seem to be particularly competitive, and ready to attempt to outperform others whenever an opportunity presents itself. Such competitiveness sometimes is displayed in contexts in which cooperation would clearly be a better strategy (Madsen & Shapira, 1970; Miller & Thomas, 1972). Depending upon one's culture, then, these early-developed tendencies may be subsequently displayed in a variety of contexts such as striving for academic excellence (teacher approval) and later personal economic gain.

With respect to father-absence, the absence (stable presence) of a (valued) male authority figure in the family also constitutes a "sign," facilitating the early development of predilections to adopt a particular style of relationship to members of the opposite sex. This early-developed set may then color the subsequently-developed behavioral systems involved in relationships with mates and offspring.

At this juncture, it is unclear whether these early-developed predilections require additional inputs for their maintenance/validation (cf. Rutter, 1984) or whether they suffice to sensitize youngsters to respond to certain constellations of cues encountered in later life. Whatever the case, they illustrate how this model of development could accommodate the effects of early experience on later behavior and heterotypic (cf. Kagan, 1971) continuity in development (Emde & Harmon, 1984).

# CHAPTER 10

# Summary and Implications

This monograph is based upon the assumptions that (a) despite the uncertainties inherent in reductionistic accounts, human behavioral development can be understood in biological terms, and (b) such models may illuminate phenomena which pose difficulties for strictly "psychological" formulations. Thus, I have attempted to consistently apply the oft-repeated, and more often ignored maxim that *all* development involves the co-action ("interaction") of genes and environment.

## GENE-ENVIRONMENT CO-ACTION

### Maturation and Experience

At the level of mechanism, the distinction between maturation and experience becomes hazy, and the so-called continuum of environmental influence is more accurately seen as a continuum of probabilities of encountering the necessary environmental conditions for gene-expression. That is, "maturational" events can simply be seen as ontogenetic changes which are initiated and sustained by conditions that prevail under almost all circumstances capable of supporting human life, whereas developmental changes called "learning" typically depend upon conditions that are encountered in quite specific situations. In short, the continuum of interest is not how open or closed the genetic system is, but how ubiquitous or how situationally specific are the environmental conditions for activation of genetic potentials.

This formulation re-emphasizes the significance of environmental conditions for all growth and the importance of analyzing the antecedents of "maturational" change while stressing at the same time that all (behavioral) development ultimately involves gene-action (e.g., Goelet, Castelluci, Schacher, & Kandel, 1986; Sutcliffe, 1984).

*Sign stimuli.* On the assumption that humans are the products of evolution, and from what we know of other species, it seems likely that many critical environmental inputs for the expression of fundamental, human behavioral characteristics amount to what have been called sign stimuli. This conception implies that the effective conditions for the development of species-typical attributes amount to sets of schematic features, features that, in our evolutionary past, were reliable indicators of conditions under which the display of those qualities promoted individual fitness. Moreover, a number of these pivotal events, particularly those necessary for the development of species-typical attributes, may be only dimly perceived, if noticed at all (Lumsden & Wilson, 1981; Stent, 1975). In contrast, assuming that our behavior is adaptive, we should be much more keenly aware of, and attuned to, subtle nuances of complex stimuli that index variations within the domains in which a priori predictability is minimal, as in the case of some social relationships.

*Effects of stimulation.* From a reductionist perspective, all phenotypic attributes can be seen as the products of environmentally induced and supported gene-action. Inheritance does not guarantee gene-expression; not all genes are activated—at any one time or over a lifetime. The way(s) in which many typical genes function under specified environmental conditions depend not only upon these conditions themselves, but also upon the activities of many other genes. Biological processes must be "regulated" at all levels, and for the full expression of a characteristic, several epigenetic steps must be completed, each of which may depend upon different constellations of environmental inputs. The epigenetic links between genes and phenotypes can be understood in terms of genetically determined, organismic (cellular) processes which are dependent upon environmental inputs to induce, facilitate, validate, maintain, and integrate growth of the structures to which they give rise. To the extent that these environmental inputs depend upon the existence of organismic structure in order to get through (e.g., via receptors) or to deliver the message (e.g., via endocrine secretions), and insofar as the developing organism acts on its surroundings, the momentary phenotype acts as a mediator of transactions between genome and environment.

### Evolution and Development

*Heterochrony.* Because natural selection is both conservative and opportunistic, many facets of evolutionary change can be understood as the products of alterations in the growth-*rates* of various component structures rather than fundamental alterations in kind (Gould, 1977; Raff & Kaufman, 1983; Wake & Larson, 1987). Genes specifying the relative timing, duration, and rate of growth of any attribute tend to be inherited independently of one another. Therefore, the ontogenies of various characteristics of an organism are linked only to the degree that they yield workable phenotypes. The relative ontogenetic independence of gene-environment coactions underlying various phenotypic features provides a wealth of raw material ("components") for natural selection. Growth, then, does not occur uniformly throughout the organism: The attributes of such apparently unitary structures such as the brain case, the lower jaw, or even the various anatomical areas within the brain typically are the result of growth in several quasi-independent components (Gould, 1977; Tanner, 1970). These components develop at different rates. In short, ontogeny is heterochronous.

*Stages.* Insofar as natural selection can only act on the genetic potentials to develop characteristics that do achieve phenotypic expression, and because this process begins at conception, every step in the life cycle is under selective pressure. This means that each stage of species-typical growth reflects not just a phenotypic response to prior transactions with the environment, but also anticipatory adaptations to conditions typical of that point in the life cycle. That is, the various organismic components must be organized and regulated to ensure that the growing fetus, child, or juvenile can effectively exploit its surroundings. These organized configurations of components, functional systems, thus will be stage-specific and, as such, may involve unique coordinations of components which will subsequently be reorganized to meet the demands of adaptation peculiar to subsequent stages of growth. Examples of such stage-specific reorganizations can be found across a wide range of activities from the development of the cardiac cycle (Arey, 1954) to the development of abstract thought (Piaget, 1962; Inhelder & Piaget, 1958). The problem of motivation of behavior can be seen as a special case of the more general issue of understanding the range of behavioral organizations available in the short-term, and peculiar to a particular developmental phase, for example, the onset of stranger anxiety coinciding with the onset of locomotion.

The model of stages in development does not necessarily mean that there are complete metamorphoses in every realm. What it does mean is that we should not necessarily expect behaviors appearing in one functional context in early life to be components of behavioral systems serving the same or similar ends in later stages. Moreover, behaviors which do predict across stages need not resemble one another (cf. Kagan's, 1971, "homotypic" continuity): An activity measured at one stage in development may predict another, apparently unrelated behavior measured at a later date (cf. Kagan's, 1971, "heterotypic continuity").

*Continuity.* Our model can account for several forms of heterotypic continuity beyond the reappearance of a specific act (e.g., smiling) in different contexts. One possibility is that the different behavioral systems involved all include one or more regulatory components in common. Heterotypic shifts across successive stages also can result from the reintegration of different regulatory sub-components ("A" and "B") of an early system into two different, later-appearing systems, the first involving "A" and the second involving "B." Finally, a component regulating one system such as a perceptual capacity can affect the functioning of an early system, for example, hypothalamic control of the pituitary, and that, in turn, as a result of the operation of the early system, can induce or facilitate development of certain features of a later-appearing system, for example adrenal response to stress, without otherwise involving directly shared elements. These hypothetical developmental changes thus might explain how early experiences can affect the expression of later-appearing behaviors. For example, the phenomena of early imprinting of later sexual preferences might exemplify homotypic continuity insofar as recognition of species mates is a shared element in both the filial and mating systems.

*Canalization.* Because developmental processes are under intense selection pressure and since many genes are involved in the determination of a phenotype, development of basic, species-specific attributes tends to be buffered. That is, basic characteristics will achieve phenotypic expression under a wide variety of conditions, as a result of the joint action of many genes which act to stabilize or canalize developmental responses to environmental conditions. Presumably, once activated, the products of some gene-complexes act to keep growth on course despite temporary perturbations such as those due to disease or brief periods of undernutrition. The phenomenon of "catch-up" growth (cf. Tanner, 1962; 1970) indicates that developmental trajectories are targeted and will be followed despite brief encounters with conditions appropriate for the activation of slightly different targets (Waddington, 1957).

In other cases, species-typical characteristics may simply be dependent upon the evolution of responsiveness to sign stimuli that are ubiquitous (present in all settings capable of sustaining human life) or to any subset of a broader array of alternative sign stimuli which typify human habitats. Thus the development of a number of species-typical, hominid characteristics in very different habitats may reflect the *irrelevance* of many of the features that distinguish one milieu from another.

In addition, the basic design features of biological structure (including the genetic code itself) involve redundancies: Living systems tend to be overengineered in that malfunction in one subcomponent often can be compensated for by the rest of a system or as a result of the operation of other, anatomically/physiologically different systems. Thus, for most children, a single, potentially damaging event such as perinatal stress does not inevitably lead to subnormal functioning. Rather, developmental deviations are more commonly associated with the presence of *several* risk factors such as perinatal stress combined with poverty and a lack of intellectual stimulation (Werner & Smith, 1982).

*Active growth.* The assumption that growth is an active process in which the young tend to provoke as well as respond to caregiving activities suggests that not only does one's inherited potentials for growth constrain what one can be, but many developmental processes, once induced, cause one to selectively process and actively attempt to gain the input required for continued growth along a particular pathway.

Just as the developing organism signals its mother's uterus to prepare to receive it, many facets of infants' and children's behavior seem geared to obtaining the kinds of stimulation required for continued growth. In the realm of motor development, newly-acquired capacities often are performed repeatedly, playfully, and apparently "for their own sake." Only later on, when they have become more or less automatized, will the same activities be deployed in the service of other ends, suggesting that, as the neural substrates underlying new coordinations begin to develop, they require a certain amount of use in order to be maintained, validated, and integrated.

*Constraints.* If each stage of growth represents a unique configuration of phenotypic attributes geared to promote efficient exploitation of the average, expectable environment both for immediate survival and to facilitate further development along a limited range of species-typical trajectories, then one's responsiveness to input as well as one's motor repertoire is likely to be constrained. That is, in its transactions with the environment, the phenotype filters input. Filtering occurs at least three levels: (a) the receptors, which determine the quality or range of effective environmental input; (b) central relays which also determine the precision of possible discriminations; and (c) central processors which, as species-specific features, constrain the "algorithms" by which patterns of nerve activity gain meaning (e.g., Ballard et al., 1983).

As Piaget (1954) put it, children "construct" reality, constructions which are illustrated both in children and adults by visual and auditory illusions and categorical perceptions. The active, constructive transactions of children are further exemplified by early language acquisition. It seems that young children *generate* their own productive grammars on the basis of a set of algorithms or hypotheses for extracting syntactic meaning from what they hear and for conveying meaning via what they say (e.g., Slobin, 1973; 1982). Nor is language acquisition the only social domain in which we can observe the child's active contribution. Although imitation is sometimes considered to be a passive form of learning, the ability to emulate another is really quite remarkable when one considers the fact that, in order to imitate, visual and/or auditory input must be translated into motor actions, actions which, in infants, involve segments of their anatomy which they have never seen (Meltzoff & Moore, 1985).

## CONCEPTUAL IMPLICATIONS

The model of gene-environment coaction and the ontogenetic reorganization of functional systems presented here has a number of implications for the ways in which we conceptualize the determinants of development.

### Effects of the Environment

First and foremost, this model is intended to underscore the idea that environmental influences of whatever kind ultimately involve gene-action. No phenotypic characteristic can be determined by purely genetic or purely environmental factors.

*Epigenesis.* Gene actions are influenced by environmental input in a variety of ways which can be roughly classified according to their effects on epigenetic processes in organis or tissues. Insofar as these phases of epigenesis are distinct, for the development of any particular attribute (or component thereof) there will be discontinuity of input. For example, many of the major outlines of human behavior are induced by what we have called ubiquitous stimuli, such as the neural substrates for binocular vision, which probably originate prenatally. The facilitation, maintenance, and validation of these feature-detectors require postnatal visual input, and the integration (use) of the products of one's visual apparatus changes as visual depth information becomes an integral part of other developing functional systems, including locomotion (Bertenthal et al., 1984). The latter developments may depend upon vision only tangentially, if at all.

To the extent that we have been successful in identifying influences on behavioral development, the majority of our findings have focused upon facilitative or integrative conditions. Indeed, a number of apparently contradictory findings may simply reflect differences in the "point of entry" in the growth process. There is no empirical reason whatsoever to expect that the same inputs will suffice to evoke and then sustain all phases of epigenesis—whether the tuning of auditory receptors or the discovering of word-meaning.

*Multiple pathways.* The view that individuals inherit a genome specifying a norm of reaction implies that several developmental pathways may be potentially available. Some of these pathways will represent alternative strategies or facultative responses to specific environmental conditions, an unremarkable concept. However, by postulating that these modes of adjustment reflect inherited potential we are also suggesting that their variety and number will be limited (at least within the range of known human habitats) and that the possibility of expression of some of these potentials will be limited in time and number.

That is, not only will there be critical periods for the fine tuning of major human potentials, but if behavior involves a multiplicity of elements organized in time, and developmental "choice points" are encountered, then the hereditary mix and environmental settings optimal for the expression of one set of organizations of elements may be suboptimal for (or inimical to) the development of another one. Even if the systems are not mutually exclusive, it is possible that maximizing the expression of one kind of organization may involve sacrificing another kind which involves elements from the first.

Finally, given the fact that individual heredities differ, we cannot assume that the same environment that is optimal for, say, the development of competitiveness for one individual will necessarily be optimal for achieving an equal degree of development of the same trait in another. While we may hope to be able to identify settings that should reliably initiate and support certain typically human developmental outcomes for most people, there will be a few for whom species-typical development will be impossible in all but the most unusual surroundings. That is, since several different patterns of deviance can be identified, it is likely that individuals who are genetically predisposed to express different behavioral patterns would require different environments in order to develop more species-typical behavioral phenotypes.

### Individual Differences

This last point highlights the implications of this model for the understanding of individual differences. Insofar as complex behavior reflects the coordinated activity of component elements, the model suggests that behavioral variations can result from differences in any one of the several components making up the system in question. Correspondingly, the same phenotypic behavior also can arise from somewhat different variants of components. Moreover, there are normal degrees of variation which, in some cases, border on qualitative differences. These too can be interpreted as the results of genetically-guided developmental trajectories in response to different environmental inputs—one's inherited "norm of reaction." In some cases they represent alternative strategies which are potentials that are presumably expressed to varying degrees by all humans and activated (at specified points in development) by situational cues, for example, the use of word order or inflection to specify syntactical meaning. In other instances, they may represent alternative developmental trajectories analogous to the commitment of cells in differentiating embryonic tissues.

Given their genetic uniqueness, individuals will vary in terms of the degree of which each facet of their growth is canalized, the number (or range) of facultative adjustments to different surroundings that they can make readily, and even the probability of following a particular alternative developmental pathway. Such variations would be due to differences in the inherited potential to develop structures mediating the thresholds for environmental activation of a particular developmental trajectory and/or to differences in the genetic competence to respond once threshold has been reached. However, all these individual differences are bounded; they are variations within the general confines of human anatomy and behavior.

Even assuming that as many as one-fifth of the identified, human genetic polymorphisms underlie the development of functionally equivalent proteins, there would remain polymorphisms amounting to about one fifth of the *total* number of known human proteins. Thus, we would expect that most people should have the *potential* to develop in a variety of ways, a few of which may be expressed only under extreme conditions. Indeed, there may even be latent developmental possibilities which could become activated in situations which we have yet to encounter (cf. Lewontin et al., 1984).

In short, we must expect genetic variation not only in the degree to which one can express a characteristic, but in the rates at which it will develop, and in the environmental conditions that will be required to ensure its maximal expression. Furthermore, if the arguments presented here are correct, the environmental conditions required to induce, to facilitate, to functionally validate, maintain, and ultimately, to integrate the (sub)systems involved in each of the components of a system underlying behavior are likely to be heterogeneous.

### Childrearing

The view that growth is active, targeted, and progresses through a series of functionally organized, (adaptive) stages wherein youngsters seek and provoke input casts the process of childrearing in a somewhat different light. As opposed to being required in order to shape or *construct* appropriate behavior and/or to *block* the expression of disapproved modes of conduct, adult influences are better conceived as supportive in that they provide the context for the expression of certain facets of the child's range of potentials. These potentials for growth and development are determined by the *child's* heredity and their expression results from a complex co-action of genome and (caregiving) setting.

Children's developmental possibilities at any point depend upon their hereditary potentials, their current phenotypes (the developmental status of their receptors, information filtering and processing capabilities, ability to integrate, store, and *react to* information, etc.) and the setting (caregiving practices, material and cultural surroundings) in which further growth is to take place. This model posits that environmental influences which include, but are not limited to, caregiving and cultural practices, act to initiate and sustain the expression of genetic potentials for the growth of *specific* substrates for a range of behaviors. Whether any particular potential can be expressed depends upon the suite of genes active at that point (the current phenotype) as well as the external inputs available.

*Peers.* So long as the necessary inputs to sustain vegetative function are otherwise available, social exchanges limited to age-mates can provide the matrix within which a variety of social skills can develop—from mastery of age-appropriate language (Luria & Yudovich, 1959) to a sense of social obligation (Freud & Dann, 1951). Even among children who receive their primary care from adults, interactions with (elder) siblings or familiar age-mates can evoke "more advanced" levels of play with objects and precocious displays of the tendency to consider the playmate's perspective (e.g., Dunn & Kendrick, 1979; Rubenstein & Howes, 1976).

*Parents.* Parenting, in this view, is still vital, but for somewhat different reasons than those typically offered. In the first place, the reductionistic model presented here suggests that parental care ultimately must be analyzed in terms of the stimuli that can be shown to affect offspring function. Many of the effective inputs important for major developmental trends probably will turn out to be sign stimuli. Moreover, induction, validation, and maintenance of species-typical development are probably dependent upon any one, or a subset, of stimuli simply indicating the presence of potential caregivers. Beyond a (yet-to-be-defined) minimum level, variation in the quality of early care is more likely to affect rates (facilitate growth) rather than the form of change. Especially for the induction and integration of the development of a number of more basic human attributes (in addition to simple vegetative survival), there may be minimum threshold levels of (sign) stimulation for *any* ontogenetic response. Furthermore, there also probably exist upper bounds of stimulation above which increased exposure to input will either be ineffective or actually detrimental to species-typical growth.

Contrary to the notion that parental care shapes child behavior largely, if not exclusively via instruction and/or exhortation, direct observation of parents and their young offspring in American homes indicates that the children spend much of their time simply watching their mothers. Moreover, as compared with child-centered, quality day care environments, children at home receive more brief verbal commands (vs. detailed instructions) and are more likely to become engaged in activities—and to leave them—on their own (Prescott, 1978; Rubenstein & Howes, 1979).

Observations of mothers interacting with their infants indicate that up to 80% of the bouts of imitation are due to the *mother's* imitating her baby (Pawlby, 1977). If we can assume that the baby's perceptual-motor matching works *both ways*, then the significance of reciprocal imitation in early infancy may be to signal the baby that it is in the care of an attentive, responsive person, that is, someone who is clearly aware of what the infant is doing. The baby's "random" action and "diffuse excitement" when an adult is nearby might then be considered provocative behavior, designed to elicit *parental* activity (cf. Waxler & Radke-Yarrow, 1975).

Although attachment behavior in infancy may lead to proximity-maintenance by infants, the educative effects of such proximity may be incidental. In fact, given sufficient mothering to support vegetative and motor development and a minimum of additional stimulation to support the formation of an attachment, toddlers may use their caregivers as props for their own forays into the unknown. Parental enthusiasm or guidance *may* focus children's attention on certain features of the environment, but the mere presence of a (relaxed) attachment-figure often suffices to support active commerce with the surroundings. That is, in the absence of parental alarm signals, young children seem to seek out and even to create their own opportunities to gain important experiences as a result of their exploratory and playful activities (Ainsworth et al., 1974; Rheingold & Eckerman, 1971). If we can extrapolate from studies suggesting that motor activity may be necessary for fine-tuning sensory analyzers, then passive exposure to animate and inanimate complexity, as afforded to infants in strollers or carried against their mothers' bodies in slings, may be no substitute for active exploration (Bertenthal et al., 1984; Goldberg, 1977; Held & Hein, 1968).

*Provocation.* The young begin to affect parents at fertilization and subsequently influence all aspects of parental life (Harper, 1975). Parenting is as much reaction as planned action, and children control at least the timing of a significant proportion of the exchanges they have with their parents. Often the quality and the course of interactions are largely determined by offspring—although the outcomes are not always to their liking (see e.g., Patterson, 1980). Beyond the quality of a child's reaction, caregiving is also determined by the number of youngsters who must receive it. For the development of such behavior as early compliance with adult demands, it seems that the essential element in such exchanges is the caregiver's willingness to allow *the infant* to pace and direct exchanges (e.g., Martin, 1981; Schaffer, 1977). Although the mother's contingent responding is considered to be crucial in the process, the initiative is the baby's. Thus, in many respects the whole process is more a matter of the baby shaping the mother's behavior (her contingent responses) than the reverse. This effect becomes particularly noticeable when siblings are twins or closely spaced in age (Lytton, 1980; White et al., 1979). That is, youngster's early characteristics/behaviors may *provoke* inputs that will affect (induce/facilitate) the development of new capacities or predilections. Indeed, it often seems that many of the more important outcomes of care-giving style do not result from deliberate educative attempts on the part of caregivers, and that much of childrearing involves *re*actions to youngsters' spontaneous activities, or unanticipated consequences of the caregiving milieu. For example, assuming that the confounding factor of shared heredity (cf. Plomin, 1984; Scarr & McCartney, 1983) proves to be only part of the picture, we may note that, whereas firstborns tend to acquire single words such as object names first, later-born children are more likely to utter phrases (much as others use words) with instrumental significance. This connection hardly seems to be a matter of design, yet birth order may represent an important determinant of the strategies young children use to develop linguistic competence (Nelson, 1981).

Given evidence that phenotypic differences in many traits are nearly as great among (nontwin) siblings *within* families as they are across unre-lated children in different families (e.g., Plomin & Daniels, 1987; Scarr & Kidd, 1983), we may also benefit from paying attention to the ways in which youngsters affect their surroundings. Scarr (1969) reported that the best predictor of the degree to which twins were treated alike was a labora-tory analysis of their zygosity, not their mother's belief as to whether they were identicals or fraternals. Thus the interactions between genotype and environment will be complex, involving not only differential responsive-ness to input but differences in (phenotypic) capacity to provoke (care-giver) response.

## IMPLICATIONS FOR RESEARCH

The model of growth presented here also has a number of implications for approaching several long-standing problems and raises several additional issues concerning effective data-gathering strategies.

### Stages and the Question of Developmental Continuity

The model of ontogenetic reorganization of behavioral components postu-lates both the existence of (adaptive) stages and discontinuities in devel-opment.

*Stages.* According to this model, stages in the development of complex, adaptive behavior should be reflected by unique patterns of behavioral organization. That is, as they grow older children would be expected to utilize somewhat different strategies in order to achieve various ends. Thus this model highlights the importance of describing and analyzing precisely the suite of skills, and so on underlying performance of the same tasks at different points in the life cycle. Moreover, it suggests that phases of reorganization should be correlated with demonstrable changes in organismic (brain) function (e.g., Chugani & Phelps, 1986; Manil, Desmedt, Debecker, & Chorazyna, 1967).

*Continuity.* Continuities in development might be expected in relatively limited realms, for example, in certain early-developing components contributing to global behaviors. However, in terms of more complex activities, discontinuities would be the rule. According to the model presented here, the rate of change in performance of any task would not suffice to identify a change in substrate (*contra* Fisher, Pipp, & Bullock, 1984). Only a demonstration of a change in the *patterning* of the contributors to performance would demonstrate discontinuities. Discontinuities in pattern could be indexed by changing factor-structures of (sets of) measures relevant to performance, or the actual temporal organization of actions involved in a complex performance itself. Discontinuity thus could result from the inclusion of a new tactic or skill in solving some task (cf. Kagan, 1984) or a change in the order in, or in the degree to which, component elements are linked to one another (cf. Bryant, 1985; Connell & Furman, 1984).

This model also suggests that the discontinuities suggested by linkages between early experience and later behavior may be explicable by analyses of the organizational dynamics of the functional systems involved. It suggests that apparently very different behavioral systems will share some component processes across stages. However, insofar as we portray stages of organization as constraining or filtering organismic responsiveness to input, this model also requires that one *demonstrate* that putative early experiences actually are registered and/or evoke some overt reaction in order to support a hypothesis of a developmental linkage.

Finally, insofar as component processes may (or may not) be dedicated to specific functional systems, this model discourages either identifying specific actions or capacities with a single molar, functional class of behavior, or of postulating a priori that a single component (e.g., a disparity detector) serves several processes. Each functional system should be investigated on its own and shared components should be demonstrated by means of experimental tests in which the putative common component is required to function simultaneously in service of conflicting tasks (cf. Kinsbourne & Hiscock, 1983).

### Effects of Caregiving

Since the model of growth presented here emphasizes both the co-action of heredity and environment and the active nature of growth processes, it suggests that traditional, correlative studies of the effects of upbringing practices are insufficient to demonstrate how childrearing tactics influeence behavior.

*Shared heredity.* To the extent that parents and offspring share the same genes, even where child behavioral outcomes are predictable from earlier parental caregiving, causal linkages cannot be inferred directly (Hardy-Brown, 1983). Unambiguous antecedent-consequent relationships can only be derived from studies (a) using adopted/foster children who are unrelated to their foster parents (b) with neonatal assessments of the infants and pre-adoptive evaluations of the characteristics of the parents-and siblings-to-be; and (c) with repeated, detailed observations of the physical and social surroundings, especially the ways in which parents, siblings, and the focal children interact with each other.

*Provocative behavior.* We have suggested that certain events associated with the presence of younger and/or older siblings act as sign stimuli which color the ways in which youngsters react to still other facets of their (social) surroundings. If so, inherited predispositions and context could interact to affect the quality of the reactions of the focal child and easily account for the otherwise surprisingly great amount of within-family variance. That is, to the extent that different children react differently to the "same" situations, they may "provoke" different inputs. Therefore, in order to meaningfully evaluate the significance of caregiving practices one must be able to estimate how much variance is attributable to offspring behavior, for example, the child's social responsiveness, soothability, and so on. This means extensive, detailed observations of behavioral exchanges across many unrelated families and/or prenatal assessment of parental reactions so that parental style can be partialed out from the effects of offspring action and reaction.

## Analytic Models

*Quantification.* We have suggested that some of the stimuli necessary and sufficient for the expression of many species-specific attributes may be ubiquitous, essentially unavoidable in settings capable of sustaining human life. If so, phenotypic variation may be skewed among (inbred) populations, or show high degrees of heritability where substantial genetic variation does occur. In either case, the frequency distribution of individual measurements should be an important datum. In our discussion of the nature of the growth process, we have also raised the possibility that there may exist both upper and lower thresholds for stimulation to affect gene-expression. That is, environmental inputs and developmental responses may not be linearly related, or they may stand in linear dose-response relationships to one another only over a very limited segment of the range of environmental variation. Therefore, nonlinear models need to be utilized more often and scatterplots of the distributions of (co)variables will be required to make a case for the (in)effectiveness of any potential inputs.

*Description.* Insofar as the effective stimuli for expressing genetic potentials can vary from ubiquitous signs to situationally-specific indices of local conditions, this model calls for intensive analyses of the nature of the stimulus along the lines of classical ethology (e.g., Tinbergen, 1951). Similarly, the concept of component contributors to organized behavior will require equally precise description and analysis of both overt responses (e.g., Thelen, 1985) and of putative underlying processes. In the latter case, our reductionist approach suggests that we may gain much from studies of (neuro) physiological functioning in order to identify both components or modules that provide the substrates for commerce with the environment (cf. Aslin et al., 1983; Banks & Salapatek, 1983; Gazzaniga, 1985; Goldman-Rakic, 1985; Wiesel, 1982), and the effective stimuli for activating them.

## Problem Areas

This conception of gene-environment co-action and the effects of the environmental input on organismic growth can serve to rekindle interest in the study of "maturational" events. From this perspective, it should be possible to identify the events necessary and/or sufficient to evoke and support the development of species-typical attributes. Although some facets of human growth may be induced, validated, and maintained by input so general as oxygen and warmth, it is likely that the facilitation and (degree of) integration of many of these characteristics will vary with identifiable environmental differences.

## Selection of Subjects

The adaptationist position and the concept of ubiquitous stimuli both require intensive description and analysis of behavioral development across the full range of human habitats. Studies using special populations (e.g., Décarie, 1969; Freud & Dann, 1951) can help us identify which inputs are not essential and/or which inputs may serve as alternative equivalents for evoking and supporting species-typical growth. However, these investigations in themselves will be insufficient to test adaptationist hypotheses. To do that and to establish (rough) boundaries on the range of human behavioral variation, and to assess the range of environmental conditions associated with such variation, extensive cross-cultural, developmental investigations are essential.

I submit that, along with the failures to appreciate the various influences of environment on epigenesis (Gottlieb, 1976) and the role of shared heredity (Scarr & McCartney, 1983) our meager success in identifying the antecedents and correlates of human behavioral variation (Maccoby &

Martin, 1983) reflects a profound lack of detailed descriptions of either human environments or of human behavioral variation (Bronfenbrenner, 1979).

As Dobzhansky (1972, p. 67) put it: "The complexity of nature should not be evaded. The only way to simplify nature is to study it as it is, not as we would have liked it to be."

# References

Abramov, I., Gordon, J., Hendrickson, A., Hainline, L., Dobson, V., & LaBossiere, E. (1982). The retina of the newborn human infant. *Science, 217,* 265–267.

Acredolo, L.P. (1987). Early development of spatial orientation in humans. In P. Ellen & C. Thinus-Blanc (Eds.), *Cognitive processes and spatial orientation in animals and man.* (Vol. II, pp. 185–201). Dondrecht, Netherlands: Martinus Nijhoff.

Adelson, E.H., & Movshon, J.A. (1982). Phenomenal coherence of moving visual patterns. *Nature, 300,* 523–525.

Adolph, E.F. (1968). *Origins of physiological regulations.* New York: Academic Press.

Aguilar, M.J., & Williamson, M.L. (1968). Observations on growth and development of the brain. in D.B. Cheek (Ed.), *Human growth* (pp. 592–605). Philadelphia: Lea & Febiger.

Ainsworth, M.D.S. (1963). The development of infant-mother interaction among the Ganda. In B.M. Foss (Ed.) *Determinants of infant behaviour.* II. (pp. 67–112). London: Methuen.

Ainsworth, M.D.S. (1969). Object relations, dependency and attachment: A theoretical review of the infant-mother relationship. *Child Development, 40,* 969–1025.

Ainsworth, M.D.S. (1977). Infant development and mother-infant interaction among Ganda and America families. In P.H. Leiderman, S.R. Tulkin, & A. Rosenfeld (Eds.), *Culture and infancy: Variations in the human experience* (pp. 119–149). New York: Academic.

Ainsworth, M.D.S., Bell, S.M.V., & Stayton, D.J. (1971). Individual differences in strange-situation behaviour of one-year-olds. In H.R. Schaffer (Ed.), *The origins of human social relations* (pp. 17–52). New York: Academic Press.

Ainsworth, M.D.S., Bell, S.M., & Stayton, D.J. (1974). Infant-mother attachment and social development: 'Socialisation" as a product of reciprocal responsiveness to signals. In M.P.M. Richards (Ed.), *The integration of a child into a social world.* (pp. 99–135). Cambridge: Cambridge University Press.

Ainsworth, M.D.S., & Wittig, B.A. (1969). Attachment and exploratory behavior of one-year-olds in a strange situation. In B.M. Foss (Eds.), *Determinants of infant behaviour,* IV (pp. 111–136). London: Methuen.

Aleksandrowicz, M.K. (1974). The effect of pain relieving drugs administered during labor and delivery on the behavior of the newborn: A review. *Merrill-Palmer Quarterly, 20,* 121–141.

Alexander, R.D. (1974). The evolution of social behavior. *Annual Review of Ecology and Systematics, 5,* 325–383.

Alexander, R.D. (1979a). *Darwinism and human affairs.* Seattle: University of Washington Press.

Alexander, R.D. (1981, March). *The biology of moral systems: The natural history of ethics.* Storer Life Sciences Lectures, University of California, Davis.

Alland, A., Jr. (1972). *The human imperative.* New York: Columbia University Press.

Allport, G.W. (1937). *Personality. A psychological interpretation.* New York: Henry Holt.

Altman, J. (1985). Tuning in to neurotransmitters. *Nature, 315,* 537.

Altman, J., Das, G., & Sudarshan, K. (1970). The influence of nutrition on neural and behavioral development: I. Critical review of some data on the growth of the body and the brain following dietary deprivation during gestation and lactation. *Developmental Psychobiology, 3*(4), 281–301.

Ambros, V. (1984). Heterochronic mutants of the nematode *caenorhalbditis elegans. Science, 226,* 409–416.

Ambrose, J.A. (1961). The development of the smiling response in early infancy. In B.M. Foss (Ed.), *Determinants of infant behaviouir* (pp. 170–195). New York: Wiley.

Ambrose, J.A. (Ed.) (1969). *Stimulation in early infancy.* New York: Academic Press.

Amiel-Tison, C. (1985). Pediatric contribution to the present knowledge on the neuro-behavioural staus of infants at birth. In J. Mehler & R. Fox (Eds.), *Neonate cognition* (pp. 365–380). Hillsdale, NJ: Lawrence Erlbaum Associates.

Amsterdam, B. (1972). Mirror self-image reactions before age two. *Developmental Psychobiology., 5,* 297–305.

Anastasi, A. (1958). Heredity, environment, and the question of how? *Psychological Review, 65,* 197–208.

Anderson, J.W. (1972). Attachment behaviour out of doors. In N. Blurton-Jones (Ed.), *Ethological studies of child behaviour* (pp. 199–226). Cambridge: Cambridge University Press.

Anderson, K.V. (1984). Information for the dorsal-ventral pattern of the Drosophila embryo is stored as maternal mRNA. *Nature, 311,* 223–227.

Anokhin, P.K. (1964). Systemogenesis as a general regulator of brain development. In W.A. Himwich & H.E. Himwich (Eds.), *The developing brain. Progress in brain research,* Vol. 9 (pp. 54–86). Amsterdam: Elsevier.

Archer, S.M., Dubin, M.W., & Stark, L.A. (1982). Abnormal development of kitten retino-geniculate connectivity in the absence of action potentials. *Science, 217,* 743–745.

Arey, L.B. (1954). *Developmental anatomy* (6th ed.). Philadelphia: W.B. Saunders.

Arvidson, K., & Friberg, U. (1980). Human taste: Response and taste bud number in fugiform papillae. *Science, 209,* 807–808.

Aslin, R.N. (1981). Experiential influences and sensitive periods in development: A unified model. In R.N. Aslin & M.R. Petersen (Eds.), *Development of perception,* Vol. 2 (pp. 45–93). New York: Academic Press.

Aslin, R.N. (1985). Effects of experience on sensory and perceptual development: Implications for infant cognition. In J. Mehler & R. Fox (Eds.) *Neonate cog-*

*nition* (pp. 157–183). Hillsdale, NJ: Lawrence Erlbaum Associates.

Aslin, R.N., Pisoni, D.B., & Jusczyk, P.W. (1983). Auditory development and speech perception in infancy. In P.H. Mussen (Ed.) *Handbook of child psychology.* Vol. II. (4th ed.) (pp. 573–687). New York: Wiley.

Axelrod, R., & Hamilton, W. (1981). The evolution of cooperation. *Science, 211,* 1390–1396.

Baillargeon, R., Spelke, E.S., & Wasserman, S. (1985). Object permanence in five-month-old infants. *Cognition, 20,* 191–208.

Baker, E., Berry, T., Gardner, H., Nurif, E., Davis, L., & Veroff, A. (1975). Can linguistic competence be dissociated from natural language functions? *Nature, 254,* 509–510.

Balazs, R., Lewis, P.D., & Patel, A.J. (1979). Nutritional deficiencies and brain development. In F. Falkner & J.M. Tanner (Eds.). *Human growth.* Vol. 3: *Neurobiology and nutrition* (pp. 415–480). New York: Plenum Press.

Ballard, P.H., Hinton, G.E., & Sejnowski, T.J. (1983). Parallel visual computation. *Nature, 306,* 21–26.

Banks, M.S., Aslin, R.N., & Letson, R.D. (1975). Sensitive period for the development of human binocular vision. *Science, 190,* 675–677.

Banks, M.S., & Salapatek, P. (1983). Infant visual perception. In P.H. Mussen (Ed.), *Handbook of child psychology,* Vol. II. (4th ed.). (pp. 435–571). New York: Wiley.

Barlow, B.A., Narasimhan, R., & Rosenfeld A. (1972). Visual pattern analysis in machines and animals. *Science, 177,* 567–575.

Barlow, G.W. (1981). Genetics and development of behavior, with special reference to patterned motor output. In K. Immelmann, G.W. Barlow, L. Petrinovitch, & M. Main (Eds.), *Behavioral development.* (pp. 191–251). Cambridge: Cambridge University Press.

Barlow, H.B. (1975). Visual experience and cortical development. *Nature, 258,* 199–203.

Barnett, S.A. (1958). Exploratory behaviour. *British Journal of Psychology, 49,* 289–310.

Barnstable, C.J. (1982). Molecular heterogeneity and the nervous system. *Nature, 298,* 708–709.

Beach, F.A. (1976). *Human sexuality in four perspectives.* Baltimore: Johns Hopkins University Press.

Beach, F.A., & Jaynes, J. (1956). Studies of maternal retrieving in rats II: Sensory cues involved in the lactating female's response to her young. *Behaviour, 10,* 104–125.

Beauchamp, G., & Hess, E.H. (1971). The effects of cross-species rearing on the social and sexual preferences of guinea pigs. *Zeitschrift fur Tierpsychologie, 28,* 69–76.

Becker, J.M.T. (1977). A learning analysis of the development of peer-oriented behavior in nine-month-old infants. *Developmental Psychology, 13,* 481–491.

Bekoff, A. (1981). Behavioral embryology of birds and mammals: Neuroembryological studies of the development of motor behavior. In K. Immelmann, G.W. Barlow, L. Petrinovich & M. Main (Eds.), *Behavioral development* (pp. 152–163). Cambridge: Cambridge University Press.

Bekoff, M. (1972). The development of social interaction, play, and metacommunication in mammals: An ethological perspective. *Quarterly Review of Biology, 47,* 412–434.

Bekoff, M. (1974). Social play and play-soliciting by infant canids. *American Zoologist, 14,* 323–340.

Bell, R.Q. (1968). A reinterpretation of the direction of effects in studies of socialization. *Psychological Review, 75,* 81–95.

Bell, R.Q., & Harper, L.V. (1977). *Child effects on adults.* Hillsdale, NJ: Lawrence Erlbaum.

Belsky, J., & Steinberg, L. (1978). The effects of day care: A critical review. *Child Development, 49,* 929–949.

Benfey, M., & Aguayo, A.J. (1982). Extensive elongation of axons from rat brain into peripheral nerve grafts. *Nature, 296,* 150–152.

Bensaude, O., Babinet, C., Morange, M., & Jacob, F. (1983). Heat shock proteins, first major products of zygotic gene activity in mouse embryo. *Nature, 305,* 331–332.

Bentley, D., & Keshishian, H. (1982). Pathfinding by peripheral pioneer neurons in grasshoppers. *Science, 218,* 1082–1088.

Bentley, D., & Caudy, M. (1983). Pioneer axons lose directed growth after selective killing of guidepost cells. *Nature, 304,* 62–65.

Berg, W.K., & Berg, K.M. (1979). Psychophysiological development in infancy: State, sensory function, and attention. In J.D. Osofsky (Ed.), *Handbook of infant development* (pp. 283–343). New York: Wiley.

Bergen, J.R., & Julesz, B. (1983). Parallel versus serial processing in rapid pattern discrimination, *Nature, 303,* 696–698.

Bergler, P.J., Negus, N.C., Sanders, E.H., & Gardner, P.D. (1981). Chemical triggering of reproduction in *Microtus montanus. Science, 214,* 69–70.

Bergmann, R.L., & Bergmann, K.E. (1979). Nutrition and growth in infancy. In F. Falkner & J.M. Tanner (Eds.), *Human growth.* Vol. 3. *Neurobiology and nutrition* (pp. 331–360). New York: Plenum Press.

Berlot, J., & Goodman, C.S. (1984). Guidance of peripheral pioneer neurons in the grasshopper: Adhesive hierarchy of epithelial and neuronal surfaces. *Science, 223,* 493–496.

Bertenthal, B.I., Campos, J.J., & Barrett K.C. (1984). Self-produced locomotion. In R.N. Emde & R.J. Harmon (Eds.) *Continuities and discontinuities in development* (pp. 175–210). New York: Plenum.

Bettelheim, B. (1969). *The children of the dream.* Toronto: Collier-Macmillan.

Bijou, S.W., & Baer, D.M. (1961). *Child development: A systematic and empirical theory.* Vol. I. New York: Appleton.

Birky, C.W. Jr. (1983). Relaxed cellular controls and organelle heredity. *Science, 222,* 468–475.

Bitterman, M.E. (1975). The comparative analysis of learning. *Science, 188,* 699–709.

Black, I.B. (1982). Stages of neurotransmitter development in autonomic neurons. *Science, 215,* 1198–1203.

Blaffer-Hrdy, S. (1976). Care and exploitation of nonhuman primate infants by conspecifics other than the mother. *Advances in the Study of Behavior, 6,* 101–158.

Blake, R., & Cormack, R.H. (1979). Psychophysical evidence for a monocular visual cortex in stereoblind humans. *Science, 203,* 274–276.

Blau, H.M., Pavlath, G.K., Hardeman, E.C., Chiu, C.P., Silberstein, L., Webster, S.G., Miller, S.C., & Miller, C. (1985). Plasticity of the differentiated state. *Science, 230,* 758–766.

Bloom, K. (1974). Eye contact as a setting event for infant learning. *Journal of Experimental Child Psychology, 17,* 250–263.

Bloom, K. (1975). Social elicitation of infant vocal behavior, *Journal of Experimental Child Psychology, 20,* 51–58.

Bloom, K., & Erickson, M.T. (1971, April). *The role of eye contact in the social reinforcement of infant vocalizations.* Paper presented at the biennial meeting of the Society for Research in Child Development, Minneapolis, MN.

Bloom, K., & Esposito, A. (1975). Social conditioning and its proper control procedures. *Journal of Experimental Child Psychology, 19,* 209–222.

Bloom, L. (1970). *Language development: Form and function in emerging grammars.* Cambridge, MA: MIT Press.

Bloom, L. (1975). Language development. In F.D. Horowitz (Ed.), *Review of child development research.* Vol. 4 (pp. 245–303). Chicago: University of Chicago Press.

Bloom, L. (1983). Tensions in psycholinguistics, *Science, 220,* 843–845.

Blount, B.G. (1981). The development of language in children. In R.H. Munroe, R.L. Munroe, & B.B. Whiting (Eds.), *Handbook of cross-cultural human development* (pp. 379–402). New York: Garland STPM Press.

Blurton-Jones, N.G. (1967). An ethological study of some aspects of social behaviour of children in nursery school. In D. Morris (Ed.), *Primate ethology,* (pp. 347–368). Chicago: Aldine.

Blythe, I.M., Bromley, J.M., Kennard, C., & Ruddock, K.N. (1986). Visual discrimination of target displacement remains after damage to the striate cortex in humans. *Nature, 320,* 619–621.

Bornstein, M.H. (1975). Hue is an absolute code for young children. *Nature, 256,* 309–310.

Bornstein, M.H. (1985). Infant into adult: Unity to diversity in the development of visual categorization. In J. Mehler & R. Fox (Eds.). *Neonate cognition* (pp. 115–138). Hillsdale, NJ: Lawrence Erlbaum.

Bornstein, M.H., Dessen, W., & Weiskopf, S. (1976). The categories of hue in infancy. *Science, 191,* 201–202.

Bonner, T.I., & Brownstein, M.J. (1984). Tissue-specific deficit in the Brattleboro rat. *Nature, 310,* 17.

Boucaut, J.D., Darribère, T., Boulekbache, H., & Thiery, J.P. (1984). Prevention of gastrulation but not neurulation by antibodies to fibronectin in amphibian embryos. *Nature, 307,* 364–367.

Bourlière, F. (1964). *The natural history of mammals.* (3rd ed.). (rev. ed.). New York: Knopf.

Bower, T.G.R. (1966). Heterogeneous summation in human infants. *Animal Behaviour, 14,* 395–398.

Bower, T.G.R. (1977). *A primer of infant development.* San Francisco: W.H. Freeman.

Bower, T.G.R. (1982). *Development in infancy.* San Francisco: W.H. Freeman.

Bowerman, M. (1981). Language development. In H.C. Triandis & A. Heron (Eds.), *Handbook of cross-cultural psychology: Vol. 4, Developmental psychology* (pp. 93–155). Boston: Allyn & Bacon.

Bowlby, J. (1952). *Maternal care and mental health.* (2nd ed.). Geneva: World Health Organization.

Bowlby, J. (1958). The nature of the child's tie to his mother. *International Journal of Psycho-Analysis, 39,* 350–373.

Bowlby, J. (1969). *Attachment and loss: Vol. 1. Attachment.* New York: Basic Books.

Bowlby, J. (1973). *Attachment and loss: Vol. 2. Separation anxiety and anger.* New York: Basic Books.

Bowlby, J. (1982). *Attachment,* 2nd Ed. New York: Basic Books.

Braddick, O., Atkinson, J., Julesz, B., Kropfl, J., Bodis-Wollner, I., & Raab, E. (1980). Cortical binocularity in infants. *Nature, 288,* 363–365.

Braddick, O.J., Wattam-Bell, J., & Atkinson, J. (1986). Orientation-specific cortical responses develop in early infancy. *Nature, 320,* 617–619.

Brainerd, C.J., & Allen, T.W. (1971). Training and conservation of density conservation: Effects of feedback and consecutive similar stimuli. *Child Development, 42,* 693–704.

Brannigan, C.R., & Humphries, D.A. (1972). Human non-verbal behaviour, a means of communication. In N.G. Blurton-Jones (Ed.), *Ethological studies of child behaviour* (pp. 37–64). Cambridge: Cambridge University Press.

Brannon, J.B. (1968). A comparison of syntactic structures in the speech of three- and four-year-old children. *Language and Speech, 11,* 171–181.

Breger, L. (1974). *From instinct to identity/The development of personality.* New Jersey: Prentice Hall.

Bregman, B.S., & Goldberger, M.E. (1982). Anatomical plasticity and sparing function after spinal cord damage in neonatal cats. *Science, 217,* 553–555.

Bretherton, I. (1985). Attachment theory. Retrospect and prospect. *Monographs of the Society for Research in Child Development, 50,* (1–2), 3–35, Serial no. 209.

Bretherton, I., & Waters, E. (1985). (Eds.). Growing points of attachment theory and research. *Monographs of the Society for Research in Child Development, 50,* (1–2) Serial no. 209.

Breznitz, S., & Kugelmass, S. (1967). Intentionality in moral judgement: Developmental stages. *Child Development, 38,* 469–480.

Bridger, W.H. (1962). Sensory discrimination and autonomic function in the newborn. *Journal of the American Academy of Child Psychiatry, 1,* 67–82.

Brody, S., & Axelrad, S. (1971). Maternal stimulation and social responsiveness of infants. In H.R. Schaffer (Ed.), *The origins of human social relations* (pp. 195–210). New York: Academic Press.

Bromage, T.G. (1985). Reevaluating the age at death of fossil hominids. *Nature, 317,* 525–527.

Bronfenbrenner, U. (1970). *Two worlds of childhood: U.S. and U.S.S.R.* New York: Russell Sage Foundation.

Bronfenbrenner, U. (1979). *The ecology of human development.* Cambridge, MA: Harvard University Press.

Bronson, G.W. (1969). Vision in infancy: Structure-function relationships. In R.J.

Robinson (Ed.), *Brain and early behaviour* (pp. 207–210). New York: Academic Press.

Bronson, G.W. (1971). Fear of the unfamiliar in human infants. In H.R. Schaffer (Ed.), *The origins of human social relations*, (pp. 59–66). New York: Academic Press.

Bronson, G.W. (1972). Infants' reactions to an unfamiliar persons and novel objects. *Monographs of the Society for Research in Child Development, 38* (3), Serial No. 148.

Bronson, G.W. (1974). The postnatal growth of visual capacity. *Child Development, 45,* 873–890.

Brooks, J., & Lewis, M. (1974). The effect of time on attachment as measured in a free play situation. *Child Development, 45,* 311–316.

Brooks, V., & Hochberg, J. (1960). A psychophysical study of "cuteness." *Perceptual and Motor Skills, 11,* 205.

Brown, C.M. (1984). Computer vision and natural constraints. *Science, 226,* 1299–1305.

Brown, D.D. (1981). Gene expression in Eukaryotes. *Science, 211,* 667–674.

Brown, D.L., & Salinger, W.L. (1975). Loss of X-cells in lateral genicuate nucleus with monocular paralysis: Neural plasticity in the adult cat. *Science, 189,* 1011–1012.

Brown, M.C., & Booth, C.M. (1983). Postnatal development of the adult pattern of motor axon distribution. *Nature, 304,* 741–742.

Brown, M.C., & Ironton, R. (1977). Motor neurons sprouting induced by prolonged tetrodotoxin block of nerve action potential. *Nature, 265,* 459–461.

Brown, R. (1958). *Words and things.* Glencoe, IL: Free Press.

Brown, R. (1973). *A first language.* Cambridge, MA: Harvard University Press.

Bruce, D.J. (1965). Language and cognition: Studies of the verbal behavior of children. *Acta Psychologica, 24,* 264–280.

Bruce, J.E., & Ayala, J.F. (1978). Humans and apes are genetically very similar. *Nature, 276,* 264–265.

Bruner, J.S. (1977). Early social interaction and language acquisition. In H.R. Schaffer (Ed.), *Studies in mother-infant interaction* (pp. 271–289). New York: Academic Press.

Bruner, J.S., & Bruner, B.M. (1968). On voluntary action and its hierarchical structure. *International Journal of Psychology, 3,* 239–255.

Bryan, J.H., & Walbek, N.H. (1970). Preaching and practicing generosity: Children's actions and reactions. *Child Development, 41,* 329–353.

Bryant, B.K. (1985). The neighborhood walk: Sources of support in middle childhood. *Monographs of the Society for Research in Child Development, 50* (3), serial no. 210.

Bryant, B.K., & Crockenberg, S.B. (1980). Correlates and dimensions of prosocial behavior: A study of female siblings with their mothers. *Child Development, 51,* 529–544.

Bryant, P.E., & Kopytynska, H. (1976). Spontaneous measurement by young children. *Nature, 260,* 773.

Buhler, C. (1933). Social behavior in children. In C. Murchison (Ed.), *A handbook of child psychology.* 2nd Ed. (pp. 374–416). Worchester, MA: Clark University Press.

Bulmer, M.G. (1970). *The biology of twinning in man*. London: Oxford University Press.

Bunge, R., Johnson, M., & Ross, C.D. (1978). Nature and nurture in the development of the automic neuron. *Science, 199*, 1409–1416.

Bunning, E. (1967). *The physiological clock*. New York: Springer.

Burghardt, G.M. (1978). Behavioral ontogeny in reptiles: Whence, whither and why. In G.M. Burghardt & M. Bekoff (Eds.), *The development of behavior* (pp. 149–174). New York: Garland STPM Press.

Butler, S.P., Suskind, M.R., & Schanberg, S.M. (1978). Maternal behavior as a regulator of polyamine biosynthesis in brain and heart of developing rat pup. *Science, 199*, 445–446.

Butters, N., Rosen, J., & Stein, D. (1974). Recovery of behavioral functions after sequential ablation of the frontal lobes of monkeys. In D.G. Stein, J.J. Rosen, & N. Butters (Eds.), *Plasticity and recovery of function in the central nervous system* (pp. 429–466). New York: Academic Press.

Cain, W.S. (1979). To know with the nose: Keys to odor identification. *Science, 203*, 467–470.

Calhoun, L.G. (1971). Number conservation in very young children: The effect of age and mode of responding. *Child Development, 42*, 561–572.

Campbell, B.A., & Jaynes, J. (1966). Reinstatement. *Phychological Review, 73*, 478–480.

Campos, J.J., Barrett, K.C., Lamb, M.E., Goldsmith, H.H., & Stenberg, C. (1983). Socioemotional development. In P.H. Mussen (Ed.), *Handbook of child psychology* (4th Ed.), vol. II, (pp. 783–915). New York: Wiley.

Campos, J.J., Langer, A., & Krowitz, A. (1970). Cardiac responses on the visual cliff in prelocomotor human infants. *Science, 170*, 196–197.

Campos, J.J., & Stenberg, C.R. (1981). Perception, appraisal and emotion: The onset of social referencing. In M.E. Lamb & L.R. Sherrod (Eds.), *Infant social cognition* (pp. 273–314). Hillsdale, NJ: Lawrence Erlbaum.

Caplan, A.I., Fiszman, M.Y., & Eppenberger, H.M. (1983). Molecular and cell isoforms during development. *Science, 221*, 921–927.

Caplan, A.I., & Ordahl, C.P. (1978). Irreversible gene repression model for control of development. *Science, 201*, 120–130.

Carmichael, L. (1954). The onset and early development of behavior. In L. Carmichael (Ed.), *Manual of child psychology*. (2nd ed.). (pp. 60–185). New York: Wiley.

Caron, A.J., Caron, R., Caldwell, R.C., & Weiss, S.J. (1973). Infant perception of structural properties of the face. *Developmental Psychology, 9*, 385–399.

Caron, R.F. (1967). Case history presentation. Child Research Branch, NIMH, Bethesda, MD.

Carpenter, G. (1980). Epidermal growth factor is a major growth-promoting agent in human milk. *Science, 210*, 198–200.

Carpenter, G.C. (1973, March). *Mother-stranger discrimination in the early weeks of life*. Paper presented at the biennial meeting of the Society for Research in Child Development, Philadelphia, PA.

Carpenter, G.C. (1974). Visual regard of moving and stationary faces in early infancy. *Merrill-Palmer Quarterly, 20*, 181–194.

Carr, S.J., Dabbs, J.M., Jr., & Carr, T.S. (1975, April). *Mother-infant attachment: The importance of mother's distance and visual field.* Paper presented at the biennial meeting of the Society for Research in Child Development, Denver.

Carroll. W.M., Jay, B.S., McDonald, W.I., & Halliday, A.M. (1980). Two distinct patterns of visual evoked response asymmetry in human albinism. *Nature, 286,* 604–606.

Casagrande, J.B. (1966). Language universals in anthropological perspective. In J.H. Greenberg (Ed.), *Universals of language* (2nd ed.) (pp. 279–298). Cambridge, MA: MIT Press.

Cavalier-Smith, T. (1980). How selfish is DNA? *Nature, 295,* 617–618.

Chagnon, N.A., & Irons, W. (1979). *Evolutionary biology and human social behavior.* North Scituate, MA: Duxbury Press.

Changeux, J.P. (1985). Remarks on the complexity of the nervous system and its ontogenesis. In J. Mehler & R. Fox (Eds.), *Neonate cognition* (pp. 263–284). Hillsdale, NJ: Lawrence Erlbaum Associates.

Changeux, J.P., & Danchin, A. (1976). Selective stabilization of developing synapses as a mechanism for the specification of neuronal networks. *Nature, 264,* 705–712.

Cheek, D.B. (1968). Conclusion and future implications. In D.B. Cheek (Ed.), *Human growth.* (pp. 568–586). Philadelphia: Lea & Febiger.

Cherry, L.M., Case, S.M., & Wilson, A.C. (1978). Frog perspective on the morphological difference between humans and chimpanzees. *Science, 200,* 209–211.

Chugani, H.T., & Phelps, M.E. (1986). Maturational changes in cerebral function in infants determined by [18]FDG Positron Emission Tomography. *Science, 231,* 840–843.

Clifton, R.K. (1974). Heartrate conditioning in the newborn infant. *Journal of Experimental Child Psychology, 18,* 9–21.

Coddington, R.P. (1968). Study of an infant with a gastric fistula. *Psychosomatic Medicine, 30,* 172–192.

Cogoli, A., Tschopp, A., & Fuchs-Bislin, P. (1984). Cell sensitivity to gravity. *Science, 225,* 228–230.

Cohan, C.S., & Kater, S.B. (1986). Suppression of neurite elongation and growth cone motility by electrical activity. *Science, 232,* 1638–1640.

Cohen, B., & Klein, J.F. (1968). Referent communication in school age children. *Child Development, 39,* 597–609.

Cohen, L.B., DeLoache, J.S., & Strauss, M.S. (1979). Infant visual perception. In J.D. Osofsky (Ed.), *Handbook of infant development* (pp. 393–438). New York: Wiley.

Cohen, N.J., & Squire, L.R. (1980). Preserved learning and retention of pattern-analyzing skill in amnesia: Dissociation of knowing how and knowing that. *Science, 210,* 207–210.

Cohen, P. (1982). The role of protein phosphorylation in neural and hormonal control of cellular activity. *Nature, 296,* 613–619.

Cole, M., Gay, J., Glick, J., & Sharp, D. (1971). *The cultural context of learning and thinking.* New York: Basic Books.

Coleman, P.D., & Riesen, A.H. (1968). Environmental effects on cortical dendritic fields. *Journal of Anatomy, 102*, 363–374.

Collins, R.C., & Olney, J.W. (1982). Discrimination and imitation of facial expressions by neonates. *Science, 218*, 179–181.

Colman, N., Hettiarachchy, N., & Herbert, V. (1981). Detection of a milk factor that facilitates folate uptake by intestinal cells. *Science, 221*, 1427–1429.

Condry, J., & Siman, M. (1974). Characteristics of peer- and adult-oriented children. *Journal of Marriage and the Family, 36*, 543–554.

Connell, J.P., & Furman, W. (1984). The study of transitions: Conceptual and methodological issues. In R.N. Emde & R.T. Harmon (Eds.), *Continuities and discontinuities in development* (pp. 153–173). New York: Plenum.

Cooke, J. (1986). Permanent distortion of positional systems of *Xenopus* embryos by brief early preturbation in gravity. *Nature, 319*, 60–63.

Cooper, T.A. (1984). A single troponin T gene regulated by different programs in cardiac and skeletal muscle development. *Science, 226*, 979–982.

Cooper, W.E., & Lainsten, M.L. (1974). Feature processing in production and perception of speech. *Nature, 252*, 121–123.

Coulombre, A.J. (1970). Development of the vertibrate motor system. In F.O. Schmitt (Ed.), *The neurosciences, second study program*, (pp. 108–116). Cambridge, MA: MIT Press.

Count, E.W. (1973). *Being and becoming human. Essays on the biogram.* New York: Van Nostrand.

Cowan, W.M., Fawcett, J.W., O'Leary, D.D.M., & Stanfield, B.B. (1984). Regressive events in neurogenesis. *Science, 225*, 1258–1265.

Cravioto, J. (1968). Nutritional deficiencies and mental performance in childhood. In D.C. Glass (Ed.), *Environmental influences* (pp. 3–51). New York: Rockefeller University Press.

Cravioto, J., & Delicardie, E.R. (1979). Nutrition, mental development, and learning. In F. Faulkner & J.M. Tanner (Eds.), *Human growth*, vol. 3 (pp. 481–511). New York: Plenum.

Creel, D., Garber, S.R., King, R.A., & Witkop, C.J. Jr. (1980). Auditory brainstem anomalies in human albinos. *Science, 209*, 1253–1255.

Crockenberg, S.B. (1981). Infant irritability, mother responsiveness and social support influences on the security of infant-mother attachment. *Child Development, 52*, 857–865.

Crook, J.H. (1983). On attributing consciousness to animals. *Nature, 303*, 11–14.

Crowne, D.P., Richardson, C.M., & Ward, G. (1983). Brief deprivation of vision after unilateral lesions of the frontal eye field prevents contralateral inattention. *Science, 220*, 257–259.

Cunningham, T.J. (1976). Early eye removal produces excessive bilateral branching in the rat: Application of cobalt filling method. *Science, 194*, 857–859.

Curtis, A.S.G., & Sheehar, G.M. (1978). The control of cell division by tension or diffusion. *Nature, 274*, 52–53.

Dale, P.S. (1976). *Language development: Structure and function* (2nd ed.). New York: Holt, Rinehart & Winston.

Damasio, A., Bellugi, U., Damasio, H., Poizner, H., & Van Gilder, J. (1986). Sign language aphasia during left-hemisphere injection. *Nature, 322*, 363–365.

Damon, W. (1983). *Social and personality development*. New York: W.W. Norton & Company, Inc.

Dansky, D.L., & Silverman, I.W. (1976). Effects of play on associative fluency in pre-school children. In J.S. Bruner, A. Jolly & K. Sylva (Eds.), *Play: Its role in development and evolution* (pp. 650–659). New York: Basic Books.

Dansky, J.L. (1985). Questioning "A paradigm question:" A commentary on Simon and Smith. *Merrill-Palmer Quarterly, 31*, 279–284.

Darwin, C. (1859/1962). *The origin of species*. New York: Collier.

Dasen, P.R., & Heron, A. (1981). Cross-cultural tests of Piaget's theory. In H.C. Triandis & A. Heron (Eds.), *Handbook of cross-cultural psychology: Vol. 4* (pp. 295–341). Boston: Allyn & Bacon.

Davidson, E.H., & Britten, R.J. (1979). Regulation and gene expression: Possible role of repetitive sequences. *Science, 204*, 1052–1060.

Davies, A.M., Thoenen, H., & Barde, Y.A. (1986). Different factors from the central nervous system and periphery regulate the survival of sensory neurones. *Nature, 319*, 497–499.

Davis, K. (1964). Isolated children. In R.L. Coser (Ed.), *The family: Its structure and functions* (pp. 394–398) New York: St. Martin's Press.

Dawkins, R. (1976a). *The selfish gene*. New York: Oxford University Press.

Dawkins, R. (1976b). Hierarchical organization: A candidate principle for ethology. In P.P.G. Bateson & R.A. Hinde (Eds.), *Growing points in ethology* (pp. 7–54). Cambridge: Cambridge University Press.

Dawkins, R. (1985). What was all the fuss about? (Book Reviews). Time frames: The rethinking of darwinian evolution and the theory of punctuated equilibria. *Nature, 316*, 683–684.

Décarie, T.G. (1969). A study of the mental and emotional development of the thalidomide child. In B.M. Foss (Ed.), *Determinants of infant behaviour. IV* (pp. 167–187). London: Methuen.

Décarie, T.G. (1974). *The infant's reaction to strangers*. New York: International Universities Press.

DeCasper, A.J., & Fifer, W.P. (1980). Of human bonding: Newborns prefer their mothers' voices. *Science, 208*, 1174–1176.

DeCasper, A.J., & Spence, M.J. (1986). Prenatal maternal speech influences newborn's perception of speech sounds. *Infant Behavior and Development, 9*, 133–150.

Dennis, I., Hampton, J.A., & Lea, S.E.G. (1973). New problem in concept formation. *Nature, 243*, 101–102.

Desjardins, C., Bronson, F.H., & Blank, L. (1986). Genetic selection for reproductive photoresponsiveness in deer mice. *Nature, 322*, 172–173.

de Weid, D. (1984). Central target for the behavioural effects of vasopressin neuropeptides. *Nature, 308*, 276–277.

Diberardino, M.A., Hoffner, N.J., & Etkin, L.D. (1984). Activation of dormant genes in specialized cells. *Science, 224*, 946–951.

Dinis-Domini, S., Glowinski, J., & Prochiantz, A. (1984). Glial heterogeneity may define the three-dimensional shape of mouse mesencephalic dopaminergic neurons. *Nature, 307*, 641–643.

Dittrichova, J. (1969). Development of sleep in infancy. In R.J. Robinson (Ed.),

*Brain and early behaviour* (pp. 193–201). London and New York: Academic Press.

D'Mello, S., & Willemsen, E. (1969). The development of the number concept: A scalogram analysis. *Child Development, 40,* 681–688.

Dobzhansky, T. (1951). *Genetics and the origin of species* (3rd ed.). New York: Columbia University Press.

Dobzhansky, T. (1960). Evolution and environment. In S. Tax (Ed.), *The evolution of life: Vol. 1: Evolution after Darwin* (pp. 403–428). Chicago: University of Chicago Press.

Dobzhansky, T. (1962). *Mankind evolving.* New Haven: Yale University Press.

Dobzhansky, T. (1970). *Genetics of the evolutionary process.* New York: Columbia University Press.

Dobzhansky, T. (1972). Genetics and the races of man. In B. Campbell (Ed.), *Sexual selection and descent of man* (pp. 59–86). Chicago: Aldine.

Dodd, B.J. (1972). Effects of social and vocal stimulation of infant babbling. *Developmental Psychology, 7,* 80–83.

Donaldson, M., & Balfour, G. (1968). Less is more: A study of language comprehension in children. *British Journal of Psychology, 59,* 461–471.

Donnee, L.J. (1973, March). *Infants' developmental scanning patterns to face and nonface stimuli under various auditory conditions.* Paper presented at the biennial meeting of the Society for Research in Child Development, Philadelphia.

Donovan, B.T., & van der Werff ten Bosch, J.J. (1965). *Physiology of puberty.* Baltimore: Williams & Wilkins.

Doolittle, F., & Sapienza, C. (1980). Selfish genes, the phenotype paradigm and evolution. *Nature, 284,* 601–606.

Draper, P., & Harpending, H. (1982). Father absence and reproductive strategy: An evolutionary perspective. *Journal of Anthropological Research, 38,* 255–273.

Dubos, R. (1968). Environmental determinants of human life. In D.C. Glass (Ed.), *Environmental influences* (pp. 138–154). New York: Rockefeller University Press.

Dugdale, A.E. (1986). Evolution and infant feeding. *Lancet,* 22 March, 670–673.

Dunn, J., & Kendrick, C. (1979). Interaction between young siblings in the context of family relationships. In M. Lewis & L.A. Rosenblum (Eds.), *The child in its family.* (pp. 143–168). New York: Plenum.

Dyson-Hudson, R., & van Dusen, R. (1972). Food-sharing among young children. *Ecology of Food and Nutrition, 1,* 319–324.

Eckerman, C.O., Whatley, J.L., & McGehee, L.J. (1979). Approaching and contacting the object another manipulates: A social skill of the 1-year-old. *Developmental Psychology, 15,* 585–593.

Edwards, C.P. (1981). The comparative study of the development of moral judgment and reasoning. In R.H. Munroe, R.L. Munroe, & B.B. Whiting (Eds.), *Handbook of cross-cultural human development* (pp. 501–528). New York: Garland STPM Press.

Eibl-Eibesfeldt, I. (1970). *Ethology, the biology of behavior.* New York: Holt, Rinehart & Winston.

Eichorn, D. (1970). Physiological development. In P.H. Mussen (Ed.), *Manual of child psychology: Vol. 1* (3rd ed.) (pp. 157–286). New York: Wiley.

Eimas, P.D. (1975). Speech perception in early infancy. In L.B. Cohen & P. Salapatek (Eds.), *Infant perception: From sensation to cognition.* (Vol. II, pp. 193–231). New York: Academic Press.

Eimas, P.D. (1978). Developmental aspects of speech perception. In R. Held, H.W. Leibowitz, & H.L. Teuber (Eds.), *Handbook of sensory physiology.* (Vol. VIII). *Perception* (pp. 357–374). New York: Springer.

Eimas, P.D. (1985). Constraints on a model of infant speech perception. In J. Mehler & R. Fox (Eds.), *Neonate cognition* (pp. 185–198). Hillsdale, NJ: Lawrence Erlbaum.

Eimas, P.D., & Miller, J.L. (1978). Effects of selective adaptation on the perception of speech and visual patterns. In R.D. Walk & H.L. Pick (Eds.), *Perception and experience* (pp. 307–345). New York: Plenum Press.

Eimas, P.D., Siqueland, E.R., Jusczyk, P., & Vigorito, J. (1971). Speech perception in infants. *Science, 171,* 303–306.

Eisenberg, J.F., & Kleiman, D. (1983). *Advances in the study of mammalian behavior.* American Society of Mammlogists Special Publication No. 7.

El'Konin, D.B. (1969). Some results of the study of the psychological development of preschool-age children. In M. Cole & I. Maltzman (Eds.), *A handbook of contemporary Soviet psychology* (pp. 163–208). New York: Basic Books.

Ember, C.R. (1973). Feminine task assignment and the social behavior of boys. *Ethos, 1,* 424–439.

Emde, R.N., Gaensbauer, T.J., & Harmon, R.J. (1976). *Emotional expression in infancy.* New York: International Universities Press.

Emde, R.N., & Harmon, R.J. (1984). *Continuities and discontinuities in development.* New York: Plenum.

Erikson, E.H. (1950). *Childhood and society.* New York: Norton.

Erikson, E.H. (1959). Identity and the life cycle. *Psychological Issues 1,* Monograph 1.

Escalona, S.K. (1968). *The roots of individuality.* Chicago: Aldine.

Ewert, J.P., Capranica, R.R., & Ingle, D.J. (Eds.). (1983). *Advances in vertibrate neuroethology.* New York: Plenum.

Fagen, R. (1981). *Animal play behavior.* New York: Oxford University Press.

Farley, J. (1983). Membrane changes in a single photoreceptor cause associative learning in *Hermissenda. Science, 221,* 1201–1202.

Feitelson, D. (1977). Cross-cultural studies of representational play. In B. Tizard & D. Harvey (Eds.), *Biology of play* (pp. 6–14). Philadelphia: J.B. Lippincott.

Fencl, M. de M., Sillman, R.J., Cohen, J., & Tulchinsky, D. (1980). Direct evidence of sudden rise in fetal corticoids late in human gestation. *Nature, 287,* 225–226.

Fernald, T.M., Cohen, D., Garcia, R., & Greenberg, R. (1985). Four-month-old infants prefer to listen to motherese. *Infant Behavior and Development, 8,* 181–195.

Festinger, L. (1957). *A theory of cognitive dissonance.* Stanford: Stanford University Press.

Field, T.M., Cohen, D., Garcia, R., & Greenberg, R. (1984). Mother-stranger face discrimination by the newborn. *Infant Behavior and Development, 7,* 19–25.

Finkelstein, N.W., Dent, C., Gallacher, K., & Ramey, C. (1978). Social behavior of infants and toddlers in a day-care environment. *Developmental Psychology, 14,* 257–262.

Firestone, G.L., Payvar, F., & Yamamoto, K.R. (1982). Glucocorticoid regulation of protein processing and compartmentalization. *Nature, 300,* 221–225.

Fishbein, H.D. (1976). *Evolution, development, and children's learning.* Cincinnati: Goodyear.

Fisher, K.W., Pipp, S.L., & Bullock, D. (1984). Detecting developmental discontinuities. In R.M. Emde & R.J. Harmon (Eds.), *Continuities and discontinuities in development,* (pp. 95–121). New York: Plenum.

Fisher, R.A. (1930). *The genetical theory of natural selection.* Oxford: Oxford University Press.

Fitzgerald, H.E. (1968). Autonomic pupillary reflex activity during early infancy and its relation to social and nonsocial visual stimuli. *Journal of Experimental Child Psychology, 6,* 470–482.

Flavell, J.H. (1970). Developmental studies of mediated memory. In H.W. Reese & L.P. Lipsitt (Eds.), *Advances in child development and behavior.* (Vol. 5, pp. 182–211). New York: Academic Press.

Fleischer, R.C., Johnston, R.F., & Klitz, W.J. (1983). Allozymic heterozygosity and morphological variation in house sparrows. *Nature, 304,* 628–629.

Flynn, J.P., Vanegas, H., Foote, W., & Edwards, S. (1970). Neural mechanisms involved in a cat's attack on a rat. In R.E. Whalen, R.F. Thompson, M. Verzeano, & N.M. Weinberger (Eds.), *The neural control of behavior* (pp. 135–173). New York: Academic Press.

Fox, M.W. (1970). Neurobehavioral development and the genotype-environment interaction. *Quarterly Review of Biology, 45,* 131–147.

Fox, N. (1975, April). *Development and determinants of separation protest in Israeli kibbutz children.* Paper presented at the meeting of the Society for Research in Child Development, Denver, Colorado.

Fox, R., Aslin, R.N., Shea, S.L., & Dumais, S.T. (1980). Stereopsis in human infants. *Science, 207,* 323–324.

Fox, T.D. (1985). Diverged genetic codes in protozoans and a bacterium. *Nature, 314,* 132–133.

Fraiberg, S. (1975). The development of human attachments in infants blind from birth. *Merrill-Palmer Quarterly, 21,* 315–334.

Frankel, D.G., & Arbel, T. (1980). Group formation by two-year-olds. *International Journal of Behavioral Development, 3,* 287–289.

Freedman, D.G. (1974). *Human infancy: An evolutionary perspective.* Hillsdale, NJ: Lawrence Erlbaum.

Freedman, D.G. (1979). *Human sociobiology: A holistic approach.* New York: Free Press.

Freedman, D.G., Boverman, H., & Freedman, N. (1966, October). *Effect of kinesthetic stimulation on weight gain and on smiling in premature infants.* Paper presented at the annual meeting of the American Orthopsychiatric Association. San Francisco, CA.

Freeman, R.D., & Bonds, A.B. (1979). Cortical plasticity in monocularly deprived immobilized kittens depends on eye movement. *Science, 206,* 1093–1095.

Freeman, R.D., & Thibos, L.N. (1973). Electrophysiological evidence that abnormal early visual experience can modify the human brain. *Science, 180,* 876–878.

Freud, A., & Burlingham, D. (1944). *War and children* (2nd Ed.). New York: International Universities Press.

Freud, A., & Dann, S. (1951). An experiment in group upbringing. *Psychoanalytic Study of the Child, 2,* 127–168.

Freud, S. (1900). *The interpretation of dreams.* London: George Allen & Unwin.

Friedlander, M.J. (1982). Structure of physiologically classified neurones in the kitten dorsal lateral geniculate nucleus. *Nature, 300,* 180–182.

Frisch, R.E., & McArthur, J.W. (1974). Menstrual cycles: Fatness as a determinant of minimum weight for height necessary for their maintenance and onset. *Science, 185,* 949–951.

Frost, B.J., & Nakayama, K. (1983). Single visual neurons code opposing motion independent of direction. *Science, 220,* 744–745.

Fry, D.B. (1966). The development of the phonological system in the normal and the deaf child. In F. Smith & G.A. Miller (Eds.), *The gensis of language* (pp. 187–206). Cambridge, MA: MIT Press.

Fuchs, A.R., Fuchs, F., Husslein, P., Soloff, M., & Fernstrom, M.J. (1982). Oxytocin receptors and human parturition: A dual role for oxytocin in the initiation of labor. *Science, 215,* 1396–1398.

Fullard, W., & Reiling, A.M. (1976). An investigation of Lorenz' "babyness." *Child Development, 47,* 1191–1193.

Fuller, J.L., & Clark, L.D. (1968). Genotype and behavioral vulnerability to isolation in dogs. *Journal of Comparative and Physiological Psychology, 66,* 151–156.

Fuller, J.L., & Thompson, R.W. (1960). *Behavior genetics.* New York: Wiley.

Furth, H.G. (1966). *Thinking without language: Psychological implications of deafness.* New York: Free Press.

Gadgil, M. (1982). Changes with age in the strategy of social behavior. In P.P.G. Bateson & P.H. Klopfer (Eds.), *Perspectives in ethology, Vol. 5, Ontogeny* (pp. 489–501). New York: Plenum.

Gage, F.A., Bjorklund, A., & Steinevi, U. (1984). Denervation releases a neuronal survival factor in adult rat hippocampus. *Nature, 308,* 637–639.

Galef, B.G. Jr. (1981). The ecology of weaining: Parasitism and the achievement of independence by altricial mammals. In D.J. Gubernick & P.H. Klopfer (Eds.), *Parental care in mammals.* (pp. 211–241). New York: Plenum.

Garcia, J., Hankins, W.G., & Rusiniak, K.W. (1974). Behavioral regulation of milieu interne in man and rat. *Science, 185,* 824–831.

Gardner, B.T., & Wallach, L. (1965). Shapes of figures identified as a baby's head. *Perceptual and Motor Skills, 20,* 135–142.

Gazzaniga, M.S. (1985). *The social brain.* New York: Basic Books.

Gelman, R., & Gallistel, C.R. (1978). *The child's understanding of number.* Cambridge, MA: Harvard University Press.

George, F.W., Milewich, L., & Wilson, J.D. (1978). Oestrogen content of the embryonic rabbit ovary. *Nature, 274,* 172–173.

George, F.W., & Wilson, J.D. (1980). Endocrine differentiation of the fetal rabbit ovary in culture. *Nature, 283,* 861–863.

Gesell, A. (1954). The ontogenesis of infant behavior. In L. Carmichael (Ed.), *Manual of child psychology* (2nd ed.) (pp. 335–373). New York: Wiley.

Gewirtz, J.L. (1965). The course of infant smiling in four childrearing environments in Israel. In B.M. Foss (Ed.), *Determinants of infant behaviour. III* (pp. 205–248). London: Methuen.

Ghiselin, M.T. (1974). *The economy of nature and the evolution of sex.* Berkeley and Los Angeles: University of California Press.

Gilbert, W. (1978). Why genes in pieces? *Nature, 271,* 501.

Gilbert, W. (1985). Genes-in-pieces revisited. *Science, 228,* 823–824.

Gilchrist, A.L. (1977). Perceived lightness depends on perceived spatial arrangement. *Science, 195,* 185–187.

Gimlich, R.L., & Cooke, J. (1983). Cell lineage and the induction of second nervous systems in amphibian development. *Nature, 306,* 471–473.

Ginsburg, B.E. (1969). Genotypic variables affecting responses to postnatal stimulation. In A. Ambrose (Ed.), *Stimulation in early infancy* (pp. 73–96). New York: Academic Press.

Glass, J.D. (1977). Alpha blocking: Absence in visuobehavioral deprivation. *Science, 198,* 58–60.

Glass, L., Silverman, W.A., & Sinclair, J.C. (1968). Effect of the thermal environment on cold resistance and growth of small infants after the first week of life. *Pediatrics, 14,* 1033–1046.

Goelet, P., Castellucci, V.F., Schacher, S., & Kandel, E.R. (1986). The long and the short of long-term memory—A molecular framework. *Nature, 322,* 419–422.

Goldberg, A. (1977). Infant development and mother-infant interaction in urban Zambia. In P.H. Leiderman, S.R. Tulkin, & A. Rosenfeld (Eds.), *Culture and infancy: Variations in the human experience* (pp. 211–243). New York: Academic Press.

Goldberger, R.F. (1974). Autogenous regulation of gene expression. *Science, 183,* 810–816.

Goldblum, R.M., Ahlstedt, S., Carlsson, B., Hanson, L.A., Jodal, U., Lindin-Janson, G., & Sohl-Akerland, A. (1975). Antibody-forming cells in human colostrum after oral immunization. *Nature, 257,* 797–799.

Goldin-Meadow, S., & Feldman, H. (1977). The development of language-like communication without a language model. *Science, 197,* 401–403.

Goldin-Meadow, S., & Mylander, C. (1983). Gestural communication in deaf children: Noneffect of parental input on language development. *Science, 221,* 372–374.

Goldman, P.S. (1976). CNS maturation and the ontogeny of behavior. *Advances in the Study of Behavior, 7,* 2–71.

Goldman-Rakic, P.S. (1985). Toward a neurobiology of cognitive development. In J. Mehler & R. Fox. (Eds.), *Neonate cognition* (pp. 285–306). Hillsdale, NJ: Lawrence Erlbaum Associates.

Goldsmith, H.H. (1984). Continuity of personality. A genetic perspective. In R.N. Emde & R.J. Harmon. (Eds.), *Continuities and discontinuities in development.* (pp. 403–413). New York: Plenum.

Golomb, C., & Cornelius, C.B. (1977). Symbolic play and its cognitive significance. *Developmental Psychology, 13,* 246–252.

Goode, A.W., & Rambaut, P.C. (1985). The skeleton in space. *Nature, 317,* 203–204.

Goren, C. (1975, April). *Form perception, innate form preferences and visually mediated head-turning in human newborns.* Paper presented at the meeting of the Society for Research in Child Development, Denver, CO.

Gottfried, A.W., Wallace-Lande, P., Sherman-Brown, S., King, J., & Coen, C. (1981). Physical and social environment of newborn infants in special care units. *Science, 214,* 673–675.

Gottlieb, G. (1970). Ontogensis of sensory function in birds and mammals. In E. Tobach, L.R. Aronson, & E. Shaw (Eds.), *The biopsychology of development* (pp. 67–127). New York: Academic Press.

Gottlieb, G. (1976). The roles of experience in the development of behavior and the nervous system. In G. Gottlieb (Ed.), *Studies on the development of behavior and the nervous system. Vol. 3: Neural and behavioral specificity* (pp. 23–54). New York: Academic Press.

Gottlieb, M.D. (1987). Local retinal regions control local eye growth and myopia. *Science, 237,* 73–77.

Gould, S.J. (1977). *Ontogeny and phylogeny.* Cambridge, MA: Belknap Press.

Gould, S.J. (1982). Darwinism and the expansion of evolutionary theory. *Science, 216,* 380–387.

Grafstein, B. (1971). Transneuronal transfer of radioactivity in the central nervous system. *Science, 172,* 177–179.

Green, M., Chilcoat, M., & Strohmeyer, C.F. III (1983). Rapid motion after-effect seen within uniform flickering test fields. *Nature, 304,* 61–62.

Greenbaum, C.W., & Landau, R. (1977). Mothers' speech and the early development of vocal behavior: Findings from a cross-cultural observation study in Israel. In P.H. Leiderman, S.R. Tulkin, & A. Rosenfeld (Eds.), *Culture and infancy* (pp. 245–270). New York: Academic Press.

Greenberg, D.J. (1971). Accelerating visual complexity levels in the human infant. *Child Development, 42,* 905–918.

Greenberg, J.H. (1966). Some universals in grammar with particular reference to the order of meaningful elements. In J.H. Greenberg (Ed.), *Universals of language* (2nd ed.) (pp. 73–113). Cambridge, MA: MIT Press.

Greenberg, M.E., Ziff, E.B., & Green, L.A. (1986). Stimulation of neural acetylcholine receptors induces rapid gene transcription. *Science, 234,* 80–83.

Greenough, W.T., & Schwark, H.D. (1984). Age-related aspects of experience effects upon brain structure. In R.N. Emde & R.J. Harmon (Eds.), *Continuities and discontinuities in development* (pp. 69–91). New York: Plenum.

Gregory, R.L., & Harris, J.P. (1984). Real and apparent movement nulled. *Nature, 307,* 729–730.

Grumbach, M.M. (1980). The neuroendocrinology of puberty. *Hospital Practice, April,* 51–60.

Grumbach, M.M., Grave, G.D., & Mayer, F.E. (1974). *The control of the onset of puberty.* New York: Wiley.

Grumet, M., Rutishauser, U., & Edelman, G.M. (1983). Neuron-glia adhesion is inhibited by antibodies to neural determinants. *Science, 222,* 60–62.

Gryboski, J.D. (1959). Suck and swallow in the premature infant. *Pediatrics, 43,* 96–102.

Gubernick, D.J. (1981). Parent and infant attachment in mammals. In D.J. Gubernick & P.H. Klopfer (Eds.), *Parental care in mammals* (pp. 243–305). New York: Plenum.

Gubernick, D.J., & Alberts, J.R. (1984). A specialization of taste aversion learning during suckling and its weaning-associated transformation. *Developmental Psycholobiology, 17,* 613–618.

Guillery, R.W. (1986). Routes for development. *Nature, 323,* 394–395.

Guthrie, K., & Hudson, L.M. (1979). Training conservation through symbolic play: A second look. *Child Development, 50,* 1269–1271.

Hadley, R.D., Kater, S.B., & Cohan, C.S. (1983). Electrical synapse formation depends on interaction of mutually growing neurites. *Science, 221,* 466–468.

Haith, M.M. (1980). *Rules that babies look by.* Hillsdale, NJ: Lawrence Erlbaum Associates.

Haldane, J.B.S. (1932). *The causes of evolution.* New York: Harper.

Hamer, K.H., & Missakian, E. (1978). A longitudinal study of social play in synanon/peer-reared children. In E.O. Smith (Ed.), *Social play in primates* (pp. 297–319). New York: Academic Press.

Hamilton, W.D. (1964). The genetical evolution of social behaviour. Parts I and II. *Journal of Theoretical Biology, 7,* 1–52.

Hamilton, W.D. (1971). Selection of selfish and altruistic behavior in some extreme models. In J.F. Eisenberg & W.S. Dillon (Eds.), *Man and beast: Comparative social behavior* (pp. 57–92). Washington, DC: Smithsonian Institution Press.

Hanley, M.R. (1985). Neuropeptides as mitogens. *Nature, 315,* 14–15.

Hardy-Brown, K. (1983). Universals and individual differences: Disentangling two approaches to the study of language acquisition. *Developmental Psychology, 19,* 610–624.

Hardy-Brown, K., Plomin, R., & De Fries, J.C. (1981). Genetic and environmental influences on rate of communicative development in the first year of life. *Developmental Psychology, 17,* 704–717.

Harlow, H.F. (1969). Age-mate or peer affectional system. *Advances in the Study of Behavior, 2,* 334–383.

Harlow, H.F., & Mears, C. (1979). *The human model: Primate perspectives.* Washington, DC: V.H. Winston.

Harper, L.V. (1970). Ontogenic and phylogenetic functions of the parent-offspring relationship in mammals. *Advances in the Study of Behavior, 3,* 75–117.

Harper, L.V. (1972). The transition from filial to reproductive function of coitus-related responses in young guinea pigs. *Developmental Psychobiology, 5,* 21–34.

Harper, L.V. (1975). The scope of offspring effects: From caregiver to culture. *Psychological Bulletin 82,* 784–801.

Harper, L.V. (1976). Behavior. In J.E. Wagner & P.J. Manning (Eds.), *The biology of the guinea pig* (pp. 31–49). New York: Academic Press.

Harper, L.V. (1981). Effects of offspring upon parents. In D.J. Gubernick & P.H. Klopfer (Eds.) *Parental care in mammals* (pp. 117–177). New York: Plenum Press.

Harper, L.V., & Huie, K.S. (1978). The development of sex differences in human behavior: Cultural imposition or a convergence of evolved response-tendencies and cultural adaptations? In G.M. Burghardt & M. Bekoff (Eds.), *The development of behavior: Comparative and evolutionary aspects* (pp. 297–318). New York: Garland.

Harper, L.V., & Huie, K.S. (1987). Relations among preschool children's adult and peer contacts and later academic achievement. *Child Development, 58,* 1051–1065.

Harris, A., Whittingham, D.G., & Wilson, L. (1982). Cytoplasmic control of pre-implantation development 'in vitro' in the mouse. *Nature, 299,* 460–463.

Harris, L.R., Blakemore, C., & Donaghy, M. (1980). Integration of visual and auditory space in the mammalian superior colliculus. *Nature, 288,* 56–59.

Harter, S. (1983). Developmental perspectives on the self-system. In P.H. Mussen (Ed.), *Handbook of child psychology* (4th ed.). Vol. IV (pp. 275–385). New York: Wiley.

Hartshorne, H., & May, M.A. (1930/1955). Studies in the organization of character. In R.G. Kuhlen & G.G. Thompson (Eds.), *Psychological studies of human development* (pp. 311–320). New York: Appleton-Century-Crofts.

Hartup, W.W. (1983). Peer relations. In P.H. Mussen (Ed.), *Handbook of child psychology* (4th ed.). Vol. IV (pp. 103–196). New York: Wiley.

Harvey, P.H. (1986). Energetic costs of reproduction. *Nature, 321,* 648–649.

Hausfater, G., & Hrdy, S.B. (1984). *Infanticide: Comparative and evolutionary perspectives.* New York: Aldine.

Haviland, J. (1975, April). *Individual differences in affect.* Paper presented at the meeting of the Society for Research in Child Development, Denver, CO.

Haviland, J.M., & Lelwica, M. (1987). The induced-affect response: 10-week-old infants' responses to three emotional expressions. *Developmental Psychology, 23,* 97–104.

Haydon, P.G. (1984). Serotonin selectively inhibits growth cone motility and synaptogenesis of specific identified neurons. *Science, 226,* 561–564.

Hebb, D.O. (1973). A return to Jensen and his social science critics. *American Psychologist, 28,* 947–961.

Held, R. (1985). Binocular vision—Behavioral and neuronal development. In J. Mehler & R. Fox (Eds.), *Neonate cognition* (pp. 37–44). Hillsdale, NJ: Lawrence Erlbaum.

Held, R., & Hein, A. (1968). Movement produced stimulation in the development of visually guided behavior. In N.S. Endler, L.R. Boulter, & H. Osser (Eds.), *Contemporary issues in developmental psychology* (pp. 364–369). New York: Holt, Rinehart & Winston.

Hess, E.H. (1970). Ethology and developmental psychology. In P.H. Mussen (Ed.), *Carmichael's manual of child psychology* (3rd ed.). Vol. 1 (pp. 1–38). New York: Wiley.

Hinde, R.A. (1959). Behavior and speciation in birds and lower vertebrates. *Biological Review, 34,* 85–128.

Hinde, R.A. (1966). *Animal behaviour.* New York: McGraw-Hill.

Hinde, R.A., & Stevenson-Hinde, J. (1973). *Constraints on learning.* London: Academic Press.

Ho, R.K., Ball, E.E., & Goodman, C.S. (1983). Muscle pioneers: Large meso-dermal cells that erect a scaffold for developing muscles and moto-neurones in grasshopper embryos. *Nature, 301,* 66–69.

Hockett, C.F. (1973). *Man's place in nature.* New York: McGraw-Hill.

Hofer, M.A. (1981). *The roots of human behavior.* San Francisco: W.H. Freeman.

Hoffman, M.L. (1970). Moral development. In P.H. Mussen (Ed.), *Carmichael's manual of child psychology* (3rd ed.). Vol. 2 (pp. 261–359). New York: Wiley.

Hohmann, A., & Creutzfeldt, O.D. (1975). Squint and the development of binocularity in humans. *Nature, 254,* 613–614.

Holliday, R., & Pugh, J.E. (1975). DNA modification mechanisms and gene activity during development. *Science, 187,* 226–232.

Hooker, D. (1952). *The prenatal origin behavior.* Lawrence, KS: University of Kansas Press.

Hopfield, J., & Tank, D.W. (1986). Computing with neural circuits: A model. *Science, 233,* 625–633.

Horn, G., Rose, S.P.R., & Bateson, P.P.G. (1973). Experience and plasticity in the central nervous system. *Science, 181,* 506–514.

Hubel, D.H. (1982). Exploration of the primary visual cortex, 1955-78. *Nature, 299,* 515–524.

Hubel, D.H., Wiesel, T.N., & Stryker, M.P. (1977). Orientation columns in Macaque monkey visual cortex demonstrated by 2-deoxyglucose autoradiographic technique. *Nature, 269,* 328–330.

Hudspeth, A.J. (1985). The cellular basis of hearing: The biophysics of hair cells, *Science, 230,* 745–752.

Hulsebosch, C.E., Coggeshall, R.E., & Perez-Polo, J.R. (1984). Increased numbers of thoracic dorsal root axons in rats given antibodies to nerve growth factor. *Science, 225,* 525–526.

Humphrey, N.K. (1976). The social function of intellect. In P.P.G. Bateson & R.A. Hinde (Eds.), *Growing points in ethology.* (pp. 303–317). Cambridge: Cambridge University Press.

Humphrey, T. (1969). Postnatal repetition of human prenatal activity sequences with some suggestions of their neuroanatomical bases. In R.J. Robinson (Ed.), *Brain and early behaviour* (pp. 43–85). New York: Academic Press.

Hutt, S.J. (1970). Specific and diversive exploration. In H.W. Reese & L.P. Lipsitt (Eds.), *Advances in child development and behavior* (Vol. 5, pp. 120–180). New York: Academic Press.

Hutt, S.J., Hutt, C., Lenard, H.G., Bernuth, H.V., & Muntjewerff, W.J. (1968). Auditory responsivity in the human neonate. *Nature, 218,* 888–890.

Huttenlocher, P.R. (1979). Synaptic density in human frontal cortex-Developmental changes and effects of aging. *Brain Research, 163,* 195–205.

Huttenlocher, P.R., De Courten, C., Garey, L.J., & van der Loos, H. (1982). Synaptogenesis in human visual cortex—Evidence for synapse elimination during normal development. *Neuroscience Letters, 33,* 247–252.

Ianuzzo, D., Williams, C., Chen, V., O'Brien, P., & Patel, P. (1977). Thyroidal trophic influence on skeletal muscle myosin. *Nature, 270,* 74–76.

Immelmann, K., Barlow, G.W., Petrinovich, L., & Main, M. (1981). General introduction. In K. Immelman, G.W. Barlow, L. Petrinovich, & M. Main (Eds.) *Behavioral development* (pp. 1–18). Cambridge: Cambridge University Press.

Inhelder, B., & Piaget, J. (1958). *The growth of logical thinking from childhood to adolescence*. New York: Basic Books.

Inhelder, B., Sinclair, H., & Bovet, M. (1974). *Learning and the development of cognition*. Cambridge, MA: Harvard University Press.

Insausti, R., Blakemore, C., & Cowan, W.M. (1984). Ganglion cell death during development of ipsilateral retino-collicular projection in golden hamster. *Nature, 308*, 362–364.

Ip, N.Y. (1984). Pattern of presynaptic nerve activity can determine the type of neurotransmitter regulating a postsynaptic event. *Nature, 311*, 472–474.

Ito, M., & Seo, M.L. (1983). Avoidance of neonatal cortical lesions by developing somatosensory barrels. *Nature, 301*, 600–602.

Jacob, F. (1977). Evolution and tinkering. *Science, 196*, 1161–1166.

Jacobson, M. (1970). *Developmental neurobiology*. New York: Holt, Rinehart, & Winston.

Jakobson, R. (1968). *Child language, aphasia, and phonological universals*. The Hague: Mouton.

James, W. (1890). *The principles of psychology: Vol. 1*. New York: Henry Holt.

Jay, M.F., & Sparks, D.S. (1984). Auditory receptive fields in primate superior coliculus shift with changes in eye position. *Nature, 309*, 345–347.

Jerne, N. (1985). The generative grammar of the immune system. *Science, 229*, 1057–1059.

Jersild, R.T. (1954). Emotional development. In L. Carmichael (Ed.), *Manual of child psychology* (2nd ed.) (pp. 833–917). New York: Wiley.

Jesperson, O. (1925). *Die sprache*. Cited by Eibl-Eibesfeldt (1970).

Jessell, T.M., & Yamamoto, M. (1980). Development of spinal sensory systems. *Nature, 288*, 640–641.

Johnson, G.B. (1974). Enzyme polymorphism and metabolism. *Science, 184*, 28–37.

Johnson, E.J., & Yip, H.K. (1985). Central nervous system and peripheral nerve growth factor provide trophic support critical to mature sensory neuronal survival. *Nature, 314*, 751–752.

Johnson, P., & Salisbury, D.M. (1975). Breathing and sucking during feeding in the newborn. In M.A. Hofer (Ed.), *Parent-infant interaction*. Ciba Foundation Symposium 33 (new series, pp. 119–135). Amsterdam: Elsevier.

Jonakait, G.M., Bohn, M.C., & Black, I.B. (1980). Maternal glucocorticoid hormones influence neurotransmitter phenotypic expression in embryos. *Science, 210*, 551–553.

Jones, H.E. (1960). The longitudinal method in the study of personality. In I. Iscoe & H. Stevenson (Eds.), *Personality development in children* (pp. 3–37). Austin, TX: University of Texas Press.

Jones, S., & Moss, H.A. (1971). Age, state, and maternal behavior associated with infant vocalizations. *Child Development, 42*, 1039–1051.

Jones-Molfese, V.J. (1975, April). *Preferences of infants for regular and distorted speech.* Paper presented at the meeting of the Society for Research in Child Development, Denver, CO.

Jukes, T.H. (1980). Silent nucleotide substitutions and the molecular evolutionary clock. *Science, 210,* 973–977.

Jusczyk, P.W. (1985). On characterizing the development of speech perception. In J. Mehler & R. Fox (Eds.), *Neonate cognition* (pp. 199–229). Hillsdale, NJ: Lawrence Erlbaum Associates.

Kabat, D. (1972). Gene selection in hemoglobin and in antibody-synthesizing cells. *Science, 175,* 134–140.

Kagan, J. (1970). Attention and psychological change in the young child. *Science, 170,* 826–831.

Kagan, J. (1971). *Change and continuity in infancy.* New York: Wiley.

Kagan, J. (1977). The uses of cross-cultural research in early development. In P.H. Leiderman, S.R. Tulkin & A. Rosenfeld (Ed.), *Culture and infancy: Variations in the human experience* (pp. 271–285). New York: Academic Press.

Kagan, J. (1984). Continuity and change in the opening years of life. In R.N. Emde & R.J. Harmon (Eds.), *Continuities and discontinuities in development* (pp. 15–39). New York: Plenum.

Kagan, J., Kearsley, R.B., & Zelazo, P.R. (1978). *Infancy. Its place in human development.* Cambridge, MA: Harvard University Press.

Kagan, J., & Kogan, N. (1970). Individual variation in cognitive processes. In P.H. Mussen (Ed.), *Carmichael's manual of child psychology* (3rd ed.). Vol. 1 (pp. 1273–1365). New York: Wiley.

Kalnins, I.V., & Bruner, J.S. (1973). Infant sucking used to change the clarity of a visual display. In L.J. Stone, H.T. Smith, & L.B. Murphy (Eds.), *The competent infant.* (pp. 707–713). New York: Basic Books.

Kandel, E.R. (1983, January). *Classical conditioning: Insights into the relationship between associative and nonassociative learning.* Storer Life Sciences Lectures, University of California at Davis.

Kaspar, J.C., & Lowenstein, R. (1971). The effect of social interaction on activity levels in six- to eight-year-old boys. *Child Development, 42,* 1294–1298.

Kaufman, M., Pinsky, L., & Feder-Hollander, R. (1981). Defective up-regulation of the androgen receptor in human androgen insensitivity. *Nature, 293,* 735–736.

Kendrick, C., & Dunn, J. (1980). Caring for a second baby: Effects on interaction between mother and firstborn. *Developmental Psychology, 16,* 303–311.

Kennell, J.H., Voos, D.K., & Klaus, M.H. (1979). Parent-infant bonding. In J.D. Osofsky (Ed.), *Handbook of infant development* (pp. 786–798). New York: Wiley.

Kessen, W., Haith, M.M., & Salapatek, P. (1970). Human infancy: A bibliography and guide. In P.H. Mussen (Ed.), *Manual of child psychology* (3rd ed.). Vol. 1 (pp. 287–445). New York: Wiley.

Kety, S.S., & Elkes, J. (Eds.). (1961). *Regional neurochemistry.* New York:Pergamon Press.

Kim, I., & Pollitt, E. (1987). Differences in the pattern of weight growth of nutritionally at-risk and well nourished infants. *American Journa of Clinical Nutrition. 46,* 31–35.

Kimura, M. (1983). The neutral theory of molecular evolution. *Nature, 306*, 713–714.

King, M.C., & Wilson, A.C. (1975). Evolution at two levels in humans and chimpanzees. *Science, 188*, 107–115.

Kinsbourne, M., & Hiscock, M. (1983). The normal and deviant development of functional lateralization of the brain. In P.H. Mussen (Ed.), *Handbook of child psychology* (4th ed.) Vol. II (pp. 157–280). New York: Wiley.

Klinnert, M.D. (1984). The regulation of infant behavior by maternal facial expression. *Infant Behavior and Development, 7*, 447–465.

Knudsen, E.I. (1983). Early auditory experience aligns the auditory map of space in the optic tectum of the barn owl. *Science, 222*, 939–942.

Kolata, G. (1985). What causes nearsightedness? *Science, 229*, 1249–1251.

Konner, M.J. (1972). Aspects of the developmental ethology of a foraging people. In *Ethological studies of child behaviour* (pp. 285–304). Cambridge: Cambridge University Press.

Konner, M. (1977). Evolution of human behavioral development. In P.H. Leiderman, S.R. Tulkin, & A. Rosenfeld (Eds.) *Culture and infancy.* (pp. 69–109). New York: Academic Press.

Konner, M. (1982). *The tangled wing.* New York: Harper Colophon Books.

Kopp, C.B. (1971, April). *Inhibition of crying: A comparison of stimuli.* Paper presented at the meeting of the Society for Research in Child Development, Minneapolis, MN.

Kopp, C.B., Sigman, M., & Parmalee, A.H. (1973). Ordinality and sensory-motor series. *Child Development, 44*, 821–823.

Kopp, C.B., Sigman, M., Parmelee, A.H. Jr., & Jeffrey, W.E. (1975). Neurological organization and visual fixation in infants at 40 weeks conceptual age. *Developmental Psychobiology, 8*, 165–170.

Korner, A.F. (1968). REM organization in neonates. *Archives of General Psychiatry, 19*, 330–340.

Korner, A.F. (1969). Neonatal startles, smiles, erections and reflex sucks as related to state, sex, and individuality. *Child Development, 40*, 1039–1053.

Korner, A.F. (1979). Maternal rhythms and waterbeds: A form of intervention with premature infants. In E.B. Thoman (Ed.), *Origin of the infant's social responsiveness* (pp. 95–124). Hillsdale, NJ: Lawrence Erlbaum Associates.

Korner, A., & Thoman, E. (1972). The relative efficacy of contact and vestibular-proprioceptive stimulation in soothing neonates. *Child Development, 43*, 443–453.

Koshland, D.E., Jr., Goldbeter, A., & Stock, J.B. (1982). Amplification and adaptation in regulatory and sensory systems. *Science, 217*, 220–225.

Kotrla, K.J. (1984). Transient expression of a surface antigen on a small subset of neurones during embryonic development. *Nature, 311*, 151–153.

Krieger, D.T. (1983). Brain Peptides: what, where and why? *Science, 222*, 975–985.

Kuhl, P. (1985). Categorization of speech by infants. In J. Mehler & R. Fox (Eds.), *Neonate cognition* (pp. 231–262). Hillsdale, NJ: Lawrence Erlbaum Associates.

Kuhl, P.K. (1978). Predispositions for the perception of speech-sound categories: A species-specific phenomenon? In F.D. Minifie & L.L. Lloyd (Eds.), *Com-

*munication and cognitive abilities—Early behavioral assessment* (pp. 229–255). Baltimore: University Park Press.

Kuhl, P.K., & Meltzoff, A.N. (1982). The bimodal perception of speech in infancy. *Science, 218,* 1138–1141.

Kuhl, P.K., & Miller, J.D. (1975). Speech perception by the chinchilla: Voiced-voiceless distinction in alveolar plosive consonants. *Science, 190,* 69–72.

Kuhn, C.M., Butler, S., & Schanberg, S.M. (1978). Selective depression of serum growth hormone during maternal deprivation in rat pups, *Science, 201,* 1034–1036.

Kuppermann, B.D., & Kasamatsu, T. (1983). Changes in geniculate cell size following brief monocular blockade of retinal activity in kittens. *Nature, 306,* 465–468.

La Gamma, E.F., Adler, J.E., & Black, I.B. (1984). Impulse activity differentially regulates [leu] enkephalin and catecholamine characters in the adrenal medulla. *Science, 224,* 1102–1104.

Landauer, T.K., & Whiting, J.W.M. (1981). Correlates and consequences of stress in infancy. In R.H. Munroe, R.L. Munroe, & B.B. Whiting (Eds.), *Handbook of cross-cultural human development* (pp. 355–375). New York: Garland STPM Press.

Lane, B., & Anderton, B. (1982). Focus on filaments: Embryology to pathology. *Nature, 298,* 706–707.

Lappan, J.S., & Fuqua, M.A. (1983). Accurate visual measurement of three-dimensional moving patterns. *Science, 221,* 480–482.

LaVail, J.H., & LaVail, M.M. (1972). Retrograde axonal transport in the central nervous system. *Science, 176,* 1416–1418.

Lazar, R.M., Tanvaroff, M., Nir, Y., Freund, B., O'Reilly, R., Kirkpatrick, D., & Kapoor, N. (1983). Language recovery following isolation for severe combined immunodeficiency disease. *Nature, 306,* 54–55.

Lazarides, E., & Nelson, W.J. (1983). Erythrocyte form of spectrin in cerebellum: Appearance at a specific stage in the terminal differentiation of neurons. *Science, 222,* 931–933.

Leehey, S.C., Moskowitz-Cook, A., Brill, S., & Held, R. (1975). Orientational anistropy in infant vision. *Science, 190,* 900–902.

Leiderman, P.H., Tulkin, S.R., & Rosenfeld, A. (1977). *Culture and infancy: Variations in the human experience.* New York: Academic Press.

Lenneberg, E.H. (1967). *Biological foundations of language.* New York: Wiley.

Lenneberg, E.H., Rebelsky, F.G., & Nichols, I.A. (1965). The vocalizations of infants born to deaf and hearing parents. *Vita Humana, 8,* 23–37.

Leonard, M., Rhymes, S., & Solnit, A. (1966). Failure to thrive in infants. *American Journal of Diseases in Children,* III, 600–612.

Lester, B.M., Kotelchuck, M., Spelke, E., Sellers, M.J., & Klein, R.E. (1974). Separation protest in Guatemalan infants: Cross-cultural and cognitive findings. *Developmental Psychology, 10,* 79–85.

Leuba, C., & Friedlander, B. (1968). Effects of controlled audio-visual reinforcement of infants' manipulative play in the home. *Journal of Experimental Child Psychology, 6,* 87–99.

Leventhal, A.G., & Hirsch, H.V.B. (1975). Cortical effect of early selective exposure to diagonal lines. *Science, 190,* 902–904.

Levi, A. (1985). Molecular cloning of a gene sequence regulated by nerve growth factor. *Science, 229,* 393–397.

LeVine, R. (1973). *Culture, behavior and personality.* Chicago: Aldine.

Levy, D.M. (1955). Oppositional syndromes and oppositional behavior. In P.H. Hoch & J. Zubin (Eds.), *Psychopathology of childhood.* (pp. 204–226). New York: Grune & Stratton.

Lewin, R. (1981). Seeds of change in embryonic development. *Science, 214,* 42–44.

Lewin, R. (1982). Evolution can be a problem for evolutionists. *Science, 216,* 1212–1213.

Lewin, R. (1984). Practice catches theory in recognition. *Science, 223,* 1049–1051.

Lewis, J. (1984). Morphogenesis by fibroblast traction, *Nature, 307,* 413–414.

Lewis, M., & Brooks, J. (1975). Infants' social perception: A constructionist view. In L.B. Cohen & P. Salapatek (Eds.) *Infant perception: From sensation to cognition* (Vol. II, pp. 102–148). New York: Academic Press.

Lewis, M., & Brooks-Gunn, J. (1979). *Social cognition and the acquisition of self.* New York: Plenum.

Lewis, M., & Freedle, R. (1973). Mother-infant dyad: The cradle of meaning. In K. Pliner, L. Krames, & T. Alloway (Eds.), *Communication and affect: Language and thought* (pp. 127–155). New York: Academic Press.

Lewis, M., & Rosenblum, L.A. (Eds.). (1975). *Friendship and peer relations.* New York: Wiley.

Lewontin, R.C., Rose, S., & Kamin, L.J. (1984). *Not in our genes,* New York: Pantheon Books.

Leyhausen, P. (1956). Verhaltensstudien bei katzen. *Zeitschrift fur Tierpsychologie,* Beiheft 2.

Li, W.H., Gojobori, T., & Nei, N. (1981). Pseudogenes as a paradigm of neutral evolution. *Nature, 292,* 237–239.

Liberman, A., Cooper, F.S., Shankweiler, D.P., & Studdert-Kennedy, M. (1967). Perception of the speech code. *Psychological Review, 74,* 451–461.

Lichtman, J., & Purves, D. (1983). Activity-mediated neural change. *Nature, 301,* 563–564.

Lieberman, P. (1975). The evolution of speech and language. In J.F. Kavanagh & J.E. Cutting (Eds.), *The role of speech in language* (pp. 83–106). Cambridge, MA: MIT Press.

Lieberman, P. (1984). *The biology and evolution of language.* Cambridge, MA: Harvard University Press.

Lim, H.W. (1984). Immunoreactive arginine-vasopressin in Brattleboro rat ovary. *Nature, 310,* 61–64.

Lim, R., & Miller, T.F. (1984). Sequential interaction of glia maturation factor with insulin. *Science, 223,* 1403–1404.

Lindblom, B. (1986, May). *Themes in the evolutionary biology of language.* Colloquium presentation, University of California, Davis.

Lipsitt, L.P. (1969). Learning capacities of the human infant. In R.J. Robinson (Ed.), *Brain and early behavior: Development in the fetus and infant* (pp. 227–245). New York: Academic Press.

Lister, A. (1984). Evolutionary case histories from the fossil record. *Nature, 309,* 114.

Loehlin, J.C., Lindzey, G., & Spuhler, J.N. (1975). *Race differences in intelli-*

*gence.* San Francisco: W.H. Freeman.

Lorenz, K. (1935/1957). Companionship in bird life. In C.H. Schiller (Ed.), *Instinctive behavior* (pp. 82–128). New York: International Universities Press.

Lorenz, K. (1956). Plays and vacuum activities. In P.P. Grassé (Ed.), *L'Instinct dans le comportement des animaux et de l'homme* (pp. 633–638). Paris: Masson.

Lorenz, K. (1965). *Evolution and modification of behavior.* Chicago: University of Chicago Press.

Lott, D.F. (1984). Intraspecific variation in the social systems of wild vertebrates. *Behaviour, 88,* 266–325.

Lowell, R.B. (1985). Selection for increased safety factors of biological structure as environmental unpredictability increases. *Science, 228,* 1009–1011.

Lumsden, A.G.S., & Davies, A.M. (1983). Earliest sensory nerve fibres are guided to peripheral targets by attractants other than nerve growth factor. *Nature, 306,* 786–788.

Lumsden, A.G.S., & Davies, A.M. (1986). Chemotrophic effect of specific target epithelium in the developing mammalian nervous system. *Nature, 323,* 538–539.

Lumsden, C.J., & Wilson, E.O. (1981). *Genes, mind, and culture.* Cambridge, MA: Harvard University Press.

Lund, R.D. (1978). *Development and plasticity of the brain.* New York: Oxford University Press.

Luria, A.R. (1961). *The role of speech in the regulation of normal and abnormal behavior.* New York: Liveright.

Luria, A.R. (1966). *Human brain and psychological processes.* New York: Harper & Row.

Luria, A.R. (1980). *Higher cortical functions in man* (2nd ed.). New York: Consultants Bureau.

Luria, A.R., & Yudovich, F.I. (1959). *Speech and the development of mental processes in the child.* London: Staples Press.

Lytton, H. (1980). *Parent-child interaction: The socialization process observed in twin and singleton families.* New York: Plenum.

Maccoby, E.E., & Jacklin, C.N. (1974). *The psychology of sex differences.* Stanford, CA: Stanford University Press.

Maccoby, E.E., & Martin, J.K. (1983). Socialization in the context of the family: Parent-child interaction. In P.H. Mussen. (Ed.), *Handbook of child psychology* (4th ed.). Vol. IV (pp. 1–101). New York: Wiley.

Maccoby, E., & Masters, J.C. (1970). Attachment and dependency. In P.H. Mussen (Ed.), *Manual of child psychology* (3rd ed.). Vol. I (pp. 73–157). New York: Wiley.

Macfarlane, J.A. (1975). Olfaction in the development of social preferences in the human neonate. In M.A. Hofer (Ed.), *Parent-infant interaction.* CIBA Foundation Symposium No. 33 (new series, pp. 103–117). Amsterdam: Elsevier.

MacKain, K., Studdert-Kennedy, M., Speiker, S., & Stern, D. (1983). Infant intermodal speech perception is a left-hemisphere function. *Science, 219,* 1347–1349.

Maddox, J. (1983). Is biology now part of physics? *Nature, 306*, 311.

Madsen, M.C., & Shapira, A. (1970). Cooperative and competitive behavior of urban Afro-American, Anglo-American, Mexican-American & Mexican village children. *Developmental Psychology, 3*, 16–20.

Main, M., Kaplan, N., & Cassidy, J. (1985). Security in infancy, childhood and adulthood: A move to level of representation. *Monographs of the Society for Research in Child Development, 50*, (1–2), 66–104. Serial no. 209.

Malrieu, P.H. (1962). Vie sociale et prélangage dans la première année. *Journal de Psychologie Normale Pathologique, 59*, 139–165.

Manil, J., Desmedt, J.E., Debecker, J., & Chorazyna, H. (1967). Les potentiels cerebraux évoqués par la stimulation de la main chez le nouveau-né normal. *Révue Neurologuique, 117*, 53–61.

Mansfield, R.J.W. (1974). Neural basis of orientation perception in primate vision. *Science, 186*, 1133–1134.

Markert, C.L., Shaklee, J.B., & Whitt, G.S. (1975). Evolution of a gene. *Science, 189*, 102–114.

Markert, C.L., & Ursprung, H. (1971). *Developmental genetics*. Englewood Cliffs, NJ: Prentice-Hall.

Marler, P. (1961). The filtering of external stimuli during instinctive behaviour. In W.H. Thorpe & O.L. Zangiwill (Eds.), *Current problems in animal behaviour* (pp. 150–166). Cambridge: Cambridge University Press.

Marler, P.R., & Hamilton, W.J. III (1966). *Mechanisms of animal behavior*. New York: Wiley.

Martin, B. (1975). Parent-child relations. In F.D. Horowitz (Ed.), *Review of Child Development Research*. Vol. 4 (pp. 463–540). Chicago: University of Chicago Press.

Martin, J.A. (1981). A longitudinal study of the consequences of early mother-infant interaction: A microanalytic study. *Monographs of the Society of Research in Child Development, 46* (3), (Serial No. 190).

Marvin, R.S. (1977). An ethological-cognitive model for the attenuation of mother-child attachment behavior. In T. Alloway, K. Pliner, & L. Krames (Eds.), *Advances in the study of communication and affect. Vol. 3: Attachment behavior* (pp. 25–60). New York: Plenum.

Marx, J.L. (1984). New clues to developmental timing. *Science, 226*, 425–426.

Maslow, A.H. (1954). *Motivation and personality*. New York: Harper.

Massé, G. (1962). Comparison de la osseuse de jeunes enfants de Dakar et de Boston. *Modern problems in pediatrics*, VII, 199–201.

Maurer, D. (1985). Infants' perception of facedness. In T.A. Field & N.A. Fox (Eds.), *Social perception in infants* (pp. 73–100). Norwood, NJ: Ablex.

Mayr, E. (1970). *Populations, species and evolution*. Cambridge, MA: Belknap Press.

Mayr, E. (1974). Behavior programs and evolutionary strategies. *American Scientist, 62*, 650–659.

McAllister, L.B., Scheller, R.H., Kandel, E.R., & Axel, R. (1983). In situ hybridization to study the origin and fate of identified neurons. *Science, 222*, 800–808.

McCall, R.B. (1981). Nature-nurture and the two realms of development: A proposed integration with respect to mental development. *Child Development,* *52,* 1–12.

McClintock, B. (1984). The significance of responses of the genome to challenge. *Science, 226,* 792–801.

McComas, A., Sica, R., & Banerjee, S. (1978). Central nervous system effects of limb amputation in man. *Nature, 271,* 73–74.

McGregor, W.G., Kuhn, R.W., & Jaffe, R.B. (1983). Biologically active chorionic gonadotropin synthesis by the human fetus. *Science, 220,* 306–308.

McKay, R.D.G., Hockfield, S., Johansen, J., Thompson, I., & Frederiksen, K. (1983). Surface molecules identify groups of growing axons. *Science, 222,* 788–794.

McLaren, A. (1984). Mammalian development: Methods and success of nuclear transplantation in mammals. *Nature, 309,* 671–672.

McMahon, D. (1974). Chemical messengers in development: A hypothesis. *Science, 185,* 1012–1021.

McNeill, D. (1970). The development of language. In P.H. Mussen (Ed.), *Manual of child psychology* (3rd ed.). Vol. 1 (pp. 1061–1161). New York: Wiley.

McWilliams, J.R., & Lynch, G. (1983). Rate of synaptic replacement in denervated rat hippocampus declines precipitously from the juvenile period to adulthood. *Science, 221,* 572–574.

Mead, M., & Newton, N. (1967). Cultural patterning of perinatal behavior. In S.A. Richardson & A.F. Guttmacher (Eds.), *Childbearing: Its social and psychological aspects* (pp. 142–244). Baltimore: Williams & Wilkins.

Medawar, B.P. (1984). A view from the left: A review of *Not in our genes. Nature, 310,* 255–256.

Mehler, J., & Bever, T.G. (1967). Cognitive capacity of very young children. *Science, 158,* 141–142.

Meltzoff, A.N., & Borton, R.N. (1979). Inter-modal matching by human neonates. *Nature, 282,* 403–404.

Meltzoff, A.N., & Moore, M.K. (1985). Cognitive foundations and social functions of imitation and intermodal representation in infancy. In J. Mehler & R. Fox (Eds.), *Neonate cognition* (pp. 139–156). Hillsdale, NJ: Lawrence Erlbaum.

Mendelson, M.J., & Haith, M.M. (1976). The relation between audition and vision in the human newborn. *Monograph of the Society for Research in Child Development, 41* (4), Serial no. 167.

Menyuk, P. (1969). *Sentences children use.* Cambridge, MA: MIT Press.

Menyuk, P. (1977). *Language and maturation.* Cambridge, MA: MIT Press.

Meredith, H.V. (1973). Somatological development. In B. Wolman (Ed.), *Handbook of general psychology* (pp. 230–241). New York: Prentice-Hall.

Meredith, M.A., & Stein, B.E. (1983). Interactions among converging sensory inputs in the superior colliculus. *Science, 221,* 389–391.

Meredith, M.A., & Stein, B.E. (1985). Descending efferents from the superior colliculus relay integrated multisensory information. *Science, 227,* 657–659.

Merzenich, M.M., Nelson, R.J., Stryker, M.P., Cynader, M.S., Schoppmann, A., & Zook, J.M. (1984). Somatosensory cortical map changes following digit amputation in adult monkeys. *Journal of Comparative Neurology, 224,* 591–605.

Milkovic, K., & Milkovic, S. (1966). Adrenocorticotropic hormone secretion in the fetus and infant. In L. Martini & W.F. Ganong (Eds.), *Neuroendocrinology,* Vol. I (pp. 371–405). New York: Academic Press.

Millar, S. (1968). *The psychology of play.* Baltimore: Penguin Books.

Miller, A.G., & Thomas, R. (1972). Cooperation and competition among Blackfoot indian and urban Canadian children. *Child Development, 43,* 1104–1110.

Miller, P.H., Kessel, F.S., & Flavell, J.H. (1970). Thinking about people thinking about people thinking about . . . : A study of social cognitive development. *Child Development, 41,* 613–623.

Miller, S.A. (1971). Extinction of conservation: A methodological and theoretical analysis. *Merrill-Palmer Quarterly 17,* 319–334.

Mills, M., & Melhuish, E. (1974). Recognition of mother's voice in early infancy. *Nature, 252,* 123–124.

Mohindra, I., Held, R., Gwiazda, J., & Brill, S. (1973). Astigmatism in infants. *Science, 202,* 329–331.

Money, J. (1976). Human hermaphroditism. In F.A. Beach (Ed.), *Human sexuality in four perspectives* (pp. 62–86). Baltimore: Johns Hopkins University Press.

Money, J., & Ehrhardt, A.A. (1972). *Man and woman, boy and girl.* Baltimore: Johns Hopkins University Press.

Moore, D. (1983). Binaural maps in the brain. *Nature, 301,* 463–464.

Morrone, M.C., & Burr, D.C. (1986). Evidence for the existence and development of visual inhibition in humans. *Nature, 321,* 235–237.

Morrone, M.C., Burr, D.C., & Ross, J. (1983). Added noise restores recognizability of coarse quantitized images. *Nature, 305,* 226–228.

Mower, G.D., Christen, W.G., & Caplan, C.J. (1983). Very brief visual experience eliminates plasticity in the cat visual cortex. *Science, 221,* 178–180.

Mudge, A.W. (1984). Schwann cells induce morphological transformation of sensory neurones in vitro. *Nature, 309,* 367–369.

Mueller, E. (1972). The maintenance of verbal exchanges between young children. *Child Development, 43,* 930–938.

Muggle-Harris, A., Whittingham, D.G., & Wilson, L. (1982). Cytoplasmic control of preimplantation development *in vitro* in the mouse. *Nature, 299,* 460–462.

Muller-Schwartze, D. (1968). Play deprivation in deer. *Behaviour, 31,* 144–162.

Muller-Schwartze, D., Stagge, B., & Muller-Schwartze, C. (1982). Play behavior: Persistence, decrease and energetic compensation during food shortage in deer fawns. *Science, 215,* 85–87.

Mussen, P.H. (Ed.). (1983). *Handbook of child psychology* (4th ed.). New York: Wiley.

Mussen, P.H., Conger, J.J., & Kagan, J. (1979). *Child development and personality* (5th ed.). New York: Harper & Row.

Mussen, P.H., Conger, J.J., Kagan, J., & Huston, A.C. (1984). *Child development and personality* (6th ed.). New York: Harper & Row.

Nakatsuji, N., & Johnson, K.E. (1984). Experimental manipulation of a contact guidance system in amphibian gastrulation by mechanical tension. *Nature, 307,* 453–455.

Nathans, J., Thomas, D., & Hogness, D.S. (1986). Molecular genetics of human color vision: The genes encoding blue, green and red pigments. *Science, 232,* 193–202.

Neel, J.V. (1970). Lessons from a "primitive" people. *Science, 170,* 815–822.

Nelson, K.E. (1968). Organization of visual tracking responses in human infants. *Journal of Experimental Child Psychology, 6,* 194–201.

Nelson, K. (1981). Individual differences in language development: Implications for development and language. *Developmental Psychology, 17,* 170–187.

Nestler, E.J., & Greengard, P. (1982). Nerve impulses increase the phosphorylation state of protein I in rabbit superior cervical ganglion. *Nature, 296,* 452–454.

Neville, H.J. (1985). Effects of early sensory and language experience on the development of the human brain, In J. Mehler & R. Fox (Eds.), *Neonate cognition* (pp. 349–363). Hillsdale, NJ: Lawrence Erlbaum.

Noonan, F.P., Halliday, W.J., Morton, H., & Clunic, G.J.A. (1979). Early pregnancy factor is immuno-suppressive. *Nature, 278,* 649–651.

Novotny, M., Jemiolo, B., Harvey, S., Wiesler, A., & Marchlewska-Kaj, A. (1986). Adrenal-mediated endogenous metabolites inhibit puberty in female mice. *Science, 231,* 722–724.

Nucci, L.P., & Turiel, E. (1978). Social interactions and the development of social concepts in preschool children. *Child Development, 49,* 400–407.

Nunnally, J.C., & Lemond, L.C. (1973). Exploratory behavior and human development. In H.W. Reese (Ed.), *Advances in child development and behavior,* Vol. 8, (pp. 59–109). New York: Academic Press.

Nussey, S.S., Ang, V., Jenkins, J.S., Chowdrey, H.S., & Bisset, G.W. (1984). Brattleboro rat adrenal contains vasopressin. *Nature, 310,* 64–66.

O'Connor, M. (1975). The nursery school environment. *Developmental Psychology, 11,* 556–561.

Ojemann, G., & Mateer, C. (1979). Human language cortex: Localization of memory, syntax and sequential motor-phoneme identifications. *Science, 205,* 1401–1408.

Olding, L.B., & Oldstone, M.B.A. (1974). Lymphocytes from human newborns abrogate mitosis of their mother's lymphocytes. *Nature, 249,* 161–162.

Oldstone, M.B.A., Tishon, A., & Moretta, L. (1977). Ative thymus derived suppressor lymphocytes in human cord blood. *Nature, 269,* 333–335.

Oller, D.K., & Eilers, R.E. (1988). The role of audition in infant babbling. *Child Development, 59,* 441–449.

Olson, G.M., & Sherman, T. (1983). Attention, learning and memory in infants. In P.H. Mussen (Ed.), *Handbook of child psychology* (4th ed.). Vol. II. (pp. 1001–1080). New York: Wiley.

O'Malley, B.W., & Means, A.R. (1974). Female steroid hormones and target cell nuclei. *Science, 183,* 610–619.

Opie, I., & Opie, P. (1969). *Children's games in street and playground.* New York: International Universities Press.

Oppenheim, R.W., & Nunez, R. (1982). Electrical stimulation of hindlimb increases neuronal cell death in chick embryo. *Nature, 295,* 57–59.

O'Reilly, E., & Steger, J.A. (1970). Children's use of context in judgment of weight.

*Child Development, 41,* 1095–1101.

Orgel, L.E., Crick, F.H.C., & Sapienza, C. (1980). Selfish DNA. *Nature, 288,* 645–646.

Oster, H. (1981). "Recognition" of emotional expression in infancy? In M.E. Lamb & L.R. Sherrod (Eds.), *Infant social cognition* (pp. 85–125). Hillsdale, NJ: Lawrence Erlbaum.

Oyama, S. (1982). A reformulation of the idea of maturation. In P.P.G. Bateson & P.H. Klopfer (Eds.), *Perspectives in ethology. Vol. 5, Ontogeny.* (pp. 101–131). New York: Plenum.

Oyama, S. (1985). *The ontogeny of information.* Cambridge: Cambridge University Press.

Palermo, D.S. (1975). Developmental aspects of speech perception: Problems for a motor theory. In J.F. Kavanagh & J.E. Cutting (Eds.), *The role of speech in language* (pp. 149–154). Cambridge, MA: MIT Press.

Palmer, A.R., & King, A.J. (1982). The representation of auditory space in the mammalian superior colliculus. *Nature, 299,* 248–249.

Palmerino, C.C., Rusiniak, K.W., & Garcia, J. (1980). Flavor-illness aversions: The peculiar roles of odor and taste in memory for poison. *Science, 208,* 753–755.

Palmiter, R.D., Norstedt, G., Gelinas, R.E., Hammer, R.E., & Brinster, R.L. (1983). Metallothionein-human GH fusion genes stimulate growth of mice. *Science, 222,* 809–814.

Papousek, H. (1969). Individual variability in learned responses in human infants. In R.J. Robinson, Ed. *Brain and early behaviour* (pp. 251–263). London: Academic Press.

Paradise, E.B., & Curcio, F. (1974). Relationship of cognitive and affective behaviors to fear of strangers in male infants. *Developmental Psychology, 10,* 476–483.

Parke, R.D., & Slaby, R.G., (1983). The development of aggression. In P.H. Mussen (Ed.), *Handbook of child psychology* (4th ed.). Vol. IV (pp. 547–641). New York: Wiley.

Parker, M. (1983). Enhancer elements activated by steroid hormones? *Nature, 304,* 687–688.

Parmelee, A.H. Jr., Schulte, F.J., Akiyama, Y., Waldehar, H.W., Schultz, M.A., & Stern, E.S. (1968). Maturation of EGG activity during sleep in premature infants. *Electroencephalography and Clinical Neurophysiology, 24,* 319–329.

Parmelee, A.J., & Sigman, M.D. (1983). Perinatal brain development and behavior. In P.H. Mussen (Ed.), *Handbook of child psychology* (4th ed.). Vol. II (pp. 95–155). New York: Wiley.

Patterson, G.R. (1980). Mothers: The unacknowledged victims. *Monographs of the Society for Research in Child Development, 45* (5), Serial No. 186.

Paulson, E. (1985). A transposon-like element in human DNA. *Nature, 316,* 359–361.

Pawlby, J.S. (1977). Imitative interaction. In H.R. Schaffer (Ed.), *Studies in mother-infant interaction* (pp. 203–224). New York: Academic Press.

Pedersen, P.E., Stewart, W.B., Greer, C.A., & Shepherd, G.M. (1983). Evidence for olfactory function in utero. *Science, 221,* 478–480.

Peiper, A. (1963). *Cerebral function in infancy and childhood.* New York: Consultants Bureau.

Perlmutter, R.M. (1985). Developmentally controlled expression of immunoglobulin VH genes. *Science, 227,* 1597–1600.

Perry, V.H., & Linden, R. (1982). Evidence for dendritic competition in the developing retina. *Nature, 297,* 683–685.

Persaud, K., & Dodd, G. (1982). Analysis of discrimination mechanisms in the mammalian olfactory system using a model nose. *Nature, 299,* 352–355.

Petrig, B., Julesz, B., Kropfl, W., Baumgartner, G., & Anliker, M. (1981). Development of stereopsis and cortical binocularity in human infants: Electrophysiological evidence. *Science, 213,* 1402–1404.

Pettigrew, J.D. (1984). Mobile maps in the brain. *Nature, 309,* 307–308.

Phillips, J.R. (1973). Syntax and vocabulary of mother's speech to young children: Age and sex comparisons. *Child Development, 44,* 182–185.

Piaget, J. (1928). *Judgement and reasoning in the child.* London: Routledge & Kegan Paul.

Piaget, J. (1929). *The child's conception of the world.* London: Routledge & Kegan Paul.

Piaget, J. (1932). *The moral judgment of the child.* Glencoe, IL: Free Press.

Piaget, J. (1952). *The origins of intelligence in children.* New York: International Universities Press.

Piaget, J. (1954). *The construction of reality in the child.* New York: Basic Books.

Piaget, J. (1962). *Play, dreams and imitation in childhood.* New York: Norton.

Piaget, J. (1970). Piaget's theory. In P.H. Mussen (Ed.), *Carmichael's manual of child psychology* (3rd ed.). Vol. 1 (pp. 703–732). New York: Wiley.

Piaget, J. (1971). *Biology and knowledge (An essay on the relations between organic regulations and cognitive processes).* Chicago: University of Chicago Press.

Pipp, S., Jennings, S., & Fischer, K.W. (1987). Acquisition of self and mother knowledge in infancy. *Developmental Psychology, 23,* 86–96.

Plomin, R. (1981). Ethological behavioral genetics and development. In K. Immelmann, G.W. Barlow, L. Petrinovich, & M. Main (Eds.), *Behavioral development* (pp. 252–276). Cambridge: Cambridge University Press.

Plomin, R. (1983). Developmental behavioral genetics. *Child Development, 54,* 253–259.

Plomin, R. (1984, March). *The genetics of the environment: A model and data from developmental behavioral genetics.* Presented at the biennial meeting of the Southwestern Society for Research in Human Development, Denver, CO.

Plomin, R.. & Daniels, D. (1987). Why are children in the same family so different from one another? *Behavioral and Brain Sciences 10,* 1–59.

Plomin, R., De Fries, J.C., & Loehlin, J.C. (1977). Genotype-environment interaction and correlation in the analysis of human behavior. *Psychological Bulletin, 84,* 803–822.

Plotkin, H.C., & Odling-Smee, F.F. (1979). Learning, change and evolution: An inquiry into the teleonomy of learning. *Advances in the Study of Behavior, 10,* 1–41.

Poggio, T., Torre, V., & Koch, C. (1985). Computational vision and regularization theory. *Nature, 317,* 314–319.

Polak, P.R., Emde, R.N., & Spitz, R.A. (1964). The smiling response to the human face. I: Methodology, quantification and natural history. *Journal of Nervous and Mental Diseases, 39,* 103–109.

Poppel, E. (1986). Long-range colour-generating interactions across the retina. *Nature, 320,* 523–525.

Porter, F.L., Miller, R.H., & Marshall, R.E. (1986). Neonatal pain cries: Effect of circumcision on acoustic features and perceived urgency. *Child Development, 57,* 790–802.

Powell, G.F., Brasel, J.A., & Blizzard, R.M. (1967). Emotional deprivation and growth retardation simulating idiopathic hypopituitarism. I. Clinical evaluation of the syndrome. *New England Journal of Medicine, 276,* 1271–1278.

Prader, A. (1962). Chemistry of growth and development. *Modern Problems in Pediatrics, 7,* 91–102.

Prechtl, H.F.R. (1969). Discussion (The infant: Physiological and behavioral studies.) In R.J. Robinson (Ed.), *Brain and early behaviour: Development in the fetus and infant* (pp. 131–138). London: Academic Press.

Preiss, A., Rosenberg, U.B., Kienlin, A., Seifert, E., & Jackle, H. (1985). Molecular genetics of *Kruppel,* a gene required for segmentation of the *Drosophila* embryo. *Nature, 313,* 27–32.

Prescott, E. (1978). Is day care as good as a good home? *Young Children, 33,* 13–19.

Pribylova, H. (1968). The importance of thermoreceptive regions for the chemical thermoregulation of the newborn. *Biologica Neonatorum, 12,* 13–22.

Price-Williams, D. (1981). Concrete and formal operations. In R.H. Munroe, R.L. Munroe, & B.B. Whiting (Eds.), *Handbook of cross-cultural human development* (pp. 403–422). New York: Garland STPM Press.

Prochiantz, A., Daquet, M.C., Herbert, A., & Glowinski, J. (1981). Specific stimulation of "in vitro" maturation of mesencephalic dopaminergic neurones by striatal membranes. *Nature, 293,* 570–572.

Provence, S., & Lipton, R. (1962). *Infants in institutions.* New York: International Universities Press.

Ptito, M., & Lepore, F. (1983). Interocular transfer in cats with early callosal transection. *Nature, 301,* 513–515.

Purves, D., & Hadley, R.D. (1985). Changes in the dentritic branching of adult mammalian neurones revealed by repeated imaging in situ. *Nature, 315,* 404–406.

Purves, D., & Lichtman, J.W. (1985). Geometrical differences among homologous neurons in mammals. *Science, 228,* 298–302.

Purvis, K., Calandra, R., Naess, D., Attramadal, A., Torjesen, P.A., & Hansson, V. (1977). Do androgens increase Leydig cell sensitivity to luteinising hormone? *Nature, 265,* 169–170.

Pylyshyn, Z.W. (1985). Plasticity and invariance in cognitive development. In J. Mehler & R. Fox (Eds.), *Neonate cognition* (pp. 403–415). Hillsdale, NJ: Lawrence Erlbaum.

Radke-Yarrow, M., Zahn-Waxler, C., & Chapman, M. (1983). Children's prosocial disposition and behavior. In P.H. Mussen (Ed.), *Handbook of Child Psychology* (4th ed.), IV, (pp. 469–545). New York: Wiley.

Raff, R.A., Anstrom, J.A., Huffman, C.J., Leaf, D.S., Loo, J.H., Showman, R.M., & Wells, D.E. (1984). Origin of a gene regulatory mechanism in the evolution of echinoderms. *Nature, 310,* 312–314.

Raff, R.A., & Kaufman, T. (1983). *Embryos, genes and evolution.* New York: Macmillan.

Rakic, P. (1981). Development of visual centers in the primate brain depends on binocular competition before birth. *Science, 214,* 928–931.

Rakic, P., Bourgeois, J.P., Eckenhoff, M.F., Zecevic, N., & Goldman-Rakic, P.S. (1986). Concurrent overproduction of synapses in diverse regions of the primate cerebral cortex. *Science, 232,* 232–235.

Rakic, P., & Riley, K.P. (1983a). Overproduction and elimination of retinal axons in the fetal Rhesus monkeys. *Science, 219,* 1441–1444.

Rakic, P., & Riley, K.P. (1983b). Regulation of axon number in primate optic nerve by prenatal binocular competition. *Nature, 305,* 135–137.

Rastan, S., & Cattanach, B.M. (1983). Interaction between the Xce locus and imprinting of the paternal X chromosome in mouse yolk-sac endoderm. *Nature, 303,* 635–637.

Reed, E. (1975). Genetic anomalies in development. In F.D. Horowitz (Ed.), *Review of child development research,* Vol. 4 (pp. 59–99). Chicago: University of Chicago Press.

Regan, D., & Beverly, K.I. (1973). Disparity detectors in human depth perception: Evidence for directional selectivity. *Science, 181,* 877–879.

Reisenauer, A.M. (1985). Abrupt induction of a membrane digestive enzyme by its intraintestinal substrate. *Science, 227,* 70–72.

Renaud, L.P., Martin, J.B., & Brazeau, P. (1975). Depressant action of TRH, LH-RH and somatostatin on activity of central neurones. *Nature, 255,* 233–235.

Rendel, J.M. (1967). *Canalization and gene control.* London: Logos Press.

Rest, J.R. (1983). Morality. In P.H. Mussen (Ed.), *Handbook of child psychology* (4th ed.). Vol. III (pp. 556–629). New York: Wiley.

Rheingold, H.L. (1961). The effect of environmental stimulation upon social and exploratory behavior in the human infant. In B.M. Foss (Ed.), *Determinants of infant behaviour.* (pp. 143–171). New York: Wiley.

Rheingold, H.L. (1963). Controlling the infant's exploratory behavior. In B.M. Foss (Ed.), *Determinants of infant behaviour II* (pp. 171–175). London: Methuen.

Rheingold, H.L. (1969). The effect of a strange environment on the behavior of infants. In B.M. Foss (Ed.), *Determinants of infant behaviour.* IV. (pp. 137–166). London: Methuen.

Rheingold, H.L., & Bayley, N. (1959). The later effects of an experimental modification of mothering. *Child Development, 30,* 363–372.

Rheingold, H.L., & Eckerman, C.O. (1971). Departures from the mother. In H.R. Schaffer (Ed.), *The origins of human social relations* (pp. 73–78). New York: Academic Press.

Rheingold, H.L., & Eckerman, C.O. (1973). Fear of the stranger: A critical examination. In H.W. Reese (Ed.), *Advances in child development and behavior.* Vol. 8. (pp. 185–222). New York: Academic Press.

Rheingold, H.L., & Samuels, H.R. (1969). Maintaining the positive behavior of infants by increased stimulation. *Developmental Psychology, 1,* 520–527.

Ribble, M.A. (1943). *The rights of infants.* New York: Columbia University Press.

Richards, M.P.M. (1970). The development of behaviour and its social context. *New Scientist, 46,* 638.

Richards, M.P.M. (1974). First steps in becoming social. In M.P.M. Richards (Ed.),

*The integration of a child into a social world* (pp. 83–97). London: Cambridge University Press.

Richards, W. (1970). Stereopsis and stereoblindness. *Brain Research, 10,* 380–388.

Riddle, D.L., Swanson, M.M., & Albert, P.S. (1981). Interacting genes in nematode dauer larva formation. *Nature, 290,* 668–671.

Ritchie, B.F. (1973). Theories of learning: A consumer report. In B. Wolman (Ed.), *Handbook of general psychology* (pp. 451–460). New York: Prentice-Hall.

Roberts, W.W. (1970). Hypothalamic mechanisms for motivational and species-typical behavior. In R.E. Whalen, R.F. Thompson, M. Verzeano, & N.M. Weinberger (Eds.), *The neural control of behavior* (pp. 175–206). New York: Academic Press.

Robertson, M. (1976). Sounds and signals. *Nature, 264,* 399–401.

Robinson, R.J. (1969). *Brain and early behaviour.* New York: Academic Press.

Robson, K.S. (1967). The role of eye-to-eye contact in maternal-infant attachment. *Journal of Child Psychology and Psychiatry, 8,* 13–25.

Rogers, B., & Koenderink, J. (1985). Monocular aniseikonia: A motion parallax analogue of the disparity-induced effect. *Nature, 322,* 62–63.

Roper, R., & Hinde, R.A. (1978). Social behavior in a play group: Consistency and complexity. *Child Development, 49,* 570–579.

Rose, K.D., & Brown, T.M. (1984). Gradual phyletic evolution at the generic level in early Eocene omomyid primates. *Nature, 309,* 250–252.

Rosen, C.D. (1974). The effects of sociodramatic play on problem-solving behavior among culturally disadvantaged preschool children. *Child Development, 45,* 920–927.

Rosenblatt, D. (1977). Developmental trends in infant play. In B. Tizard & D. Harvey (Eds.), *Biology of play.* (pp. 33–44). Philadelphia: J.B. Lippincott.

Rosenhaan, D., Frederick, F., & Burrowes, A. (1968). Effects of co-observer's sanctions and adult presence on imitative aggression. *Child Development, 39,* 291–302.

Rosenzweig, M.R. (1971). Effects of environment on development of brain and behavior. In E. Tobach, L.R. Aronson, & E. Shaw (Eds.), *The biopsychology of development* (pp. 303–342). New York: Academic Press.

Rothenberg, B.B., & Courtney, R.G. (1969). A developmental study of nonconservation choices in young children. *Merrill-Palmer Quarterly, 15,* 363–373.

Rothenberg, B., & Orost, J.H. (1969). The training of conservation of number in young children. *Child Development, 40,* 707–726.

Rowe, D.C., & Plomin, R. (1981). The importance on nonshared (E1) environmental influences in behavioral development. *Developmental Psychology, 17,* 517–531.

Rubenstein, J., & Howes, C. (1976). The effects of peers on toddler interaction with mother and toys. *Child Development, 47,* 597–605.

Rubenstein, J., & Howes, C. (1979). Caregiving and infant behavior in daycare and in homes. *Developmental Psychology, 15,* 1–24.

Russell, M.J. (1976). Human olfactory communication. *Nature, 260,* 520–522.

Rutishauser, U. (1984). Developmental biology of a neural cell adhesion molecule. *Nature, 310,* 549–553.

Rutter, M. (1984). Continuities and discontinuities in socioemotional development.

In R.N. Emde & R.J. Harmon (Eds.), *Continuities and discontinuities in development* (pp. 41–68). New York: Plenum.

Ryan, S.M., Hegion, A.G., & Flavell, J.H. (1970). Nonverbal mnemonic mediation in preschool children. *Child Development, 41,* 539–550.

Sackett, G.P., Ruppenthal, G.C., Fahrenbruch, C.E., Holm, R.A., & Greenough, W.T. (1981). Social isolation rearing effects in monkeys vary with genotype. *Developmental Psychology, 17,* 313–318.

Sadoul, R., Hirn, M. Deagostini-Bazin, H., Gorriolis, C., & Rougon, G. (1983). Adult and embryonic mouse neural cell adhesion molecules have different binding properties. *Nature, 304,* 347–349.

Sagi, A., Lamb, M.E., Lewkowicz, K.S., Shoham, R., Dirr, R., & Estes, D. (1985). Security of infant-mother-father and -metapelet attachments among kibbutz-reared Israeli children. In I. Bretherton & E. Waters (Eds.), Growing points of attachment threory and research. *Monographs of the Society for Research in Child Development, 50* (1–2), 257–275. Serial no. 209.

Saji, M., & Reis, D.J. (1987). Delayed transneuronal death of substrata nigra neurons prevented by gamma-Aminobutyric acid agonist. *Science, 235,* 66–69.

Salapatek, P. (1975). Pattern perception in early infancy. In L.B. Cohen & P. Salapatek (Eds.), *Infant perception: From sensation to cognition.* Vol. 1 (pp. 133–248). New York: Academic Press.

Salmons, S., & Streiter, F.A. (1976). Significance of impulse activity in the transformation of skeletal muscle type. *Nature, 263,* 30–34.

Saltz, E., Dixon, D., & Johnson, J. (1977). Training disadvantaged preschoolers on various fantasy activities: Effects on cognitive functioning and impulse control. *Child Development, 48,* 367–380.

Sameroff, A.J., & Cavanaugh, P.J. (1979). Learning in infancy: A developmental perspective. In J.D. Osofsky (Ed.), *Handbook of infant development* (pp. 344–392). New York: Wiley.

Sameroff, A.J., & Chandler, M.J. (1975). Reproductive risk and the continuum of caretaking casualty. In F.D. Horowitz (Ed.), *Review of child development research.* Vol. 4 (pp. 187–244). Chicago: University of Chicago Press.

Sanes, J. (1984). More nerve growth factors? *Nature, 307,* 500.

Sargent, T.D., & Dawid, I.B. (1983). Differential gene expression in the gastrula of "Xenopus laevis." *Science, 222,* 135–139.

Sayegh, Y., & Dennis, W. (1965). The effect of supplementary experiences upon the behavioral development of infants in institutions. *Child Development, 36,* 81–90.

Scarr, S. (1969). Social introversion-extraversion as a heritable response. *Child Development, 40,* 823–832.

Scarr, S., & Kidd, K.K. (1983). Developmental behavioral genetics. In P.H. Mussen (Ed.), *Handbook of child psychology* (4th ed.). Vol. II (pp. 343–433). New York: Wiley.

Scarr, S., & McCartney, K. (1983). How people make their own environments: A theory of genotype→environment effects. *Child Development, 54,* 424–435.

Scarr-Salapatek, S. (1971). Race, social class, and I.Q. *Science, 174,* 1285–1295.

Scarr-Salapatek, S. (1975). Genetics and the development of intelligence. In F.D.

Horowitz (Ed.), *Review of child development research*, Vol. 4 (pp. 1–57). Chicago: University of Chicago Press.

Scarr-Salapatek, S. (1976). Genetic determinants of infant development: An overstated case. In L.P. Lipsitt (Ed.), *Developmental psychobiology* (pp. 59–80). Hillsdale, NJ: Lawrence Erlbaum.

Schaffer, H.R. (1963). Some issues for research in the study of attachment behaviour. In B.M. Foss (Ed.), *Determinants of infant behaviour II* (pp. 179–199). New York: Wiley.

Schaffer, H.R. (1971). Cognitive structure and early social behavior. In H.R. Schaffer (Ed.), *The origins of human social relations* (pp. 247–262). New York: Academic Press.

Schaffer, H.R. (1977). Early interactive development. In H.R. Schaffer (Ed.), *Studies in mother-infant interaction* (pp. 3–15). London: Academic Press.

Schaffer, H.R., Greenwood, A., & Parry, M.H. (1972). The onset of wariness. *Child Development, 43,* 165–175.

Schankler, D.M. (1981). Local extinction and ecological re-entry of early Eocene mammals. *Nature, 293,* 135–138.

Schiller, P.H. (1957). Innate motor action as a basis of learning. In C.H. Schiller (Ed.), *Instinctive behavior* (pp. 264–287). New York: International Universities Press.

Schiller, R.H. (1982). Central connections of retinal ON and OFF pathways. *Nature, 297,* 580–583.

Schneider-Rosen, K., Braunwald, K.G., Carlson, V., & Acchetti, D. (1985). Current perspectives in attachment theory: Illustration from the study of maltreated infants. In I. Bretherton & E. Waters (Eds.), Growing points of attachment theory and research. *Monographs of the Society for Research on Child Development, 50* (1–2), 194–210. Serial no. 209.

Schneirla, T.C. (1965). Aspects of stimulation and organization in approach/withdrawal processes underlying vertebrate behavioral development. *Advances in the study of behavior, 1,* 2–74.

Schneirla, T.C., Rosenblatt, J.S., & Tobach, E. (1963). Maternal behavior in the cat. In H.L. Rheingold (Ed.), *Maternal behavior in mammals* (pp. 122–168). New York: Wiley.

Schwartz, A., Campos, J.J., Baisel, E., & Amatore, B. (1971, April). *Cardiac and behavioral correlates of infant stress: Visual cliff and maternal separation.* Paper presented at the Biennial Meeting of the Society for Research in Child Development. Minneapolis, MN.

Schwartz, G.M., Izard, C.E., & Ansul, S.E. (1985). 5-month old's ability to discriminate facial expressions of emotion. *Infant Behavior and Development, 8,* 65–77.

Scofidi, F.A., Field, T.M., Schanberg, S.M., Bauer, C.R., Velga-Lahr, N., Garcia, R., Poirier, J., Nystom, G., & Kuhn, C.M. (1986). Effects of tactile/kinesthetic stimulation on the clinical course of sleep/wake behavior of preterm neonates. *Infant Behavior and Development, 9,* 91–105.

Seifert, R.A., Schwartz, S., & Bowen-Pope, D.F. (1984). Developmentally regulated production of platelet-derived growth factor-like molecules. *Nature, 311,* 669–671.

Seneglaub, D.R., & Finlay, B.L. (1981). Early removal of one eye reduces normally occurring cell death in the remaining eye. *Science, 213,* 573–574.

Shadlen, M., & Carney, T. (1986). Mechanisms of human motion perception revealed by new cyclopean illusion. *Science, 232,* 95–97.

Shea, B.T. (1983). Paedomorphosis and neoteny in the pygmy chimpanzee. *Science, 222,* 521–523.

Shea, S.L., Aslin, R.N., & McCulloch, D. (1987). Binocular VEP summation in infants and adults with abnormal binocular histories. *Investigative Opthalmology and Visual Science, 28,* 152–161.

Sheldrake, A.R. (1974). The ageing, growth and death of cells. *Nature, 250,* 381–384.

Shepard, R.N., & Zare, S.L. (1983). Path-guided apparent motion. *Science, 220,* 632–634.

Shepherd, J.C.W. (1984). Fly and frog homoeo domains show homologies with yeast mating type regulatory proteins. *Nature, 310,* 70–71.

Siegelman, M., Fried, V.A., Bond, M.W., Weissman, I.L., St. John, T., & Smith, H.T. (1986). Cell surface molecule associated with lymphocyte homing is a ubiquitinated branched chain glycoprotein. *Science, 231,* 823–828.

Silitto, A.M., Kemp, J.A., & Blakemore, C. (1981). The role of GABA ergic inhibition in the cortical effects of monocular deprivation. *Nature, 291,* 318–320.

Silman, R.E., Chard, T., Lowry, P.J., Smith, I., & Young, I.M. (1976). Human foetal pituitary peptides and parturition. *Nature, 260,* 716–718.

Silman, R.E., Holland, D., Chard, T., Lowry, P.J., & Hope, J. (1978). The ACTH "family tree" of the Rhesus monkey changes with development. *Nature, 276,* 526–528.

Silver, I., & Ogawa, M.Y. (1983). Postnatally induced formation of the corpus callosum in the acallosal mice on glial-coated cellulose bridges. *Science, 220,* 1067–1069.

Simmel, M.L. (1966). Developmental aspects of the body scheme. *Child Development Monograph, 37(1),* 83–95.

Simon, T., & Smith, P.K. (1985). Play and problem solving: A paradigm questioned. *Merrill-Palmer Quarterly, 31,* 265–277.

Simpson, G.G. (1950). *The meaning of evolution.* New Haven: Yale University Press.

Simpson, G.G. (1972). The evolutionary concept of man. In B. Campbell (Ed.), *Sexual selection and descent of man* (pp. 17–39). Chicago: Aldine.

Siperstein, G.N. (1973, March). *Differential modification of neonatal behavior.* Paper presented at the meeting of the Society for Research in Child Development, Philadelphia, PA.

Sirinathsinghji, D.J.S., Rees, L.H., Rivier, J., & Vale, W. (1983). Corticotropin-releasing factor is a potent inhibitor of sexual receptivity in the female rat. *Nature, 305,* 232–235.

Skinner, B.F. (1981). Selection by consequences. *Science, 213,* 501–504.

Slack, J. (1984). A rosetta stone for pattern formation in animals? *Nature, 311,* 364–365.

Slobin, D.I. (1973). Cognitive prerequisites for the development of grammar. In C.A. Ferguson & D.I. Slobin (Eds.), *Studies of child language development* (pp. 175–208). New York: Holt, Rinehart & Winston.

Slobin, D. (1982). Universal and particular in the acquisition of language. In E. Wanner & L.R. Gleitman (Eds.), *Language acquisition: The state of the art* (pp. 128–170). Cambridge: Cambridge University Press.

Sluckin, A.W., & Smith, P.K. (1977). Two approaches to the concept of dominance in preschool children. *Child Development, 48*, 917–923.

Smith, A., & Over, R. (1975). Tilt aftereffects with subjective contours. *Nature, 257*, 581–582.

Smith, P.K., & Connolly, K. (1980). *The ecology of preschool behaviour.* Cambridge: Cambridge University Press.

Smith, P.K., & Whitney, S. (1987). Play and associative fluency: Experimenter effects may be responsible for previous positive findings. *Developmental Psychology, 23*, 49–53.

Smith, R.G., & Appel, S.H. (1983). Extracts of skeletal muscle increase neurite outgrowth and cholinergic activity of fetal rat spinal motor neurons. *Science, 219*, 1079–1081.

Smith, W.J. (1977). *The behavior of communicating. An ethological approach.* Cambridge, MA: Harvard University Press.

Snow, C.E. (1972). Mother's speech to children learning language. *Child Development, 43*, 549–564.

Snow, M.H.L., & Tam, P.P.L. (1980). Timing in embryological development. *Nature, 286*, 107.

Snyder, S.H. (1980). Brain peptides as neurotransmitters. *Science, 209*, 976–983.

Sokoloff, A.N. (1969). Studies of the speech mechanisms of thinking. In M. Cole & I. Maltzman (Eds.), *A handbook of contemporary Soviet psychology* (pp. 531–573). New York: Basic Books.

Sonderegger, P., Rishman, M., Bokoum, M., Bauer, H., & Nelson, P. (1983). Axonal proteins of presynaptic neurons during synaptogenesis. *Science, 221*, 1294–1296.

Spelke, E.G. (1985). Perception of unity, persistence, and identity: Thoughts on infants' conceptions of objects. In J. Mehler & R. Fox, (Eds.), *Neonate cognition* (pp. 89–113). Hillsdale, NJ: Lawrence Erlbaum Associates.

Spelsberg, T.C., Webster, R.A., & Pikler, G.M. (1976). Chromosomal proteins regulate steroid binding to chromatin. *Nature, 262*, 65–67.

Spemann, H. (1938). *Embryonic development and induction.* New Haven, CT: Yale University Press.

Sperry, R.W. (1968). Plasticity of neural maturation. *Developmental Biology Supplement, 2*, 306–327.

Spinelli, D.N., & Jensen, F.E. (1979). Plasticity: The mirror of experience. *Science, 203*, 75–78.

Spiro, M.E. (1979). *Gender and culture: Kibbutz women revisited.* Durham, NC: Duke University Press.

Spitz, R.A. (1945). Hospitalism. An inquiry into the genesis of psychiatric conditions in early childhood. *Psychoanalytic Study of the Child, 1*, 53–74.

Spitz, R.A. (1946a). Hospitalism: A follow-up report. *Psychoanalytic Study of the Child, 2*, 113–117.

Spitz, R.A. (1946b). Anaclitic depression: An inquiry into the genesis of psychiatric conditions in early childhood. *Psychoanalytic Study of the Child, 2*, 313–342.

Spitz, R.A. (1950). Anxiety in infancy: A study of its manifestations in the first year of life. *International Journal of Psycho-Analysis, 31*, 138–143.

Spitz, R.A., & Wolf, K.M. (1946). The origin of the smiling response. *Genetic Psychology Monographs, 34*, 57–125.

Squire, L.R. (1986). Mechanisms of memory. *Science, 232*, 1612–1619.

Sroufe, L.A. (1979). Socioemotional development. In J.D. Osofsky (Ed.), *Handbook of infant development* (pp. 462–516). New York: Wiley.

Sroufe, L., & Waters, E. (1975). The ontogenesis of smiling and laughter: A perspective on the organization of development in infancy. *Psychological Review, 83*, 173–189.

Stahn, R., Fabricus, H.A., & Hartleitner, W. (1978). Suppression of human T-cell colony formation during pregnancy. *Nature, 276*, 831–832.

Stanfield, B.B., O'Leary, D.D.M., & Fricks, C. (1982). Selective collateral elimination in early postnatal development restricts cortical distribution of rat pyrimidal tract neurons. *Nature, 298*, 371–373.

Starkey, P., & Cooper, R.G., Jr. (1980). Perception of numbers by human infants. *Science, 210*, 1033–1034.

Starkey, P., Spelke, E.S., & Gelman, R. (1983). Detection of intermodal numerical correspondences by human infants. *Science, 222*, 179–181.

Stebbins, G.L., & Ayala, J.F. (1981). Is a new evolutionary synthesis necessary? *Science, 213*, 967–971.

Stent, G.S. (1975). Limits to scientific understanding of man. *Science, 187*, 1052–1057.

Stern, D.N., Jaffe, J., Beebe, B., & Bennett, S.L. (1975). Vocalizing in unison and in alternation: Two modes of communication within the mother-infant dyad. *Annals of the New York Academy of Sciences, 263*, 89–100.

Sternglanz, S.H., Gray, J.L., & Murakami, M. (1977). Adult preferences for infantile facial features: An ethological approach. *Animal Behaviour, 25*, 108–115.

Stevens, C.F. (1985). Molecular tinkerings that tailor the acetylecholine receptor. *Nature, 313*, 353–354.

Stiles, C.D. (1984). Autocrine control of growth? *Nature, 311*, 604–605.

Stott, L.H. (1961). An empirical approach to motivation based on the behavior of a young child. *Journal of Child Psychology and Psychiatry, 2*, 97–117.

St. Pierre, T.E. (1981). The role of group size and physical setting on toddlers' social interactions with peers. Unpublished master's thesis, University of California at Davis.

Strange, W., & Jenkins, J.J. (1978). Role of linguistic experience in the perception of speech. In R.D. Walk & H.L. Pick, Jr. (Eds.), *Perception and experience* (pp. 125–169). New York: Plenum Press.

Strayer, F.F. (1980). Social ecology of the preschool peer group. In W.A. Collins (Ed.), *Minnesota symposia on child psychology, Vol. 13* (pp. 165–196). Hillsdale, NJ: Erlbaum.

Struhl, G. (1984). A universal genetic key to body plan? *Nature, 310*, 10–11.

Südhof, T.C., Russell, D.W., Goldstein, J.L., Brown, M.S., Sanchez-Pescador, R., & Bell, G.I. (1985). Casette of eight exons shared by genes for LDL receptor and EGF precursor. *Science, 228*, 893–895.

Sullivan, H.S. (1953). *The interpersonal theory of psychiatry.* New York: Norton.

Sutcliffe, J.G. (1984). Control of neuronal gene expression. *Science, 225,* 1308–1316.

Swanson, L.W. (1985). Novel developmental specificity in the nervous system of transgenic animals expressing growth hormone fusion genes. *Nature, 317,* 363–366.

Sylva, K., Bruner, J.S., & Genova, P. (1976). The role of play in the problem-solving of children 3–5 years old. In J.S. Bruner, A. Jolly & K. Sylva (Eds.), *Play: Its role in development and evolution* (pp. 244–257). New York: Basic Books.

Taghert, P.H., Doe, C.D., & Goodman, C.S. (1984). Cell determination and regulation during development of neuroblasts and neurones in grasshopper embryo. *Nature, 307,* 163–165.

Tanner, J.M. (1962). *Growth at adolescence* (2nd ed.). Oxford: Blackwell.

Tanner, J.M. (1970). Physical growth. In P.H. Mussen (Ed.), *Carmichael's manual of child psychology* (3rd ed.). Vol. 1 (pp. 77–155). New York: Wiley.

Taylor, A. (1968). Institutionalized infants' concept formation ability. *American Journal of Orthopsychiatry, 38,* 110–115.

Tcheng, F.C.Y., & Laroche, J.L. (1965). Phases de sommeil et sourires spontanes. *Acta Psychologica, 24,* 1–28.

Ter Vrugt, D., & Pederson, D.R. (1973). The effects of vertical rocking frequencies on the arousal level in two-month-old infants. *Child Development, 44,* 205–209.

Teuber, H.L., & Rudel, R.G. (1962). Behavior after cerebral lesion in children or adults. *Developmental Medicine and Child Neurology, 4,* 3–20.

Thelen, E. (1985). Developmental origins of motor coordination: Leg movements in human infants. *Developmental Psychobiology, 18,* 1–22.

Theorell, K., Prechtl, H.F.R., Blair, A.W., & Lind, J. (1973). Behavioural state cycles of normal newborn infants. *Developmental Medicine and Child Neurology, 15,* 597–605.

Thoday, J.M. (1975). Non-Darwinian "evolution" and biological processes. *Nature, 255,* 675.

Thoman, E.B. (Ed.). (1979). *Origins of the infant's social responsiveness.* Hillsdale, NJ: Lawrence Erlbaum Associates.

Thompson, J.N. (1975). Qualitative variation and gene number. *Nature, 258,* 665–668.

Thompson, J.N., Jr., & Woodruff, R.C. (1978). Mutator genes-pacemakers of evolution. *Nature, 274,* 317–321.

Thompson, W. (1983). Synapse elimination in neonatal rat muscle is sensitive to pattern of muscle use. *Nature, 302,* 614–616.

Thompson, W.R., & Grusec, J.E. (1970). Studies of early experience. In P.H. Mussen (Ed.), *Carmichael's manual of child psychology* (3rd ed.). Vol. 1 (pp. 565–654). New York: Wiley.

Thomson, K. (1984). Reductionism and other -isms in biology. *American Scientist, 72,* 388–390.

Thorpe, W.H. (1963). *Learning and instinct in animals* (2nd ed.). Cambridge, MA: Harvard University Press.

Tinbergen, N. (1951). *The study of instinct.* Oxford: Oxford University Press.

Tizard, B., Cooperman, O., Joseph, A., & Tizard, J. (1972). Environmental effects on language development: A study of young children in long-stay residential nurseries. *Child Development, 43,* 337–358.

Tizard, J., & Tizard, B. (1971). The social development of two-year-old children in residential nurseries. In H.R. Schaffer (Ed.), *The origins of human social relations* (pp. 147–161). New York: Academic Press.

Tizard, J., & Tizard, B. (1974). The institution as an environment for development. In M.P.M. Richards (Ed.), *The integration of a child into a social world* (pp. 137–152). London: Cambridge University Press.

Trivers, R. (1971). The evolution of reciprocal altruism. *Quarterly Review of Biology, 46,* 35–57.

Trivers, R.L. (1974). Parent-offspring conflict. *American Zoologist, 14,* 249–264.

Tulkin, S.R. (1977). Social class differences in maternal and infant behavior. In P.H. Leiderman, S.R. Tulkin, & A. Rosenfeld (Eds.), *Culture and infancy: Variations in the human experience.* (pp. 495–537). New York: Academic Press.

Ullman, S. (1979). *The interpretation of motion.* Cambridge, MA: MIT Press.

Ullrey, G. (1986, April). *Non-organic failture to thrive.* Paper presented at a colloquium sponsored by the graduate group in child development. University of California, Davis.

Ungar, F., Geiger, B., & Ben-Zéev, A. (1986). Cell contact- and shape-dependent regulation of vinculin synthesis in cultured fibroblasts. *Nature, 319,* 787–791.

Valverde, F. (1967). Apical dendritic spines of the visual cortex and light deprivation in the mouse. *Experimental Brain Research, 3,* 337–352.

Vandell, D.L. (1980). Sociability with peer and mother during the first year. *Developmental Psychology, 16,* 355–361.

van den Berghe, P.L. (1973). *Age and sex in human societies: A biosocial perspective.* Belmont, CA: Wadsworth Publishing Co.

Van der Loos, H., & Woolsey, T.A. (1973). Somatosensory cortex: Structural alterations following early injury to sense organs. *Science, 179,* 395–397.

Van Lieshout, K. (1972). Structure of social interaction in preschool children: Stability over time and relation to concurrent and contigently antecedent and consequent behavior. In F.J. Monks, W.W. Hartup, & J. de Wit (Eds.), *Determinants of behavioral development,* (pp. 597–604). New York: Academic Press.

Vidyasagar, T.R. (1976). Orientation specific color adaptation at a binocular site. *Nature, 261,* 39–40.

Vine, I. (1973). The role of facial-visual signalling in early social development. In M. von Cranach & I. Vine (Eds.), *Social communication and movement* (pp. 195–298). London: Academic Press.

von der Heydt, R., Peterhans, E., & Baumgartner, G. (1984). Illusory contours and cortical neuron responses. *Science, 224,* 1260–1262.

von Senden, M. (1960). *Space and sight.* Glencoe, IL: The Free Press.

von Uexkull, J. (1934/1957). A stroll through the world of animals and men. In C. Schiller (Ed.), *Instinctive behavior* (pp. 5–80). New York: International Universities Press.

Vrba, E.S. (1983). Macroevolutionary trends: New perspectives on the roles of adaptation and incidental effect. *Science, 221*, 387–389.

Vygotsky, L.S. (1962). *Thought and language.* New York: Wiley.

Wachs, T. (1983). The use and abuse of environment in behavior-genetic research. *Child Development, 54*, 396–407.

Wachs, T., Uzgiris, I., & Hunt, J. (1971). Cognitive development in infants of different age levels and from different environmental backgrounds: An exploratory investigation. *Merrill-Palmer Quarterly, 17*, 283–319.

Wachs, T.D., & Gruen, G.E. (1982). *Early experience and human development.* New York: Plenum Press.

Waddington, C.H. (1957). *The strategy of the genes.* London: George, Allen & Unwin.

Waddington, C.H. (1962). *New patterns in genetics and development.* New York: Columbia University Press.

Waddington, C.H. (1971). Concepts of development. In E. Tobach, L.R. Aronson, & E. Shaw (Eds.), *The biopsychology of development* (pp. 17–23). New York: Academic Press.

Wake, D.B., & Larson, A. (1987). A multidimensional analysis of an evolving lineage. *Science, 237*, 42–48.

Walsh, R.P. (1969). Generalization of self-control in children. *Journal of Educational Research, 62*, 464–466.

Walthall, W.W. (1984). Rules for neural development revealed by chimaeric sensory system in crickets. *Nature, 311*, 57–59.

Warner, A.E. (1984). Antibodies to gap-junctional protein selectivity disrupt junctional communication in the early amphibian embryo. *Nature, 311*, 13–19.

Wasz-Hockert, O., Partanen, T., Vuorenkoski, V., Valanne, E., & Michelsson, K. (1964). Effect of training on ability to identify preverbal vocalizations. *Developmental Medicine and Child Neurology, 6*, 393–396.

Waterlow, J.C., Ashworth, A., & Griffiths, M. (1980). Faltering infant growth in less-developed countries. *Lancet, (2)*, 1176–1178.

Watson, J.S. (1967). Memory and "contingency analysis" in infant learning. *Merrill-Palmer Quarterly, 13*, 55–76.

Watson, J.S. (1972). Smiling, cooing and "the game." *Merrill-Palmer Quarterly, 18*, 323–339.

Watson, J.S. (1979). Perception of contingency as a determinant of social responsiveness. In E.B. Thoman (Ed.), *Origins of the infant's social responsiveness.* (pp. 33–64). Hillsdale, NJ: Lawrence Erlbaum Associates.

Watson, J.S. (1981). Contingency experience in behavioral development. In K. Immelmann, G.W. Barlow, L. Petrinovich, & M. Main (Eds.), *Behavioral development.* (pp. 83–89). Cambridge: Cambridge University Press.

Watson, J.S., & Ramey, C.T. (1972). Reactions to response-contingent stimulation in early infancy. *Merrill-Palmer Quarterly, 18*, 219–227.

Watt, R.J. (1985). Structured representation in low-level vision. *Nature, 313*, 266–267.

Waxler, C.Z., & Radke-Yarrow, M.R. (1975). An observational study of maternal models. *Developmental Psychology, 11*, 485–494.

Webster, D.B., & Webster, M. (1977). Neonatal sound deprivation affects brain stem auditory nucleus. *Archives of Otolaryngology, 103*, 393–396.

Weill, C.L., & Greene, D.P. (1984). Prevention of natural motoneurone cell death by dibutryrl cyclic GMP. *Nature, 308*, 452–454.

Weisberg, P. (1963). Social and nonsocial conditioning of infant vocalizations. *Child Development, 34*, 377–388.

Weiss, P. (1970). Neural development in biological perspective. In F.O. Schmitt (Ed.), *The neurosciences. Second study program* (pp. 53–61). New York: Rockefeller University Press.

Wellman, H.M., & Lemper, J.D. (1977). The naturalistic communicative abilities of two-year-olds. *Child Development, 48*, 1052–1057.

Werker, J.F., & Tees, R.C. (1984). Cross-language speech-perception: Evidence for perceptual reorganization during the first year of life. *Infant Behavior and Development, 7*, 49–63.

Werner, E.E., & Smith, R.S. (1982). *Vulnerable but invincible: A longitudinal study of resilient children and youth.* New York: McGraw-Hill.

Werner, H. (1948). *Comparative psychology of mental development* (Rev. ed.). Chicago: Follett.

Wertheimer, M. (1961). Psychomotor coordination of auditory and visual space at birth. *Science, 134*, 1692.

Whitaker, H., & Ojemann, G. (1977). Graded localization of naming from electrical simulation mapping of left cerebral cortex. *Nature, 270*, 50–51.

White, B.L. (1971). *Human infants: Experience and psychological development.* Englewood Cliffs, NJ: Prentice-Hall.

White, B.L., Kaban, B.T., & Attanucci, J.S. (1979). *The origins of human competence.* Lexington, MA: D.C. Heath.

White, T.D. (1980). Evolutionary implications of Pliocene hominid footprints. *Science, 208*, 175–176.

Wiesel, T.N. (1982). Postnatal development of the visual cortex and the influence of environment. *Nature, 299*, 583–591.

Wilcox, B.M., & Clayton, F.L. (1968). Infant visual fixation on motion pictures of the human face. *Journal of Experimental Child Psychology, 6*, 22–32.

Wild, H.M. (1985). Primate cortical area V4 important for color constancy but not wave-length discrimination. *Nature, 313*, 133–135.

Williams, B.J. (1981). A critical review of models in sociobiology. *Annual Review of Anthropology, 10*, 163–192.

Williams, G.C. (1975). *Sex and evolution.* Princeton, NJ: Princeton University Press.

Willoughby, R.H., & Trachy, S. (1971). Conservation of number in very young children: A failure to replicate Mehler and Bever. *Merrill-Palmer Quarterly, 17*, 205–209.

Wilson, E.O. (1975). *Sociobiology, the new synthesis.* Cambridge, MA: Belknap Press.

Wilson, E.O. (1978). *On human nature.* Cambridge, MA: Harvard University Press.

Winick, M., Meyer, K.K., & Harris, R.C. (1975). Malnutrition and environmental enrichment by early adoption. *Science, 190*, 1173–1175.

Wolff, P.H. (1963). The early development of smiling. In B.M. Foss (Ed.), *Determinants of infant behaviour*, II (pp. 113–134). New York: Wiley.

Wolff, P.H. (1966). The causes, controls and organization of behavior in the neonate. *Psychological Issues, 5*, (Whole no. 1).

Wolff, P.H. (1969). The natural history of crying and other vocalizations in infancy. In B.M. Foss (Ed.), *Determinants of infant behaviour*, IV (pp. 81–109). New York: Wiley.

Wolfram, S. (1984). Cellular automata as models of complexity. *Nature, 311*, 419–424.

Wong-Riley, M., & Carroll, E.W. (1984). Effect of impulse blockage on cytochrome oxidase activity in monkey visual system. *Nature, 307*, 262–264.

Wood, W.G. (1985). Control of haemoglobin switching by a developmental clock? *Nature, 313*, 320–322.

Woodland, H., & Jones, E. (1986). Developmental biology: Unscrambling egg structures. *Nature, 319*, 261–262.

Woodruff, R.C., Thompson, J.N., Jr., & Lyman, R.F. (1979). Intraspecific hybridisation and the release of mutator activity. *Nature, 278*, 277–279.

Woolsey, T.A., & Van der Loos, H. (1970). The structural organization of layer IV in the somatosensory region (SI) of mouse cerebral cortex. *Brain Research, 17*, 205–242.

Wright, S. (1949). Adaptation and selection. In G.L. Jepsen, G.G. Simpson, & E. Mayr (Eds.), *Genetics, paleontology and evolution* (pp. 365–389). Princeton, NJ: Princeton University Press.

Wright, S. (1960). Physiological genetics, ecology of populations and natural selection. In S. Tax (Ed.), *The evolution life.* (pp. 429–475). Chicago: University of Chicago Press.

Yarrow, L.J. (1963). Research in dimensions of early maternal care. *Merrill-Palmer Quarterly, 9*, 101–114.

Yarrow, L.J., Pedersen, F.A., & Rubenstein, J. (1977). Mother-infant interaction and development in infancy. In P.H. Leiderman, S.R. Tulkin & A. Rosenfeld (Eds.), *Culture and infancy: Variations in the human experience* (pp. 539–584). New York: Academic Press.

Yarrow, L.J., Rubenstein, J.L., Pedersen, F.A., & Jankowski, J.J. (1972). Dimensions of early stimulation and their differential effects on infant development. *Merrill-Palmer Quarterly, 18*, 205–218.

Yonas, A., Bechtold, A.G., Frankel, D., Gordon, F.R., McRoberts, G., Norcia, A., & Sternfels, S. (1977). Development of sensitivity to information for impending collision. *Perception and Psychophysics, 21*, 97–104.

Yuwiler, A. (1971). Problems in assessing biochemical ontogeny. In M.B. Sterman, D.J. McGinty, & A.M. Adinolfi (Eds.), *Brain development and behavior* (pp. 43–58). New York: Academic Press.

Zamenhof, A., van Marthens, E., & Gravel, E. (1971). DNA (Cell number) in neonatal rat brain: Second generation ($F_2$) alteration by maternal ($F_0$) dietary protein restriction. *Science, 172*, 850–851.

Zaprozhets, A.V. (1969). Some psychological problems of sensory training in early childhood and the preschool period. In M. Cole & I. Maltzman (Eds.), *A handbook of contemporary Soviet psychology.* (pp. 86–120). New York: Basic Books.

Zola-Morgan, S., Squire, L.R., & Mishkin, M. (1982). The neuro-anatomy of amnesia: Amygdala-hippocampus versus temporal stem. *Science, 218*, 1337–1339.

# Author Index

# Subject Index